Survivor Transitional Narratives of Nazi-Era Destruction

A Modern History of Politics and Violence

A Modern History of Politics and Violence is a new book series that scrutinizes the diverse history of political violence in the modern world. It includes original studies, edited collections and reference works that explore the cultural settings and key actors that have allowed violent solutions to become seen as desirable somehow at certain points in history.

Published:

British Fascist Antisemitism and Jewish Responses, 1932–40, Daniel Tilles (2014)
A British Fascist in the Second World War, Claudia Baldoli and Brendan Fleming (2014)
Civil Uprisings in Modern Sudan, W. J. Berridge (2015)
Colin Jordan and Britain's Neo-Nazi Social Movement, Paul Jackson (2016)
Transnational Fascism in the Twentieth Century, Matteo Albanese and Pablo del Hierro (2016)
The Victims of Slavery, Colonization and the Holocaust, Kitty Millet (2017)

Forthcoming:

The Comparative History of Fascism in Eastern Europe, Constantin Iordachi (2017)
The Image of the Soldier in German Culture, 1871–1933, Paul Fox (2018)

Survivor Transitional Narratives of Nazi-Era Destruction

The Second Liberation

Dennis B. Klein

BLOOMSBURY ACADEMIC
LONDON • NEW YORK • OXFORD • NEW DELHI • SYDNEY

BLOOMSBURY ACADEMIC
Bloomsbury Publishing Plc
50 Bedford Square, London, WC1B 3DP, UK
1385 Broadway, New York, NY 10018, USA

BLOOMSBURY, BLOOMSBURY ACADEMIC and the Diana logo
are trademarks of Bloomsbury Publishing Plc

First published 2018
Paperback edition first published 2019

Series design: Clare Turner.
Cover image: Women stand in line for food during the liberation of Guson Concentration
Camp, near Linz, Austria, 1945 (© CORBIS / Getty Images).

A catalogue record for this book is available from the British Library.

Library of Congress Cataloging-in-Publication Data
Names: Klein, Dennis B., author.
Title: Survivor transitional narratives of Nazi-era destruction : the second
liberation / Dennis B. Klein.
Description: London ; New York : Bloomsbury Academic, an imprint of
Bloomsbury Publishing Inc, [2018] | Series: A modern history of politics
and violence ; 9 | Includes bibliographical references and index.
Identifiers: LCCN 2017018348| ISBN 9781350037144 (hb) | ISBN 9781350037151 (epub)
Subjects: LCSH: Holocaust, Jewish (1939-1945)--Historiography. | Holocaust,
Jewish (1939-1945)--Moral and ethical aspects.
Classification: LCC D804.348 .K54 2017 | DDC 940.53/180922–dc23 LC record available at
https://lccn.loc.gov/2017018348

ISBN: HB: 978-1-3500-3714-4
PB: 978-1-3501-1231-5
ePDF: 978-1-3500-3716-8
eBook: 978-1-3500-3715-1

Series: A Modern History of Politics and Violence

Typeset by Fakenham Prepress Solutions, Fakenham, Norfolk NR21 8NN

To find out more about our authors and books visit
www.bloomsbury.com and sign up for our newsletters.

Alongside justice there is wickedness,
Alongside righteousness there is wickedness.

Ecclesiastes 3:16

Contents

Acknowledgments

This book began with a single conversation with a member of the Tavistock Institute in London. I was interested in the phenomenon of forgiveness, though at the time I wasn't thinking about its relationships with mass violence or, for that matter, its existence in any historical context. The idea just intrigued me: I wondered about its discordant properties, its cautionary as well as generous characteristics. Subsequently, I began the inquiry—the proto-stages of this book—with Michael Rustin, who offered his time and invaluable erudition that led me to think critically and theoretically about forgiveness. There are others in London who I would like to thank for their warm hospitality and support, in particular, Russell and Mandy Caller, and Leonard and Loren Loeb. During this period, a decade ago, I was fortunate to meet up with Jill Scott, who was, herself, working on a book dealing with the subject. She alerted me to a conference scheduled to take place in Cape Town on the legacy of South Africa's Truth and Reconciliation Commission. Since the question of forgiveness figured prominently in its proceedings, I submitted a proposal, which resulted in the first "test" of my thoughts on the subject. There, I met Pumla Gobodo-Madikizela, then at the University of Cape Town, who served as chair of the TRC's public hearings in the West Cape region. Her inspiration materialized in an article I wrote for a volume she edited in 2009. Eventually, I caught up with Avishai Margalit in Jerusalem, whose work on a project about the vicissitudes of betrayal significantly supported my commitment to exploring this emotion. These were exceptional experiences and exceptional encounters.

Back in the States, I benefited immensely from others on my way to completing this book. Here, I want to invoke another concept, "affinity space." The idea refers to the way people are drawn to common concerns: We find ourselves by finding each other mutually, not unlike Freud's notion of uncanny, "chance" encounters. The special magnetic pull of ideas on a circle of people may have something to do with the formation of a cohort of colleagues and friends around the themes of this book. It brought me into contact with individuals whose inspiration is woven everywhere into this work. Eliezer Diamond alerted me to biblical inquiries into forgiveness; Abraham Rubin and Peter Banki convinced me of the significance of Vladimir Jankélévitch and his relevance to my argument; Devin O. Pendas pointed me to the social climate implicated in the West German state's zeal, in the 1950s and 1960s, for putting the sordid Nazi past behind, forever; Jeffrey Blustein, in his intellectual commitment to fathoming forgiveness and memory, introduced me, with his signature compassion, to the exciting nascent stages transitional justice movement; Dominick LaCapra read an early version of my argument and offered severe, extraordinary advice; Magdalena Zoklos showed an interest in my work-in-progress and provided a welcome platform for it in her anthology on Jean Améry. I owe a special debt to Kitty J. Millet, who invaluably supported my interrogation of survivors' subjectivity and historical specificity and, overall, encouraged this project from beginning to end.

Home possesses a special meaning in this book: As a place or, rather, a state of mind, that feels familiar, intimate, and reassuring, Améry pined for it, though he confessed that it was, after the Nazi destruction, inaccessible. Fortunately, the influence of my colleagues, friends, and family were not only unusually accessible but also instrumental. I owe a special debt to my colleagues at Kean University who, for some twenty years, provided the crucial scaffolding for this book—in particular, to Dawood Farahi, the university's president; Jeffrey Toney, the academic provost; Suzanne Bousquet, my dean (and now associate provost); Jonathan Mercantini, my department chair (and now acting dean); Sue Gronewold, my fellow historian and interlocutor; and to all my history department colleagues and students, my colleagues and students in the Masters of Arts in Holocaust and Genocide Studies program and Jewish Studies program, and my colleagues in the faculty seminar. It is impossible to imagine this book without them. I am especially grateful to Brandon Moye, a recent MA in Holocaust and Genocide Studies graduate, who assisted me immeasurably and steadfastly with this book's construction. During my 2014–15 sabbatical, the Able Bakery in Maplewood, NJ, served as my satellite office, an environment par excellence for easing my intellectual journey; to its staff, my thanks. I want to thank Rob Handelman and Angela DeCandia as well. They facilitated my emotional journey through some pretty challenging moments. Muriel Jorgensen, Mildred Schwartz, and Jeffrey Tannenbaum, in reading portions of the manuscript, somehow combined supportive friendship with pointed criticism, a real talent.

The real homeland magic occurs ultimately in the presence of family. My brothers, Roger and Richard, along with partner, Jacqi, and wife, Gail, joined humor with interest to lift this enterprise often from its weighty moorings. My children, now adults, are a constant source of special inspiration, as they surely were at each stage of this book. To them and their families, my deepest gratitude: Aaron, his wife, Dina, and their children, my grandchildren, Jayden, Zachy and Emmie; Leah, her husband, Josh, and their son (yes, my grandson), Jonah; and Rachel, my youngest, who, like her brother, sister, and their families, possesses considerable promise and the gift of love, joy, and sparkling expressiveness. To my wife, Libby, I dedicate this book. I know of no one—along with my mother and father, whose memory endures—who inspires me with such remarkable strength, wisdom, and unbroken radiance. Counter-narratives are vital in our lives: they interrupt our tribulations with dreams and words of aspirations. Tribulations are also part of marriage, but Libby remained and remains constant, a reminder of our incandescent and lasting love for each other.

Introduction: Unseen

This study is an attempt to anchor Nazi-era survivors to circumstances that inspired and explain their notable emergence on the historical stage. Among the questions we are concerned with are: What was happening in the 1960s that fueled the decision of an aggregate of survivors to mass a public campaign for memory, giving vent to stories that they consulted to that point only in circumscribed settings? What does the delivery of their accounts to an audience who were not only anonymous but also inhospitable tell us about their dynamic outward orientation—not just toward the Nazi past but toward an ancestral past as well? And not only backward to the past but also to an immediate, magnetic present, and, surprisingly, intensely forward to a tentative future, too? We recognize an emphasis in survivors' accounts and other post-atrocity narratives on the commission of massive political and social crimes, mainly by bearing witness and often with a didactic purpose. This customary interpretation, however, limits the value of post-atrocity accounts by occluding their significance as a process of reworking relationships with an unrepentant world they inherited and so considerably distrusted. They are often slotted as "memoir" but could simultaneously be understood as prolegomena.

Part of the reason for this inattention is the common practice of analyzing survivors' accounts in isolation of the circumstances that enfranchised them. Seen as esoteric testaments, scholars from the 1960s onward sought to rescue the victim's "voice" from its positivist predators who, in exalting documentary evidence—the facts—as the province of verifiable proof and objective truth, diminished witnesses' memories as unreliable—merely subjective and sentimental—or as derivative confirmation of their empirically validated arguments. This view was exemplified by the political philosopher Hannah Arendt, who covered the 1961 Eichmann trial for the *New Yorker*. The proceedings provided a major platform for survivors of Nazi-era destruction. Though they offered little evidence in support of the case for the prosecution, they succeeded at drawing worldwide attention to atrocity victims' emotional ordeal. Arendt disparaged their testimony as "embroidery."[1] In disagreement, others, particularly "deep-memory" theorists, championed attention to emotional expressions from the "inside," where they claimed to harvest "deep" truths. We agree with Annette Wieviorka in criticizing the over-attention to singular feelings and emotions. However, we do not believe, as she did, that the only alternative and best practice is historical reconstruction: history authorized by historians.[2] Victims, who serve as witnesses to atrocity, disclose dimensions of persecution that schematic interpretations miss. We don't have to engage the question of authenticity to rely on their accounts for grasping what Primo Levi termed the "unseen from the outside."[3]

Victims are, indeed, worth listening to closely, but when their voices are reduced to deracinated emotions, or when they are lumped together in the sweep of historical oppression—a relatively recent flourish in genocide scholarship—the immediacy and specificity of their lived experiences disappear. Jürgen Zimmerer, for example, argued that Nazi victims in equal measure were subjected to the regime's colonial aggression, which, in turn, amounted to radicalized variants of recurrent colonial practices: "Attending to the colonial dimension in German history for an understanding of Nazi politics enables the recognition of various types of precursors and models."[4] A. Dirk Moses maintained that the Holocaust was a late event on a historical continuum of "transnational" racialized thinking: "In Hitler, the imperial models of centuries of human history crystallized into a single, total, imperial fantasy of genocidal conquest and exploitation." Jews, he said, were a manifestation of the "traditional colonial Other: Dirty, lazy, stateless, uncivilized. They were treated in the customary colonial manner: labor, food, and security considerations combined to determine their fate."[5] As Donald Bloxham wrote in the introduction to his book *The Final Solution: A Genocide*, "The evolution and dynamics of the final solution are at the centre of the book, but that is to the larger end of asking how and how far the Holocaust fits into the broader patterns of the human past."[6] Part of the reason for decontextualizing victims and designating them as cosmopolitan was to argue against "identity-specific" politics, against survivors' claim that their Nazi-era experiences were unique based on a need, in Bloxham's words, "to give a special significance to the past suffering of Jews in the name of present communal identity."[7] Cosmopolitan victims, the argument goes, are equivalent or at least more alike than different. Their experiences may "seem unprecedented," Zimmerer argued, but they resulted from practices that, "on closer inspection, [proved] to be radicalized versions of forms found in earlier colonial times."[8] As such, they are not qualified to evaluate victimization because, as stakeholders, they overemphasize the specificity of their identities.

Marianne Hirsch and Leo Spitzer pointedly argued against specificity. Concerned about the appropriation of survivors' accounts for specious ulterior purposes, such as the influence of a national–Zionist narrative on witnesses' testimonies during the Eichmann trial, they asserted another way of regarding them that was congruent with "our age of globalization." They wanted to glean "the human elements of survival that can become the links between the diverse catastrophes of our time."[9] There are surely "transnational" and "cosmopolitan" dimensions of survival, as Daniel Levy and Natan Sznaider observed,[10] and there are beneficial occasions for comparative analysis. But their primary objection to the abuses of "nationalist and identity politics"[11] prevented them from recognizing the role of immediate circumstances in eliciting, rather than determining, survivors' responses. They claimed that "a cosmopolitan memory ... does not in any sense aim to diminish or relativize the experiences and suffering of European Holocaust survivors,"[12] just as Levy and Sznaider argued that it can take account of "local sensibilities,"[13] but they privileged the "human elements of survival" as an antidote to "a hyperbolic discourse of uniqueness and exceptionalism."[14]

"Linking diverse catastrophes" is a worthy endeavor if it begins the investigation with an affirmation of their profound diversity, but that was not a priority for Hirsch and Spitzer and their allies.[15] Their preferences for "de-contextualizing" Holocaust memory from "its European specificity" (Hirsch and Spitzer 2009), and for imagining collective memories that "transcend ethnic and national boundaries" (Levy and Sznaider 2002) make clear the limitations imposed by narrative theories on narrative expression. Exalting the human element and emotional anguish in the depths and dynamics of survivors' accounts usefully underscores the phenomenon that survivors possess and express a voice. But, by ignoring the historical circumstances that gave rise to expression and communication, they elided *what* survivors said and to *whom.*[16]

Accounting for historical injustice is a lived process of recording as well as a record of wrongdoing. As a process, an account is a survivor's engagement with their contemporaries and a search for a place among them as urgent matters unfold. They tell us something about the tribulations of surviving as they do about the impossible, anterior conditions that threatened survival. Memory is prospective as it is retrospective. We are, therefore, concerned with the context of open-air, communicated accounts and with how survivors endeavored to negotiate contemporary opinions, both informal and codified. Embedded in provocative circumstances, they did so conscious of their vocation as survivors in the process of surviving, communicating what it means to endure in a combative, tenuous, and restive world after atrocity.

The subject under investigation is survivors' decisive acts of worldly engagement to disquiet world opinion. Many elected to assert their deeply personal stories directly and provocatively to their contemporaries, a remote audience, for the first time in the 1960s. This claim is, admittedly, contentious since there is a corpus of recent scholarship that argues that survivors were vocal well before that decade, and that any suggestion they were not, that they were silent until then, is specious.[17] The notion of "silence" as we mean it here, then, requires clarification. These scholars note that survivors were active witnesses as early as the war. Their activities, however, were largely devoted to chronicling their ordeal. They were surely vocal, as Hasia Diner argued in her study of the United States, where many survivors relocated. But as she showed, they not only summoned the past but often did so in limited, familiar settings—primarily in the postwar "Jewish public sphere" among other survivors, friends and community, and family members.[18] When they addressed a wider public, primarily in Europe, they were committed to collecting testimonies and making them available for others, notably represented by David Boder's testimonies project in the displaced persons (DP) camps in 1946.[19] Laura Jockusch's impressive research showed the existence, during and immediately after the war, of a spate of survivor-inspired Jewish historical commissions and documentation centers that gathered some 18,000 testimonies,[20] including London's Wiener Library, Paris's *Centre de Documentation Juive Contemporaine*, and Warsaw's *Centralna Żydowska Komisja Historyczna*. As Jockusch made clear, their endeavors were confined to chronicling and preserving stories for research, analysis, education, and expert judicial testimony. They did so, she added, for self-understanding and self-recovery in a spirit of revenge, grief, and commemoration.[21] Simon Wiesenthal's Jewish Historical Documentation Center, established in Vienna after the war, possessed a broader mission but with a dedicated practical purpose: to locate and, with the help of the Allies, to bring former Nazis to justice. When Wiesenthal published *The Sunflower* in 1969, however, a different rhetoric emerged, one more hortatory than documentary, more moral protest than deposition. In his account, he was committed to refuting rather than redressing his world's commonplace refrain, "Forgive and forget."[22] Speaking up this way was a measure of breaking a silence that had obstructed a direct engagement with his contemporaries. It was immediate and urgent, at turns defiant and searching. Four years earlier, Jean Améry published *At the Mind's Limits* specifically to get his message out: "After twenty years of silence," he, like Wiesenthal, started to write about his ordeal—not to his "comrades in fate," since "they know what it is all about," but boldly "to the Germans" who seemed disturbingly and hopelessly unaffected.[23] We believe, then, that what distinguished survivors in the 1960s from the period before was their decision to broadcast their accounts for the purpose of excoriating and exhorting public opinion.

Scholars determined to debunk the myth of silence offer an errant concession to the idea that there was, indeed, something new in the 1960s—that the wider society was, in fact, ready and willing to listen. What was actually new, however, was survivors' commitment to engaging with a society that was, on the contrary, set against listening.

The climate of public opinion during this period was, indeed, hostile, but unlike the general silence that discouraged survivors by 1950 from their historical activity, leading them "to turn inward and keep their stories to themselves,"[24] the wall of silence in the 1960s galvanized survivors to speak out. Survivors' decision to amplify their stories occurred against the backdrop of two immediate European developments centered in Germany: the Frankfurt Auschwitz trial (1963–5) and the West German debate over the prescriptibility, or the enforcement, of the twenty-year statutes of limitations for prosecuting egregious Nazi crimes. A longer-term development authorizing a suspension of prosecution in order to put the past to rest began at the start of the Federal Republic of Germany in 1949 with amnesty legislation escorting former Nazi party and Wehrmacht members, as well as convicted war criminals, into German society. During the country's first two years alone, amnesty legislation benefited close to 800,000 people. As the May 1965 statutory deadline approached, survivors joined others in concerted opposition to what one observer called "strategies of oblivion."[25] Survivors were especially vigorous, admonishing their contemporaries for their complacent indifference to Nazi crimes, whose nativism and racism they believed still lingered. Wiesenthal observed the substantial public pressure to comply with statutory legislation that would prohibit further prosecution of former Nazis. Like other survivors, he vehemently objected: the world "urges that we draw a line and close the account as if nothing had ever happened."[26] Determined to resist—an expression of moral and emotional liberation—they produced a genre of narrative accounts committed primarily to recalling endemic and protracted Nazi-era criminality.

The 1960s were a period of considerable social unrest, inspired by a resurgence of the disfranchised in world affairs—colonies were in revolt for their independence; U.S. African-Americans were demonstrating for their civil rights; students were mobilizing for free speech; survivors were granted recognition as witnesses in courts of law. As John Gillis noted, collective memory became thoroughly contested, as workers, women, and minorities posited counter-memories to elites' "official" narratives of triumphant nationalism.[27] Améry noted the élan of survivors' resistance against German self-righteousness: more than isolated expression, they sensed a turn of events giving rise to a self-styled survivor cohort: "This solidarity is part of my person and a weapon in the battle to regain my dignity."[28] Unlike the first liberation from the death camps, this one was self-determined. It also showed signs of aspirations by sounding a yearning for worldly engagement that they felt would take decades before the time was right for expression. Améry noted the delay before the battle for dignity was joined: "We emerged from the camp stripped, robbed, emptied out, disoriented—and it was a long time before we were able even to learn the ordinary language of freedom."[29] Survivors were unsure if or how they were ever to re-engage with the larger world. One survivor recalled, "I remember after liberation, I suffered probably more from the loneliness and the isolation, more than during the Holocaust … Feeling of, yes, I'm alive, but that's it."[30] Another found the prospects terribly unsettling: "Soon the euphoria and hysteria were over. It was joy, yes—we were free, the gates were open—but where were we to go? … We had no place to go, and nobody was waiting for us anywhere. We were alive, yes. We were liberated from death, from the fear of death, but the fear of life started."[31] But all was not hopeless. Some were able to sense new life in unexpected encounters with others. In one arresting reminiscence, another survivor recalled, "It was only when the British distributed a bowl of rice and hot milk that we understood that we might one day be human beings again."[32] The rice and milk kept him alive but it was the helping gesture that gave him reason to believe there was something more to life. Améry remembered a similar incident during his incarceration at Auschwitz: "An orderly from the sick barracks once gave me a plate of sweetened grits." He ate it ravenously, he reported, but he was surprised that the moment inspired "an extraordinary spiritual euphoria." He explained that it was "the phenomenon of human kindness" that lifted his spirits.[33] Of course, the moment didn't last, but the impression of another's concern did. If that hadn't resonated, Améry, and others like him, wouldn't have interjected references to these experiences in accounts that were otherwise dedicated to condemnation. It activated a desire to be "human beings again."

Memories like these alert us to expressions that lived on in the shadow of narrative condemnation. A generation after their physical liberation, survivors were not only committed to recalling atrocities and reproaching their contemporaries' evasiveness but were also open to possibilities "beyond physical survival," Améry noted, to "survive the nightmare morally also."[34] While acknowledging the importance of survivors' stories of survival, statements of reproach, and appeals to retributive justice, this study is concerned with forward-looking expressions that interrupted backward-looking statements in narrative swerves expressed sideways as confessions, counterfactuals, dreams, and digressions. In accounts given over to bearing resolute witness to past crimes, these fragmentary moments of narrative derailment surprise us. Like manifest narratives—narratives that are declarative and assertive, recalling a dark past, counter-narratives—parallel narratives—that are allusive and connotative—are historically rooted. Their allusions to fellow-feeling, as primitive an emotion as that is, evoked social relationships that predated their destruction when Jews coexisted with their compatriots. Often characterized as social integration or assimilation, their interaction with neighbors was more than an adoption of the larger society's external markers—language, dress, and customs—buttressed by statutory civil rights and secular education, as well as conversion, intermarriage, and other rites of passage.[35] Whether or not Jews did fit in; whether their relationships were "thick" or "thin"; whether their common post-Enlightenment strategy of inclusion was reasonable and successful, or fatally misguided, if not delusional, are matters of a long-running scholarly debate. We acknowledge and then supersede that debate in order to draw attention to underlying beliefs that fueled aspirations to fit in, often in spite of the realities. In the train of recent scholarship exploring the subjective experiences of Jews' post-emancipation quest for social acceptance,[36] we pay special attention to Jews' emotional attachments to their social counterparts. Even if their ancestral quest for connections collided with realities of social tensions that acquired ominous and sometimes tragic dimensions, west-central European Jews, for over a century and half before their destruction, expected the promise of common humanity, underwritten by their historical emancipation, to withstand setbacks and eventually materialize. The rupture that occurred with the campaign to destroy Jews gave rise to survivors' conclusions about a broken world, observations that informed their strong narratives. But importantly, something of their previous, antediluvian aspirations—a residual zeal—also survived. Exactly how is the main subject of our investigation. For now, it is sufficient to observe the dispositions in these weaker narratives: a search for human sympathy or references to "brotherhood," a term favored by survivor Vladimir Jankélévitch, who published his accounts in the mid-1960s; indeed, an urgent wish, a yearning, for a human connection: "We have waited for word for a long time, a single word of understanding and sympathy. We have wished for it, this fraternal word! … We would have received it with gratitude, with tears in our eyes."[37]

Though we refer to a number of survivors residing in Europe at different times for useful observations, Améry, Jankélévitch, and Wiesenthal will demand our special attention. The problem of representativeness is an occupational hazard in historical analysis. Perhaps with the exception of the Annales school's fascination with longue durée or the structural predilections of Marxist history and historical sociology, historical investigations must face the problem and explain their selections. Why choose three middle-class Jewish men from West-Central Europe in active moral revolt at the same time? To begin with, we make a modest claim to generalization: context matters; hence, our attention to a specific period of time. Our argument indicates that ideas and actions do not spring from the heart alone but intersect with exigent circumstances. We agree with the French philosopher Maurice Halbwachs that: "It is in society that people normally acquire their memories."[38] Responses might be creative and heartfelt, but even the most original emerge from the crucible of current social existence. Others will disagree, but we hope to show just how significant context is in explaining themes and narratives in survivors' aggregate accounts. The west-central European locus is important as well. Here was a perfect storm. As the Frankfurt Auschwitz trial threatened to be the final act of state for prosecuting former Nazis, survivors confronted a reprise of their oblivion and that, as an echo of their shattering ordeal, they could not tolerate. Remaining silent was no longer an option.

Limiting further our choice to Jewish survivors provides an opportunity for exploring the role of ancestral memories in the architecture of strong and weak narratives. The juxtaposition of two memory narratives—the ordeal of consummate Jewish destruction and historical expectations of their broad social acceptance—produced signature expressions of resentment and betrayal in strong narratives as well as a counter-narrative recasting of expectations into a longing for human fellowship. This aspect of our argument is suggestively generalizable by drawing attention to the influence of pre-traumatic memories on how ethnic groups recall and negotiate their experiences with atrocity. Further restricting our subject to Jewish men exposes the emotional intensity of Jewish aspirations to belong; that is, belonging not only as expedient but also as urgent matters of identity and ambition. As Paula Hyman showed, Jewish men were traditionally in the vanguard of taking advantage of new opportunities provided by the sweep of Enlightenment humanism and the regime of political rights.[39] Our trio of survivors also represents a single socioeconomic class; this is apposite too. As educated writers dedicated to their literary craft, they embodied middle-class values. Améry and Jankélévitch were especially distinguished by philosophical reflection; Wiesenthal, too, was reflective, rarely missing a chance to glean significance from his encounters with violence. These predilections allowed them to speak for themselves, but just as important, the decision to publish their accounts represents a determination, beyond a literary calling, to make all-important connections with the larger world. I confess that my appreciation of their impressive probity is a personal reason for my selection. Even within these parameters I selected three writers for the narrative contrast they offer. On the one hand, Jankélévitch and Wiesenthal show considerable forward-looking propensities in this genre, arguably its most concentrated considerations of forgiveness. Améry, on the other hand, dwelled on defeated expectations and his earned resentments. The range of their work will help make our case, for themes of betrayal are also notable in Wiesenthal's and Jankélévitch's accounts, just as aspirations are in Améry's. Each account slices our argument differently, but as a whole they indicate rupture in strong narratives and interruptions in weak, counter-narratives; recrimination in the former as well as a palimpsest of ancestral memories in the latter.

We are most interested in exploring the work, both its construction and its historical context. But a word about their authors is fitting. Jean Améry's reputation as an adamant defender of resentment rests on a series of essays he published in 1966 entitled *Jenseits von Schuld und Sühne: Bewältigungsversuche eines Überwältigten*. The English title, *At the Mind's Limits*, is the same as the title of the first essay in which he argued that the "concrete reality" of Auschwitz ruled out intellectual and metaphysical considerations of "ultimate questions"; dying trumped thoughts of death.[40] Auschwitz, he asserted, ended his dedication to studying philosophy and literature, yet like so much else in his reflections, what he claimed and what unfolds were often at odds, for there is scarcely better evidence of the life of the mind than these essays. Born Hans Mayer, just before the First World War, in 1912, he grew up in the western Austrian province of Vorarlberg. Even after he left Austria in 1938, once the Nazis annexed the country, his bitterness toward his compatriots' German-nationalist enthusiasm did not break the continuity of writing in German.[41] The *nom de plume* he took on in exile further betrayed traces of his former homeland: Jean is analogous in French to Hans, and Améry is an anagram of his given surname Mayer. Indeed, the essay from *At the Mind's Limits*, "How Much Home Does a Person Need?," is a dramatic, if difficult, evocation of his homeland—its "Alpine valleys and folk rituals."[42] His youthful family life was distant from his father's Jewish heritage and surely from the culture of his grandfather, whose Hebrew was fluent.[43] As he recalled, "With Jews as Jews I share practically nothing: no language, no cultural tradition, no childhood memories."[44] After his father's death from his wounds in battle in 1916, his mother, who was Roman Catholic, raised him, eventually moving to Vienna. In short, Améry's Jewish background reached the vanishing point of assimilation. Along with countless others possessing faint traces of Jewish heritage, he awakened rudely to that virtually forgotten reality in the 1930s with the fatal labeling exercises of racial decrees. But there is potency in what he didn't forget. What did he mean when he always knew he was a Jew? He declared that his neighbors constantly reminded him of that.[45] Notably in his youthful quest to be a "human being,"[46] he betrayed the behavior of an assimilated Jew. It was possible to be a human being, he said, "only if you are a German, a Frenchman, a Christian, a member of whatever identifiable social group."[47] He tried to present himself as "an impressive German youth."[48] That was the requisite detour for a Jew who aspired to belong. That he was "excluded from the fate of the German community"[49] did not abort his inclinations; it lived on in his accounts, now as emotional longing.

After the *Anschluss* in March 1938, Améry fled his homeland for Belgium, which was at war with Germany. Arrested in 1940 by the Belgians as a German "enemy alien," he was deported to camps in Southern France, including the Gurs concentration camp. In 1941, he escaped by way of Paris to occupied Belgium and joined the Resistance.[50] For him, participating in the movement marked a significant departure from his experiences in Austria: it was a "new life" that transformed his Jewish existence from an object, "forsaken" by others, to a rebelling Jew who became a subject of his own destiny.[51] In July 1943, he was arrested by the Gestapo for disseminating anti-Nazi materials among the German occupying forces in Belgium. For several days the SS—the agency of the Nazi regime for security, surveillance, and terror—detained him for interrogation. That experience became the subject of his essay "Torture," in which he deftly plumbs the subjective experience of the victim. Learning nothing of value, his tormentors shipped him off to Auschwitz III, the Buna-Monowitz labor camp, where, for a year, he labored at the I-G Farben industrial site. Toward the end of the war, he was reassigned to Buchenwald and then to Bergen-Belsen before his liberation in April 1945. From then on he resided in Brussels and soon turned to writing for German-language Swiss publications, adopting in 1955 a "French-sounding pen name."[52] A generation later, he collected several essays written in the mid-1960s into the volume *At the Mind's Limits*. These essays represent his only concentrated investigation of his tribulations under the Nazis. Even an account of his intellectual development, published in 1971 as *Unmeisterliche Wanderjahre*, avoided discussion of his ordeal.[53] Instead, he wrote about cultural subjects—jazz, celebrities, aging, and consumer society, subjects which he anticipated briefly in *At the Mind's Limits* as manifestations of a purely functional, emotionless, and rootless "technological-scientific" world.[54] His 1976 inquiry on suicide, *Hand an sich Legen*, appeared two years before he took his own life, raising the unavoidable question about his inability to shake off desperation or at least the corrosive effects of compulsive resentment inherited from his Nazi-era experiences. It may be true that his "Attempts to Overcome by One Who Has Been Overcome," the subtitle in English of the German essays, *Jenseits von Schuld und Sühne: Bewältigungsversuche eines Überwältigten*, expressed the limits of physical survival that no measure of determination could exceed, though articulated as a subtitle, the attempts, themselves, indicate the counter-narrative tenacity of moral survival after atrocity. Whether or not they helped him to regain his dignity; whether, if they ultimately failed, that failure accounted for his suicide, is anybody's guess.

Vladimir Jankélévitch's prodigious work on the subject of forgiveness is an important contribution to a field that has gained considerable currency from the 1990s generated by political debates in South Africa and elsewhere over the prospects of reconciliation after internecine national violence. He published the inquiry after France, his homeland, declared the imprescriptibility of radical crimes—that is, their exemption from statutory limitations—three years before. He was, however, in no mood to celebrate. Developments in Germany left the question of statutes of limitations unresolved, a problem that preoccupied him and demanded his response in an article he began to write in 1965 as the Frankfurt Auschwitz trial was drawing to a close. His deliberations on Germany's recalcitrance were more than a public intellectual's formidable analysis or the polemics of a progressive and engaged observer, though he was surely capable of both. Germany and the collaborationist Vichy regime directly disrupted his life. Though he eluded captivity, his reflections were no less indignant than Améry's. He was born to parents who had emigrated from Russia to Bourges in central France. Shortly after his birth in 1903, the family moved some 120 miles north to Paris, where he resided for most of the remainder of life.[55] If there were Eurasian influences on his intellectual development, they were overshadowed early on by his father's western orientation even before his emigration. Before moving the family Serge (Samuel) Jankélévitch took up residence in France in the 1880s—a period of unrest for Russian Jews threatened by pogroms—where he elected to study medicine for a physician's career. To satisfy his intellectual appetite, he started translating the work of pre-eminent European scholarship. Once he settled the family in France, he continued his literary work, becoming the first to translate Freud's work into French. He translated other German scholarship as well, including works by the German idealists G. W. F. Hegel, Johann Gottlieb Fichte, and Friedrich Wilhelm Joseph von Schelling. By the 1920s, when he was especially prolific, his son, reflecting Serge's erudition, studied philosophy at prestigious universities, notably under the considerable influence of Henri Bergson, taking first place in the *aggrégation*, a national examination for students who aspired to teach the subject. While teaching at the French Institute in Prague, he completed his doctoral thesis on Schelling, publishing it in 1933 as the culmination of his studies at the Sorbonne.

In a 1931 letter, Jankélévitch wrote about the distance he started to feel from mainstream French philosophy. While the divergence is clear, and especially noteworthy after the Second World War, it's hard to imagine that this was the only, or even primary, reason for the isolation he was feeling—and probably cultivated—as an outsider. After all, he held appointments at the Sorbonne, including a chair in moral philosophy, for almost thirty years—virtually to the end of his life in 1985. Being a Jew certainly contributed to feeling déclassé. Though French culture tempted him,[56] and Jewish religious observance wasn't important, the rise of fascism between the two world wars forced him, like Améry and so many other Jews, to re-examine his heritage. Whatever his reluctance to identify as a Jew, he started to address the problems of racism and antisemitism during the Second World War and, afterward, in lectures at the *Colloques des intellectuels juifs de langue française* (the annual Colloquia of French-Speaking Jewish Intellectuals) on his Jewish ancestry among other topics. The immediate circumstances surely stimulated these interests but it appears they were long-standing. If nothing else, his father's Jewish religious knowledge, exhibited in his 1947 book *Mishnah: le Shabbat* (commentaries on the Jewish Sabbath)[57] suggests a lifelong, if subtle, influence. The turning point that set in motion his concerns for worldly affairs occurred shortly after he was mobilized for combat against Germany in August 1939. After some ten months of service, as France went down to defeat, he was injured in the military effort to repel the German aggression. Upon his release from convalescence, he repaired to Toulouse in the south of France in hopes for a university appointment. Even though developments in Vichy France threatened Jews, he retained a faith in French law and its provision of benefits to French citizens with military service that would permit him to continue teaching. The authorities' decision in late 1940 to rescind the provision, an act that barred Jews from public service, was a substantial setback. At this point, Jankélévitch decided to live a clandestine life, furthering his pariah sensibilities to the end of the war in France and, indeed, for the rest of his life. Denied a teaching position, he organized secret lectures in the city's cafés and circulated his writings underground among students.

Historically, Toulouse had a progressive reputation, one likely reason for making it his home. Nearby was the transit camp Saint-Sulpice-la-Pointe. At first, "foreign" Jews were interned there, but starting in the spring of 1942, Jews, including those who were naturalized French citizens, were rounded up for deportation to Auschwitz, Majdanek, and Sobibor. Jankélévitch joined the resistance movement in 1941 and began drafting pamphlets on racism for dissemination the following year for the *Mouvement nationale contre le racism*, a movement hospitable to Jews committed to hiding children from round-ups and spiriting them to safety. He remained involved in resistance efforts for the duration of the war. Recognizing that his French citizenship granted him uncertain immunities, his activities were exceptionally perilous. The liberation of France, in late summer 1944, ended his fugitive existence. He returned to the academy, assuming a position at Lille, where he published *Traité des vertus* (*Treatise on the Virtues*) in 1949 and, in 1951 (the year his father died), at the Sorbonne. *Traité des vertus*, which he started working on in hiding during the war, raised themes that originated from his studies of Bergson and threaded his philosophy in general—the virtues of spontaneity, moral action, and the impermanence of everything—themes that assailed the totalistic triumphalism of Nazi ideology.[58]

Jankélévitch's productive output after the war, including *Forgiveness*, did not escape from the shadow of destruction. The experience of surviving the onslaught, he maintained, "ravaged our lives."[59] He refused to recognize German culture, neither its language nor its philosophy. The decision marginalized him from mainstream postwar French philosophical thought, which gravitated to Nietzsche and Martin Heidegger. This is one primary reason why his work, including his fertile contributions to forgiveness theory, remained obscure in international philosophical circles for a half century since the war. He started to explore concepts of forgiveness in a course dedicated to the subject in 1962–3 and in a lecture, entitled "*Introduction au theme du Pardon*" ("Introduction to the Theme of Forgiveness"), at the 1963 *Colloque,* whose gathering around the topic he helped organize. The relevant publications that followed—his 1965 article *Pardonner?* ("Should We Pardon Them?") and his 1967 book *Le Pardon* (*Forgiveness*)—demand our special concern, for they wrestle with the legacy of what he referred to as "the six million dead of Auschwitz"[60] as well as with widespread inclinations to erase this past as if it *were* past. The outlines of his 1965 article surfaced in the January 3 edition of *Le Monde*, and later that year in *Le Revue administrative* under the title *L'Imprescriptible*. For this study, we consulted its expanded version, published in 1971 (and translated into English in 1996), but note its origins in the mid-1960s to preserve its direct relationship to the debates over statutory limitations. *Forgiveness*, too, is an elaboration of themes he first explored in the 1963 *Colloque* lecture. The book shed the contextual framework that distinguished his 1965 polemic, but occasional references to the German debates, which, he decried, amounted to a "prescriptive delay,"[61] and to crimes' acts and actors, make clear that its theoretical construct is anchored in the tribulations of surviving.

Simon Wiesenthal's largely familiar life and work presents an entirely different task than Jankélévitch's: it requires unlearning what we know in order to grasp the significance of his account, *Die Sonnenblume* (*The Sunflower: On the Possibilities and Limits and Forgiveness*), a popular work that he also regarded as his most important.[62] As demanding as the contradiction is between Jankélévitch's 1965 merciless diatribe and his 1967 tome of generosity, the incongruity of Wiesenthal's acclaimed postwar dedication to bringing Nazi-era criminals to justice and his 1969 account of extra-judicial, interpersonal rapprochement is utterly perplexing. There are surely ample references in *The Sunflower* to perpetrator malfeasance, but, like Jankélévitch's two works on forgiveness, it is our contention that the dissimilarities of Wiesenthal's endeavors are significant for representing two parallel, irreconcilable narrative concerns. *The Sunflower*, along with Anne Frank's *Diary of Young Girl*, Elie Wiesel's *Night*, Art Spiegelman's *Maus*, and Primo Levi's *Survival in Auschwitz*, among other popular accounts, is standard issue for classroom reading; like them, it presents an interpretive problem. *The Sunflower* is often read out of context as a personal journey that floats above the contemporary circumstances that inspired it. To be sure, Wiesenthal's account of his search for something human in conversations he had with a dying SS officer makes a remarkable story, but we need to foreground his concerns in the text, as well as beyond it in his Nazi-hunting mission, with the world's preferences to forget the Nazi past "as if nothing had ever happened." Both Jankélévitch and Wiesenthal were in search of common ground and considered forgiving their enemies. But they strongly condemned their enemies at the same time.

Wiesenthal is the "middle child" of the three survivors under scrutiny—his 1908 birth placing him a few years older and younger than Améry and

Jankélévitch, respectively. Over the course of his life, his relationships to the larger world might best be characterized as liminal or, as Tom Segev observed, "belonging and not belonging."[63] For most of his first thirty-five years, including four years (1939–43) under Soviet and Nazi rule, he spent his time in and around Lvov, then in Poland. (Under Nazi occupation, from 1941 to 1945, Lvov was known as Lemberg; today, as a city in western Ukraine, it is known as Lviv.) In a portentous coincidence, Lvov was the stomping grounds for two Jewish thinkers who were among the most important figures in the burgeoning, postwar movement for cosmopolitan justice: One was Hersch Lauterpacht, who was born near Lvov in 1897; he is credited with the concept of crimes against humanity and was one of the most active international lawyers campaigning for human rights. The other was Raphael Lemkin, who entered the university in Lvov in 1920, shortly after Lauterpacht left it for Vienna; he was responsible for the term "genocide" and exerted decisive influence on the United Nations' ratification of the 1948 genocide convention.[64] Wiesenthal's decision to live in Linz, Austria, from 1945 to 1961, and afterward in Vienna until his death in 2005, confirmed his distance from a region whose intolerance toward Jews he had witnessed. But it also involved a western magnetism that, from his earliest days growing up in the small village of Buczacz, some 100 miles southeast of Lvov, drew his attention to central Europe. "We were the pioneers of German culture in the East," he recalled. German was the spoken language in his childhood home; his mother often cited classic German literature.[65] Buczacz—which was also home to the Emanuel Ringelblum, the leader of the acclaimed research project in the Warsaw Ghetto, and S. Y. Agnon, a Nobel laureate for literature—belonged to the autonomous region of Galicia on the eastern edge of the Austro-Hungarian Empire. His parents, Rosa and Asher (Henczel), were strong supporters of the dual monarchy with Vienna as its capital. Asher, a wholesale merchant trading in sugar, served as a reservist in the Imperial Austrian army during the First World War, giving his life in the line of duty on the Russian front. Wiesenthal's western orientation became evident when he attended the German Technical School and the Czech Technical University in Prague for four years, from 1928 to 1932. Enamored of the city's cultural and social freedoms, he became part of its alluring open, cosmopolitan life.[66] He was impressed with the ease of Jews' participation in its social life, commenting to his biographer, Hella Pick, "Living at close quarters with such a mixed group was an entirely novel experience. It was exhilarating."[67] For Wiesenthal, Linz, and especially Vienna, recaptured that spirit. He prized his adopted homeland and sought to uphold "our country's" postwar image by rooting out "all the wild growths of Nazism."[68]

His reference in *The Sunflower* to the existence of a "single community" that presumed that "one must answer for the other"[69] echoed these influences.

Wiesenthal's first exposure to the monarchy's capital occurred after his father's death when his mother, Rosa, left Buczacz for Vienna in 1915, with her parents, Wiesenthal, and his brother, Hillel. Their stay was short. Within a couple years, they returned to their Polish village, remaining there for several years—although Wiesenthal briefly returned to Vienna—until the family further fragmented with the death of Hillel, in 1923, and his mother's remarriage and relocation to the foothills of the Carpathian Mountains three years later. Wiesenthal remained behind until his departure for good to chart a new course in the field of architecture in Prague. Upon his return from the city, in 1932, he resided in Lvov, where he earned a diploma from the city's technical university which enabled him to work for an architectural firm in Poland. The escalation of antisemitic hostilities during the decade disrupted his ambitions, a development that he recounted in *The Sunflower*. Expressions of anti-Jewish discrimination did less to awaken or reawaken his Jewish self-awareness, as it did for Améry and Jankélévitch, than to reinforce it, for his involvement in Jewish life was already, by then, firmly anchored and would remain that way. His youthful environment was strongly ethnic. Between 50 and 70 percent of Buczacz's population was Jewish. Though he did not grow up in a Jewish-religious home and was not a practicing Jew,[70] his grandparents were observant and he, as a very young child, attended *cheder*, a school where Jewish children traditionally receive a Hebrew and religious education. When Rosa resettled the family in Vienna in 1915, she moved in with distant relatives who lived in the city's Jewish quarter.

Wiesenthal described his university days in Lvov with consternation: ascendant expressions of antisemitic intolerance departed dramatically from the open society he prized. He left for Prague in large part because Lvov's Polytechnic Institute restricted Jews from enrolling. But even in Prague he encountered hostilities, compelling him to leave the German Technical School after one semester for Czech Technical University across the city. Sudeten Germans, who were displaying great enthusiasm for Nazism's ascendance and a penchant for attacking Jews, became a disturbing reality.[71] It was then, in the early 1930s, that he first exhibited signs of political activism. He joined a combative chapter of the Revisionists, a militant Zionist faction, but soon left it for a more moderate party called the Jewish State Party.[72] At Lvov's technical university, he co-founded a student magazine called *Omnibus*, and contributed political cartoons that were mainly anti-Nazi.[73] His commitment to the burgeoning new state of Israel continued after the war, when he worked for organizations that prepared displaced persons and refugees for emigration.

In *The Sunflower*, Wiesenthal reflected on his disillusionment at the behavior of his compatriots who turned against Jews. He recalled local citizens who were mute when his ghetto labor detail marched by, and local students who threatened Jews, while other students and school authorities failed to speak out.[74] In June 1941, as Germany advanced on the Soviets, Ukrainian auxiliary troops wearing German fatigues—witnesses from the region reported recognizing them as their former neighbors—ferreted Jews from their hiding places for punishment, a role Wiesenthal would adopt in reverse after the war. In 1941, he was caught and taken to Brigidki prison in Lvov. One incident made a formative impression: a former acquaintance, who served with the Ukrainian auxiliary police, helped him escape from the prison. Many survivors reported that he often remembered decent Germans who helped save his life.[75] The next couple of years, when he was an inmate in the Lemberg (Lvov) ghetto serving the Ostbahn Works, the repair facility for Lvov's Eastern Railroad, constituted the subject of *The Sunflower*. The experience, along with his confinement in the nearby Janowska concentration camp, proved less unbearable than what was to come, however. In 1943, he escaped from Janowska and joined a group of Jewish partisans, but in June 1944, the Gestapo caught up with him and inflicted inordinate misery on him during his final year of captivity, before liberation. During this period, he spent time in several camps—the Lackie Wielkie slave labor camp, the Kraków-Płaszów concentration camp, and, eventually, after a Nazi-steered westward retreat of attrition from the advancing Soviet military, the Mauthausen concentration camp, from which U.S. troops liberated him and others on May 5, 1945. Before the Nazis invaded, in 1941, Lvov had between 160,000 and 170,000 Jews: in 1945, Wiesenthal was among the some 3,000 who survived.[76] Within just weeks, he embarked on a mission that was to mark his postwar reputation. He persuaded the camp's U.S. military commander to enlist him in efforts to bring Nazi criminals to justice.

Wiesenthal's involvement in the statutory limitations' debate catapulted him into the international limelight. His contributions to heightening the conscience of his country, Austria, and the world, are noteworthy. They did not require embellishment, though he exhibited a tendency to exaggerate his role in bringing war criminals to justice—Segev noted his inclination to "fantasize."[77] Wiesenthal started working on commissions in Linz for the U.S. War Crimes Unit in 1945, and later for the Office of Strategic Services (OSS) and for the Counter Intelligence Corps (CIC). He was disheartened by his Austrian compatriots' resistance to proposals for extending the prescribed period for prosecuting war criminals, but he believed they could be brought around. He believed this in spite of his "years of suffering" and the doubts they inflicted "on my faith that justice existed in the world." Both he and the world had changed: "It was impossible for me simply to restart my life from the point at which it had been so ruthlessly disrupted." But his faith endured, partly because of the strength of his youthful identification with German culture and the "single community" it represented, and partly because he came to see that faith in anything depended on taking action, in this case his work on investigating Nazi crimes: "I thought the work of the commission might help me regain my faith in justice and humanity."[78] He left the CIC in 1947 to open a private office—the *Zentrum für jüdische historische Dokumentation*, the Jewish Historical Documentation Center. During this early, post-liberation period, he published a couple of books, including his 1946 work *KZ Mauthausen*, which, like many of his subsequent publications, documented the search for criminals as well as witnesses and their families. As his fame grew in the 1960s, with a deliberately public campaign for extending the prescribed period for prosecution, he started receiving invitations to lecture and meet with government officials. A number of books followed, including *Verjährung?: 200 Persönlichkeiten des öffentlichen Lebens sagen nein—Eine Dokumentation* (*Statutory Limitations?: 200 Public Figures Say No*), a report he published in 1965 on public figures who responded to his requests for extending the prescribed period in Austria as well as in Germany. (On March 31, 1965—after a two-year extension, and three months before the period of statutory limitations were to lapse—the Austrian government declared the imprescriptibility of war crimes against humanity.)[79] Segev faulted Wiesenthal for craving publicity, but we believe that his zeal was driven by something other than, or, perhaps, in addition to, his "soaring ego":[80] The more he received recognition for his successes, the more he satisfied his cosmopolitan aspirations. Segev recognized how important it was for him to become "part of Austrian society."[81]

Our main task is to observe the "unseen from the outside." In order to do so, we begin with an analysis of the multiple narratives that coexist in the text, paying special attention to unseen forward-looking counter-narratives, our concern in Chapter 1. Survivors sometimes strayed from their assertive, often third-person, manifest observations to express or dream about possibilities. As digression, these swerves appear "weak" and immaterial, but we believe they express their own truths. We note that these counter-narrative expressions are not subversive in the text, for primary, declarative narratives, set against disturbing history and dispiriting contemporary opinion, are never compromised. These swerves interrupt rather than disrupt the text and, as such, exist "*despite* the misdeed," as Jankélévitch observed.[82] In addition to preserving the independence of both narratives, we argue against "deep-memory" theorists that neither one—neither stated positions nor allusive dispositions—is more authentic than the other. Moreover, we believe that historical memories as well as traumatic recall, privileged by deep-memory theory, live on in counter-narratives. This is the subject discussed in Chapter 2. Counter-narratives, we maintain, often articulated expressions of fellow-feeling, swerves that aroused memories of life for Jews before their destruction. These memories are replete in both Améry's and Wiesenthal's accounts. Pre-traumatic memories are not to be confused with nostalgia. Strong narratives recalling destruction and the collapse of trust in the world didn't permit a sentimental return to former times. It is well documented that modern Jewry, residing before the war in societies characterized by close relationships, was largely integrated, but there is a considerable debate over the degree of Jewish social engagement in European society before their communities' destruction. Scholars argue either for "thick" relationships of trust in Eastern and West-Central Europe, or for "thin" relationships of unstable coexistence, relationships that looked especially thin, retrospectively, through the prism of destruction. But these reasoned, objective accounts understate or miss the subjective experiences of Jews and the dynamism of their affective, ancestral memories. In spite or even in light of open hostilities, assimilated Jews were fundamentally and emotionally attached to European society: they felt or wanted to feel at home regardless of how their compatriots actually and, sometimes, fatally felt about them. The rupture that occurred with the campaign to destroy Jews fueled survivors' conclusions about a broken world, observations inflected with emotional despair that informed their strong narratives. But surprisingly, a residual zeal for a human connection based on grounded loyalties survived in transitional counter-narratives. It emerged in post-conflict counter-narratives either as memories that recognized in their assailants the compatriots they once knew, or as a longing for human fellowship.

The habit of reading survivors' accounts as narratives that gaze backward to Nazi-era crimes and seek to coax their contemporaries to do the same diminishes the capacity for seeing developments in counter-narratives that are in a process of reworking social relationships. This optic is especially misleading when reading essays written by Améry. As a writer dedicated to admonishing his contemporaries' moral complacency, he is widely considered as the champion of resentment. Chapter 3 argues that even in an account dedicated to recalling the past, there are narratives in Améry's testimonies that lean forward. Our argument pivots on his plaintive expressions of isolation and loneliness, an emotional price he paid for surrendering his faith in humanity. The argument calls attention to his search for release from what he called the trap of resentment that paved the way to narrative interruptions. But while his search for release responds to his narratives of condemnation, we show how it proceeds in the direction of something new without revising or "correcting" them. For Améry, daydreams and digressions served to evoke emotions of homesickness. Though he could never merely resume relationships as they existed before the war—retrospectively, he called them fraudulent—the sense of belonging to a community, of feeling at home, inspired a yearning for a human connection. Counter-narratives are weak in the text, leaving strong, distancing narratives of reproach intact, but their forward-looking perseverance is noteworthy. The first step in this direction is apparent in Améry's decision to reach out to his contemporaries with his account in an act of earnest communication.

Chapters 4 and 5 explore oblique narratives of betrayal and forgiveness. While scholars commonly refer to survivors' narratives of betrayal, this study draws attention to their structural significance and plumbs these narratives for their historical origins and transitional implications. In this chapter we look at narratives that explore relationships between victims and victimizers and note the regularity of references to memories of broken covenants. In contrast to manifest narratives referring to scenes of naked violence and reckless disregard, counter-narratives recalled violated expectations, a collapse of a nascent faith in their compatriots' dependability. In the field of psychology, where the experience of having been betrayed would naturally belong as a subject for study, scholars have characterized the experience as a non-negotiable disruption of human relationships; reactions to it are regarded as pathological or retributive. This book argues, however, that the reactions to betrayal, as severe as they are, constitute a liminal emotion. Theories of mourning indicate that experiencing loss, especially in relationships of intimate attachment, can inspire a search for new relationships as a means of displacing and compensating for previous ones. Survival was a state of mind as well as a state of existence: betrayal possesses an afterlife.

There is a different reason for the elision of forgiveness in interpretations of survivors' accounts: survivors flatly refused to forgive their adversaries, preferring instead to observe and denounce historical and contemporary injuries. There is also considerable semantic confusion about the term that obscures recognition of forgiving dispositions in counter-narratives. The argument in Chapter 5 sheds light on their existence in the text by interrogating and contextualizing its discourse. Our effort to do so might seem ingenuous and overly intrusive, but in response, we begin with an inquiry into the climate in the 1960s when survivors, in reaction to the ascendant public outcry to forgive and forget, were preoccupied with the question of forgiveness. Survivors' refusal to forgive was predicated on an understanding of what forgiveness conventionally means: an erasure of the offense and a pass for offenders. Our analysis shows that survivors, in fact, articulated an atypical version that permitted anger and memories of criminal assault. Though they couldn't label it as "forgiveness" as such, which, as they understood the term, wasn't possible, they were disposed to distinguishing acts from actors, crimes from criminals, acknowledging in the process "the person"—indeed, yearning for the connection—while denouncing prodigiously his misdeeds. They could never forget, as strong narratives that bear witness make clear. They demanded accountability. But their evaluation of the offender amounted to a reconceptualization of forgiveness that, in Améry's terms, looked forward to "a continued existence of the world."[83]

Chapter 6 concludes the book with a look at the implications of survivors' accounts for societies in transition after atrocity, an especially urgent exercise in light of the growth of massive political violence with the end of the Cold War. In particular, we are interested in interrogating the transitional justice (TJ) movement since it looks ambitiously beyond remediating the ruinous effects of social collapse to proposals for transforming successor societies. Its mainstream theories, however, especially its conceptions of reconciliation, are in need of perspectives from atrocity witnesses to strengthen the transition. The inclusion of witnesses in this development is coming at a time when civil society, and not only state actors and official criminal proceedings, are effectively resetting the stage. Survivors' public recollections of European Jewry's destruction propose a new, emotionally inflected paradigm for negotiating post-conflict transitions in two respects. By recognizing the precariousness of social relationships, they posit an unstable successor order that demands an attitude of suspicion rather than the exalted TJ notion of reconciliation that privileges a rational order of consensus and mutual respect. Second, the influence of ancestral memories on their longing for fellowship activated a forward-looking search for a social order imbued with compassion rather than one constructed out of utilitarian social arrangements based on calculated and contractual reciprocal agreements for reconciling parties in conflict. To suggest, as TJ theorists do, that mutual respect is sufficient for reconciliation neglects the imperatives of the heart. Linking backward- and forward-looking perspectives is elusive for survivors—indeed, they are discordant and irreconcilable—but the paradigm recognizes that likely transitions demand perpetual, responsible action for negotiating the terms of a post-atrocity future.

A note about procedure before embarking. Our argument adopts a method that works back and forth between considerations of conceptual constructs and an inspection of survivors' accounts, revising constructs along the way until arriving at a position that elucidates survivors' dynamic perspectives. As an aspect of this method, I include a literature review in each chapter relating to specific problems. Because the nature of our overall investigation demands a multidisciplinary inquiry, I decided to present a suitable disciplinary perspective for each chapter. For discussions about counter-narratives (Chapter 1) and Améry's plural narratives (Chapter 3), I employ a literary analysis; I use historical constructs for looking at Jews' participation in modern European societies (Chapter 2), psychological concepts for interrogating the phenomenon of betrayal (Chapter 4), philosophical constructs for evaluating dispositions of forgiveness (Chapter 5), and legal postulates for exploring societies in transition (Chapter 6). No matter the perspective, my overall goal is to show an inconclusive tension in survivors' accounts between a narrative thesis of backward-looking recrimination and a counter-narrative antithesis of forward-looking, compassionate attachment. It is inconclusive insofar as we privilege solutions, but our hope is to show that a dynamic account of human behavior, especially primitive human behavior, means that there are no conclusions and implores vigorous caution about extremes in one direction or another—too much distrust, too much trust.

With regard to methodological conventions, there are a number of observations I wish to make. My objective is to locate the existence of counter-narratives in survivors' accounts and to augment their main concerns and directions in order to "round out the facts or heighten the colors," as Levi wrote.[84] I therefore consult original texts in native languages when I believe a particular word or phrase offers special insight. Quotations used for illustration often underscore words for emphasis. Since at no time do I add emphasis, I see no need to indicate "emphasis in the original" and therefore dispense with the practice. I also refrain from using the term "Holocaust" to refer to the destruction of European Jewry during the Nazi period. There are three reasons for replacing it with other referents. With a single exception, the accounts we are mainly considering did not deploy the term, and even that exception—Jankélévitch's "*holocauste*"—could be explained by the period of time when the expanded version of "Should We Pardon Them?"—released in 1965 and reissued in 1971—was published: By the 1970s, "Holocaust" was emerging as the term of choice.[85] Jankélévitch favored instead the terms "crime" and "crimes," using them seventy-three times in "Should We Pardon Them?," as well as "catastrophe" (five times) and "genocide" (four times). In *Le Pardon*, he privileged the terms "*faute*" and "*méfait*," which his translator, Andrew Kelley, usually rendered as "misdeed" (eighty times)—non-specific terms suitable for a work devoted to ultimate questions. Améry often used the term "Katastrophe," though his English translators, Sidney Rosenfeld and Stella P. Rosenfeld, strayed from the text of his final essay, "*Über Zwang und Unmöglichkeit, Jude zu sein*" ("On the Necessity and Impossibility of Being a Jew") by substituting the word "Holocaust" when they brought out the work in 1980. Améry provided a second, more substantial reason for omitting the term: The idea implied by "Holocaust" that "a beating or death in the gas chamber was the renewed suffering of the Lord" struck him as transcendent and incommensurate with what he called the naked "concrete reality" of his experiences.[86] Its theological connotations, he remarked, "stood open, wide open onto the world that was not the world of Auschwitz."[87] The critic Ruth Wisse concurred: referring to "a sacrificial figure in a denationalized saga of evil and innocence," it stands outside of history.[88] I use the signifiers "destruction" and "wartime" to restore specificity, though there's no intention to conflate the genocidal campaign with the Second World War. A third reason involves the implication of uniqueness that the "Holocaust" has acquired. Without getting into this quagmire, I hope that this study's concentration on survivors of Nazi-era destruction provides organizing principles for investigating other instances of moral survival after atrocity.

The term "survivor" presents semantic problems as well. I recall attending a lecture about victims' experiences during the Nazi era that dissolved into personal arguments among its auditors about who suffered more and under what circumstances outlasting the predators qualified as "survival." Could it be that an episode of *Curb Your Enthusiasm* got to the kernel of competitive claims by crossing the line of propriety in order to show a Nazi-era victim and a reality show "survivor" arguing over what constitutes authentic survival? How can we include Jankélévitch in our triad with Améry and Wiesenthal when he avoided captivity? In essentialist terms, I see surviving atrocity as outliving life-threatening and hopelessly degrading experiences. In the subjective terms exalted by Améry, I also honor accounts that were written with an awareness of a vocation, of a mission to communicate after atrocity what life was like and became after encounters with rapacious hostility and aggression. It would be an unfortunate and mistaken excision to dismiss Jankélévitch's valuable insights into the phenomenon of moral survival because he managed, under perennial duress, to dodge detection and the killing centers, including the proximate transit camp Saint-Sulpice-la-Pointe. The term "survivors" in this study refers mainly to our three featured subjects as a literary expedience; the reader is invited to see comparisons with other survivors and under different historical circumstances, but I do not imply that they are exemplary. Elsewhere, I use the term "accounts" to refer to their published work. I sometimes use the term "stories," Levi's term for rounding out facts, but it can give the misleading impression that they stray from truth-telling. "Memoirs" is a more common designation for the genre that is associated with survivors, but that term, in addition to suggesting a backward-looking enterprise that only partly represents survivors' narratives, conveys the sense of a finished retrospection when, on the contrary, survivors feel the past is never past. "Accounts" is more neutral; it also implies considered observations for reflection.

The work of survivors I am interested in mine experiences for their transformative properties. Améry's commitment to discussing "the content of my experiences" was marginally important compared with his efforts at exploring what it means "for the person who has survived torture."[89] Jankélévitch regarded forgiveness as a different order of magnitude, a disposition toward re-evaluating the offender instead of ruminating over what is lost: "It is the whole lighting of my relations with the guilty person that is modified, it is the whole orientation of our relations that finds itself inverted, overturned, and overwhelmed![90] As reflections, accounts are disclosures that do more to raise questions than posit answers: "The crux of the matter is, of course, the question of forgiveness," Wiesenthal maintained.[91] Questions: That's how survivors preferred it, for not only were relationships in the present interminably negotiable, but the past, if immutable, was never settled. "Clarification," wrote Améry a few years after *At the Mind's Limits*, "would amount to disposal, settlement of the case, which can then be placed in the files of history. My book is meant to aid in preventing precisely this."[92]

1

Traumatic Memories and Historical Memories

Witnesses' accounts after atrocity

We are concerned in this chapter with a specific problem: the question of survivors' memories after atrocity, not their record of atrocity. For the past half-century, scholars have distinguished memory from history, construction from a reconstruction of the past. Our concern, however, is not a rehash of postmodern theory that posits interpretation as a projection of local convictions.[1] To be sure, the influence of present circumstances on memory is a vital aspect of our inquiry, but we are also concerned with how past existence informed memory, which is different from documentary reconstruction. Often, "memory" (construction) and "history" (reconstruction) compete for scholarly attention;[2] survivors' accounts show us that narratives inspired by the present and the past exist in the same text. Both inflect memories after atrocity, but since "presentism" in memory construction and the pastness of the past in memory-as-recall accomplish different tasks, distinctive narratives in these accounts coexist in separate registers. It is their disharmony that demands our attention. While the intricacies of memory are by now a familiar phenomenon, it is worth exploring this unusual constellation in depth: What is the nature of present-informed memories in survivors' accounts and how are they different from past-informed memories? Why do both types of remembrances exist in the same text and, when they do, what is their relationship? Importantly, what do memories grounded in the past tell us that present evocations of the past don't or can't, and vice versa?

In answering these questions, we will look at witnesses to atrocity—to Nazi-era destruction, in particular—in relationship to the event. When, in 1940, Emanuel Ringelblum founded a research project in the Warsaw Ghetto, he and his fellow inmates, some fifty to sixty intellectuals, set about secretly collecting evidence of German crimes. Their purpose was to provide as faithful a description as possible of the events they observed—torture, deportation, and murder—events as they were actually happening.[3] Their aspirations echoed the signature ideal of historical inquiry since the early nineteenth century. Its authority, technically known as positivism, was an entrenched article of erudition and commonly remains so. A couple of years later, jurist Raphael Lemkin, in his famous chapter in *Axis Rule in Occupied Europe,* where he coined and defined the term "genocide," wrote about the practical value of witnesses' depositions for exposing the unfolding crisis in Nazi-occupied Europe. Their reports, he believed, would trigger a response leading to intervention. He never doubted that they provided an accurate replication of "inhumane and intolerable conditions." The only problem was their credibility, not because they were unreliable but rather because they were "so gruesome that people refused to believe them."[4] Eventually, witnesses' accounts acquired prestige for dispelling such disbelief.

Hannah Arendt, who filed reports on the Eichmann trial from Jerusalem to the *New Yorker* in the early 1960s, and subsequently published the account in 1963 as *Eichmann in Jerusalem*, confirmed the standard for historical integrity that governed the role of witnesses' depositions in chronicling the destruction of European Jewry. As long as they rehearsed German crimes "without embroidery," she said, witnesses were valuable as documentary sources. Citing one witness who spoke about the expulsion of Polish Jews from Germany in 1938—the first in a series of events that led to Kristallnacht—she recorded with approval his Spartan description of their abject conditions as they were taken by train to the Polish border: "The S.S. men were whipping us, those who lingered they hit, and blood was flowing on the road. They tore away our suitcases from us, they treated us in a most brutal way, this was the first time that I'd seen the wild brutality of the Germans."[5] She expressed concern, however, about their limitations as testimony, concurring with justice Robert Jackson, the chief prosecutor at the Nuremberg trial. Witnesses, he said, would "always be chargeable with bias, faulty recollection, and even perjury." Documents, on the other hand, unlike witnesses, "could not be accused of partiality, forgetfulness, or invention."[6] By the time of Arendt's trial account, however, witnesses' subjective expression was gaining favor over documentary objectivity for historical truth, and she knew it. The prosecution invited witnesses to tell their stories and to express their agony regardless of their bearing on the case, a spectacle that disturbed her for permitting "tales of horror" to distract the proceedings from establishing the record.[7] But the chief prosecutor, Gideon Hausner, was clear in his intentions: it was their "blood cries" that deserved a special hearing.[8] He was less interested in a documentary record, he observed after the trial, than in a "living record of a gigantic human and national disaster" that would "reach the hearts of men."[9] Not a catalog of crimes but the suffering they produced in those who survived, and countless others who did not, was the impetus to condemnation. In order to bring home "the fantastic, unbelievable apparition that emerges from Nazi documents,"[10] testimonies of experience sounded a deeper truth—the legacy of the offense and its difficult but imperative negotiation—than the material facts of the offense.

The 1960s were a period when victims of atrocity acquired standing and a stake in shaping historical accounts. Elie Wiesel observed the formation of a new canon of expressive language: "If the Greeks invented tragedy, the Romans the epistle, and the Renaissance the sonnet, our generation invented a new literature, that of testimony."[11] It was testimony that distinguished witnesses as historical actors living with the past, as survivors burdened with laden memories. The watershed marking the rise of the witness in this new role came about when the Nazi era emerged as a subject of considerable discussion in Germany and elsewhere in Europe.

Survivors, who deliberately recounted their experiences, did not always elect to do so in public. It's one thing to talk about the difficult past with other survivors or among family members, and another to strangers where memories are no longer secure. The decision to go public with intimate memories is partly idiosyncratic. The tendency to privilege dramatic emotional expression inspired survivors, who sought recognition, to testify, often to condemn. It came at a price, as Annette Wieviorka argued. Testimony that "appealed to the heart, not the mind" diminished historical truth for the sake of psychological truth.[12] By decontextualizing its subject, it displaced the historical specificity of genocide. Another reason for the decision to make their memories public was the influence of current events, a phenomenon Wieviorka observed in the Eichmann trial. Embracing the view of Ben-Gurion, Israel's prime minister, Hausner summoned witnesses whose testimonies, he felt, would galvanize younger generations who, in his words, were "absorbed … in the building and guarding of a new state."[13] In this, she asserted, were "lessons" for the future,[14] specifically for the relatively new state's future, for as Arendt noted, the trial took place in Israel and not before an international criminal court whose concern was universal, the commission of crimes against humanity.[15] Wieviorka, who articulated the danger of testimonies serving therapeutic purposes, recognized that witnesses responded to social imperatives: the trial "was addressed to [Israel's] present time, to the nation's youth."[16] Wieviorka is correct in her analysis as far as it went. Current events did escort intimate memories to the public sphere, but the relationship between present circumstances and survivors' accounts deserves further analysis. It certainly wasn't always a one-way mandate. Survivors in Europe conversely brought their memories to bear on national opinion, government policies, and legal proceedings just a few of years after the Eichmann trial.

The French philosopher Maurice Halbwachs famously argued for the "social frameworks of memory": "It is in society that people normally acquire their memories."[17] External circumstances—present-time exigencies and the "slant" of groups to which individuals belong[18]—fuel the process of recall, not "some nook of my mind to which I alone have access."[19] The argument may well explain why survivors felt a special inducement to recount their ordeal, but it doesn't explain why they decided to reach beyond their closest associates to anonymous readers. There were surely a number of developments in the 1960s that localized their memories, developments that survivors recognized and related to their own accounts. "The horrible can make no claim to singularity," wrote Jean Améry in 1966.[20] In preparing to publish an account about his imprisonment by the SS in Belgium, where he was an active member of the Resistance, and, in particular, about his affliction in the Breendonk fortress at the behest of torturers "where no scream penetrated to the outside,"[21] a notice about the South Vietnamese capture and torture of Vietcong rebels caught his attention. He noted similar practices elsewhere before recounting his own experiences—the unspeakable abuses in South African, Angolese, and Congolese prisons—and observed the numerous books and pamphlets reporting about torture and its "horror" in French Algerian jails during the preceding decade.[22] "American sheriffs who [*sic*] howling dogs on black civil rights protesters" concerned him as well.[23] Vladimir Jankélévitch, who was a member of the French Resistance, invoked comparisons with other atrocities, including the colonial "torture in Algeria," to declare "the uniqueness of Auschwitz."[24] His reference to "segregationist violence in the United States"[25] suggests his awareness of the ascendant U.S. civil rights movement. Mention of Albert Memmi would have illustrated a more direct lineage. His 1961 melancholy self-reflection, *Portrait of a Jew*, excoriated France's colonial behavior in Tunisia, his homeland, a reference that aroused associations with his plight as a Jew, including his flight from Tunisia's Nazi occupation.[26]

It is tempting to presume that an evocation of Nazi-era memories, nourished by comparisons with other hegemonic abuses, would prod strictly personal and private memories into the public sphere. Michael Rothberg makes a compelling case for "multidirectional memory," but not for its "impetus" to articulation in public, which he noted in passing. It is persuasive that decolonization forced "a recognition of racialized state violence," including Nazi atrocities,[27] but Halbwachs, in writing about social memory, suggests a credible explanation for survivors' decisions to make a public case out of it: "We will see that, most frequently, we appeal to our memory only in order to answer questions which others have asked of us, or that we suppose they could have asked us."[28] The remark confirms Wieviorka's observation of an immediate impetus to witnesses' public pronouncements: At a moment of Zionist opportunity, they testified to the agony of Jewish victimization and to the priority of personal and national survival. In fact, the day's questions influenced what witnesses recalled, shaping their testimony "to conform to what they imagine the public wants"[29]—graphic accounts designed to awaken a national resolve. Other scholars posit similar arguments for depositions given by survivors in Europe. Jeffrey C. Alexander broadly observed the relationship between "trauma representations," including narratives of Nazi-era destruction, and a wider audience's concerns, such as attention to the responsibilities of ordinary citizens in the destruction process.[30] Ruth Wisse argued that survivors became strangers to themselves by relinquishing the "authentic" stories closer to their personal memories of volition under extreme conditions, in order to satisfy European intellectuals' fascination with the Christian motif of the suffering, helpless, virtuous victim.[31]

Survivors were not only responsive to contemporary questions, they often regarded them as urgent.[32] But their answers were not always inclined to satisfy. On the contrary, Améry, Jankélévitch, and Simon Wiesenthal broke a period of silence—a silence that had confined their accounts to limited circumstances—to admonish their contemporaries. The early to mid-1960s were a time of growing impatience in Europe over a preoccupation with the Nazi past in legal proceedings, an impatience coaxed by the impending enforcement of statutory limitations. Survivors were unsettled by appeals to leave the past behind and move forward. The general mood threatened them for two reasons: It reminded them of the dreadful time when they were abused with merciless disregard; and it smugly consigned the Nazi period of national disgrace—for them, a historical watershed—to useless insignificance. What propelled Améry's references to discursive global violence was his fear that no one will care. "The screams penetrated as little into the world as did once my own strange and uncanny howls from the vault of Breendonk."[33] Will memories of victims simply vanish? "Where and who are all the others [who were tortured] about whom one learned nothing at all, and of whom one will probably never hear anything?"[34] The juxtaposition of colonial-era and Nazi-era indifference to torment was more than a mnemonic device. While anticolonial movements abetted and even stimulated attention to the Nazi past, his decision to enter the collective discourse emerged from a realization that the "revolt of public conscience" had all but expired.[35]

Like Améry, Jankélévitch compared atrocities to fuel his protest against his contemporaries' moral evasion of "the exceptional quality of genocide": "I have said that the problem of Auschwitz for distinguished intellects seems to inhere in these words: How to unburden ourselves of it?"[36] His 1965 article "Should We Pardon Them?" was a broadside against what he called "the definitive quietus promised to the criminals who committed this crime."[37] The promise was the exercise of statutory limitations, when "forgetfulness would become in a sense official and normative."[38] That, he wrote repetitively, was intolerable and could not proceed without a commensurate response: resolute and punishing protest against past crimes and "the forgetfulness that completed it."[39] Wiesenthal, who devoted his account to writing a story about his unexpected encounter, during his ghetto internment, with an SS officer on his deathbed, referred sparingly to the wider audience, his readers. But when he did, it was acerbic. After the war, he decided to find the officer's mother to get "a clearer picture of his personality."[40] In characteristic fashion, he was inclined to find favor in her; she was "clearly kindhearted, a good mother and a good wife."[41] He went as far as to speculate about their "common link" that transcended their poignant differences: she, who grieved for her son and "the ruins of her [German] people"; he, who "might have been among her son's victims."[42] But when she proclaimed that her neighbors were not responsible for Jews' murder, Wiesenthal demurred: "No German can shrug off the responsibility."[43] The strength of the conviction energizing his admonishment is clear from the way it overpowered contiguous observations. He said that she, herself, wasn't responsible; "she was not the recipient of my reproaches." Yet all Germans, even if not personally accountable, "must share the shame of it."[44] Jews, too, played a role in the preconditions of hostilities, a point that he implied in response to her question, "You are not German?" Signaling the ascribed distance between them, he replied, "No, I am a Jew."[45] But his rebuke of each and every German, as well as his belief in a common bond, was paramount: "As a member of a guilty nation he cannot simply walk away like a passenger leaving a tramcar, whenever he chooses. And the non-guilty must dissociate themselves publicly from the guilty."[46]

Counter-narratives: Omnipotent and impotent

The distinctions we drew at the beginning of this chapter—between a constructed and a reconstructed past, and between present- and past-informed memories, which is our concern—recalls Michel Foucault's famous notion of "counter-memory" as residual conceptions of the past that disrupt official assertions of historical continuity.[47] Twelve years later, in 1989, Pierre Nora familiarly articulated a similar distinction: the contrast between memory and history. He, too, found official, or positivist, history wanting. As a tool of national authority, it creates the dogmatic impression that the nation and its politics are unified, preordained, and teleological, indeed, sacred and inviolable. Against this, "memory" struggles for expression, "no longer quite life, not yet death."[48] In its fruition, it represents "the remnants of experience still lived in the warmth of tradition, in the silence of custom, in the repetition of the ancestral."[49] Unlike history, which is organized, descriptive, and intellectual, memory is "a perpetually actual phenomenon."[50] It is "affective and magical."[51] It doesn't take much to see where Nora's sympathies reside, but what I find striking is the value of applying this cultural and political analysis of authority to the architecture of texts.

Texts betray multiple narratives—factual and fictional, expressive and measured, personal and neutral. The most influential theorists of narrativity in survivors' accounts, which we will evaluate, hold different views of their relationships, though there is consensus among some theorists in finding narratives that struggle against positivist tendencies. Our argument veers from this position. We recognize narrative diversity rather than struggle, and find that positivism doesn't play as important a role in accounts that we are primarily concerned with here—accounts that are distinguished by reflection—as they do in accounts devoted to reconstruction. Reflective accounts are particularly valuable for exploring the role of memory in the survival process, memory after atrocity. Reflection is not only self-affirming but also represents an awareness of the quest for self-affirmation, establishing, and not just granting, the survivor's standing. It expedites the transition from experience to intelligibility, exhibiting a desire to interpret and communicate emotional meaning. It also helps us to distinguish between what survivors aspired to say and what otherwise demanded expression.[52] In these accounts (and not only in these accounts), declarative statements coexist with plaintive expressions. Indeed, there is a marked distinction between the two narratives, the former stronger and more assertive in tone than the latter. We already saw evidence of strong narratives in the present-informed rhetoric of protest. "The non-guilty must dissociate themselves publicly from the guilty," Wiesenthal wrote; Jankélévitch raged against Nazi belligerence and "the forgetfulness that completed it." The language of Améry's reflections is pointedly declarative, as in his observation about present-day Germans, "who must continue to bear the responsibility for those twelve years" since they failed to end it.[53] Wiesenthal, Jankélévitch, and Améry each stepped into the role of "the witness," making statements about the Nazi past and the German present. In the assertion, in their expressions of protest and reprimand, and in their very stance as custodians of historical and moral truth, they maintained a distance from their readers. As Améry proclaimed, he was not inclined to rid himself of his resentments—the hallmark of the survivor-as-public witness—nor, we should note, could he.[54] "Bearing witness," the phrase that most often characterizes survivors' depositions, constitutes a narrative that resolutely looks backward. As for narratives of expressive pathos, it is our task to show their contradistinction as alive and present, worldly engaged, and, though informed by memory, gazing forward to the uncharted future.

There are important differences between Nora's cultural observations lamenting history's conquest of a natural and spontaneous consciousness, and the argument, which I am proposing, for the coexistence in survivors' accounts of strong and "weak" narratives. Above all, Nora was concerned with national power. Ours is located at the other end of the political spectrum: its victims. National Socialism manufactured words and images to buttress its claim to heroic national deliverance. For the regime, the destruction of European Jewry was redemptive; for survivors, it was the abyss. As useful as the distinction between history and memory is for a textual analysis of survivors' multiple narratives, as a paradigm of power, it has no bearing. Narratives that bear witness, for example, do not presume historical continuity. On the contrary, their "official" accounts seek to show the rupture between past and present. Jankélévitch made the point assertively in referring to Nazi criminality: "The reactions that it inspires are above all despair and a feeling of powerlessness before the irreparable. One can do nothing. One cannot give life back."[55] Note Jankélévitch's formal tone of intellection. While what the passage says—"despair and a feeling of powerlessness"—is too immense for the third-person voice that expresses it, Jankelevitch's purpose here is to proclaim futility rather than disclose true feelings. Even so, there is surely emotion. The observation is acrid. Acrimony inflects his statement of brokenness. Améry, too, made clear his sense of despair. He wrote poignantly about loss, "the loss of home by an expellee from the Third Reich,"[56] and in writing about it, his purpose is precisely to assert a reality to an audience that preferred not to listen or care.

A second, related distinction between Nora's notion of history and survivors' sure accounts is the relationship between past and present. There is emphatically nothing teleological in survivors' accounts, certainly not in the sense Nora meant it when he wrote that official history exalts its "heroes, origins, and myth."[57] A third adjustment, in adopting Nora's analysis for the narrative structure of survivors' work, is to the relationship he asserted between history and memory. Nora posited a predatory nation-state and its totalizing mythmaking when he wrote about history's "eradication" of memory,[58] "its true mission."[59] Our argument is necessarily quite different, for as strong as witness-narratives are, and as opposed as they are to counter-narratives, both in their forceful tone and in their severe attention to the informative past, the two narratives are heterogeneous rather than in hostile conflict. Counter-narratives possess the ancestral warmth Nora reserved for memory that is not only still alive, as he noted, but is truly energetic. They are, as he noted, weak by comparison, but they reveal their pluck whenever they interrupt strong narratives.

While the contrast Nora draws between history and memory is vivid and an intriguing interpretive framework for parsing multiple narratives in survivors' accounts, other scholars have observed it directly in the text, making the case from literary and psychological, and well as philosophical, perspectives, and, unsurprisingly, arriving at varying conclusions. Much scholarly activity has illumined the existence of "deep" narrative references to the destruction process. These accounts of atrocity disturb testimonies' "common" narratives, a recital of events that privileges, as Lawrence L. Langer wrote, "the idea of continuity, and even of chronology."[60] The distinction originated from Holocaust survivor Charlotte Delbo's formulation of what she called "deep memory"—"the memory of the senses"—and "external memory"—"the memory connected with thinking processes"[61]—with sense/deep memory serving as "counter-time" (Langer's term) recording, typically, "the odor of burning flesh."[62] As she made clear, these counter-narratives represent the rawest possible reconstruction of realities—realities that defy vernacular articulation:

> Did you know that suffering is limitless
> that horror cannot be circumscribed
> Did you know this
> You who know.[63]

Even though Langer asserted that deep memory "coexists" with consoling, sanitized narrative "relief one feels from the fact of survival,"[64] there is no narrative parity: deep memory's "subtext" is the testimony's "*essence*."[65] Deprival, not survival, is the authentic account—"the doom of those closest to him," citing one survivor's testimony, "who did *not* survive"—not redemptive stories about how "he managed to stay alive."[66] There is no convalescence: "For the victims, the Holocaust is a communal wound that cannot heal."[67]

In deep-memory theory, common memory deflects our attention from a radically different order of existence. Fortress-like, it clings to Enlightenment ideals of human progress and heroic agency despite deep memories of destructive zeal. W. G. Sebald invoked this kind of narrative evasion in *On the Natural History of Destruction*, his inquiry into cultural memories of the devastation Germans endured as a result of RAF offensive bombing campaign during the Second World War.[68] In spite of the carnage, Germans managed at best an anemic accounting, he argued. No one who witnessed the destruction, "incomprehensible in its extremity," could have possibly escaped with an "undisturbed mind."[69] But the ruinous reality "pales when described in such stereotypical phrases as 'prey to the flames,' 'that fateful night,' 'all was let loose,' 'we were staring into the inferno,' 'the dreadful fate of the cities of Germany,' and so on and so forth."[70] Langer compared these kinds of locutions to conventional, "consciously contrived" literary devices.[71] As Sebald wrote, "Their function is to cover up and neutralize experiences beyond our ability to comprehend,"[72] or stated directly, recalling Nora, "to banish memory."[73] He preferred a written record that sounded "the authenticity" of experience proportionate to reality.[74] Such accounts included "fragmented memories of nights spent in the bunkers"[75] and other evocations of "disgust and revulsion … the fears of general dissolution that threatened the collapse of all order, with humans running wild and descending into lawlessness and irreversible ruin."[76]

In spite of its putative fraudulence, common memory competes in survivors' accounts with deep memory for narrative expression. Primo Levi confirmed the point in reflecting about his story, *The Truce*. Compared to earlier work, it was "a more 'self-conscious' book, more methodical, more literary, the language much more profoundly elaborated. It tells the truth, but a filtered truth."[77] For him, both registers of memory were authoritative, for he also asserted the irrepressible force of disquieting memories that recalled "bizarre, marginal moments of reprieve":[78] "I have not forgotten a single thing."[79] They interrupted "compressed identity" in order to "reacquire for a moment its lineaments."[80]

"Without any deliberate effort, memory continues to restore to me events, faces, words, sensations, as if at that time my mind had gone through a period of exalted receptivity, during which not a detail was lost," adding emphatically, it "imperiously demanded to be told."[81] Entering this discourse, historian Saul Friedländer argued that the task of history was to honor the authority of common and deep memory. The historian is responsible for "rendering as truthful an account as documents and testimonials will allow."[82] But, as necessary as "the distancing effect of intellectual work" is,[83] the historical quest must permit survivors' memories to unsettle standard narrative sequence, "the facile linear progression of the narration." This requires a self-consciously "sporadic but forceful" measure of commentary by means of a strategic "voice-over":[84] "The *Alltagsgeschichte* of German society has its necessary shadow: the *Alltagsgeschichte* of the victims."[85]

Shoshana Felman argued for similarly distinctive narratives, contrasting the documentary record with "the shock of an *encounter* with events ... history as an experience."[86] Like Langer, she valorized deep memory's counter-narrative. Framing her argument with the two most famous legal trials related to the Nazi era, the Nuremberg and Eichmann trials, she characterized witnesses as messengers whose stories "re-traumatized" the experience, and thus, in comparing accounts with artistic expression, convey something that is "*more than*" the "*totality of facts* and events."[87] In her view, counter-memories, like deep memory, are more authentic, if ultimately ineffable and unmasterable, than legal and historical positivism. Unlike deep memory, however, they refer to the present experience, to "*hallucinated timelessness*," which amounts to reliving the original violation endlessly as traumatic repetition.[88] Perhaps exemplifying an approximation of the truth of the event is an account Sebald cited that was written in 1955 by Gert Ledig, *Die Vergeltung* (*Retribution*):

> It tells of the dreadful end of a group of anti-aircraft auxiliaries barely out of childhood, a priest who has lost his faith, the excesses of a company of soldiers heavily under the influence of alcohol; it deals with rape, murder, and suicide; and it returns again and again to the torments of the human body—teeth and jaws broken, lungs shredded, chests slashed open, skulls burst apart, trickling blood, grotesquely dislocated and crushed limbs, shattered pelvises, people buried under mounds of concrete slabs and still trying to move, waves of detonations, avalanches of rubble, clouds of dust fire and smoke.[89]

Encounters with events bring the events close to the present, while antiseptic, objective documentation, the legal remedy, keeps it distant.

Marianne Hirsch and Leo Spitzer also relegated factual information to the value of traumatic re-enactment in witnesses' accounts, particularly when it is visual—in gestures, muteness, and resistance discernible in video and courtroom testimonies, and in documentary films—in order to disclose the "'Auschwitz self' that is located in the body and outside speech."[90] But they cautioned against the implications of an esoteric and apparently inaccessible idiom. The "unspeakability of trauma" suggested "the utter impossibility of fully bearing witness to this particular traumatic past."[91] The problem is the lost opportunity of communication. It might well be impossible to get close to the truth of the event, they said, but it's still necessary to try, for witnesses possess a "wealth of knowledge" and are "eager to testify."[92] Jorge Semprun, a memoirist and member of the Resistance in France against the Nazi occupation, exemplified their argument. He claimed, "You can tell all about this experience … Even if you wind up repeating yourself. Even if you remain caught up in it, prolonging death, if necessary—reviving it endlessly in the nooks and crannies of the story. Even if you become no more than the language of this death, and live at its expense, fatally."[93]

Critics of deep-memory theory posit a second narrative of their own. Recognizing narratives of traumatic repetition, Susan Rubin Suleiman, Sidra DeKoven Ezrachi, and Dominick LaCapra noted strategies in survivors' accounts that worked at making sense of traumatic experiences. Relying on the classical theories of Freud and his nineteenth-century predecessor, Pierre Janet, Suleiman referred to the process as "narrative memory" (Janet's term), a development more dynamic in the text than the subtext of deep memory. Ezrahi characterized it as "an ongoing renegotiation" of historical realities that would otherwise remain static and inflexible.[94] In other words, narrative memory involved efforts at "working through." As an example, Suleiman wrote about Semprun's late discovery of an intervention on his behalf, when he was an inmate at Buchenwald. Having assumed during his internment and afterward that he was registered as a "student," he revealed in one account how he learned that, in fact, the scribe registered him as "*Stukkateur,*" a useful worker skilled in stucco. The story "forced me to rethink things," for the survivor, who saw how he could be "caught up" in death, confirmed life, recalling how the scribe "probably saved me" from a fatal selection. By referring to the scribe as "My German communist"—an expression denoting kinship—he also confirmed a common humanity.[95] LaCapra noted that the renegotiation involves an awareness of the "here and now," which is different from what happened "back then"[96]—an important difference from traumatic re-enactment, the "unmediated truth," as

Langer wrote,[97] which erases the distance between the present and the past. Narrative and traumatic memory constitute survivors' possible trajectories, trapped, in the case of traumatic repetition, by the past in compulsive identification with loss, or freed in counter-narrative by a compensatory search for new beginnings.

Significantly, narrative memory and working through are a consequence of the expressive act constituted in the act of writing. Unlike spontaneous testimonies in documentary film, videos, or courtroom proceedings, storytelling, wrote Ezrahi, is an "intertextual process" that resists "the black hole." The narrator of Jurek Becker's novel, *Jakob der Lügner* (*Jacob the Liar*)—the protagonist's friend—faithfully recounts and simultaneously invents the circumstances of a ghetto's existence and destruction. Invention is the story's conceit: it created a more bearable reality. Jacob, the subject of the story and a ghetto inmate, broadcast "news" of hope, the imminence of liberation, on his invented radio. But as a fiction that was more acceptable than what really happened, invention served as an alternative, compensatory reality that, as Ezrahi observed, "counters the growing despair." The 1969 novel, she noted, was an early example of counter-narrative.[98]

Storytelling and other recorded expressions offer survivors a process for working through by managing intense and excessive emotions, providing, as LaCapra observed, "some measure of conscious control, critical distance and perspective."[99] Retrospection, a process that Langer critiqued as a refraction of direct address, served the purpose of transmuting traumatic memories into what Susanne Langer called "the articulation of feelings," expressing emotions that are not "deep" but are not, for that reason, any less authentic.[100] It was, accordingly, the act of rewriting that spared Semprun from endlessly reliving the past, just as it forced him to "rethink" what and who saved him from disaster and likely death. "Intellection," wrote Jankélévitch, can achieve an understanding of the other person. It "reduces anger as aspirin reduces a fever. Whether it is a matter of indignation or irritation, of rancor or shame, lucid knowledge is in all things the great sedative; it soothes suffering, takes the heat off tenacious sulkiness, decongests the inflammation of anger, and 'relaxes' the aggressive and strained man."[101] For survivor and Nobel laureate Imre Kertész, writing served to work through traumatic memory: "Whenever I think of the traumatic impact of Auschwitz, I end up dwelling on the vitality and creativity of those living today. Thus, in thinking about Auschwitz, I reflect, paradoxically, not on the past but on the future." It met his "need to step out of the mesmerizing crowd, out of History," which was a burden whose totality and authenticity he was not willing to approximate. Writing was his refuge: "For whom does a writer write, then? The answer is obvious: he writes for himself."[102]

LaCapra, Ezrahi, and others made the important point that working through, in spite of its suggestive finality, is an ongoing process. As part of the process, it involves reflection, retrospection, and regulation—influences, they assert, that moderate and compensate for traumatic memory—"keeping death at bay," Ezrahi commented, "for a time at least."[103] The argument for retrospection distinguishes them from deep-memory theorists who argued instead for psychological introspection to unmediated truth. I don't agree, however, that counter-narratives are necessarily "intertextual," as working-through theorists argued. Freud's influence is particularly evident here. Narrative memory, as Suleiman claimed, is a "revision" of traumatic memory,[104] just as renegotiation, for LaCapra, is "the muting or mitigation of trauma."[105] More than revision, Suleiman continued, it "implies a mastery or overcoming of trauma."[106] Ezrahi added that the process of renegotiation could undermine, as well as mitigate, the immobility of the past.[107] The regnant postulate of counter-narrativity therefore construes counter-narratives as interdependent with witness narratives: a renegotiation of traumatic memory or, conversely, Nora's historical conquest of common memory's redemptive and anesthetic relief from desolation. As dynamic as texts are—this is particularly evident in traumatic regulation—we believe that counter-narratives express possibilities that possess their own forward-looking significance independent of their effect on other narratives.

Let us consider the structure of the three accounts we are concerned with for evidence of narrative independence. For Jankélévitch, the authority of "human essence" is the moral compass of his public expression in the 1960s. Extracting terms from classical philosophy for his 1967 master work, *Forgiveness*, he wrote: "My love is addressed to the pure hominity of the man and to the naked ipseity [essence] of his person in general,"[108] adding, "of all the values, love for humans is the most sacred."[109] Yet, the conviction did nothing to mute, much less overcome, his acrimony. As he remarked, "The judgment of condemnation has stayed the same."[110] If anything, what he condemned contradicted what he loved, for "indifference to crimes against humanity, … indifference to crimes against the essence and hominity of the person is the most sacrilegious of all misdeeds."[111] No one would disagree that *Forgiveness* is a work of considerable "conscious control" with an awareness of the "here and now." It clearly sublimated excessive rage. But it was more than an exercise in coming to terms with the past. His assertion of love for humanity was a superlative statement—it is the most sacred value; human existence is a first principle, an "elementary and vital right"[112]—and therefore referred not only back to the "black hole" but also forward to the future. Indeed, by remaining alert to misdeeds, to a brokenness that the future must accommodate, he showed little interest in working through.

Améry's inclinations barely permitted attenuation of moral outrage. But when he did stray from condemnation, a human dimension emerged. In his essay "How Much Home Does a Person Need?," he evoked memories of his pre-war homeland that, more than nostalgia, expressed a longing for human attachment: I "still suffer from homesickness, a nasty, gnawing sickness."[113] Even though he had come to recognize the fatal miscalculation of his former sense of security, he acknowledged that "rootedness in a homeland" was essential.[114] These inspired memories were visionary, not revisionary. Like Jankélévitch's, they articulated a condition of a social order that would meet his wish for something grounded, as remote as home seemed to him. Indeed, as the phrase "rootedness in homeland" suggests, the wish included remnants of the past, an inflection of the familiar, though it sailed to a different shore. It did not compromise his incendiary memories, as his considerable accounts of Nazi-inspired torment make clear: "Torture has an indelible character. Whoever was tortured, stays tortured. Torture is ineradicably burned into him."[115] These strong, witness narratives remained inflexible and immune to negotiation. Indeed, they formed the basis of what he believed was another non-negotiable human condition: the manifest potential for human cruelty.

Of the three survivors we are examining, Wiesenthal comes closest to engaging a process of narrative mitigation. In recounting his surreal meeting with a dying SS officer, he found ways of understanding, though not excusing, his crimes, stating that they were a result of indoctrination. He believed the officer was repentant, "even though he did not admit it in so many words."[116] His expression of sympathy, even warmth, for the enemy is surprising. But he doesn't let us forget the circumstances of the encounter. He sets his story in a forced-labor environment. Nearby residents were unmoved, a point that he directed as much to his complacent contemporaries as he did to the mesmerizing crowd of onlookers. Killing was endemic. His faith in humanity was broken: "Life in a concentration camp taught me differently." It was impossible to believe in anything, he said, after witnessing a new era of shameless and serial contempt.[117] In *The Sunflower*—a work whose consideration of forgiveness is strikingly generous—two narratives, in fact, compete for attention. Neither one was in service to, or more authentic than, the other. His search for humanity instead opened other possibilities.

The argument for counter-narratives as unmediated truth or dynamic palliative presumes a stratification of memories. This is especially conspicuous in deep-memory allusions to "the Auschwitz self," which, in Langer's terms, is "the buried self": deep memory "burrows beneath the surface of the narrative to excavate episodes that corrrode the comforts of common memory."[118] These memories colonize accounts as "subtext." Other critics, writing about narrative memories that work through and renegotiate traumatic memory, postulate a process invading the fixation on loss. Their argument recalls Freud's theories of mourning. The process of mourning loss, he argued, had the effect of attenuating repressed traumatic injury and the pathology of "melancholia" that tended to reproduce loss or violence.[119] Freud explored the process of mitigation in "Remembering, Repeating, and Working-Through" (1914), an investigation into the influence of analysis on interrupting repressed memory and its grip on compulsive repetition.[120] In an earlier argument, I favored this vertical model and its homage to subterranean narrative truth as authentic and as narrative possibility.[121] But I now believe that memories are situated horizontally,[122] with witness narratives looking backward and counter-narratives looking forward. At times, Langer appears to suggest narrative parity in observing that deep memory and common memory exist in two heterogeneous registers, a "permanent duality, not exactly a split or a doubling but a parallel existence."[123] If parallel, however, there is still interplay, with common memory serving as faux-redemptive response to traumatic memories. "The unfolding story brings relief," though no satisfaction.[124]

We need to re-evaluate the presumption that the vocation of counter-narratives "counters the growing despair." LaCapra, in making the case, after Freud, that working through is open-ended,[125] posited a "limited *process*"[126] with a purpose: it "may enable more desirable configurations."[127] Ezrahi referred to "divergent sensibilities," which "are actually part of the same dialectic" between urgent representation and the unrepresentable, suggesting, as dialectics sometimes do, intertextual developments, a narrative supersession.[128] There are surely indications in survivors' accounts of interplay between narratives: Améry's repetitive references to feeling abandoned[129] inspired a search for some form of worldly engagement. In this, the memories are not dissociated, as Bessel A. van der Kolk has argued.[130] They are not so compartmentalized and fragmented that there is no interaction between them. But to argue that the interplay is responsible for producing new configurations or a dialectical synthesis is misleading. Survivors' accounts do not recapitulate Nietzsche's famous discourse on the "Dionysian" and the "Apollonian" predispositions in human creativity.[131] While there are Apollonian inclinations toward emotional calibration with a potential for controlling, if not eviscerating, Dionysian tendencies toward ecstatic, amorphous, and amoral fury exceeding all boundaries and form, the two spirited forces do not manifestly require each other to keep each other in check or work themselves out in dynamic interplay toward creative accomplishment. Jankélévitch, in asserting the sacrilege of vital rights and the imperatives of forgiveness in the same text, made clear that the two themes are necessarily, at bottom, irreducible: for him, there is no attenuation of traumatic memory in spite of forgiveness's generosity. "In order to forgive, we must first remember," he observed,[132] but then insisted that "forgiveness is omnipotent and impotent." It "forgets all,"[133] and yet "the judgment of condemnation" hasn't wavered. It's hard to reconcile both sides of the equation, but that is importantly the point he made: traumatic memory and narrative forgiveness share the imaginary but each remain "imperious."[134] Forgiveness, he said, is a "revolutionary inversion of our vindictive tendencies," not, however, their conversion. It radiates infinitely, or so it wants to, only to concede the next moment to "irremediable evil."[135]

> The human spirit oscillates between these two triumphs that are simultaneously true, yet alternately conceived: for they contradict one another. And the reciprocity of these two contradictories is reciprocal to the point of vertigo … No! there is no last word.[136]

The paradigm of oscillation—what he elsewhere called "the play of contraries"[137]—is a significant articulation of counter-narratives' conduct. However much they give and receive from witness narratives, they are impotent in altering traumatic memories and the acrimony they arouse. They do not relieve or console or initiate a process, even a limited process. If Semprun's late discovery forced him to "rethink things," a later discovery—a reminder of irremediable evil—again intruded. For he could not forget the "bitterly cold" days, "when snow covered the camp, as it would later cover my memory."[138] Counter-narratives interrupted what Jankélévitch termed the "ultimate … Hell of despair,"[139] but "the last word is always the penultimate word."[140] Perhaps this is what working-through theorists mean by an open-ended process: as Ezrahi observed, narrative memory postpones death "for a time at least," though Jankélévitch preferred to conceptualize counter-narratives less as an interaction than as an action. In this formulation, the picture that emerges is a mosaic of memories in "insoluble conflict"[141]—two discrete narratives that make up, but do not form, a whole. The world that survivors imagined would somehow have to incorporate an undiluted and unreserved, though controlled, recognition of ineradicable evil as well as, in Nora's terms, "the remnants of experience still lived in the warmth of tradition, in the silence of custom, in the repetition of the ancestral."

The vocation of counter-narratives

If counter-narratives are impotent, do they then exist merely as an alternative to primary narratives that bear witness, admonish belated generations, or express relief? If they do not serve a corrective or compensatory intertextual purpose, do they do something more than balance the text? Deep-memory and working-through theorists have established a significant feature of survivors' counter-narratives: they show how they express the authority of the survivor's voice. Of course, strong, declarative narratives constitute prima facie evidence of victims' acquired standing. As literary critic Terrence Des Pres observed, "The fact that this literature exists, that survivors produced these documents … is evidence of a profoundly human process,"[142] or as Améry wrote, "What matters to me is the description of the subjective state of the victim."[143] But counter-narratives are notable for their urgent expression; deep-memory theorists recognized this in evocations of traumatic memories. Working-through theorists noticed urgency as well. Suleiman observed the emergence of agency in Semprun's story about a visit with a dying inmate at the Buchenwald infirmary. Greeted with the exclamation, "No, not you," he replied, "No, not I, François, I am not going to die. Not this night, in any case, I promise you. I will survive this night, I will try to survive many other nights in order to remember."[144] When critics suggest that accounts are sometimes implausible, it is because survivors assert their authority over intractable circumstances. Semprun, it appears, invented François as his death mask in order to show that he is a survivor.[145]

Wiesenthal, too, some suggest, also made up his deathbed story. Heinrich Böll, the well-known German critic, presumed fabrication when he wrote him with suggestions for rewriting the account in order to make the dying SS officer more real, and not the good boy Germans might adopt as a symbol. He also recommended that he associate him properly with the Wehrmacht so that his crimes would indict the German army for its criminal record.[146] But fabricated in the details or not, the story, by transforming the enemy into a complex figure he could then relate to, transformed Wiesenthal from a victim to a survivor. Victims, he wrote in witness narratives, were passive and helpless.

They "obeyed apathetically, without a will of their own, like automatons."[147] Counter-narratives, however, presented a different estimation of his internment: "I needed badly to remain strong, for only the strong in these dire times had a hope of survival."[148]

Bruno Bettelheim's claims to independent thinking and action in Dachau and Buchenwald, where he spent the years 1938–9, occasionally belie credibility. He recounted an incident when he "provoked an SS official." Not only did he claim to escape punishment for the act of disobedience; afterward, he actually received permission for his release from imprisonment.[149] The incident's compression into a single time frame might explain our disbelief, but the important point is the effect Bettelheim wanted to convey. It represents his account's counter-conceit: the lifesaving importance of self-assertion under prominent circumstances that threatened and often succeeded to reduce prisoners to childlike helplessness. "Why did I deliberately provoke an SS officer? I believe that in order not to collapse, I had to prove to myself that I had some power to influence my environment."[150] Disobeying orders doesn't exactly appear prudent, but for Bettelheim, action beat passivity for what "I needed most to survive."[151]

Attention to the authority of the victims' voice—a trend dating from the 1960s—assailed conventional historical positivism for demoting survivors' accounts. Demotion is discernible in the work of Lucy Dawidowicz, a historian recognized for her scholarly contributions toward founding the field of Holocaust Studies in the mid-1970s. She distrusted testimonies: "The transcribed testimonies I have examined have been full of errors in dates, names of participants, and places, and there are evident misunderstandings of the events themselves."[152] At best, testimony served historians as evidentiary fodder for critical analysis, confirming arguments already established by rationalist, scientific documentation. For example, Debórah Dwork and Robert van Pelt, writing about decrees in German-occupied Poland ordering Jews to wear a Star of David as a mark of their ostracism from Polish society, cited the diary of survivor Dawid Sierakowiak for illustration: "Thursday, November 16 [1939]. Lodz. We are returning to the Middle Ages. The yellow patch once again becomes part of Jewish dress."[153] Survivors naturally objected to the occlusion of their distinctive voice: "My personal task," wrote Améry, "is to justify a psychic condition that has been condemned by moralists and psychologists alike. The former regard it as a taint, the latter as a kind of sickness."[154]

Narrative theorists importantly abetted the task by justifying victims' deep truths or intertextual negotiations, but they missed the part of the communication in survivors' accounts that reached out and looked broadly to the larger world. Améry not only recalled his Nazi-era ordeal. In primary narratives, he made clear that his assertion of standing existed in context—as protest against contemporary indifference. In counter-narratives, too, he evoked former times and human attachments. But narrative theorists ignored context and therefore isolated witnesses' voices from the circumstances that variously inspired their expression. Paradoxically, these theorists prized close listening, a hallmark that particularly distinguishes deep-memory analysis by urging the value of listening to witnesses from the "inside."[155] Joining the indictment of documented knowledge for predetermining what is relevant about victims' experiences, psychoanalyst Dori Laub exhorted investigators to hear "new, diverging, unexpected information,"[156] information historians tended to neglect, like "the anguish of one's memories."[157] Grasping witnesses' voices within and confined by the text, however, risks compressing memories into composite expression of deracinated, exceptional torment—"the anguish of one's memories." Victimization, however, is not interchangeable. Anguish, like all experience, is an anterior and posterior emotion that recalls specific formative circumstances—violations of neighbors' trust, social indifference, and their tormentors—and attaches negative and positive responses to it for a new worldview. As Wiesel commented in a dialogue with Semprun, one's Auschwitz is not another's.[158]

This, as we have seen, is related to Wieviorka's concern. In developing an account of the Nazi past, all that seemed to matter, she wrote critically, were feelings and emotions, memories of "painful episodes."[159] Interpreters invested in listening to the authentic disorder of victims' experiences, in preserving traumatic memory as unmediated truth or in anchoring it as an object for negotiation, displaced historical reconstruction with "an archive of survival."[160] She lamented what she called a "historiographical revolution": "the substitution of testimonies, supposedly real history, for the history of historians,"[161] and she worried when it came to "invade the public sphere."[162] Wieviorka dates the revolution to the Eichmann trial when "the advent of the witness profoundly transformed the very conditions for writing"[163] about the Nazi past; its effects persist to the present day, as she rightly observed. Her argument for elevating historical diligence over the "juxtaposition of stories"[164] is valuable for an analysis of the past, which was her concern, and for our analysis of the circumstances when survivors elected to present their accounts for public scrutiny. The conclusion she drew, however, was overstated, a throwback to the principles of historical positivism. For her, testimonies obstructed historical knowledge: The right of each person to her memory "can come into conflict with an imperative of the historian's profession, the imperative of an obstinate quest for the truth."[165] Though she conceded that "testimony contains extraordinary riches," that is, more than factual truth, a "subtle and just as indispensable truth of an epoch and of an experience,"[166] it merely summons "the power" of an event or evokes desultory phenomena such as traumatic violence and its repercussions. Nothing, she insisted, is more important than understanding the event, and that, she argued, requires a coherent historical narrative and the "reflection, thought, and rigor" that it incites.[167]

There is surely something more to counter-narratives than expressing their authors' urgent voice, but they have had a hard time escaping their reputation as phenomenological or intertextual expression. Having emerged persuasively from the shadow of legal and historical positivism, it is typecast for an occasional disruption, as deep memory, or as a mitigating influence, as dynamic process. All we seem to get from them is a sense of the experience—Hausner's "unbelievable apparition"—or the promise of negotiating it. Strong, declarative narratives are another matter. Gazing intently back in time, they signify a message or communicate a purpose by bearing witness to past crimes, condemning belated generations for their dispossession of the past, or proclaiming a redemptive, triumphant victory over the past. We've already seen the strength of passages written by Améry, Jankélévitch, and Wiesenthal admonishing their contemporaries' evasion of their responsibilities for national renewal. Améry recognized, in protesting against moral inertia, that the nation might be "goaded" into rejecting everything, "but absolutely everything, that it accomplished in the days of its own degradation."[168] Jankélévitch also saw admonishment as instrumental. Like Wiesenthal, he asserted the "sacred flame of disquiet," describing his world's "amnesia" as "shameful."[169] Even if they had little faith in the efficacy of condemnation, the pronouncements helped drive their strong narratives.

While counter-narratives ardently assert a hope or need for survival, strong, indicative narratives are prescriptive. "Remain strong" was Wiesenthal's strategy for escaping the abyss that others, who "obeyed apathetically, without a will of their own, like automatons," couldn't.[170] Bettelheim was thoroughly explicit. He wrote his account to show "what it takes to remain autonomous in any mass society."[171] Levi famously described the conditions of survival in "the power to refuse our consent," explaining, "We must polish our shoes, not because the regulation states it, but for dignity and propriety. We must walk erect, without dragging our feet, not in homage to Prussian discipline but to remain alive, not to begin to die."[172] Survival as triumphant, as a statement of having survived, is a positive assertion with a negative aversion: it declares an endurance of will against the tribulations of a hostile opposition—the abyss of SS cruelty; the pressures of mass society; "Prussian discipline"; and, I would add, the unconcern of belated generations.

Establishing the record is, according to Alvin Rosenfeld, the primary function of testimony: witnesses were, after all, in a position to show how devastating destruction "actually was."[173] Bearing witness is truth-telling,[174] often the substance of narrative deposition that, in the positivist tradition, declares an empirical and verifiable account in contrast to the "unmediated truth," "the thing itself,"[175] that deep-memory theorists reserve for true witnessing.[176] As material evidence, "the enormity of human loss" is its province;[177] for Rosenfeld, loss sometimes included post-traumatic emotional distress. Unconcerned beyond literary tradition with contextualizing accounts, Rosenfeld asserted that survivors were devoted to writing narratives of catastrophe, quoting as evidence a passage by Wiesel: "The progression of the inhuman transcends the exploration of the human,"[178] and remarking that Levi chronicled "the devolution of a man."[179] For Rosenthal, bearing witness is a matter of "wicked illumination."[180] A member of Ringelblum's Warsaw Ghetto chroniclers confirmed the empirical-truth value of their project: "I consider it a sacred duty for everyone, whether proficient or not, to write down everything he has seen or heard from others about what the Germans have done … It must be recorded without a single fact left out." His purpose was manifold: to inform those who were not witnesses and might be skeptical: "And when the time comes—as it surely will—let the world read and know what the murderers have done"; to serve as a basis for commemoration: "When the mourners write about this time, this will be their most important material"; or to inspire revenge: "When those who will avenge us will come to settle accounts, they will be able to rely on [our writings]."[181]

Bearing witness, like condemnation, responds to regnant opinions at the time of recall. We have seen how witnesses were mobilized to help inspire a Zionist awakening, but witnesses didn't always require prodding. An atmosphere of political demonstrations for national liberation from colonial control stimulated survivors to recall their own experiences with persecution. Witnesses recalled Nazi-era crimes to defeat denial or, after the Second World War, to deter a German resurgence. Survivors who elected to go public with their stories in the 1960s recalled places and events to assail common and cavalier misconceptions. "Although you may previously have walked by the gate of the Gestapo headquarters countless times," Améry wrote, "it has other perspectives, other ornaments, other ashlars when you cross its threshold as a prisoner" to face his tormentors, "whose light blinds us and burns us to the bone."[182] Jankélévitch evoked "the German insult, the insult that tramples underfoot, that uses women's hair as a mineral substance,"[183] to defy facile comparisons between the greediness of exploiting low-cost labor for surplus profit and Auschwitz's radical offenses.[184]

Other common strong narratives include variations of the demand "never again," an assertion Levi articulated when, in contrast to an impulse he felt at liberation to raze everything that reminded him of the Nazi architecture of destruction—barracks, barbed wire, ovens—he later realized their significance as "a Warning Monument."[185] For many survivors, achieving clarity about their experience was significant enough. "I didn't understand, though I wanted to," Wiesel wrote. "Ask any survivor and you will hear the same thing: above all, we tried to understand. Why all these deaths? What was the point of this death factory? How do I account for the demented mind that devised this black hole of history called Birkenau?"[186]

By contrast, intimate expressions inhabiting counter-narratives receive little credit for signification. For deep-memory theorists, they are the "thing itself," resisting elaboration. For working-through theorists, they are cast in supporting roles responsible for moderating the blinding effects of traumatic memory. Then again, we shouldn't be surprised: counter-narratives are not always easy to grasp, especially in contrast to the prominence of consolidated and declarative statements in primary narratives. That may be because they are extra-textual, exceeding the boundaries of textual interplay. We note passages that engage worldly relationships even as they negotiate traumatic memories. Within their narrative milieus, they exhibit desire rather than contempt, dreams rather than anguish, even compassion and love rather than disparagement. When survivors confessed to the futility of their expectations for recognition and worldly reform—"nothing of the sort will happen," Améry wrote;[187] for Jankélévitch, "our horror" was "mute and impotent"[188]—their expectations mutated to dreams, the stuff of counter-narratives. As imaginative expression inflected wishfully, counter-narratives seem aimless. They are also transient, occasionally interrupting strong narratives but not disrupting them because survivors, at the same time, resolutely recalled the past—indeed, they ruminated about it. In our view, they are the province of possibilities overshadowed by the immensity of resentment and resignation. They are "weak" narratives—tentative and wishful, sometimes connotative, and seemingly out of place. Indeed, they represent a valuable index of what Levi called "unseen" realities.[189] But that's what makes them intriguing and suggestive, a valuable subject for scrutiny. These unseen realities are memories that gave rise to transitional, forward-looking expression.

We inherit from narrative theorists an interest in bringing the unseen to light. For them, the project involved an exposure of truths truer than the claims of historical and legal positivism. "The psychological and emotional milieu of the struggle for survival," as Geoffrey Hartman observed,[190] disclosed greater insight than factual, documentary evidence. By looking at accounts from the inside, from the victim's perspective, LaCapra, though cautioning against "extreme identification" with the victim, arrived at conclusions missed by an "objectifying methodology." In opposition to Raul Hilberg's critical assessment of Jewish Council members—the SS-appointed community leaders responsible for implementing Nazi orders, often at the expense of fellow Jews—he consulted testimonies to argue for their hopeless dilemma.[191] Omer Bartov utilized accounts recorded by Ukrainian survivors to show, in contrast to conventional documentation, the complexity of survival in circumstances of interethnic massacres: "The distinction between rescue and denunciation was often blurred and at times nonexistent, as was the distinction between perpetrators and victims."[192] In one instance, a survivor recounted that a Ukrainian nationalist, who hid him and his mother, was responsible for killing Jews and Poles.[193] Accounts also exposed the sham of the bystander figure "since everyone took part in the events, whether they suffered or profited from them."[194] This picture—one more nuanced than a rationalist historiography that, for Bartov, "distorts and ultimately falsifies the historical record"[195]—draws our attention to what Levi regarded as "unseen from the outside":[196] the "gray zone." Resisting schematic description, he referred to the divergence and convergence of "masters and servants" in the Lager where the oppressed pandered to the authorities for privilege, aiding the summary collapse of moral order.[197] He observed new codes of behavior that required "that you take care of yourself first of all."[198] The offer to help another inmate, he observed, simply didn't exist.[199] This kind of conduct was not limited to time or place or party: all were implicated.[200] There is much new truth in counter-narratives, though our argument cast them as distinctive from other claims—those in strong narratives—not in opposition to falsification. Bartov's argument deserves consideration on its own merits. The enemy, he affirmed, was often at one point an ally. As one survivor observed: "I would say 80 percent [of my family] were killed by the Ukrainians who were our friends."[201]

It is our contention that the phenomenon of betrayal is an unseen reality that requires close inspection. Not only is its narrative expression frequently articulated; it also represents a memory that inspired survivors to forward-looking considerations. As much as survivors starkly condemned violent behavior, their evocation of shocking violations—the breakdown of trust—recalled the presumed bond with their compatriots. Memories of violated expectations were more like reminiscences of a human connection they historically prized and prospectively longed for, though the traumatic disruption deeply and indelibly chastened their conceptions of humanity. They are ancestral, retaining implicit warmth and traces of affection, as Nora observed. Felman wrote about survivors' "shock of an *encounter* with events," an observation that pointed to their subjective experiences with trauma, but we need to add that the encounter, itself, constituted a *relationship*. As Bartov observed, survivors often recalled "the relationship between Jewish populations and their local gentile surroundings," and it is these narratives, as well as occasional references to Jewish culture, reactions to events, and experiences of torment and survival, that require manifestation and analysis so that we can see them from the outside where we are.[202] These memories require attention but, more than that, the kind of inspection that strong, backward-looking narratives of condemnation receive so that we can see and interpret what Améry meant when, after resolving to maintain a "moral chasm" between survivors and their adversaries, he added, "for now."[203]

By examining counter-narratives, we can interpret survivors' vigorous reactions to the debate over statutory limitations as multifaceted. What is apparent is their resentment of the silence, the cold indifference, and the view that whatever isn't self-serving is disposable. But the brazenness also recalled encounters a generation before when their compatriots, with whom they felt an affinity, indeed, a historical attachment, violently betrayed their trust with similar behavior. Their counter-narratives permitted them to indulge those antecedent, intimate memories and to interrogate their relationships with belated generations. Expressions of longing for a human connection are another unseen, emotional reality. Jankélévitch was direct in expressing the ideal of "brotherhood"[204] (though he recognized its impermanence): "The truth that intellection," or "lived comprehension,"[205] "wants to re-establish is that of an amicable world in which man will cease to curse his brother and will live in peace of mind and of heart. In that, intellection implies an effort and relates to the future."[206] Améry, in expressing his homesickness, even as he recanted the emotion, and Wiesenthal, whose story produced something human about an SS officer who committed heinous crimes, also show a side of survivors' accounts that gets lost in accounts whose *raison d'être* is to record misdeeds. But here, again, is a truth—the emotional significance of steadfast, if compromised, human relationships—that exists alongside backward-looking narratives, poised toward looking outward to a world survivors want to address in what Jankélévitch called a "second person" voice,[207] and forward, warily, to a world they were open to negotiating.

A question remains that won't go away: Why are counter-narratives "unseen"? Why do they seem out of place in survivors' accounts, as an afterthought, perhaps, or as intrusive thoughts? Why are they sometimes connotative and not, like strong, witness narratives, denotative? Langer posited one reason: they are "buried" because deep memories of traumatic re-enactment are painful and require repression or at least dissimulation. Or perhaps oblique references to the value of human relationships exist merely as a foil for condemnation, as a measure of shaming their detractors; hence, their ancillary, counter-narrative significance. Jankélévitch's evaluation of his contemporaries' indifference as "sacrilegious," an affront to the "essence" of humanity, appears to confirm this explanation. These answers have merit and usefully show the existence of interplay within the text. But, consistent with the argument for narrative independence, there is another reason for "weak" narratives in at least some survivors' accounts. They derive from memories of their roles in acts of betrayal that survivors were ashamed about and often preferred to gloss over.

Wiesenthal recalled one such incident involving the SS's frequent but futile search for the ghetto's children. He castigated "SS Group Leader Katzmann—the notorious Katzmann" for the tragedy that ensued. "His brutish brain conceived a devilish plan: He would start a kindergarten!" Katzmann required the Jewish Council's support; gradually the children's parents also agreed to sending them to the kindergarten. Like so many other similar stories, this one reached its betrayal denouement with a dramatic reversal of expectations. Inmates, upon hearing the plan, believed it was "a sign of a more humane attitude," though Wiesenthal qualified the idea as one based more in expedience than in generosity, since, as he reported, some heard that an international commission was about to visit the ghetto for evidence of appropriate treatment. "A committee from the Red Cross was anxiously awaited. But it never came. Instead"—the term signaling the epochal moment of fatal surprise—"Instead, one morning three SS trucks arrived and took all the children away to the gas chambers." It wasn't only the kindergarten that was "deserted." Whatever faith he and other victims somehow still had in Germans' humanity also deserted them—or at least until the next time, as the story's coda suggests. On reflection, Wiesenthal wondered, *sotto voce*, why Jews presumed their enemies' good, or at least reasonable, intentions. He answered that Jews were "eternal and incorrigible optimists."[208] If placed in context, the remark refers to the belief modern Jewry sustained for generations in the fellowship of common humanity, often against contrary evidence. Jews, in this grim account, were innocent, the victims of sordid motives. But the added comment, which seems unrelated to the story's point, implicated Jews for their susceptibility to any conceivable sign of fellowship, an expectation that, in this rendering, abetted dreadful results. This is one of Wiesel's main points made in an unpublished, Hebrew edition of *Night*: "The professional optimists meant to make the present easier, but in doing do they buried the future."[209] Wiesenthal elsewhere confessed that the picture he formed of the dying SS officer "was kinder than the reality,"[210] an observation admitting to emotional inclinations that, in hindsight, appeared wrongfully permissive. We, of course, are more lenient in recognizing that hope was among few tactics victims had at their disposal. But that's not how Wiesenthal saw it: Jews were unwitting enablers.

An episode Améry later regretted reveals a confession of naïveté that he felt contributed to his arrest by the Gestapo. As a member of the Resistance, he joined his group in distributing anti-Nazi propaganda to German occupation troops, believing that this "could convince the German soldiers of the terrible madness of Hitler and his war."[211] The observation suggests that the soldiers, unlike Hitler, were actors amenable to rational or even moral suasion. That simple perception, he remarked in retrospect, required correction, indeed, a revision—not, as Suleiman argued, for emotional management, but rather for an entirely new worldview. Instead of reversing course, the soldiers, he later surmised, passed along the fliers up the chain of command to security agents, who then arrested him for what turned out to be brutal interrogation.[212] As belated commentary, his speculation was the result of an acquired wisdom, "an enormous perception at a later stage,"[213] that redacted a story of heroism and courage into one decrying "feeble" acts of sabotage whose innocence led to his capture.[214] He started the story rather prosaically: what led to his arrest was plainly his actions, "a matter of [distributing] fliers."[215] But the story conveyed something else as well: they were not Germans who happened to be soldiers, as he had believed; they were soldiers first in service to Nazism. The story he wanted to tell—an account of his arrest—was also a crestfallen memory of groundless faith in his countrymen.

Jankélévitch's confession of a formerly fraudulent belief in his countrymen's good will was also indirect, an acknowledgment that is implicit in his belated recognition of love's risks in "our world of enmity that is dug full of hiding places and subterranean galleries." What he learned "from our misery" is that the one who receives love has to first merit it. Better a love that is "mutual," even as "ulterior motive" and insincerity govern. Yet that, too, is "naïve."[216] Jankélévitch's moral volte-face rested on recognizing the perils of expecting too much from others, which he said he gained from his activity in the Resistance: A world of enmity demanded action. "Violence and force," even "without love," is the "heroic choice" when "essential values" are at stake. The "fight against fanatics," he observed, is still merely "the least of all evils," praiseworthy but insufficient.[217] Action, for Jankélévitch, is superior to blind trust. In accordance with his argument for forgiveness, "unreciprocal or unilateral love"[218] is the gold standard. That, of course, sounds more quixotic than mutuality, which would threaten precisely those essential and vulnerable values he endeavored to save. But, in contrast to idle confidence in others, and in deference to the persistence of "unforgivable wickedness,"[219] he asserted expressions of caring for another. It allowed him to dream in search of a tenable future. In the meantime, it satisfied the requirement for independent action, which urgently redressed the naïve behavior that he and other survivors had come to regard as fatal.

References to the shame of illusion surfaced in other accounts. An inscription in the memorial book for Jedwabne, written some forty years after residents in this Polish village destroyed its Jewish community, lamented the conclusions drawn by community leaders after imploring a Catholic bishop for protection in the days leading up to the 1941 pogrom. The reporter recalled that he warned family members against heedlessly trusting the bishop's pledge of intervention: "The Jews placed too much confidence in his promise [to help] and refused to listen to the constant warnings that came from friendly Gentile neighbors." Once again, we are reminded about the impossible dilemmas facing Jews at each turn, for whom were they to believe, the bishop or their friendly neighbors? Even though the story's details are in dispute,[220] the recorded memory is a tableau of pathos. "We here in Yedwabne [*sic*] are safe," he recalled his family members saying, "because the Bishop promised to protect us."[221] The original, 1956 Yiddish version of *Night* permitted Wiesel some latitude in expressing views among insiders. Here, and not immediately in translation, he upbraided his fellow Jews for their misguided beliefs: "In the beginning there was faith—which is childish; trust—which is vain; an illusion—which is dangerous. We believed in God, trusted in man, and lived with the illusion that every one of us has been entrusted with a sacred spark from the Shekhinah's [divine] flame; that every one of us carries in his eyes and in his soul a reflection of God's image. *That* was the source if not the cause of all our ordeals."[222] A short while later, in his unpublished, Hebrew version, he added: "We [fared] very badly not believing in fate"—that is, in signs portending their destruction. "If we had, we could have prevented many catastrophes."[223]

There are a couple of ways of interpreting what survivors regarded in hindsight as their shameful overconfidence in their compatriots. Levi believed it was a psychological response to crisis. Writing about the Lager, he remarked: "The harsher the oppression, the more widespread among the oppressed is the willingness … to collaborate" with the authorities. Though he explained it as a desire for power and privilege, the goal was plainly *protekcja*.[224] Arendt, on the other hand, took the long view. She argued that the presumption of faith in their compatriots' humanity was a historical accretion, the habit of demonstrated allegiance to the nation and state.[225] Whether Jews seized elusive opportunities for advantage, or, as we believe, were inspired by credos and proclamations throughout modern Europe that promised social acceptance, the destruction of Jews compelled a difficult self-assessment. It forced them to see their compatriots in a radically different light, but also to reflect on their own behavior, arousing a sense of concealed disgrace. No longer could they rely for their security on hope or trust or faith in reason or the holy spark or in the state's protection. It all appeared as a sham undertaking. But, while their ordeal shattered their confidence in the premise of their interrelationships, it didn't destroy the sense attachment, their taste for common fellowship. These memories lingered in counter-narratives as acute homesickness or as human compassion and love. The foundation of the previous attachment didn't vanish, but it did require reworking.

2

Historical Emotions

Narratives of encounters

On his way to an extraordinary encounter with an SS officer on his deathbed, Simon Wiesenthal noticed that the meeting place seemed eerily familiar. Objectively, there was nothing surprising about the makeshift hospital: It was one stop for him in a four-year sentence under Nazi race laws to forced labor that would include imprisonment in concentration camps. It was, in fact, part of an unwelcome detour from his nascent career as an architect, an interruption of the course he had charted for himself in his hometown of Lvov (Lemberg as it was called in German).

Wiesenthal's confinement to the Lemberg Ghetto is the subject of his well-known account *The Sunflower*. As he recalled, he was chosen by a nurse for an unexpected assignment: he was to serve at the request of an SS officer as an interlocutor for the confession he wanted to make. Wiesenthal remembered that his election was random, though his description of the circumstances referred to a meeting of eyes that appeared to single him out.[1] As he followed the nurse into the hospital along his *via dolorosa*, he recognized a staircase. He became aware that he had been here before. It was there, as "we reached the upper hall, where, not so long ago, my diploma had been handed to me."[2] He got lost in his thoughts: the hospital metamorphosed to the university he once attended. "There on the right was the way to Professor Bagierski's office and there on the left the way to Professor Derdacki's."[3] The nurse interrupted the spell, drawing him "out of the past,"[4] but not before other details established his emotional foothold "on well-known ground":[5] "I could still see [the professor's] hand making lines across my drawings with a thick pencil, a hand with a large signet ring."[6]

This was "well-known ground." The Germans seemed entirely out of place. Throughout his encounter with the SS officer, "The feeling of unreality persisted."[7] His memories commandeered his present circumstances. What startled him were not moments of homeland recognition but the German usurpation. The whole situation was "uncanny":[8] This place belonged to him. In Wiesenthal's mind, he was led not into the hospital room to meet an officer who was about to confess his crimes, but into what he recognized as the office of the Dean of Architecture. A white bed with an adjacent night table would eventually demand his attention, but first he saw "familiar objects, the writing desk, the cupboards in which our papers were kept."[9]

More than recalling a seizure of power and an occupation of territory, the key to Wiesenthal's account was its fragmentation into descriptions of what he saw and what he remembered, of what seemed out of place and what seemed at home and displaced. That's what made the occupation unreal. It disrupted the familiar, the province of the "well-known" or what Maurice Halbwachs, the pioneering French sociologist of "collective memory" and the social construction of memory from the first half of the twentieth century, called "the content of mind." For Halbwachs, "external" influences did more than introduce something new. They called attention to the difference between what was new—"a change of location, occupation, or family"—and what was already known. Importantly, the disruption did not expunge memory. All that it did was split cognition between an awareness of the external and memory of the past, for the disruption "hasn't totally ruptured his bonds with previous groups."[10] In observing the accouterments of the occupation, Wiesenthal enlisted his "content of mind," the substance of what really mattered to him. What he could still see felt visceral: the hand of his professor, the ring on his hand. He "could still see" the seminal, pre-war past when he had formed bonds with his Polish compatriots who guided him as they "handed" to him his certificate of advancement, certifying in the process his hopes and expectations.[11]

Wiesenthal's testament exemplifies evocations of warm memories in survivors' accounts otherwise devoted to narratives of torment that brought to mind formative bonds of human relatedness These counter-narratives are distinguishable not only because they are latent in accounts of human disconnection, inscribed as ambient persecution and assault, but also because they reverse narrative direction in seeking reconnections. Jean Améry, in *At the Mind's Limits,* wrote in both voices. Using a term in manifest narratives to define embodied brutality, he referred to National Socialism as a political order that "not only practiced the rule of the antiman (*Gegenmenschen*), … but had expressly established it as a principle."[12] On the other hand, he did not forget that beneath or within the antiman was an "ordinary" person,[13] someone ultimately no different from him: The antiman was what "your fellow man (*Mitmensch*) became."[14] Améry's essay on torture seeks to make ineffable connections along the way of reciting the details of his grim, irreducible physical torture. He often identified himself as a victim; in fact, the self-description is his leitmotif. His "objective description" of torture was plainly something "I finally want to get to"[15]—no less so, perhaps, than Wiesenthal's overt purpose in reconstructing his encounter with the SS officer. But he was not solely a victim, an object of contempt and abuse. More than just "the other," he also identified *with* his enemies: They tortured "his fellow man," and, again, transformed "the fellow man" into flesh.[16] Like Wiesenthal, he interrupted the description of his ordeal with counter-memories reprising what was, after all, well known.

Torture refracted the bond of human fellowship into the powerful and powerless, the torturer mutating into an antiman, the victim reduced to flesh, his spirit extinguished.[17] It is noteworthy that Améry still held on to memories of a vanished world, a "social world" with the capacity to grant "our fellow man life, ease his suffering, bridle the desire of our ego to expand."[18] Even as he condemned the torturer's sadism, he could still see the ornaments of human features embroidering the figure of "evil."[19] One of his torturers had a name, a point he recalled emphatically: "P-R-A-U-S-T." He recognized his voice: "The accent was colored by Berlin dialect." He embellished the portrait: He "had that fleshy, sanguine face."[20] He unmasked his torturers' "leather coats and pistols" and their "Gestapo faces ... as [they] might appear in a book," giving them "faces like anyone else's. Plain, ordinary faces."[21]

Like Améry's social world or Wiesenthal's personal encounters at the hospital/university, Vladimir Jankélévitch intimated a human connection in lectures he gave at the *Colloques des intellectuels juifs de langue française,* a gathering of French-Jewish intellectuals that began in 1957. Even as he sought to establish the "fact" of his Jewishness, he acknowledged his deep and ineffaceable relationship with French culture, an allure that Améry referred to as ties that "linked" him and other Jews to their "land and its people."[22] Whether or not a common fellowship existed in fact is not the point of these narratives. Accuracy is the concern of accounts bearing witness to observable and verifiable acts, the province of documentary history and strong narratives.[23] Counter-narratives make a claim to another truth, an emotional truth: As Jews, they were drawn to the social world. In their recessive accounts, they veered from "objective descriptions" to assert that they still wanted to belong—though not on the same terms as before.

Privileging emotional truth is especially important for interpreting Wiesenthal's account. Critics have questioned his fidelity to facts.[24] The SS officer, for example, appeared too good.[25] Why would an SS officer, a practicing Catholic, seek forgiveness from a Jew rather than a last sacrament? That the encounter even took place seems implausible. Documentary historians presume, however, that credible accounts are ones that record or reconstruct events when Wiesenthal's purpose, in addition to establishing the setting, was to express what was important to him: an attachment to a world he felt a part of, a world that was familiar, replete with recognizable emblems. Everything was falling apart except his memories of a social world he believed he knew and occasionally evoked.

Ancestral memories

Halbwachs's theory of collective memory provides a suggestive explanatory framework for the survival of pre-offense memories in accounts centering on an offense. These memories, as sullied as they were by disruptive events, recall "what still lives."[26] Applying the argument for continuity to survivors' memories is debatable, especially because the examples he provides—"a change in location, occupation, or family"—seem unequal to the task of explaining memories inundated with violence. The break for them was total, or almost total, a point survivors strongly assert. "Nothing has healed," Améry wrote when he reissued *At the Mind's Limits* in 1976.[27] The evidence of continuity when rupture was paramount is, however, located in counter-narratives of vestigial memories recalling emotional connections with milieus before their deterioration. Psychologists refer to these pre-traumatic narratives as episodic long-term memories that have the effect of "making me the same as the person I was in the past"[28] in spite of "differences between the person now and the person then."[29] These memories, compared with the narratives holding forth against massive wrongdoing, were ancillary. But the enduring "social memory," as Halbwachs called it, was substantial and, by keeping alive a semblance of human fellowship that appeared to remain vivid, succeeded at occasionally redirecting their accounts against their backward-looking, contemptuous grain toward a period both earlier in their lives *avant le déluge* and sometime in a future they were inclined to imagine.[30]

I prefer to regard survivors' accounts as expressions informed with ancestral instead of social memories. The difference distinguishes Halbwachs's social memory as mainly an identification "in unison" with a group (Jews)[31] from memory that seeks to identify with totemic, intergenerational stories. The notion of ancestral memories is a key postulate in arguments for reparations. Descendants often justify their claims of redress by positing inherited "family lines," in this case, in relationship to past wrongs.[32] As Richard Vernon remarked, "Some wrongs endure, however, in an embodied way, that is, in the bodies and minds of those who still suffer them despite distance in time from the original wrong."[33] The dynamic, if not the contents, is the same: descendants participate in a common, kindred story across generations, grounding them in the process in defiance of traumatic interference. Survivors, especially those who considered the implications of their ordeal in a reflective pose, identified with a group vertically, in historical perspective, as well as laterally, as social or collective memory. To revise Halbwachs's formulation, survivors identified with a synchronic, contemporary Jewish-survivor cohort and with diachronic, ancestral family lines that echoed sonic aspirations in modern Jewish history.[34]

That Jews were largely "assimilated" before the war is beyond dispute. Wiesenthal's youthful Jewish ethnic milieu in the Austro-Hungarian region of Galicia permitted his attraction to the empire's multi-ethnic culture. During his studies in 1930s Prague, he found cosmopolitan life "exhilarating."[35] His parents' support of the empire, including his father's military service in the Imperial Austrian army during the First World War, surely influenced his western orientation. Jankélévitch spent his entire life in France, where he exhibited strong ties to French culture. Both of his parents had emigrated from Russia, and though his father showed an interest in Jewish tradition—an interest that likely influenced his son's attention to Jews' distress during and after the Second World War—Jankélévitch, like Améry, did not affirm his Jewish heritage until the 1930s with the rise of antisemitism. Before then, the family was immersed in European culture. He and his father had taken to the currents of continental philosophy—his father was a consummate translator of German psychology and philosophy into French before the First World War; Vladimir was a promising interpreter of the French philosopher Henri Bergson and a noteworthy pedagogue at French universities. He served in the French military and expressed faith in the state's protection of its citizens even after the nation's German defeat in 1940. Améry, who always acknowledged his Jewish background, recalled his youthful indifference to it. Raised by a Catholic mother after his father's death in combat during the First World War, he grew up in Austria aspiring to acceptance as "an impressive German youth,[36] the gold standard of a secure social membership. As he wrote, the racial Nuremberg Laws in the mid-to-late 1930s prevented him from fully assimilating. He was explicit about the anguish he experienced due to the Germans' rejection of his German cultural credentials.

This précis of their European lives does not, however, do justice to what "assimilation" meant to these men. Against their counter-narrative swerves to exalting humanity—to the "bonds with previous groups," as Halbwachs put it—characterizing their European relationships as fitting into the larger society is a faint and merely adequate description. It doesn't capture the subjective, emotional energy, reified in postwar accounts that managed to survive the catastrophic wartime social and moral disintegration that severed Jews from the rest of European society. Indeed, classic historical evaluations of Jewish assimilation, as a distinguishing phenomenon of modern Jewish history, fail to explain the tenacity and impossible resilience of counter-narrative dreams and digressions that acclaim a human connection, an attachment that still lives even in accounts that are otherwise dedicated to condemning the campaign of Jewish destruction. Historians agree that post-emancipated European Jews—Jews in West-Central and Eastern Europe spanning the period of some 150 years from the late eighteenth century to the 1930s and 1940s—existed in compact societies. How compact Jewish integration was varied, and scholars, taking the long view, interrogate social integration as a process of assimilation by degrees. At one end of the spectrum is a relatively consonant picture of absorption, and even a "symbiosis," in dominant societies. At the other end is a dissonant picture of unease and interethnic tension. In between is a hybrid portrait of acculturation where Jews took their place openly, as state citizens, in general society—in the "neutral" or "semi-neutral" society, as Jacob Katz famously characterized it[37]—while simultaneously attending to an endogenous, self-consciously Jewish life "at home" ranging from religious observance to in-group, intramural association.[38]

Such analysis mutates to vigorous debate when scholars examine Jews' pre-war social aspirations through the prism of their wartime destruction. One position holds that social tensions adumbrated the final cataclysm. They possessed a special, corrosive power that dispels the illusion of symbiotic relationships and even defeats the credibility of Jewish emancipation with its promise of enfranchisement. From this angle, antisemitism appeared sutured to European culture; it was a condition of Jewish modernity. Assimilation was as much chimera as it was aspiration. It left Jews abjectly unprepared for self-defense. From a different perspective, eruptions of hostilities meant nothing more than a momentary atavism that would eventually fade away. Setbacks were exceptional, a historical jolt, at times a serious jolt, that did little long-term damage to a more or less integrated reality or at least to Jews' faith in its prospects. This was the position that our trio of survivors adopted. Their accounts recalled formative social ties, though not based on faith in their eventual fruition but rather as a longing for a human connection that felt as remote as it was urgent and uncertain in the shadow of their dreadful experiences.

Much of the groundbreaking scholarship exploring the antecedents of Jews' European destruction has recently centered on Eastern Europe due to opportunities for access to documentary sources since the fall of the Iron Curtain some twenty-five years ago. Eastern Europe offers a prime social laboratory for studying the interrelationships Jews had with their counterparts since Jewish life before its collapse was characteristically interethnic and intercultural, Jews among neighbors.[39] It was in these local, provincial settings, in and about villages and other open-air warrens, where about half of those murdered under Nazi control resided. What kind of village relationships existed prior to village killing? The side of the spectrum characterized by interdependent relations is illumined by historian Omer Bartov, who explored Jewish life in Southeastern Poland, in what used to be called Eastern Galicia and Western Ukraine. He asserted historically close ties with their ethnic Polish and Ukrainian neighbors. "While there were periods of strife—both domestic and with external forces—and although we should not idealize their relations, these groups knew only the reality of coexistence."[40] Interaction was constant in schools, at marketplaces, in common spaces, and even in state and military service. The relative comity did not last into the twentieth century as Ukrainian nationalism and Soviet interference marginalized "foreigners," including ethnic Poles as well as Jews. But even as terror mounted in the 1930s, interethnic relationships remained close, closer than the term "coexistence" suggests. Bartov is especially poignant when he investigated relationships in the fog of hostilities. Killing, he showed, often occurred among residents who had cared for each other; provocatively, it was "intimate." The parties in conflict, he asserted, knew each other well: As he persuasively documented, Jewish victims identified their assailants as their school friends and Christian neighbors before the war.[41] One survivor, Alicia, told the story of her friend's father who became a Ukrainian police official. Before arresting her, she recalled, he said "he loved me like a daughter."[42]

The growing documentary evidence of rescue acts in Ukraine underscores interethnic kinship. Often marginalized in the historical record by ascendant strife in interwar Eastern Europe—hostilities augmented by the economic depression; official discriminatory policies, including restrictions on attending universities; and the perception of duplicitous "Jewish Bolshevism"—rescue acts were not uncommon; in fact, argued Frank Golczewski, there were "too many" of them to ignore, suggesting that interrelationships required attention in evaluating the circumstances for Jews in pre-war Poland.[43] Stories about protecting Jews at considerable risk—in one case, as many as 1,700 Jews were saved—often refer to everyday deeds: Discovering a Jew in hiding, one policeman said, "Let him go. I know him well."[44] Natalya Lazar captured the quality of fraternal relations in her study of the century-long process of emancipation and acculturation for East European Jews in Czernowitz, the capital city of Bukowina, once a Habsburg imperial province. Looking at their involvement in the process during the interwar period, she showed how they identified with German culture, adopted its language and bourgeois values, and took to its music, philosophy, and literature. For Paul Celan, Rose Ausländer, and novelist Aharon Appelfeld writing after the war, she wrote, Bukowina was "a site of vibrant cosmopolitan culture and the Habsburg Empire's overall German–Jewish symbiosis."[45]

In her documentary analysis, Eva Hoffman sheds light on the other side of the spectrum where nominal coexistence, she asserted, is an accurate depiction. As the daughter of Polish Jews who survived the war in hiding, she looked at one village near the Russian border where more than half of its 4,600 inhabitants were Jews. Here, too, she observed, was an atmosphere of "proximity and familiarity" among Jews and ethnic Poles, but she concluded that relations were not all that close. In place of "frank exchanges or intimacy," such as Catholics attending Jewish weddings or interfaith conversations about religion,[46] Jewish and Catholic Poles limited their dealings to running business errands or having social drinks. "Before the war, most Poles and Jews did not include each other within the sphere of mutual and natural obligations."[47] Relations this thin precluded "shared structures and convictions"[48] and concealed their basic differences. In the end, these conditions were fatal: feeling "less alone, less abandoned in their most tragic hour" would have saved Jews from elimination.[49]

Scholars and contemporaries observed the process of Jewish integration in the urban centers of West-Central Europe as well. In one classic articulation, Peter Gay asserted that "Germany's Jews were woven into the very texture of German culture."[50] Social tensions were everywhere present, exacerbated by the rise of political antisemitism in the late nineteenth century, but they were non-catastrophic. With the decline of the movement toward the end of the century, Gay observed, German Jews "could read the auguries [of a successful integration] as highly favorable."[51] Even Theodor Herzl, the founder of political Zionism, betrayed his preferences for assimilation. Though he argued in his manifesto, *The Jewish State* (1896), that assimilation in Europe was bankrupt—a process subverted by political antisemitism, which he claimed was inevitable—the Jewish state, far from disinheriting the promise of enlightened humanity, was, at bottom, its continuation. Writing to exhort a following, he stated: "For ambitious young men, to whom every road of advancement is now closed ... the Jewish State throws open a bright prospect of freedom, happiness, and honor."[52] The significant difference for Herzl between European assimilation and assimilation outside Europe was the shift of responsibility for its success. We Jews, he said, could "help ourselves by other means"[53] toward fulfilling their frustrated dreams: "The exodus will thus at the same time be an ascent in class."[54]

Herzl's political-Zionist warning about the acceleration of antisemitic hostility was not his only intuitive premonition; he recognized that assimilation's progression provoked fear of Jews' economic domination: "And if the power the Jews now possess evokes rage and indignation among the anti-Semites, to what outbursts would a further increase lead?"[55] Historian Götz Aly elaborated on the position in his study of the Holocaust's "prehistory": Germans, disquieted by an "innate insecurity,"[56] were envious of post-emancipated Jews who profited disproportionately from unprecedented economic, educational, and statutory opportunities. Seeing Jews, as outsiders, achieve success inspired popular resentment and hatred, setting the stage for a certain means of racial prophylaxis.[57] Political philosopher Hannah Arendt, writing in the 1950s and 1960s, took the argument of assimilation to an extreme in *Eichmann in Jerusalem* when she provocatively impugned the Nazi-era ghetto's Jewish leadership for collaborating with the Nazi regime in selecting Jews for annihilation.[58] This, she asserted, was the logical extension of their modern allegiance to the state that provided "special services to the governments" and "their special protection from the state." Their loyalty was *sui generis*: "Of all European peoples, the Jews had been the only one without a state of their own, and had been, precisely for this reason, so eager and so suitable for alliances with governments and states as such."[59] Arendt observed that Jews always remained pariahs in modern European society," but their "foreign, exotic appeal" was, in fact, a condition of their integration: Jews were to demonstrate "humanity as a universal principle."[60] From the moment in 1791 when Jews in France were granted full citizenship, Jews believed the burden of proof was theirs to convince others of their qualifications.[61] Their "differentiation and distinction"[62] was ominous: they exposed Jews qua Jews in their new positions of power and influence, a catastrophic mixture that incited a combustible fear of extraordinary danger.

Arendt confirmed Herzl's conclusion that anti-Jewish antagonism, in Europe, was endemic. If for Gay antisemitism was non-catastrophic and short-lived, for

Herzl it was merely "dormant," and the longer it remained subterranean, "the more violently it will erupt."[63] Herzl and Arendt both posited that Jewish assimilation was a remote prospect. But even worse, it was the *reason* for antisemitism. Social conflict, in their view, acquired pre-eminence over assimilation as the condition of modern Jewish circumstances.

The historiographical debate, whenever it centered on *the reality* of the Jews' vanished social world, appropriately presents an inflected composite portrait. The societies they inhabited were friendly enough to provide at least a scaffolding of home in Europe and an adequate measure of social participation and interaction, but the structure wasn't uniformly secure. The relationships Herzl and others drew between assimilation and antisemitism indicate how far they believed Jews penetrated in society where their assimilation could appear to their detractors as a threatening Jewish infiltration. As important as these empirical evaluations were and are in assessing Jews' actual life in modern Europe, the objectivity they prize can occlude or demote the emotional aspect—the lived life—in Jews' assimilationist dreams and expectations. The problem is evident in philosopher Avishai Margalit's important work on thin and thick human relationships.[64] For him, "all humanity"[65] or a "fellow human being"[66] is an example of a thin relationship, essentially relationships among strangers.[67] In this rendering, Améry's appeal to his fellow man or Wiesenthal's longing for worldly connections was merely "benign,"[68] and the encounters between Jews and their neighbors as "accidental" coexistence,[69] "physically proximate"[70] but not within Hoffman's "sphere of mutual and natural obligations." But like Hoffman's historical, scholarly evaluation, the analysis is, itself, thin and "faceless,"[71] a detached description that corroborates the argument for a tenuous and insubstantial social interaction. Margalit's analysis accurately describes the nature of integrated societies—Herzl's "road of advancement" and "ascent in class," a quest for personal "freedom, happiness, and honor," as well as dominant groups' mediate relationships with outliers beyond what Margalit characterized as "*my* town."[72] It doesn't, however, capture how Jews *saw* or wanted to see their neighbors. Margalit argued that memories of a shared past are constituent of thick relations. "It is the cement that holds thick memories together," whereas thin relationships are "long on geography and short on memory."[73] This should have alerted him to the thickness inherent in Wiesenthal's school-day reminiscences escorting a "childish longing" (*kindisches Verlangen*) for worldly connections[74] and Améry's evocation of a "social world" of true fellowship. The fact that survivor Freddie Knoller recognized, in hindsight, that his "sense of belonging" to Viennese society "was to prove entirely delusory" shouldn't distract us or Margalit from the feeling informing a certainty that he did belong even as he recalled a different truth confirmed by events that Jews "mixed socially only with Jews, merely exchanging greetings with our Christian neighbours. Though there was nothing in appearance to distinguish us from each other, we remained strangers."[75] Margalit recognized personal or intimate relationships could be "imagined,"[76] a comment in passing that deserved elaboration. Jews, nourished by dreams of belonging, were, emotionally, in thick relationships.

With the help of scholars' attention to subjective experiences, we need to ask: Where do we find evidence of "what still lives" in survivors' counter-narratives? How do we account for survivors' pursuit of historical continuity when an objective analysis, both scholarly and in their own strong, denotative narratives, observes discontinuity—a disruption due to the vanishing prospects of assimilation against the emergence and metastasis of antisemitism? As strong as narratives of condemnation are, we need to listen to connotative narratives of encounters and the reworking of relationships, what Freud termed the "affective process" over the "intellectual function" of memories.[77] These counter-memories offer a different magnitude of information: Améry recalled it as a search for a social world exalting life that empirical studies of observable, material reality miss and descriptive witnessing disregards. Listening to the "affective process" moves us from judging the success or failure of assimilation to an evaluation of Jews' historical attachment to "*my* town," their adoptive homelands.

Recent neuroscience research helps to explain how modern Jews were prone to reinterpreting the actual thin or thinning relations between Jewish and ethnic Poles or Germans. The neural science, called "affective realism," disputes a common misconception that the human brain is a blank slate, a reactive organ receiving a stimulus followed by a response. Using an experimental technique called "continuous flash suppression (CFS)," subjects are exposed to dynamic, visual images in one eye and a static, still image in the other, which, by comparison, is "unseen." Researchers have concluded that unseen, unconscious information produces and anticipates conscious visual processing that is in conflict with the actual, projected visual images. As networks of neurons involving feelings, or affect, these preconceptions, lodged in past experiences, wrongly guess at observable reality, made up of the dynamic visual images, producing a phenomenon called "affective misattribution." This suggestive research provides an evidence-based, explanatory framework for Jews' presumptive commitment to their social worlds, deeply endowed with the worldview of Enlightenment-based contractual ideals and prescriptions that had come to constitute their predominant beliefs. Preconceptions such as these, however much they clashed with objective reality, constituted an affective reality—a reality in a different register. One implication of affective realism for our purposes is the surprising tenacity of these beliefs after atrocity: the potency of Jews' commitment to their neighbors and compatriots was so durable that it often survived their counterparts' blunt lethality. It is fair to say that, before the war, Jews' generous preconceptions of their neighbors and compatriots exemplified what the neural research term calls "naïve realism." Améry said as much: "Mankind's eternal progress was only a naïve belief of the nineteenth century."[78] After the war, however, survivors renegotiated the terms of their relationships that shifted the burden of responsibility for their disposition from their counterparts to themselves.[79]

In her study, *The Human Condition*, Arendt devoted a section to the idea of "promises." Making promises arises "directly out of the will to live together with others"[80] and, when they are kept, assures "the joy of inhabiting together."[81] Promises are, however, unreliable: either the "darkness of the human heart" or the uncharted course of human affairs can break promises. They therefore require "an agreed purpose for which alone the promises are valid and binding."[82] As codified in statutory decrees, this is how Jews understood emancipation and liberalizing policies as they were ratified in Europe in the eighteenth and nineteenth centuries: the promise of social equality and integration, economic opportunity, and the political rule of law enforced by the enlightened, distributive nation-state. But considerably more than that, the movement toward Enlightenment in the mid-eighteenth century inspired a belief in an intuitive human bond, a belief that Jews, who had more to gain than those already enfranchised, embraced and cultivated with notable expectation. Lynn Hunt argued that sympathy, or fellow-feeling, was the enlightenment's antidote to the danger of excessive individualism. It "made social life possible."[83] Literate western European society during this nascent period gravitated to fashionable epistolary novels that described an affinity, or "sympathy," among people notwithstanding their evident differences, establishing an emotional, as well as a legal, foundation for aspirations to a common humanity.[84] It inspired relationships that crossed traditional boundaries. Adam Smith, in his *Theory of Moral Sentiments* (1759), considered the question of sympathy for the tormented at the sufferance of his torturer, observing the possibility of emotional identification that allowed the spectator to feel what he feels: "By the imagination we place ourselves in his situation, we conceive ourselves enduring all the same torments, we enter as it were into his body, and become in some measure the same person with him, and thence form some idea of his sensations, and even feel something which, though weaker in degree, is not altogether unlike them."[85] It established a new and more authentic basis of human relationships, a sensibility Améry exhibited, with a twist, in observing the execution of SS officer Wajs: "When SS-man Wajs stood before the firing squad, he experienced the moral truth of his crimes. At that moment, he was with *me*."[86] The sensibility, migrating to central Europe, informed the *Sturm und Drang*, a German literary movement exemplified by Goethe's popular *Sorrows of Young Werther* (1774). Goethe's protagonist was a subject of considerable adulation, generating a cult of Werther drawn to his search for meaningful, sympathetic connections. Remarking on his attraction to Lotte, he commented: "I no longer saw her lovable beauty, no longer the gentle light of her exquisite spirit; all that disappeared. I saw a far more wonderful look in her eyes: an expression of the warmest sympathy, of the sweetest compassion."[87]

Compassion also breached the greatest wall of all: a human bond with the enemy. Werther managed that, too: "He was overcome by compassion and moved by an irresistible desire to save this man, [a murderer] whose predicament he felt deeply. He considered him, even as a criminal, to be free of real guilt, and identified himself so completely with him."[88] Against the grain of his narrative condemnation of Nazi-era cruelty, Wiesenthal confessed to compassion for his worst enemies. Much as he tried to resist the feeling, he couldn't "reject" his "feeling of sympathy" for the dying SS officer.[89] Though he didn't grant his request for forgiveness, the crucial point, in Jankélévitch's words, is the urge to proclaim "our irresistible and fraternal sympathy for human misery." Human sympathy, Jankélévitch asserted, is predicated on the belief in an "essential similarity," a bond even with "the guilty person."[90] Before the war, Jews anticipated their acceptance, appealing, if necessary, to moral principle and the court of law to defeat obstruction. Their experience with human destruction defeated their anticipation of these prospects but it didn't erase their longing for them. Expatriate Bukowinians still yearned for the old Austrian spirit and its cosmopolitan, German culture, according to one former resident of Czernowitz.[91] Longing for home was Améry's preoccupation in one of his essays: feeling abandoned by a heartless if not ruthless world, home for him was impossible but it was still necessary.[92] It was impossible for Hoffman, too, but her interrogation of a Polish village was, as she remarked, a personal inquiry as well as a historical one. The confluence is what makes her observations particularly interesting. Growing up in Poland after the war, she wrote about her determination not only to record its history or remember, "but to remember strenuously."[93]

Her subject would form a bridge to her parents, who had lived nearby. Faithful to her intentions, she explored the complex relationships between Jewish and ethnic Poles who lived side by side, relationships that alternated between cruelty and generosity and all manner of behavior in between at intervals of conflict and peace. But the account did not diminish her personal affection: "I believe that something of the atmosphere of the shtetl, of its mental habits and moral attitudes, of its human gestures and emotional language, penetrated my psyche through the words and personalities of my parents."[94] She concurred with Knoller that relations were actually thin; the two groups "remained strangers." But an intergenerational memory touched her in a way that reconnected her with "human gestures," inspiring, perhaps, Knoller's "sense of belonging." For her, an attachment to this atmosphere was as emotional as it was elusive, and it lingered in a study written more than fifty years later as an alluring, if idle, promise. There is even a hint of something latent and reminiscent in *The Jewish State* that interrupts Herzl's robust appeal to freedom. Antisemitism, he wrote, motivated his plan: it was time for Jews to leave Europe. But the problem was not its intensity. There were periods when it was more "vicious." The problem was an increase in "our sensitivity" to persecution.[95] Had Jews not "sincerely tried everywhere to merge with the national communities in which we live"; had Jews become not merely loyal patriots, but "sometimes superloyal,"[96] perhaps the "road to advancement" would have alone served to rally his movement. But antisemitism represented something more than an obstacle to circumvent. It was a source of "our suffering," of emotional distress, for "prolonged persecution has strained our nerves."[97] Zionism, for Herzl, was a "venture" marketed finally to the "well to do" and the "wealthy,"[98] but beneath the scheme for full participation in society was, as he said, "a gigantic dream,"[99] the province of affective realism where the wish for immersion in the mainstream responded to emotions that were sincerest. Home, for Herzl, was possible as well as necessary.

Sigmund Freud, Herzl's contemporary who aspired to free thinking "in my dream-life if nowhere else,"[100] found the incipient antisemitic movement at the time alarming. As much expressive as analytic, his *Interpretation of Dreams*, published four years after *The Jewish State*, articulates Freud's reflections on the quest of assimilated Jews for the fulfillment of their wishes. Freud praised Herzl after publishing the dream inquiry as "the fighter for the human rights of our people,"[101] an endorsement in the spirit of the 1848 revolution of an entreaty to make good on promises and on commitments to humanitarian progress that political liberalism, the flag-bearer of Enlightenment ideals, set in motion. His dream work was gigantic enough, though it favored psychological over Herzl's proposed resettlement excavation. In several dreams meant to illustrate psychoanalytic theory, Freud famously referred to circumstances that influenced his social life. In the "R" dream, he reflected on his wish for a state appointment to a professorship at the University of Vienna. He remarked on his surprise at how strong that wish was, a "craving" that "showed a pathological ambition."[102] "What, then, could have been the origin of the ambitiousness which produced the dream in me?" He traced it back to the period of his adolescence when Austria briefly supported a liberal government (1867–79): "The wish [in the dream] that it had done its best to fulfill was one dating back to those times." As he commented, those were days when Jews were in thrall of "cheerful hopes." He recalled his father at the time bringing home portraits of great men—men like Carl Giskra, a hero of the 1848 revolution who once wrote that "authority dwells [alone] in the people."[103] "There had even been some Jews among them," the liberals his father revered. His four Rome dreams expressed a "longing" as well, a longing "for the eternal city"[104] and, by association, for "the promised land"[105]—as much a reference to the Enlightenment as to Jewish redemption. Anticipating Halbwachs, he remarked, "We find the child and the child's impulses still living on in the dream."[106] Freud's ambition was, then, another term for assimilationist zeal, a drive whose deferred expression as a wish would have to wait for fulfillment: "For a long time to come, no doubt, I shall have to continue to satisfy [my] longing in my dreams."[107] With the rise of political antisemitism, cheerful hopes mutated to "the dreary present."[108] His promised land would be "seen from afar" due, he maintained, to the growth of reactionary antisemitism. Freud rued that Rome had become hostage to a Catholic Church that he felt turned partisan and belligerent: Just two years before he published his dream book, Catholic Vienna elected Christian Socialist Karl Lueger on an antisemitic platform. Like Herzl's sensitivities, this generation's response, following a period of considerable anticipation, was particularly distressed. Referring to his first encounter with the movement, Freud invoked his hero from his school days to guide him. It was the Carthaginian military commander Hannibal, who Freud called "a semitic general." When "everyone expected him in Rome," he led a historic campaign during the second Punic War. "To my youthful mind Hannibal and Rome symbolized the conflict between the tenacity of Jewry and the organization of the Catholic church."[109] As political antisemitism grew and political liberalism waned, Freud decided to give up on studying law at the University of Vienna. Like Hannibal, whose wish to enter Rome was "lifelong,"[110] Freud transferred his wishes to a movement of his own whose theories asserted a common, human condition. For the moment, longing for social inclusion displaced expectation.[111]

Historians have traditionally regarded witnesses' observations, including survivors' accounts, as little more than supplements to what they believe are a more rigorous, objective reconstruction of events.[112] But witnesses' accounts offer a different kind of sovereign truth: the lived experience of history "from below." By attending to affective realism, we observe something thick and ancestral in post-emancipation Jewish life. Wiesenthal used intimate language to describe his attachment: "We adored the emperor and we were ardent patriots of the Austro-Hungarian Empire."[113] So did Czernowitz poet Alfred Margul-Sperber: "Emancipated from the ghetto, Jewish youth sat at the feet of German teachers from the West and eagerly absorbed everything new, great, and beautiful that western culture and civilization could procure for them."[114] Their intensity is the predicate of betrayal's ubiquity in survivors' narrative recall. Wiesenthal felt devastated when his compatriots reneged on the promise: "I was consumed by a feeling that the world had conspired against us and our fate was accepted without a protest, without a trace of sympathy,"[115] adding vindictively, "I don't want their sympathy."[116] He mourned the breakdown of social relations he had presumed with his compatriots: "Our fathers had crept out of the confines of the [premodern] ghetto into the open world. They had worked hard and done all they could to be recognized by their fellow creatures. But it was all in vain."[117] Améry, too, recalled his aspirations before admitting that it was "an existential misunderstanding." The land and the people he called "our homeland" became a "racial disgrace."[118] Betrayal implies the truth of emotional attachments even as survivors condemned the behavior. As one Jewish resident recalled about his Polish neighbors, "During the war you started to discover that they hate your guts … they didn't want to help us."[119] Another witness was explicit: "I would say 80 percent [of my family] were killed by the Ukrainians who were our friends."[120] Surely the account of assault didn't require the reference to former friendships, but it corroborates the emotional significance and endurance of Wiesenthal's imagined return to "well-known ground." Expressions of betrayal are pivotal: they tell us about the social contract Jews endorsed before the cataclysm, their presumptions of interethnic dependability, their expectations that relationships will recover from episodic lapses, and, surprisingly, about what remains vivid as fond memories of and longing for human fellowship and compassion.

When Wiesenthal entered the hospital for his meeting with the dying SS officer, did it occur to him, in light of the hostile turn of events, that his pre-war

war "content of mind," rather than the Nazis' occupation of his former school, was exotic? Could it be that the school life, which he felt belonged to him, really didn't? Survivors had come to recognize that their superloyalties were groundless, that their beliefs in participating in Hoffman's "mutual and natural obligations" were a scandalous delusion. Wasn't it all in vain? Did Wiesenthal, then, recognize what Klein and Nichols referred to as the post-traumatic "differences between the person now and the person then" so that pre-traumatic memories "seem to belong to someone else and not to the subject"?[121] The pre-war past was well known to Wiesenthal as he claimed it was, but it was simultaneously completely unknown to him as well. Survivors' accounts resist efforts at reconciling contradictions like this, but they begin to make sense when we read them in their double voices, as narratives and counter-narratives that authorize memories in different registers. Where we find evidence of dissociation from the pre-traumatic past is in narratives condemning their compatriots' criminal behavior and rebuking themselves for groundlessly believing they "were our friends." But in counter-memories recalling those beliefs and hopes, when Jews did "all they could to be recognized by their fellow creatures," suddenly Hoffman's pre-war "mental habits and moral attitudes" and Knoller's "sense of belonging" *felt* grounded and real. What was well-known to Wiesenthal as he saw himself again at the university felt like home where people were "made of the same stuff" even if they became "murderers and their victims."[122] This was Améry's "social world" of fellow, "ordinary" men before they became antimen. At this level of recall, Wiesenthal was "the person I was in the past," as Klein and Nichols described a post-traumatic phenomenon in their discussion, noting the experience as "'I had these experiences."[123] Memories in this register were unbroken and intergenerational, exemplifying the psychological experience of "mental time travel"[124] and the philosophical notion of grounded loyalties where attachments to country are inherited or, we should add, felt that way.[125] When Améry observed, "We, however, had not lost our country, but had to realize that it had never been ours,"[126] he also believed at the same time—in retrospect, mistakenly—that it was, wondering, as did survivor Ruth Kluger, "Or had I never left?"[127]

Arendt was among the most vocal critics of what she characterized as modern Jewry's perilous disregard of ominous reality. "Just as the Jews ignored completely the growing tension between the state and society, they were also the last to be aware that circumstances had forced them into the center of the conflict. They never knew how to evaluate antisemitism."[128] Her vehemence—"how fantastic their ignorance of actual conditions in Europe"[129]—acquires historical perspective in Saul Friedländer's critique of the German 1930s: "Jews were unaware that 'the Jew' was outside the domain of natural and contractual ties and obligations."[130] Notable, he remarked, was the "inability of most European Jews to assess the seriousness of the threats that they faced."[131] There is, of course, a terrible truth in these assessments. Most west-central European Jews rejected Herzl's appeal when he delivered it at the turn of the twentieth century. They couldn't accept the argument that political antisemitism was intractable[132] and its causes were "ineradicable."[133] If antisemitic discrimination and innuendo were repugnant, few agreed with Herzl that it "increases day by day and hour by hour among the nations."[134] As Gay argued, contemporaries of the antisemitic movement, in its nascent stages, regarded it as a passing phenomenon, a momentary social retrogression.

Gershom Scholem, a German Jew who emigrated to Palestine in 1923 and became an authority on Jewish mysticism, asserted that there never was a German–Jewish dialogue where each side was "prepared to perceive the other as what he is and represents, and to respond to him." But he conceded the "passionate intensity"[135] and "the infinite intoxication of Jewish enthusiasm"[136] that sustained their search for it: "Jews attempted a dialogue with the Germans, starting from all possible points of view and situations, demandingly, imploringly, and entreatingly." To continue, however, by writing that the attempt was undertaken with "a godforsaken lack of dignity"[137] is a judgment after the fact that doesn't ratify the lived experiences of Jews who aspired to common fellowship. Tom Segev, in his biography of Wiesenthal, also minimized Jews' passionate intensity. After commenting that Wiesenthal and other Jews were "in love with progress" and that their "faith in justice was so deep," he concluded, "Like most of his friends, Wiesenthal preferred to rationalize and delude himself that the circumstances [of the Nazi threat in 1930s Poland] did not require him to uproot himself from the place that gave him his identity."[138] Unable to measure the gravity of hostilities as they transpired or foresee the eventual radical renunciation of Jewish life in Europe, Jews remained steadfast and made decisions accordingly.[139] Wiesenthal recalled that the faculty-student environment was rife with anti-Jewish contempt. A group of students—he called them "antisemitic bands"—had thrown a Jewish student over the staircase railing to the floor below during the "student riots of 1936."[140] The professors, whom he referred to in such affectionate detail down to the signet ring, "were notorious for their dislike of Jewish students."[141] Though recurrent memories[142] and disturbing, their interruption by grounded counter-memories of fellow feeling suggests that they did not—and would not—define his existence as a

Jew. They appeared as just "another fragment from the past,"[143] more erratic than cautionary. "We never took Hitler seriously," he remarked. "We only looked upon him as a crisis that would pass."[144] Historian Havi Ben Sasson observed that it wasn't until late 1942 before Polish Jews "realized that their experiences had deviated from the idealized picture they had created of the Poles."[145] What ended in 1942, however, was the idealization of the picture; the picture, itself, of a human connection continued to make an impression on survivors in their published accounts.

Shock of recognition

In her study of the preconditions of genocide in Rwanda, Lee Ann Fujii observed that attention to "the local" in massive wrongdoing marked a "micropolitical turn in the study of social violence."[146] In the 1990s, historians started looking at the local rather than the top-down, state-political origins of the destructive process in East Europe for what Jürgen Mattthäus exalted as "a deeper understanding of the dynamic process that led to the annihilation of Jewish life and culture."[147] Survivors' counter-narrative aspirations to belong provide emotional texture to the local preconditions and conditions of destruction. Jan Gross, whose seminal 2001 study *Neighbors: The Destruction of the Jewish Community in Jedwabne, Poland* concentrated on the relationships between ethnic and Jewish Poles in one small village, gets credit for inspiring studies of the local in the European-Jewish destructive process but failed to distinguish between its descriptive and subjective interpretations. On the one hand, he suggested that the villagers were not particularly intimate. To help make the point that they were neighbors, he cited one ethnic Pole who claimed that the town's Jews were "on good terms with the Poles,"[148] though how good were these terms if this resident did not regard Jews as Poles? Gross described relations remotely, remarking that "contact and interaction" were "plentiful,"[149] a thin characterization similar to Hoffman's assertion of "proximity and familiarity" among the villagers she studied. Indeed, he noted that habitually malicious theological instruction[150] and progressive suspicions of a Jewish-Soviet alliance[151] formed an undercurrent of "latent hostility"[152] that inflected their coexistence as perilously nonlethal and just below the threshold of "open confrontation" before the war.[153] Jews, he affirmed, felt unsafe in "the foreknowledge of impending pogroms."[154]

But when consulting Jewish survivors about the carnage that decimated their community in 1941, a different picture emerges. A young rabbi "fondly remembers pre-war encounters with Polish neighbors."[155] In one revealing case, Jewish community leaders, after learning about a wave of pogroms in nearby villages, visited a local bishop to seek assurance that he would protect Jews. According to one Jewish witness, they were confident—it turned out, overconfident—he would do so.[156] Their reliance on neighbors illustrates the affective side of Jews' interrelationships. Their lived experience revises documentary description, making "the local" thick for Jews. It was thick diachronically as well as synchronically for the attachment of Jews to their neighbors was a historical dynamic galvanized by humanitarian ideals and the modern evolution of the central secular state that championed citizens' social integration. Jews' allegiance to the new order was only the most visible result. Whether or not they were rewarded for their fidelity or, as Scholem acidly contended, even if Jews cried hopelessly "into the void" without an echo,[157] they imagined and believed in the eventual fulfillment of their dreams for acceptance into the fold of national and human fellowship.

These accounts remind us that the destruction process for Jews often involved assailants they felt they knew and could trust. Alicia's account of her arrest becomes interpersonal when she identified the Ukrainian policeman as her friend's father. That he once "loved me like a daughter" indicates the emotional gravity embedded in the moment of recognition but also the disorienting shock of the unexpected betrayal. As her friend's father turns aggressive, she must have wondered: but that's not really him; I don't recognize him. In that compressed instant, under these unanticipated conditions, and in view of the familiar "face," resides a shock of recognition. As evidence mounts of local collaboration with fascist regimes and the denunciation of Jews to the authorities, it becomes clear that the shock of recognition was a widespread phenomenon throughout Europe, Western as well as Eastern. Collaboration was rife in Germany. As Tony Judt observed, "The Germans could not have done what they did in occupied Norway or Belgium or Holland without the collaboration of the locals."[158] Survivors first started to speak publicly about the incrimination of German compatriots in their ordeal at trials in Germany from the late 1950s to the Frankfurt Auschwitz proceedings in the mid-1960s,[159] though testimonies were limited at this point to implicating camp guards and other Nazi leaders for their direct participation in the destruction process. In the following decade, Germans started acknowledging their collective responsibilities.[160] Jan Grabowski devoted his recent research to documenting the epidemic of confidence violations in a rural county in Southeastern Poland during the war: "There is no doubt that the great majority of Jews in hiding perished as a consequence of betrayal. They were denounced, or simply seized, tied up, and delivered by the locals to the nearest station of the Polish police, or to the German gendarmerie."[161] If Jews did not directly mingle with their neighbors who eventually betrayed them, they placed their faith in them for their protection, with fatal consequences.[162]

The term "recognition" indicates a mental act, a re-cognition. But the encounter for those who experienced it was unbearably emotional. It was an existential violation, an act of moral treason, that destroyed the predicate of relationships Jews presumed: a belief in and expectation of mutual trust and assistance, especially under dire circumstances. Jews were surely incredulous when open confrontation erupted, but they were also devastated. One story by survivor Menachem Finkelsztajn about a massacre in a village not far from Jedwabne, despondently reported, "More painful than wounds and damages we suffered this evening was the awareness that our situation was much worse on account of the Polish population taking a hostile attitude toward the Jews. And they were becoming more active and bold in their persecutions."[163] For Améry, the agony of recognition led him to one narrative conclusion: he would withdraw from a world he once loved. It was no longer possible to recapture what Halbwachs called the "best part of himself"[164] because the land and its people whom he thought he knew and who once conferred joy were insubstantial to begin with. Home was a mirage, for "we were not entitled to it."[165] Singing "native songs in our dialect" and pining for "the mountains and rivers back home" were risible, a case of mistaking a desire to belong for actually belonging.[166] He and other Jews, he protested, had to "mime" their daily lives,[167] a disparaging term for assimilation's fraudulence. Wiesenthal's shock of recognition occurred with his abrupt awakening to the university's displacement by a hospital for convalescent SS officers representing the triumph of a power-craven establishment over the hope and faith of reason a university inspires. Finkelsztajn spoke for Wiesenthal and other survivors confronting new realities: "How great was our disappointment," he remarked.[168] "No Christian let any Jew into his house or offered any help."[169]

The tension in these narratives are typically articulated in thick societies characterized by interethnic transactions among friends, teachers, neighbors, and compatriots—men and women whom survivors thought they knew and could rely on, often in spite of reversals that were serious but seemed malleable. One witness to the genocide in Srebrenica during the 1992–5 Bosnian War expressed surprise at the behavior of his wife's former classmate: "When Gavric looked at him, there was nothing. No flicker of recognition swept across his face.

One thing resonated from his squinting eyes and curled mouth: hatred."[170] Paul Rusesabagina, the manager of the Hôtel des Mille Collines in Kigali, Rwanda, which sheltered more than 1,200 refugees during the 1994 Rwandan genocide, remarked with a measure of restraint, "It was more than a surprise. It was a disappointment. I was disappointed by most of my friends, who immediately changed with that genocide. I used to see them just as gentlemen, and when I saw them with the killers, I was disappointed."[171] Recalling the 1994 genocide, Immaculée Ilibagiza told a similar story. She met a member of the notorious Interahamwe, "recognizing the man instantly." As a leader of the government-sponsored militia at the vanguard of mass murder, he plundered her parents' home and killed her mother and brother. Ilibagiza recognized him because she played with his children as a little girl.[172]

Forward-looking counter-narratives are less debilitating than backward-looking expressions of resentment, and are more curious about their local friends, neighbors, and compatriots before or beside the transgression. Instructively, the phrase "shock of recognition," attributed to Herman Melville, evokes positive reminiscences. In his "Hawthorne and His Mosses" (1850), he praised the antebellum author for eliciting "the smell of your beeches and hemlocks ... your own broad prairies ... the far roar of his Niagara," expressing the shock, the astonishment, of recognizing Hawthorne's genius in everyone "all over the world."[173]

Philosopher Paul Ricoeur corroborated the "shock of the event" as "the pleasure of recalling what I once saw, heard, felt, learned, acquired ...,[174] that minor miracle of happy memory."[175] Although Alicia's policeman was not the same person she knew, at another level, in Ricoeur's words, he also "remained the same ... I say in my heart: that's really him, that's really her. I recognize him. I recognize her."[176] Counter-narratives retain these memories against the grain of recrimination. Jankélévitch, in writing about true forgiveness after violation, asserted its merits as restoring "a *personal relation* with another person."[177] Though forgiveness wants "to last forever"[178] but can't, making the connection was important for "inaugurating positive relations between an offended person and an offender intimately reconciled."[179] Améry searched for a human connection, as well—the face, "plain ordinary faces"—as did Wiesenthal, who expressed a sympathetic attachment to the enemy. They realized and asserted in their strong narratives that Améry's "social world" vanished,[180] but it still lived in imagining how it grants his "fellow man life."

It is significant that references to human fellowship even occur in accounts devoted to bearing fierce witness. To remember that ethnic Ukrainians who killed Jewish family members "were our friends" is not only painful memory. It is also a lingering, searching evocation of "what I once saw, heard, felt, learned, acquired." As Ricoeur observed, "Something of the original impression has to have remained for me to remember it now."[181] It's no different with the antiman Améry encountered, "yelling out in pain."[182] He is radically different from the one he knew by his familiar dialect. But in seeing his fellow man embodied within, in recognizing that he is essentially the same, he is seeking an elusive human connection.

3

Narrative Disclosure: Jean Améry

Among our trio of survivors under close textual scrutiny, Jean Améry, a survivor of torture under state-police interrogation and in the camps, deserves special attention. While Vladimir Jankélévitch and Simon Wiesenthal offer insight into survivors' intermittent inclinations to look forward, Améry steadfastly insisted on looking backward, bearing resentful witness to Nazi-era crimes. His essays on his ordeal, collected in the mid-1960s into a volume called *Jenseits von Schuld und Sühne: Bewältigungsversuche eines Überwältigten* (*Beyond Guilt and Atonement: Attempts to Overcome by One Who Has Been Overcome*; translated for its publication in English as *At the Mind's Limits: Contemplations by a Survivor on Auschwitz and Its Realities*), represents an archetype of survivors' determination to condemn the radically brutal and ruthless behavior of perpetrators implicated in mass violence. Against the background of contemporary events we can see why all three survivors were resentful. At the time of their publications, European nations were mired in fierce debates over the enforcement of statutes of limitations, which would have released former Nazi criminals from prosecution. The Frankfurt Auschwitz trial, which lasted from 1963 to 1965, plausibly appeared as the last trial of its kind. Government leaders in the Federal Republic of Germany ratified a popular disposition to forgive and forget. Améry wasn't alone in prosecuting criminal malfeasance where others failed to do so, but he was notoriously resolute. He often declared that to make amends with a criminal past and a complicit present would deny if not abet what he argued was society's lingering, corrosive addiction to greed, intolerance, and deception. At the other end of the spectrum from Jankélévitch and Wiesenthal, he offered little slack and certainly no firm consideration to reworking relationships with a world he vehemently distrusted. We believe, however, that he was also an archetype of expressive complexity, for even in accounts that were energized by recrimination, there are counter-indications that characterize their narratives as bifocal. Améry's account serves as an overture to subsequent discussions of all three survivors, for if its severity permits counter-indicative possibilities, how much more would we anticipate multiple narratives in others' accounts that bear witness against extreme criminality. As always, it would be helpful were there a narrative arc we could limn in *At the Mind's Limits*, but since its narratives are mutually antithetical, they defy architectural compression. We will have to consider them instead as plural or parallel voices.

Resentments

Jean Améry is a notable observer of an era governed by calculated human destruction because he is largely considered as a survivor whose disparagement of Germans for their behavior during and after the assault against Jews was unrelenting. He earns his reputation as a quintessence of resentment for good reason. He wrote about his dedicated "retrospective grudge."[1] Nothing, it seems, could shake him from the position he held toward the SS officers who held him in captivity in 1943, after his arrest, while working for a German-speaking resistance organization in Belgium. The "business room," as Améry recalled the reference to a windowless vault inside "Reception Camp Breendonk," was the scene of unspeakable crimes. Fort Breendonk, built during the First World War for the defense of Belgium against Germany, acquired a reputation for its sadistic tormentors. Half of its prisoners survived: the rest were deported to concentration camps.[2] As Améry recalled, his torturers embodied the "radical negation of the other."[3] Referring to his internment in Auschwitz, and other camps, during the final two years of the war, he decried the ascendance of an "SS logic" promoting aggressive self-preservation that buried, he said, a "universal humane logic."[4] Améry considered himself as a "catastrophe Jew," someone who "must get along without trust in the world."[5] The self-description confirms the impression that his account is unmistakably backward-looking, a rumination on traumatic injury that redefined him: "Being a Jew means feeling the tragedy of yesterday as an inner oppression."[6] He reflected on the shadow cast by the Auschwitz number on his left forearm. It "touches the deepest and most closely intertwined roots of my existence."[7] If he is "not even sure if this is not my entire existence,"[8] he acknowledged that catastrophe at least was "the dominant force."[9]

In addition to ruthlessness, the wholesale disregard of—indeed, contempt for—moral conventions appalled him. He recounted the episode of a poet he met in 1941, while interned, for a few months, in the Gurs camp, in Southern France. When the poet was deported from the German town of Karlruhe, "no hand was lifted to protect him." The episode surely resonated with Améry—like him, the subject was a "German poet."[10] In truth, the story was his story. "The hand that was not raised in [the poet's] protection"[11] was the hand of his compatriots: hopelessly subjected to abuse, he concluded, "No help can be expected."[12] As Améry wrote tirelessly about the commission of extreme crimes, he wrote resentfully about "the certainty" he once felt that "the other person will spare me." That certainty, he felt, constituted an inviolable "social contract" that inspired an a priori "trust in the world."[13] Never before did he question the moral principle of mutual assistance: "The expectation of help, the certainty of help, is indeed one of the fundamental experiences of human beings."[14] Améry's exposure to radical crimes changed all that. Reflecting on how his compatriots had "forsaken" Jews[15] and realizing the fraudulence of the social contract constituted a scandalous awakening. "The schoolmate from the same bench, the neighbor, the teacher" on whom he had depended, even if they were not Jews, and who accordingly signified a common bond, "had become informers or bullies, at best, embarrassed opportunists."[16] Even more distressful, he came to realize that they didn't just "become" that way; their unexpected transgression wasn't just a decisive disruption. He now understood that they were always predisposed against them. The country he lost had, in fact, "never been ours."[17] A Jew, he wrote, "could not claim German culture as his possession, because his claim found no sort of social justification."[18] Perhaps what darkened his memories most was the innocence of his beliefs or, more precisely, the intensity of his homeland attachments. He confessed a romance he had with Germans—our "first love"[19]—whose exorbitance blinded him from recognizing his compatriots' true colors. As he wrote, his "mimicry"[20] of everything German was so thorough it came to define "what we were."[21] He agonized that it was all "a foolish, sham undertaking!"[22] It offered him no encouragement some twenty years later that Germans remained morally inert. "Little had changed," he lamented,[23] after recalling "a brief global hour," with the defeat of Nazi Germany of worldwide contempt for its behavior. Eventually, he repudiated the view that antisemitism throughout Europe was "an aberration."[24] Germans, he said, were hopelessly and heartlessly unrepentant, commenting: "I rebel: against my past, against history, and against a present that places the incomprehensible in the cold storage of history and thus falsifies it in a revolting way."[25]

What made resentment a strong, primary narrative in his accounts was his commitment to the emotion: The grudge he felt toward Germans and the world was something "I neither can nor want to get rid of."[26] For him, expressing anger represented a crucial transition from fear for his life to the dignity of moral protest,[27] or what he called his "personal salvation."[28] Indeed, he regarded resentment as a process of turning the tables of history away from the degradation of Jews, beginning with the death sentence promulgated by the Nuremberg Laws,[29] which led to the concentration camps and still lingered in belated estrangement, to "the reattainment of dignity," which, he felt, he must acquire "through my own effort."[30] Condemning his contemporaries meant nothing less to him than "the right to live."[31] By this he did not mean a species of natural law but, rather, an urgent and primitive human *cri de coeur*. It materialized even as his weakened body "tensed" for physical blows.[32] His dignity rallied at Auschwitz in revolt against an overseer's punch to the face by hitting back, an act for which he dearly paid but at a price he asserted was entirely worth the cost: "Painfully beaten, I was satisfied with myself."[33] He continued to prize the dignity of his expressive resentment after the war "in a climate of deceptive peace."[34] Indeed, it became a "compulsion."[35] Recalling the Hebrew words "*Sch'ma Israel*" at a performance of Arnold Schönberg's "A Survivor from Warsaw," he asserted that "'Hear, oh Israel' is not my concern. Only a 'Hear, oh world' wants angrily to break out within me."[36] It's clear that he hoped his revolt, the "moral demands of our resentment,"[37] would revise the world's appalling insouciance,[38] but even as he recognized the futility of his dream for the world's moral transformation, he valorized resentment as a personal, life-sustaining, moral necessity. With the imminence of statutory enforcement that threatened to end the prosecution of war criminals and the state-sanctioned judicial interrogation of the Nazi past, resentment and its articulation in revolt became not only imperative but also the seeds of a social movement. More than a personal mission, he recognized "my solidarity with every threatened Jew in this world"[39] who joined together in common rebellion against popular indifference. Resentment, surely a source of dispiriting anger, formed an emotional basis for the first wave of Nazi-era survivors to transform what Améry once suspected was his "neurosis" into an open rebellion: "The others are the madmen."[40]

Narrative swerves

Améry showed an inclination to abandon his preoccupation with resentment; if nothing else, the preoccupation felt hopelessly dispiriting: "Whoever has succumbed to torture can no longer feel at home in the world."[41] He recognized the price he paid for his profound acrimony, a price that deeply disturbed him. That price was loneliness: "At stake for me is the release from the abandonment that has persisted from that time until today."[42] Indeed, he ruminated how "alien and alone he felt" as a Jew in a world in which he lost trust."[43] The source of Améry's loneliness was twofold: On the one hand, it was the result of his resentments. He regarded them as his main concern, his self-styled mission, indeed, a principled entitlement. By exalting them for "their moral value and their historical validity,"[44] he formed an inextricable commitment to them. But he recognized that they had the effect of social withdrawal and self-isolation. His preoccupation with destruction and loss threatened to remain static and non-negotiable. On the other hand, his contemporaries' behavior—their heartless impatience with historical reminders—was offensive, a rejection of the "inner oppression" of his current existence that echoed "the tragedy of yesterday," his "radical negation." He suggested a second "point of healing in 1964"—likely a reference to the commencement of the Frankfurt Auschwitz trial and the vigorous debate over the period of statutory limitations whose impending lapse inspired a vocal opposition. But the will of belated generations to move resolutely forward became evident, prompting his observation several years later that "Nothing has healed," and worse, that the impetus to historical amnesia "is bursting open again [in 1976] as an infected wound."[45]

These disquieting circumstances gave rise to profound despair, "an extreme *loneliness.*"[46] Writing plaintively that "all that I can manage is to get along within my foreignness,"[47] he reproved his contemporaries, as well as his persecutors, for the sense of abandonment he endured: "I am alone, as I was when they tortured me."[48] Abandonment is a leitmotif in survivors' accounts: shortly after his release from Buchenwald, Bruno Bettelheim observed that prisoners hated "all those living outside the camp, who 'enjoyed life as if we were not rotting away.'"[49] Elie Wiesel reprimanded the world's silence, including the Jewish world's: "Why silent? Why did it not find it vital to inform us of what was going on in Germany? Why did they not warn us? Why?"[50] Vladimir Jankélévitch, a member of the French Resistance, considered the feeling of abandonment as "one of the most frightful aspects of their ordeal":[51] "The Jews," he wrote, "were alone, absolutely alone."[52] Améry reviled Germans, indeed, "the whole world," for approving the Nazi campaign of destruction; glimmers of "superficial regret" were anemic: "There was no way out."[53] Nor was there a way out in the present day when he felt Jews were not "loved" or "worthy of life."[54]

Améry's observations of dispiriting contemporary developments matured into essays for *At the Mind's Limits* when all manner of German society—survivors and other Germans—were closely observing the trial of former Nazis taking place from 1963 to 1965 in Frankfurt am Main. In a strange coincidence, the number 20 is conspicuous in the trial's main outlines: The trial started on December 20 and lasted twenty months, ending in judgment on August 20. It concluded in 1965, twenty years after the end of the Second World War, with decisions rendered for twenty defendants (two were dropped for medical reasons). The elapsed period presented the prospect of releasing former Nazis from prosecution under the West German penal code specifying a statute of limitations for extreme crimes. As Améry recalled in the first sentence of his preface to the first 1966 edition: "When the big Auschwitz trial began in Frankfurt in 1964 [*sic*], I wrote the first essay on my experiences in the Third Reich, after twenty years of silence."[55] By the time he published his essays, he recognized that he could not return home from his outpost in Brussels: It would have been an "embarrassment"[56] since "Hitler's Reich will, for the time being, continue to be regarded as an operational accident of history. Finally, however, it will be purely and simply history."[57] He devoted the essay "How Much Home Does a Person Need?" to his condition of alienation, his emotional exile, and his misery as a result of homelessness and abject aloneness. He insisted that the foreignness he felt could not be "compensated,"[58] yet he felt "trapped" in resentment: "It nails every one of us on the cross of his ruined past."[59] His use of Christian metaphor to describe his plight is ironic, for salvation eluded him. After asserting resentments' validity he wondered, "But how much longer?"[60] Desperate for release and convinced that the German moral "revolution" was anything but imminent,[61] he searched for a way out.

The search directed his reflections to a different register of memory that interrupted his narrative resentments, which he wanted neither to console nor to fetishize. Literary critic Harold Bloom called these inclinations "revisionary swerves," a phrase worth adopting, after parsing, because it indicates dispositions rather than a full-blown turn. Bloom argued that literary swerves between texts—or, as he prefers, between poems—void "an intolerable presence" of an overwhelming forerunner influence, a strong poet,[62] not unlike Améry's response to resentments' trap within the text. Counter-narratives, where these swerves reside within texts, are weak interruptions of main, backward-looking narratives. But they are not revisionary in the sense that Bloom posited. It may be true, as he argued, that "individuation" is possible only with "revisionary strife,"[63] but the deflection is not necessarily a "corrective movement," by which Bloom meant "the precursor poem went accurately up to a certain point, but then should have swerved, precisely in the direction that the new poem moves."[64] Closer to the conception of swerves as an interruption rather than a dedicated filial disruption of strong trajectories is Lucretius's *On the Nature of Things*, in which he defended Epicurus's doctrine of atoms:

> Though atoms fall straight downward through the void
> by their own weight, yet at uncertain times
> and at uncertain points, they swerve a bit—
> enough that one may say they change direction.
> And if they did not swerve, they all would fall
> downward like raindrops through the boundless void;
> no clashes would occur, no blows befall
> the atoms; nature would never have made a thing.[65]

Here is a different interpretation of swerves' trajectories. Even if counter-narratives originate as a response to primary expression—often to regulate anxiety, whatever its source—their "entire existence," in Améry's terms, continues onward in new directions without correcting or revising what came before. Clashes surely ensue; counter-narratives formed Améry's response to the "intolerable presence" of abandonment and homelessness. But their swerves ultimately stand alone; their intertextuality is limited and they are not inclined to misinterpret strong, canonic expression, as Bloom would have it. Instead, they pursue their own, sovereign interests untethered to other narratives in the plurality of narrative expression.

In one instance, Améry called a remarkable, seven-page encomium he wrote to the "human spirit" a "digression."[66] Even though it "stood on weak legs,"[67] and, he asserted, failed "to exemplify its dignity," there was something about the spirit that "was still stirring."[68] By "spirit," he meant "the phenomenon of human kindness,"[69] recalling that once, while in Auschwitz, an orderly from the sick barracks offered him something to eat. He "greedily devoured" the sweetened grits, but it was the gesture that had the greater effect: "A wild longing for things of the spirit took possession of me"—books he had read, music he had heard. The experience aroused not only momentary "intoxication" and "euphoria"[70] but also ancestral memories of his pre-war life among people "he always associated" with, a Jew among compatriots whose differences between them were palpable but were also fundamentally "humane and reasonable."[71] Much as he dwelled in his accounts on transgressive behavior, articulating and condemning the inhuman and the unreasonable, what "brought tears to my eyes"[72] started with exceptional expressions of human kindness.

Améry devoted much of his first chapter, the eponymous "At the Mind's Limits," to what he called the camp's "concrete reality," the engulfing impingement of each moment when, for example, "the Kapo roars 'left,' and the soup was watery, and the flags are clanking in the wind."[73] The intellect, whose vocation he prized for its analytic facility, humanism, and transcendent possibilities, was, like the spirit, in retreat under these unmediated circumstances, but there are several intimations when he evaded the defining authority of the "camp logic."[74] Perhaps most obvious, though a casualty of plain sight, is the intellectualized style of Améry's retrospective accounts as well as his frequent references to the "spiritual and esthetic heritage"[75] of great German thinkers—Kleist, Novalis, Nietzsche, and so forth. Both the literary style and his frame of intellectual reference testify to the moral survival of Améry's "longing for things of the spirit" and the humanity it represented. At another point during his considerable digression, he offered a "confession." In spite of his assertion that "at no time could I discover within me the possibility for belief"—upon his liberation from Bergen-Belsen he was "an agnostic"—just a couple of sentences later he recalled how he felt, and, significantly, managed to "still feel, great admiration" for his comrades' commitment to political or religious belief.[76] It is always intriguing to read Améry every time he discharged his counter-narrative lapses. On the one hand, he rejected their ideals as imaginative flights or, more revealing, as "naïve," for he had come to deeply lament his pre-war faith in reliable social relationships and in the errant presumption of a common human bond. His "intoxication" with humane expression "left behind a dreary, hangover-like feeling of emptiness and shame."[77] Yet it's important to note the existence of these lapses and, in this case, his confession, which, even if they were "exceptions,"[78] he included in the text. His comrades' beliefs in salvation were "dismaying," but they were also "impressive."[79] They were able to transcend the camp's conditions that otherwise "overwhelmed" inmates[80] by framing those conditions remotely as contingent outgrowths of modernity's turning away from God or yielding to imperatives of capitalist aggression rather than what he asserted they were: "the monstrous product of sick minds and perverted souls."[81] Améry couldn't ally with his believing comrades. Their views were "Finalistic," an attitude his skeptical predilections prevented him from endorsing. The world that emerged from the camps was irreversibly inept for eventual reconciliation. But their sense of "spiritual continuity that is interrupted nowhere, not even in Auschwitz"[82] was appealing: "I would have wished to be like them: unshakable, calm, strong."[83]

At uncertain times and at uncertain points his narratives swerve a bit and puncture his expressions of resentment. Strong narratives dominated his account. He railed against "the policeman's fist," remarking that "a part of our life ends and it can never again be revived."[84] He recognized how vehement he appeared: "Those who have followed my deliberations may well see their author as a monster, if not of vengeance, then at least of bitterness." But here again he temporized: "There may be a trace of truth in such a judgment, but only a trace."[85] Another truth, the part of his life that he did not lose, may explain the name "Jean Améry" he adopted after leaving his Austrian homeland in 1939, for, though he could no longer identify with German culture, and his given name, "Hans Mayer," "no longer made sense" after the Nazi racial theft,[86] he did not sever his ties completely: Jean is short for Johannes, the French equivalent of Hans; Améry is an anagram for Mayer. His expression of contempt for Germans was paramount, but his anterior references, and self-references, suggest an opening.

Feeling abandoned by others, he also abandoned himself to imagine a bridge to his compatriots. He dreamt that the Nazi criminal would someday experience "the moral truth of his crimes" and would "once again become a fellow man."[87] Even the German revolution "would be made good,"[88] he fancied in "an extravagant moral daydream I have abandoned myself to!"[89] Germans, "as I sometimes hope,"[90] would seek to negate their acquiescence in the Third Reich, integrate it in their moral education, and come to eradicate criminal inclinations[91]—a "negation of the negation: a highly positive, a redeeming act."[92] He eventually reawakened to his senses: "Nothing of the sort will happen ... The German revolution? Germany will not make it good."[93] But we need to acknowledge the effect of Améry's dreams not only on providing a way out of isolation and desolation but also on changing narrative directions. In counter-narratives, dreams and digressions open to a future of human connections. It might be elusive and merely wishful, but they permitted him to examine the part of his life that still lived. They inspired him to imagine a new beginning.

Perhaps the most persuasive evidence of Améry's self-disclosures is captured by his "urge" to "communicate."[94] It is hard to overestimate the significance of his craving for expression, especially in an observer who dwelled on experiences of radical helplessness and the immutability of the victim's condition. Communication was an existential act, an intrinsic value. For him, that, in itself, was a psychological volte-face, for he recognized the bankruptcy of his previous orientation.[95] This was the deepest counter-narrative swerve of all: It broke his silence and complicated his claims to foreignness. Even though he claimed that no kind of human communication could make up for the "foreignness in the world" he feels, he wrote about "euphoric moments ... [when] the bundle of limbs that is slowly recovering human semblance feels the urge to articulate the experience intellectually."[96] Survivors often regard their accounts as depositions for posterity, but the process—what Freud called an "affective process"[97]—is significant, too. As an act of expression, they confer their agency. Instead of resigning to hopeless isolation, communication transforms the victim's powerlessness into the survivor's expressive act; indeed, it means they are no longer victims.

Améry's urge to communicate involved his decision to examine his darkest thoughts and emotions in the light of day. This is considerable as well. The act of open-air *public* communication establishes a "second-person" address. Edward Casey observed that it signifies a desire to form relationships: It "is an essentially *interpersonal* action. It is undertaken not only in relation *to* others and *for* them but also *with* them in a common action of communalizing."[98] As a common action, it enabled Améry to make a human connection—even with those who negated him—that he was longing to affirm. "To the Germans," he commented, "I would like to relate a few things here."[99] He started the process of communication with Germans in a series of invited radio broadcasts for the South German Broadcasting Corporation in 1964 after twenty-six years in exile and two years before publishing *At the Mind's Limits*. The decision to broadcast in Germany reflected a glimmer of hope, soon to fade, in Germany's self-renewal. There are occasional hints in the essays to the dialogue he enacted in his radio broadcasts, such as the interjection, "Again, I hear indignant objection being raised" about his diatribes.[100] The paradox nested in the urge to connect was his determination to admonish his audience for their moral complacency: "The man of resentment cannot join in the unisonous peace chorus all around him, which cheerfully proposes: not backward let us look but forward, to a better, common future!"[101] But his election to speak and then write for his contemporaries was just a beginning, the start of a negotiable worldly relationship. As Améry wrote, "To the extent that the reader would venture to join me at all he would have no choice but to accompany me, in the same tempo, through the darkness that I illuminated step by step."[102] Germans may well have wanted to abandon survivors, but he would not abandon them. The decision to go public with his memories was very much forward-looking—ironically, in keeping with Germans' supplications though not with their disregard of historical realities. Even the phrase "to articulate the experience intellectually" possesses a forward-looking orientation. As Susanne Langer noted, when those who were wronged are ready to write and to make public their experiences, their raw emotions of anger have gone through a process of "disciplined rehearsal."[103] Regulating raw emotions is an intertextual achievement that simultaneously makes it possible to participate in public discourse.

In *The Rebel,* Camus wrote, "To talk of despair is to conquer it. Despairing literature is a contradiction in terms."[104] For Améry, the very act of communication served to ease the burden of alienation and exile, much of which was self-imposed as a result of his signature resentment. But in these formulations the audience is notably absent. Améry and other first-wave survivors recalling Nazi-era destruction for a reluctant audience were not writing out of despair alone. This cohort emerged when it did precisely because of a collective insistence on ending the period of accountability and on commencing a new period, a *Stunde Null*, burnishing a clean slate. Survivors believed the demand required a response: They refused to remain silent a second time. In the process, they acquired a voice when the alternative, an expectation of help, proved ruinous. They became interlocutors, an impossible role during the original period of endemic destruction when getting even after the "first blow" of torture was unimaginable: "You *cannot* do it when it is the other one who knocks out the tooth."[105] As interlocutors, they parried the threat of oblivion and re-entered the world. Distrusting their contemporaries as they never so completely did before, their re-engagement was both cautious and ardent, an ebb-and-flow construct. When he first broke his silence for his radio broadcasts, Améry rehearsed for common fellowship even as he reproached his contemporaries. By the time he published *At the Mind's Limits,* the vocal "peace chorus" transformed his search for promising signs to a longing for human kindness and moral human relationships.

Possibilities

In his studies on Améry, Thomas Brudholm argued that expressions of resentment, though "negative emotions," possess positive, forward-looking properties. They were "tied to a wish for a constitution (or restoration) of a moral community between former enemies," he wrote, citing Améry: "My resentments are there in order that the crime become a moral reality for the criminal."[106] Améry, of course, had come to see that such a restoration would remain a wish: Germans' corrective self-understanding was really nothing more than an "extravagant moral daydream." But wishes and dreams, like digressions and the act communication, are, themselves significant as autonomous expressions. They endure and produce their own effects independent of their outcomes. Even when rebuking Germans with visions of their moral remediation, the rebuke, itself, manifested an urge to make a connection with them and all humanity. Mirroring the narrative expression of rage against the condition of his homelessness in a country in which he no longer could live "within a

We"[107] was his counter-narrative confession to feeling homesick. He longed for a home where he could again feel secure and could even expect what is known to him to recur, again and again.[108] These homeland reminiscences, he said, represented nostalgic loss but also "constitutional elements and constants of our personality."[109] Though he knew he would never feel secure again nor expect reassurances, memories of homeland continued to stir feelings of fellowship "that we absorbed very early."[110]

At one point he imagined yet another name for himself, "Yochanan"—a Hebrew variant of Hans.[111] But this alias was too far removed from his formative, if imaginative and still wishful, ties to his German neighbors. Would "Yochanan," an "upright Israeli, conversing fluently in Hebrew, be able so completely to obliterate the white-stockinged youth who once took such pains to speak a local dialect?"[112] Nonetheless, his association with something Jewish is apparent. Améry recalled his Jewish background as practically nonexistent: "However [much] I might try to find in Jewish history my own past, in Jewish culture my own heritage, in Jewish folklore my personal recollections, the result would be nil.[113] Yet even if antisemitism "made a Jew of me,"[114] a Jew he was, especially in "solidarity" with other threatened Jews.[115] The portrait that emerges is the profile of assimilated European Jewry who, conscious of their Jewishness and its place in the world, identified with their white-stockinged German neighbors. Germans, in this view, were not seen as provincially ethnic or nationalist but, in the manner of local allegiances to other nations and religions, as the standard of humanity and perfectibility, each, according to the eighteenth-century German thinker Johann Gottfried von Herder, "adapted to a truly human life."[116] Social differences didn't matter to Améry: "I could not say today which of my acquaintances at that time was a Jew and which was not."[117] All were German; all belonged to a moral community. For Améry, "Spirited home by memories of Alpine valleys and folk rituals"[118] was an evocation of fellow-feeling. It was this background, the desire of Jew who "took such pains" to belong, and who, by speaking and looking like Germans, believed he did, that fueled his dreams of human fellowship. Such early experience, as he observed, would remain emotionally vivid and influential: "Mother tongue and native world grow with us, grow into us."[119] For him, "the simple summation of early experience" is what it means to be "Something": "Everyone must be who he was in the first years of his life, even if later these were buried under. No one can become what he cannot find in his memories."[120]

Améry often faulted himself for the naïve belief in "honeysweet human pronouncements."[121] He resisted "an inadmissible heightening of emotions."[122]

But intellection, the declarative voice of strong narratives, and the prudential distance it maintained, did not erase the sense of home he missed. He confessed to the siren song of former emotional attachments, abandoning himself to sentimentality. His counter-narrative references to home are visceral, something that he said he grasped "through the senses"—seeing, hearing, and touching. "We need a house of which we know who lived in it before us, a piece of furniture in whose small irregularities we recognize the craftsman who worked on it. We need a city whose features stir at least faint memories of the old copperplate engraving in the museum."[123] Emotional evocations of homeland (*Heimat*), wrote Simon Schama in *Landscape and Memory*, was a familiar refrain in German culture nourished by nineteenth-century Romantic writers in forging a sense of an organic national bond.[124] They remained potent for Germans to and beyond the Second World War as a salve against memories of German cities' destruction: commenting on letters he received in response to his Zürich lectures on Germany's devastation, W. G. Sebald wrote, "We have here the glorious world of our mountains, the carefree eye resting upon the beauty of our homeland."[125] Améry lamented his "pretentious nostalgia" for his homeland, but when he let his guard down, "relaxed by alcohol," he, too, affectionately recalled "the mountains and rivers back home (*heimischen Bergen and Flüssen*) … in tearful bliss … [We] secretly wiped our eyes."[126] Much as he tried "dismantling our past piece by piece"—he twice asserted the paramount value of emotional suppression[127]—a childhood notion of *Heimat* connoting a deep sense of belonging would have a lasting hold.[128] Home "still penetrates through the eye … and is assimilated in a mental process we call remembering."[129] It was not only a matter of remembering; it appears he was still searching: "What we urgently wished, and were socially bound to hate, suddenly stood before us and demanded our longing."[130] Améry knew he couldn't go back; home would no longer mean belonging. But his love of home, even if it were forbidden love—or at least forbidding love—remained intense: "Now and then traditional homesickness (*Heimweh*) also welled up and claimed its place."[131]

Améry recalled an encounter just before his arrest in exile that clarified for him how "my homeland followed after me."[132] He and other members of his resistance group met secretly in an apartment that felt safe to them even though German soldiers were living on the floor below. Disturbed one day by the noise they made, one of the Germans climbed the stairs and, entering the room, demanded quiet. Apologies apparently appeased him and he left, but the point of his story centered on the petitioner's manner of speech, a dialect he recognized from his native region. He also noticed that the soldier was an SS man and a member of the Gestapo whose task included arresting state enemies and deporting them to death camps. For the moment, however, homeland eclipsed "fear and the control of reason": "There stirred within me the mad desire to answer him in his own dialect." He felt he actually knew him, and recognized feelings of "intimate cordiality." The "good comrade" whose mission was "to wipe me out" "appeared to me suddenly as a potential friend."[133] The suddenness is important, for it betrays the primal attraction of kinship, and it was spontaneity like this that he regarded as an instance of homeland fellowship.[134] His German identification was, of course, imaginary. His "intellectual function," "the control of reason" that existed in his strong narratives, dismissed the impulse as "abstractive" or risible. As dreams or wishes, however, they possess something deeply emotional or affective. In them resides lived experience fostering an orientation to worldly engagement.

At times, what Améry imagined and wished for seemed close at hand. In his original preface, he evoked a community of "all those who wish to live together as fellow human beings"[135] and even said it was morally possible for the criminal to "join his victim as fellow human being."[136] Among his dark memories were those that recalled good Germans, brave Germans, who "broke out of the Third Reich."[137] They exemplified Germans' "better origins."[138] These observations, residing in weak narratives as departures but buttressed by suggestive dreams and desires, suspend his claim, in a stronger, indicative voice, that "resentment blocks the exit to the genuine human dimension, the future."[139] No matter the assertion, his stated position just couldn't rule out possibilities that he occasionally abandoned himself to. Their existence recast the work as heterogeneous, divergent narratives comprising a resentment conceit and intrusive second thoughts. In a familiar trope found in *At the Mind's Limits*, home was as necessary as it was impossible. It irrationally grew into him.

John Kleinig, in his 2014 inquiry into the phenomenology of loyalties, mined the famous biblical story of the *akedah* (the binding of Isaac) to show how "grounded" defining loyalties are. Here is God's test of Abraham's devotion: he is commanded to sacrifice Isaac, the son he loves. Why, the story demands, was Abraham's faith in God so great to follow the command? Kleinig argued that the defining relationship of Abraham to God provided a motive for Abraham's otherwise impossible decision. It was a decision "grounded as it has been up to that time in God's recurrent righteousness." Abraham, faced with an incomprehensible command, recognized that God was worthy of devotion, for the relationship was based on trust and protection.[140] The analogy to Améry is not perfect: there is a significant difference between covenantal relationships and wishful daydreams. Even when deliverance failed, the prophets reminded adherents of God's promise of redemption:

> For a while I forsook you,
> But with vast love I will bring you back.
> In slight anger, for a moment,
> I hid My face from you;
> But with kindness everlasting
> I will take you back in love
> —said the Lord your Redeemer[141]

For Améry, too, the predecessor order "had forsaken us" but his confidence that love would bring him back broke down. Relationships with his neighbors were, in retrospect, never promising to begin with. Still, the dynamic is fundamentally the same. Even if he had come to recognize that trust was unfounded; even if events proved that protection was, in the end, fatally specious, his former belief in his neighbors left an impression. It defined a part of his life—his emotional aspirations—that inspired a motive, grounded in belief not unlike Abraham's, to look forward—here, if only in his dreams—to a new relationship configuration in spite of the irreparable fracture. Unrequited as it was, his attachment to the world he inhabited lingered in reminiscences, providing ballast for a subsequent renegotiation. Camus was particularly discerning when he wrote:

> In the most abject misery, perpetually surrounded by a ragged mob, [the prisoner] composed a strange music which was audible to him alone. And for those of us who have been thrown into hell, mysterious melodies and the torturing images of a vanished beauty will always bring us, in the midst of crime and folly, the echo of that harmonious insurrection which bears witness, throughout the centuries, to the greatness of humanity.[142]

Améry's work was a complicated Enlightenment inheritance. On the one hand, his second thoughts indicate a surprising survival—more than "a trace"—of bedrock modern Enlightenment imperatives—humanity's greatness and a tenacious human attachment—not completely shaken by radical crimes against humanity or by his own narrative requiem to human ignominy. On the other hand, his essays sounded the disillusionment of the emancipated Jew and the counter-Enlightenment European intellectual. They posit an ascendant post-rational order of power politics and ethnic supremacy that recapitulated a divisive, might-is-right tribal ethos immune to the rule of law and a discourse of compromise and consensus. As Lawrence Langer observed in his studies of survivors' accounts, the fate of Jews made clear that the Enlightenment could not deliver on its promise of human progress and humankind's perfectibility.[143] Améry confirmed that "mankind's eternal progress was only a naïve belief of the nineteenth century."[144] His resentments condemned Germans and the world for violating the bond of trust constituting the social contract with their Jewish neighbors. The contradiction between Enlightenment and counter-Enlightenment inclinations announces a post-Enlightenment ethic. It is the tragic incongruity of these two narratives—an expressive intimacy and longing for fellowship, and his worldly loathing as well as a self-loathing for possessing such inadmissible emotions—that articulates a broken but not hopeless world. There is a notable measure of forward-looking possibilities in these essays, but it is hardly triumphant. If "no hand was lifted to protect him," if he could no longer count on others for help, he still leaned toward human fellowship. Looking forward in post-Enlightenment perspective required a new orientation. Améry came to realize that it was an expectation of mutual assistance that set all moral problems in motion: faith in others' good will created a dangerous condition of vulnerable dependency. How fatal to believe that an expectation of help was "as much a constitutional psychic element as is the struggle for existence."[145] Arriving at this "enormous perception at a later stage" in his life,[146] he recognized that the new order demanded reflection "honed and hardened by camp reality."[147] It cast in doubt notions of "inherent dignity."[148] Instead of relying on others for help, which he had come to renounce as naïve and "abstractive,"[149] the search for protection and a measure of fellowship would begin with skepticism: he would knock on the door for asylum, he wrote, but he would never be sure if anyone would hide him.[150] In other words, he didn't rule out the prospects of mutual protection and concern—indeed, he longed for it—but, taking nothing for granted, trust would have to begin with "what I *want* to feel."[151] It would be up to him, and, by extension, everyone else, to negotiate a world prone to violence, simultaneously wary and alert to possibilities.

4

Betrayal and Its Vicissitudes

Mapping betrayal

Betrayal and its effects have largely eluded systematic scrutiny. In the field of psychology, where the phenomenon would naturally belong as a subject for study, it has remained on the sidelines. Avishai Margalit, a philosopher, has recently scrutinized the transgression—mainly the misdeeds of adultery, treason, and apostasy. His inquiry reminds us that the subject's popularity in wisdom folklore and historical episodes primarily concerns acts of betrayal rather than the experience of its recipients, the subject of the present chapter. The story of Judas Iscariot stands out for his prototypical betrayal of Jesus to the authorities. Brutus figures prominently in Caesar's demise during the Roman civil war. Benedict Arnold is another classic example, as is Vidkun Quisling, the Norwegian defense minister who sold out his country to the Nazis—two names that have become synonyms for "traitor." In Mexico, a traitor is called a *Malinchisto* after La Malinche (Doña Marina), the Native American captive of conquistadors who served Hernán Cortes during his sixteenth-century New World expedition.

How people react to betrayal, what the reaction represents, and why its legacies endure and can eclipse even the effects of physical violence are significant questions that expose the dynamics of another constituent human emotion: anger. A recent assessment of "American Rage" (2016), indicated, on the one hand, that white people said they believed the American dream is dead, the American role in the world is not what it used to be, and their life is not working out the way they thought it would. The authors summed up the mood: "A plurality of whites tends to view life through a veil of disappointment." On the other hand, nonwhite Americans reported lower levels of anger than whites because they remained hopeful about their future in spite of adversities that we would expect to inspire angrier feelings. Anger, in this example, is a matter of feeling betrayed; in the survey's words, it is a response to "perceived disenfranchisement … the bitterness of a promise that didn't pan out."[1]

Betrayal, or more precisely the experience of being betrayed, is a common emotion in our everyday lives. We are surprised, as well as disturbed, when we expect something that doesn't materialize, like a friend's repayment of a debt. But it is stronger than a surprise: it is a negative emotion that begins with disappointment. The reason for disappointment is twofold: Failing to repay a debt is a disclosure of a particular or exceptional behavior that leads us to revise our estimation of someone we thought we knew. Or the behavior appears typical, intentional, and a breach of common trust; it interrupts a relationship and threatens to end it. We use the term "betrayal" in both ways. I may decide to maintain my relationship if I believe that the act wasn't typical or intentional, but I could see it as a rupture in the relationship if it subverts what Hannah Arendt called "the will to live together with others."[2] Recurrent and systematic violations amount to disillusionment more than disappointment, which, as interruptions, we can more easily get over. They recast our relationships by sundering them. The will that binds—that is, the trust between us or the persuasive appeal of a promise—withers away. We may conclude that an act of betrayal means that we can no longer rely on someone else and therefore need to withdraw from the relationship. But even if we decide the relationship is over, we might at least hold onto memories and, perhaps, keep an eye out for possibilities.

People are also affected by betrayal as a collective phenomenon, when, for example, a party to a business contract violates its stipulations or a nation contravenes the terms of a treaty. In an interview with a victim of a vicious attack on the Yazidi community in 2014, we see how prominent experiences of betrayal are in circumstances of conflict: "They tortured us, attacked our honor, our religion. We lived together with our Muslim Arab neighbors during the Iran/Iraq war, during the First Gulf War. We protected each other. Now they became our enemies."[3]

More subtle are the responses to betrayal when it is intentional or normative.[4] Intentional betrayal is contingent on specific circumstances, such as the calculations that led to Judas's, Brutus's, Arnold's, and Quisling's treachery. Normative betrayal may have intentional origins but evolves into a culture of sanctioned and even exalted behavior. When social relationships become aggressively competitive, the will to live together with others is no longer what matters. The quest for supremacy redefines relationships. As we will explore, the convention of routine betrayal defeats expectations of common, mutual, civic respect. But among parties who know each other, such as lovers, friends, and neighbors, or who, by dint of circumstances, inhabit the same moral environment, such as compatriots or what passes for humanity, acts of betrayal are especially agonizing. In this nasty climate, trust yields to suspicion; promises lose their potential to persuade categorically; reliability is a fiction or, worse, a foolish figment. Acts of recurrent and ruthless betrayal are not a matter for discrete evaluation. Instead, they constitute a normative shift to a cynical worldview. Here, too, however, no matter how tectonic the shift, traces of the former relationship might persist as latent, incandescent memory that kindles a measure of desire and hope.

The present chapter is devoted to identifying and understanding the trajectories of experiencing betrayal's transgressions in accounts written by survivors of Nazi-era destruction. They reside in narratives that explore relationships between victims and victimizers and, as accounts, express reactions to broken covenants. In contrast to strong narratives describing scenes of violence, references to acts of betrayal observe the misdeeds of moral violations. In fact, these references form the matrix of counter-narratives. As I will show, feeling betrayed is an emotion that looks forward even as it looks backward to the violation. It is a transitional emotion that underwrites transitional narratives in accounts of atrocity.

The afterlife of disillusionment from betrayal deserves particular consideration. It is a phenomenon that is especially under-theorized. In light of our present task, it is not an exaggeration to say, in the words of Jennifer J. Freyd and Pamela J. Birrel, that disillusionment rewrites history: "On discovery of betrayal, a key response is to reorganize one's perceptions of what has happened."[5] To assert that disillusionment from betrayal possesses an afterlife is important if for no other reason than it is transitional in contrast to strong narratives that look backward and condemn traumatic brutality. This much is clear enough from victims' interpretation of interpersonal acts of betrayal that are, or at least are seen as, an exceptional but not a final departure from the premise of a relationship. Depending on the severity of the act, a victim can move on, if warily. But, as I will argue, even when betrayal is normative and the act is disruptive, as in the case of Nazi-era racial assault, victims, in recalling the incident, can come to regard it as negotiable without depreciating the transgression. Counterintuitively, this is especially true between "intimates," and especially in relationships that are influenced by an ancestral history of victims' emotional attachment.

Counter-narratives of betrayal

The first hint of betrayal we encounter in survivors' accounts of Nazi-era destruction are in narratives devoted to championing resentment. As the main conceit in *At the Mind's Limits,* Jean Améry's determination to hold Germans accountable expresses a specific form of anger. When he reviled his torturers in the 1960s, he did so in two voices: he assailed them for their physical brutalization and its effect of overwhelming the victim and destroying life. So strong was his reaction that he wrote about wanting the "vile satisfaction" of punishing his enemy.[6] He excoriated younger generations who, twenty years after the war, appeared eager to ease, if not discard, the past's burden. What was important for him was to resist this kind of "false conciliatoriness" and keep "a moral chasm ... wide open."[7] In this voice, his expression of anger was divisive leaning toward retaliation. Expressing it, he said, was the reason for reissuing the book in 1977. Retribution is the emotion that governed his strong, indicative narrative.

In another voice, he wrote not just about the "antiman" but also about his "fellow man" whom he experienced as the antiman.[8] Resentment, in this sense, is different from retributive anger. The customary definition of resentment is a reaction to "perceived threats to expectations based on norms that are presumed shared in ... common life."[9] Against the narrative grain, Améry explored relationships that he suggested were not defined solely by degrading ruthlessness, even though he said they were. The assailants and even their descendants were transgressive for violating presumed normative expectations, or what he referred to as a "social contract": "The certainty that by reason of written or unwritten social contracts the other person will spare me."[10]

Betrayal is a common refrain in the observations of Jews who were victims of the lethal campaign against them. In one account written toward the end the war, Tadeusz Obręski wrote, while in hiding in Warsaw, about the decision of the Polish government-in-exile to pay tribute to a victim of the Warsaw Ghetto uprising. He was bewildered:

> Why are they awarding a medal of honor to the dead, but refraining from helping the living? ... I have been following the behavior of the Polish population from the very beginning [and] this posthumous decoration arouses in me [only] feelings of contempt. Now the Polish government decides to raise its voice? Now, when no Jews are left? ... Where was it ... during the four and a half years of occupation? Why ... didn't it order the Poles, back in 1939, to help Jews hide from the German murderers? Why did they keep silent? Why did they let, and why are they still letting, us be destroyed, here on the Aryan side?

The question, "Where was it?"—the leadership comprising his worthy compatriots—presumes that Obręski expected a better response than a useless medal. He believed that the government-in-exile possessed the potential to save Jewish lives but violated the promise by remaining silent. "This is where the main crime of the [Polish] government and of Polish society stems from: this hostility [to Jews] and this complete indifference. All of Polish society helped exterminate Jews … The Polish people betrayed three and a half million Jews. This is a fact that will be discussed in [future] history."

For Obręski, betrayal was criminal, and it stirred him to contempt. He was right about its significance in the conduct of the war, for betrayal would not only characterize survivors' subsequent accounts; it also accounted for his own fate: It appears that the Pole who took the considerable risk of hiding him eventually killed him.[11] Havi Ben-Sasson, who unearthed Obręski's "Memories and Diary," is on point in her interpretation. For Polish Jews, there existed an "unbearable gap between the positive image they had created and the reality—as they experienced it—in the later years [of the war]. As high as their hopes had soared, so deep was the depth of their disappointment." As the war entered its third year, Jews began to see their neighbors as their primary persecutors. Polish Jews from that point on saw no reason to change again their view of their neighbors or their relationships with them. Their "shattered hopes and beliefs about Polish society during the Holocaust" would "shape [the] discourse" for years to come, perhaps, she wonders, up to the present moment.[12] The question I will later explore is her contention that the betrayal was non-negotiable.

We can discern similar expressions in other accounts. A survivor who had lived in Czernowitz, "the Vienna of the East," remembered seeing a group of boys standing with clubs before the local university. It was bad enough that they appeared to be waiting for Jews, a belief confirmed by the steady restrictions that limited Jews' admission. But she was disheartened to learn who were among them: "To this day, I still cannot believe that the boys I knew, the boys I had flirted with and went to school with, would do such a thing."[13] Elie Wiesel, in a Hebrew edition of *Night* that he never published, reviled the surprising turncoat behavior of his Hungarian neighbors: "All the residents stood at the entrances of their homes, with faces filled with happiness at the misfortune they saw in their friends of yesterday."[14] Years after this unfiltered reproach, he reflected, "The further I go, the more I learn of the scope of the betrayal by the world of the living against the world of the dead."[15] He referred here to free world leaders, but the observation, upon reflection, also articulates a moral vision: "The cruelty of the enemy would have been incapable of breaking the prisoner; it was the silence of those he believed to be his friends—cruelty more cowardly, more subtle—which broke his heart."[16]

Lawrence Langer wrote in response that comments like these were not only subsidiary against the force of Wiesel's narrative protest, as I believe they were, but were also a puzzling distraction. They amount to a "momentary lapse of a stubbornly clear-sighted intelligence."[17] Langer's considerable argument for listening to the traumatic voice of the survivor and its evocation of "the ferocious nature of the event"[18] and victims' "meaningless deaths"[19] sometimes occludes recognition of authentic, simultaneous motifs in survivors' accounts, particularly the very process of surviving the destruction of European Jewry.[20] For Wiesel, surviving in a world in which not just individuals died in the camps but a vital part of humanity itself, circumspection was the prerequisite condition of the successor world.

In his chronicle of degradation in Polish–Jewish relations written and preserved clandestinely in the Warsaw Ghetto, Emanuel Ringelblum intoned in 1943 the new reality of chastening surprise. Before the war, when the occupying German authorities compelled Jews to register whatever possessions they did not already plunder, Jews made the decision to hand over their belongings to Polish Christians for safekeeping. As a measure of what he characterized as their reliance on their associates before the war, he added that Jews surrendered their valuables "on condition that the Jew should be a partner in the business." In characteristic understatement, he remarked, "It usually turned out very badly for the Jew." Ringelblum commented that Polish Christians "had been decent and honest all their lives." There were even some "noble individuals" who refused any benefits from the transaction and who exhibited extraordinary courage in hiding Jews and who, moreover, "to this day are still saving the lives of Jews on the Aryan side." But he recognized that something seismic was taking place. Their number was small, he wrote: "As happens in war, baseness predominates." The war "demoralized" people, he wrote, though he permitted himself on occasion to use somewhat stronger terms: they "appropriated Jews' possessions unscrupulously."[21] Ringelblum referred distantly to "the Jew" and described the present plight with notable restraint, though there is something reminiscent in his reference to his neighbors' basic decency, and there is a trace of hope when he acknowledged, as an aside, the presence of "noble individuals." Small as their number were, they appear to have represented for him a lingering faith in human fellowship.

As I see it, and as I believe Ringelblum saw it, too, there is pathos in his remark about the conditions Jews imposed on their neighbors as associates for what they thought was an act of entrustment. That they also assumed the transaction was mutual appears to have disheartened him. The agreement, Jews believed, was a temporary measure, an escrow arrangement, when, Ringelblum noted, their partners had no intention of remitting the debt: they treated Jews as "'deceased on leave' about to die sooner or later." The outcome—"in an overwhelming majority of cases" they kept what they apparently promised to return—cast the entire affair for Ringelblum as a critical turn of circumstances.[22] Germans and Polish Christians were clearly culpable in his account, but the story's expressive features belonged to Polish Jews—to them, for sure, but also to the radical and remarkable subversion of their social relationships. Ringelblum preferred to observe events from a reflective distance, but he could hardly suppress his awakening to the new regime of betrayal.

The theme of betrayal in accounts of destruction during the Second World War was not confined to Eastern Europe; it is conspicuous in accounts by Jews in Central-Western Europe as well. The point deserves some emphasis because the historiography of collaboration and duplicity during the Nazi era centers on circumstances of Eastern Europe—Poland, Rumania, Belorussia, Lithuania, and Ukraine.[23] Jews from both parts of Europe were emotionally attached to their milieus and expected basic assurances, even as they observed and acknowledged exceptional lapses. For East European Jews, relationships were communal and neighborly; for Jews elsewhere in Europe, relationships were entrenched in a common national culture and in common national traditions. Assimilation or acculturation was presumed and anticipated. The destruction process was different by region—local massacres in Eastern Europe accounting for roughly half of the decimation; roundups in Central-Western Europe and deportation to killing centers. But the experience of betrayal was profound across the board.

Simon Wiesenthal reflected on broken promises in *Die Sonnenblume* (*The Sunflower*), his account and reflections from the late 1960s. His sensibilities were eastern and western European. He spent most of his pre-war years in the East, the Austro-Hungarian territory of Galicia. A western influence germinated during the years he spent in Prague studying architecture, as well as in thrall of the empire's cultural appeal, but had come to predominate during his postwar years when he resided and wrote his accounts in Linz and Vienna.

Brokenness is elemental to Wiesenthal's account of Nazi captivity. Early on he evoked the ghetto's misery: hunger, exhaustion, anxiety, the cruelty of SS officers in charge, forced hard labor, and ambient death. Against this reality, he wrote about his helplessness, as someone who was "defenseless."[24] So strong was his sense of "mental paralysis"[25] that only "fate"[26] seemed to determine the outcome: the prisoner "had to learn to let himself be driven without a will of his own."[27] Reflecting on his condition of "hopelessness,"[28] he was a victim.[29] Even in an account dedicated to finding alternatives (the "sunflower"), retribution looms: "I still clung to the belief that the world one day would revenge itself on those brutes."[30]

It seems odd, then, that Wiesenthal regarded humiliation as his hardest experience.[31] In fact, it was actually "shocking humiliation" (*wie man Menschen so erniedrigte*) that demanded his attention.[32] In recounting his return with other prisoners from a work detail, the observations he made of local citizens who were staring at them overshadowed his passing reference to the day's ruinous labor. He was appalled by what he believed was their brutal indifference: "Of what concern were we to them?"[33] Comparing this encounter with persecution, he asked, "Was it not just as wicked for people to look on quietly and without protest at human beings enduring such shocking humiliation? But in their eyes were we human beings at all?"[34]

Nested in the question is the presumption of a common moral obligation. Now a target of contempt, he deeply rued that he felt "alone."[35] Abandonment and indifference echoed with the circumstances of his life before the war. Wiesenthal's decision to study architecture in Prague occurred after he was denied admission at the University of Lvov, then in Poland, where an infamous *numerus clausus* imposed a quota that limited the admission of Jews. The rejection, as momentous as it was for him personally, represented an instance of social and political betrayal.

Some thirty years later, he wrote about an incident at another local university in Lvov (in German, Lemberg) where he was working toward a Polish diploma. With depressing regularity, a number of students—the "'gilded youth' of Lemberg"[36]—brandished ribbons with the words "the day without the Jews." It wasn't so much the slander and its consequences that disturbed him, however, as the desertion by those whom he looked to for support. The school's rector failed to call in the police. Other students, who, he observed, were in the vast majority, stood by out of "cowardice and laziness. The great mass of the students were unconcerned about the Jews or indeed about order and justice."[37] Those students, who caused the most disturbances and were eventually arrested, "emerged from prison as heroes,"[38] martyrs "for their country's cause!"[39]

These episodes contributed to a loss of faith in the unspoken bond of social relationships. His world of normative expectations would no longer be the same: "I had gradually become resigned to the idea that I would never again build houses in which people would live in freedom and happiness."[40] And then, more rhapsodically, "It is impossible to believe anything in a world that has ceased to regard man as man, which repeatedly 'proves' that one is no longer a man."[41]

It is tempting to regard betrayal as a constituent survivor narrative, a part of what every Holocaust survivor must have experienced. Indeed, as Tony Judt and Jan Grabowski, among others, make clear, local collaboration with fascist authorities, including acts that exposed Jews in hiding or in flight, were endemic.[42] But circumstances that were present when survivors published their accounts also aroused the emotion. The world survivors encountered in the 1960s—a world that showed no interest in their considerable misfortune and, worse, a steady inclination, if not determination, to forget the past—rekindled memories of betrayed expectations during their ordeal. It is, of course, possible that the "double betrayal" occurred as a result of the original betrayal, focusing their attention to repeated behavior. But that observation ignores the impact of their generation's belated merciless disregard that prodded, for the first time, their acts of public protest.

The step from recollections for self-understanding to recollections as public protest involves a significant decision. It is a commitment to forming a relationship with others who are largely outside an intimate circle of family, friends, and community. Public testimony is a worldly communication, signifying a readiness to re-engage with strangers whose behavior is unknown and unpredictable. For survivors, there is an additional risk: They knew that the present time was not the same as it was before the terrible and unexpected turn of events. Once betrayed, they were aware that they had to renegotiate relationships with a world that demonstrated hostile inclinations. We are especially interested in how survivors managed the renegotiation and understood circumstances where betrayal was no longer surprising.

Recognizing betrayal as commonplace twenty years after their world's collapse, they felt compelled to bear witness in order to disturb their contemporaries' conscience and awaken a renewed moral commitment. The subject became a matter of retrospection worthy of measured scrutiny.[43] Indeed, a double betrayal is already discernible during the Nazi campaign against Jews when betrayal emerged as traumatic shock and survival was all that mattered. When Ringelblum wrote about the way matters were turning out for Jews, the way honest and decent Polish Christians exploited defenseless Jews who, as far as their adversaries were concerned, were merely on death leave, he was also conscious of what he termed a "new era in Polish–Jewish relations" with the formation of the Warsaw Ghetto. The old reliability mutated to new suspicion.

He observed the conditions of their social death:[44] "In organizing the Ghetto, the Germans aimed at isolating the Jewish population completely and segregating it entirely from the Aryan population." This meant dire privation and hopeless vulnerability. It also meant: "All economic and cultural contact between Jews and the Aryans was to be broken off completely."[45] The cultural, physical, and moral collapse of ghettoized inmates' daily lives articulated the wholesale dissolution of Jewish life, which he summed up by emphasizing the completeness, the irrevocability, of their categorical ostracism. The two instances formed a double betrayal, the first experienced as existential, the second as a metamorphosis, and together as hopeless abandonment.

The circumstances in the 1960s represented a combustible confluence of events that alarmed Améry and Wiesenthal and inspired them to recall to their contemporaries, in the process of bearing witness to destruction, their compatriots' wartime betrayal. As Améry observed in his account, Germans had contravened their "better origins"[46] and were still doing so by seeking to turn a new page on the past and declare a *Stunde Null,* or zero hour. What spurred their mission to condemn their world's indifference and self-indulgence was the Frankfurt Auschwitz trial. Ever since the war, but especially during the five years before the trial's 1963 commencement, West Germans, who were reminded again and again of the Nazi past, tried to bury the era and its commission of crimes. Many were pleased that statutes, in setting up a central office in 1958 for investigating Nazi-era crimes, mandated that it refer cases to local prosecutors, robbing it of independent power. In addition, defense attorneys and trial judges sought to disparage witnesses' testimonies by challenging survivors' fitness to serve.[47]

The Frankfurt trial generated substantial publicity, prompting many Germans, including the West German government, to invoke the statute of limitations, an act set to declare an end to prosecuting former Nazis and, by extension, Germans' overt or tacit collusion. At this point, survivors spoke out. As Wiesenthal recalled: "The world demands that we forgive and forget the heinous crimes committed against us. It urges us that we draw a line, and close the account as if nothing had ever happened."[48] For Améry, "the big Auschwitz trial" sparked his commitment to write about the past, his "experiences in the Third Reich, after twenty years of silence."[49] The debate that ensued drew German Jews into the public arena to argue for the "imprescriptibility" of extreme crimes against humanity. The argument asserted that such crimes should remain eligible for prosecution indefinitely, beyond the usual prescribed period, since they sought to expunge the first principle of human existence, that is, existence itself regardless of specific actions. As a result, Améry and Wiesenthal, among other survivors including French philosophers Emmanuel Levinas and Vladimir Jankélévitch, emerged as the original cohort of Holocaust survivors to write their accounts in defiance.

Their determination to go on record was perhaps nothing more than a reminder that survivors, in Wiesenthal's words, "cannot obliterate the hell we endured,"[50] but it was also inspired by the concern that Europe would erase the past in its apparent zeal to move on. The inclination to annihilate memory had the opposite intended effect on survivors, who recognized that this time they could defeat the repression—or at least try to, which was, itself, a significant expression. Writing strong narratives that recorded the persecution they endured would keep the past vivid for belated generations at a time when Nazi trials reached a pinnacle of unpopularity.[51] As Jankélévitch wrote, survivors were determined to recall the past "to the forgetful, the frivolous, and the indifferent."[52] In addition to publishing their accounts, Améry signed petitions against the enforcement of the statute; ten years after *The Sunflower*, Wiesenthal endorsed a considerable postcard campaign addressed to the West German chancellor that contributed to the West German Bundestag's decision to abolish the statute for radical crimes.[53]

For survivors, their accounts possessed intrinsic value. They were surely considering the influence of their reports for posterity, as we so often hear, but it is important to note that this period, marking the transition from a silence beyond self-references or documentary testimony to an outward, public protest, represented an opportunity to reverse the course of their earlier renunciation. As Améry wrote, he repudiated the "social pressure" to remain silent.[54] Choosing to write about the occurrence of normative betrayal a generation earlier was a decision that grew out of survivors' dejection over their contemporaries' heartless commitment to moving forward by leaving the past behind. It was as if the European 1960s reprised a day without the Jews.

Afterlife

We need to account for expressions that look forward, expressions that seem out of place in work devoted to reminders about past wrongdoing. Améry hinted at the future in dreams about a moral German revolution in which Germans would "once again become the fellow man."[55] Jankélévitch, in an essay "invoking these days of rage"—"the extermination camps, the hangings at Tulle, the massacre at Oradour"[56]—nonetheless made room for expressing his belief that the Frankfurt Auschwitz trial would inspire people "to realize what it was that they had diverted their thoughts from."[57] Wiesenthal retained a moral vision in spite of his story's expressions of recrimination. Even as the indifference and contempt of bystanders left him wondering about a "world that has ceased to regard man as man," he contravened the observation in his companion "sunflower" ruminations. The human connection to the dying SS officer he wrote about is so meticulously drawn out that it seems forced or, as more than one critic claimed, even fabricated.[58] Parallel to narratives recounting the officer's confessions about murder are incongruous confessions of his own: Wiesenthal felt "sympathy" for Karl.[59] Calling the officer by his first name (a pseudonym) also suggests a measure of compassion. We get this impression in the details of the account: he often referred to Karl's eyes, offhanded remarks that inflect a search for communication that words, alone, couldn't consummate. As a direct means of communication, eye contact represents a trained search for human connection. The importance of the search is especially poignant when we learn that Wiesenthal couldn't really see Karl's eyes; they were covered with bandages. Yet, "I had the feeling that he was staring at me,"[60] adding inexplicably that his eyes "looked at me through small holes in the bandages."[61] Karl appeared capable of a human response even as he recalled his participation in his unit's assault against helpless Jews. As Wiesenthal wanted to relate, Karl could never forget the incident, "least of all" one child with "dark eyes."[62]

It is incredible that Wiesenthal would want to rescue Karl's humanity in a world he had come to resent for its inhumanity, but that is an apparent contradiction we need to look at. Whether or not he took liberties in telling the story, it is at bottom an expression that accommodated in the same text two distinctive views of humankind, one that looked back to a sinister period, the other that represents a foundation for the future: "Were we truly all made of the same stuff? If so, why were some murderers and others victims? Was there in fact any personal relationship between us, between the murderers and their victims?"[63]

Wiesenthal's famous life activity, beginning in 1945, when he started investigating Nazi crimes, involved a commitment to bringing about justice. He also hoped it would help him restore his "faith in humanity."[64] Betrayal, I want to argue, is an emotion we have identified in survivors' accounts that, contrary to classic psychological studies, permits transitions from acrimony to renewed, if qualified, beliefs. Unlike expressions of condemnation, which are non-negotiable and strongly articulated, allusions to acts of betrayal, though darkly inflected, are plastic and retain a capacity for development. They constitute counter-narratives, narratives that rebut inconsolable recrimination, if subtly. The emotion lends itself to misunderstanding, for it appears inflexible and retributive, a reaction to violated expectations that inspires anger or resignation. Acts of betrayal, by sundering the moral foundations of civil society, weaken the glue of social relations. Mutuality, trust, and faith in a common future are values that lose their authority when the moral premise binding strangers into common destiny—a social contract—is broken. The surprise factor is integral to betrayal, as Jan Błoński noted about wartime Polish Jews: "There was, conscious or unconscious, an expectation that their fate would improve, the burden of humiliation would lighten, that the future would gradually become brighter. What actually happened was exactly the opposite."[65] Surprise is the emotional response to broken expectations. Experienced as shock, it is a traumatic injury.

The common emotional response to betrayal is resentment. When it begins to evolve into an expression of protest, it gives victims standing and can free them from a state of dependence, the victim's signature condition. But even then, it exhibits limitations: It doesn't necessarily produce social change. Under extreme circumstances, as Langer remarked, shaming those who egregiously violated normative expectations to self-reflection, let alone contrition, requires their willingness to show respect for the "moral intention of the protestor," and that, he asserted, was hardly likely.[66] What, then, of the future? If betrayal is as severe as it is portrayed in survivors' accounts, relationships between peers—whether they're between the citizen and the state (Obręski and Wiesel) or between compatriots (Ringelblum, Améry, and Wiesenthal)—appear not only broken but broken irrevocably. The wound of past offenses restricts relationships at best to an expedient rapprochement; on the scale of intensive human destruction that came as an awakening, survivors could hardly imagine the prospect of social harmony. (Desmond Tutu, in the context of structural persecution, championed the conception for post-apartheid South Africa as a paradigmatic alternative.) Tarnished by the offense, survivors' relationships to a world that exposed its vile predilections would more likely be unstable. Could they hope for anything more than a tenuous self-preservation?

Some of what we know about the psychology of betrayal comes from studies of childhood abuse. We are reminded that trauma affects children differently from adults (Améry, Jankélévitch, and Wiesenthal were in their thirties in 1942), but these studies define a benchmark for comparison since, as scholars and survivors observed in the case of Nazism's victims, victims of extreme and protracted cruelty were reduced to childlike helplessness.[67] Jennifer Freyd studied the phenomenon of "betrayal trauma," and, indeed, coined the term; as such, her research provides a standard of scholarship for comparison with survivors and their formative experiences with betrayal. Based on her investigations of the psychological effects of abuse—such as psychological torment or gross neglect, as well as sexual and other physical violations—by someone the child knew and trusted, her conclusions were dismal.[68] She argued that victims of betrayal would normally cease interacting with the offender, but when the victim is at the mercy of a primary caregiver, the child requires another strategy in order to preserve the relationship. She posited the idea of "traumatic amnesia" that succeeds at blocking the painful memory that would otherwise interfere with the will to attachment. Survival is the higher good, but it comes at a price: The blocked memory is processed "by other less conscious mechanisms"—such as dissociating the emotional memory from knowledge of the event or repressing memories of the event after it occurred—that will later emerge as "highly maladaptive behaviors."[69] The damage materializes as a compromised assessment of reality, an inflation or extirpation of trust, and emotional and mental distortion.[70] For Freyd, the experience of betrayal is pathological and, short of successful psychotherapy, is understood as an obstinate emotional impairment.

More accessible studies of betrayal transform clinical research into commonplace conceptions. In seeking to honor the victims' voice, Alice Miller wrote about the repercussions of stark childhood experiences with caregivers, in one case with a father "who had no respect for her soul."[71] As an analyst, she explained the daughter's behavior in adulthood: "She was constantly re-enacting the drama of her childhood in her repetition compulsion, sometimes with the roles reversed, so that *she* was the one who was superior to men, who wounded and abandoned them." She played this out by taking out her feelings of revenge on surrogate persons.[72] Miller concluded that childhood betrayal compromised prospects for authentic love. For the preponderance of humankind without the opportunities for analysis, the phenomenon of betrayal under abusive circumstances is detrimental because it seems intransigent. Do we find similar dynamics in survivors' accounts? It's hard to miss the echoes, if not salience, of emotional mutilation. Améry's rumination on his experience with torture is a dramatic illustration: "It was over for a while. It is still not over. Twenty-two years later I am still dangling over the ground by dislocated arms, panting, and accusing myself. In such an instance there is no 'repression.'"[73] Jankélévitch, too, evoked "the full horror of the catastrophe" and sounded its impossible depths: it is an "unnameable, unmentionable, terrifying thing, a thing from which one diverts one's thoughts and that no human speech dares describe."[74] Dominick LaCapra characterized it a possession by the past; Sidra DeKoven Ezrahi regarded it as static and non-negotiable despair.[75]

This is surely true for narratives recalling episodes of traumatic assault, but is it true for counter-narratives of betrayal? Psychoanalytic theories of normal development, though not directly concerned with betrayal, are actually more useful for us in this regard since survivors' accounts, as a deliberate act of retrospection, represent a stage of control over traumatic memories. The subject matter is surely dark and profoundly disquieting, and the emotions implicated in recall elude mastery, but as a written record, they demonstrate effective emotional management. This might be the result of the passage of time before many elected to recall their ordeal, or, more likely, it represents an emergence from despair as a result of a process of writing about the past systematically, disciplined by a mission to condemn morally complacent observers. In a different register of reflection, emotional reactions to shocking interpersonal or intercultural defections are more resilient and robust than arguments for costly self-preservation claim.

Melanie Klein suggested alternative trajectories by positing the requirement for post-betrayal self-preservation without serious liabilities. Studying pre-oedipal relationships, she recognized that an infant, who comes to see his mother as whole, both good and bad, and hates her for offering but failing to satisfy his insatiable needs, wants to reject her. Feeling guilty and stricken with depressive anxiety as a result of aggressive impulses toward an "object" he relies on, the sadistic urge hastens a counter-urge to repair and restore the relationship. Reparation, as Klein saw it, was not merely expedient. In normal circumstances, it reconstructs the infant's inner world, puts the infant's aggressive drives to rest, and accelerates his maturity. Though subsequent experiences of loss will reawaken anxieties, his relationships with his mother, and eventually his father and the world, shaken by the pre-oedipal betrayal, are stable.[76]

Klein's interest in the anxieties of loss and abandonment, and in the psychological work that mitigated them, alerted her to the significance of the mourning process.[77] Its theoretical foundations, established by Freud, help us understand the narrative tensions in survivors' accounts and the transitional psychodynamics of betrayal. For Freud, mourning involves stages of reactions to the loss of a person or an object that she felt attached to. By objects, Freud meant "one's country, liberty, an ideal, and so on."[78] Dejected by the loss, "the world has become poor and empty."[79] So devoted is she to mourning the loss that it "leaves nothing over for other purposes or other interests."[80] Eventually, however, just "being alive" fuels "narcissistic satisfactions" and the will to detach from the lost object.

Loss is a significant motif in survivors' accounts—the loss of spiritual and moral, as well as physical, capacity: Améry's expressive loneliness and inability to feel at home in the world[81] and his determination to keep it that way; Ringelblum's chronicle of worldly isolation; or Wiesenthal's despondent reaction to the broken bond of friendship and community. In "Mourning and Melancholia" (1917), Freud alludes to subsequent stages of the mourning process. Once detached, the mourner, becoming "free and uninhibited again,"[82] displaces the lost object with a new one, a stage missing from melancholia and its fixation on, or identification with, loss.[83] Freud's miniature essay "On Transience" (1915) looked at the displacement and the way it resolved loss, which would include betrayal, into a reattachment to other objects. The essay is a compelling read not only for its forward-looking thrust but also as self-reflective expression. It draws our attention to survivors' counter-narratives, which we might otherwise miss altogether were we to notice only backward-looking narrative acrimony. Améry insisted that his resentment "blocks the exit to the genuine human dimension, the future,"[84] but it appears that a process of mourning is active in his account. In fact, the process is responsible for the phenomenon of counter-narratives and its effect on chipping away at obstacles toward charting new pathways.

"On Transience" is one of Freud's masterful, nontechnical inquiries exhibiting his finesse with storytelling. Originating as a contribution to a collection of essays by different writers, called *Das Land Goethes*, at the invitation of the Berlin Goethe Society, it is a reminiscence of an encounter Freud had two years before with two companions, whose identities he concealed but were later revealed as the poet Rainer Maria Rilke and the writer and a colleague in Freud's circle, Lou Andreas-Salomé.[85] Freud responded to the "young but already famous poet," who felt that everything worthwhile is "fated to extinction."[86] It is likely that Freud, in the course of his conversation with Rilke during breaks at the 1913 proceedings of the International Psychoanalytic Association, was ruminating over Carl Jung's defiance of Freud's movement and the possible demise of the movement itself, but the details, as Freud knew, were not important for the essay.

Freud characterized the poet's "aching despondency"—which his other companion evidently shared—as a "revolt in their minds against mourning."[87]

He wrote the essay as a rejoinder to this position, which he would later call melancholia. He disputed "the pessimistic poet's view that the transience of what is beautiful involves any loss in its worth," remarking that whatever the duration, the beautiful is valuable "for our own emotional lives."[88] A flower that lasts for one night, he wrote, is no less lovely on that account.[89] The distinction set the stage for his explication of the mourning process: However painful and dispiriting, loss is liberating. Spontaneously (though in "Mourning and Melancholia," he remarked on the gradual progression), mourning reaches a point when it "consumed itself";[90] "our capacity for love" and attachment can eventually "take other objects instead,"[91] objects, he asserted, that were "equally or still more precious."[92]

The argument for proxy attachments after loss provides a suggestive normative framework for understanding betrayal's afterlife. Klein's conception of reparation moves us in the right direction. In her view, reparation dynamics begin with subaltern anticipation of fulfillment and proceeds to psychological defeat, an echo sounded historically in Jews' social relationships with their European compatriots. As they came to realize, their expectations produced results that were "exactly the opposite," as Błoński put it, from what they anticipated. The world they had known during its fall was radically different not only because it disclosed deplorable behavior—the concern of their strong narratives—but also because it defied a presumption of human reciprocity that they felt was fundamentally inviolable. Jankélévitch believed the new reality exposed a "shameful secret" that he never before imagined. It was "the secret of modern humanity" brought to universal awareness by craven belligerence.[93] At this point of the process, betrayal theorists, looking at childhood (and childlike) conditions of primitive dependence, recognize psychological arrest. Resolution is not an option. Relationships are non-negotiable. In this view, trajectories are limited to survival strategies at the expense of forward-looking authentic fellowship. What explains the new course that survivors charted? Exploring psychological mechanisms at the earliest stages of life, Klein maintained that the surprise of rejection inspired a secondary reflexive response, a "counter-urge" to the primary desire for retaliation. This, she said, possessed the potential, under conducive circumstances, for restoring and righting relationships. Spontaneity doesn't, however, explain survivors' development. Survivors engaged an alternative process to spontaneity in the act of writing about their past. Though Améry confessed to emotional limitations in writing about the "how" of pain, he clearly wanted to write about "what" it was.[94] As a method of self-assertion and a means of worldly reconnection, it evidently released him, and other survivors protesting against commonplace indifference, from emotional paralysis and permitted him to displace a state of hopeless dependence and its pathological repercussions with narrative expression. Writing, communicating, and, as Améry remarked, becoming "a vehemently protesting Jew"[95] generated a reparative or mourning response to loss. Klein showed that reparation progresses from a desire to bury hatred to a course of renewed possibilities. In measured expression, it can have the effect of dampening the threat of abandonment and inspiring alternatives to Jankélévitch's rage and Améry and Wiesenthal's devastating loneliness.

Freud's "On Transience" is historically significant as an essay tethered to nineteenth-century European conceptions of loss and mourning. Written during the First World War, he observed the carnage as transient if unprecedented. In fact, one of the essay's attractions is its tenacious insistence, in light of the magnitude of destruction, on the possibilities for resolving loss. For Freud, once grief "consumed itself," a capacity for love (we are "alive") rekindles the desire or drive for renewed love and attachment analogous to Klein's counter-urge. The essay's regard for the vestiges of loss provides instructive comparison with survivors' narrative negotiation of loss. There are hints of something precious in Ringelblum's rarefied "noble individuals" and in his reminiscence of Polish Christians who "had been decent and honest all their lives." Wiesenthal's conception of humanity—murderers and victims—constituting the "same stuff," also betrays what Freud called "our capacity for love." But in writing about the completeness of their social death, could they go as far as Freud, who sought to allay his despondent companions' anxieties, by regarding tarnished humanity as "equally or still more precious"?

Freud related the war's destructiveness to an ardent desire for reattachment: "Bereft [*verarmte*] of so many of its objects," life-affirming drives "have clung with all the greater intensity to what is left to us." He did not avoid the effects of war altogether. As he writes:

> [It] shattered [*brach*] our pride in the achievements of our civilization … and our hopes of a final triumph over the differences between nations and races … It revealed our instincts in all their nakedness and let loose the evil spirits [*bösen Geister*] within us which we thought had been tamed forever by centuries of continuous education by the noblest minds … [It] showed us how ephemeral was much that we had regarded as immutable [*beständig*].[96]

Yet Freud was determined to preserve his faith in human progress: "Our pride in what is common to us" has "suddenly grown stronger."[97] But did he so quickly forget about the war's devastation—the world's "evil spirits"—and how it "shattered" his hopes for a final triumph? The essay appeared on the cusp of Freud's break with the past and his theoretical revision. It foreshadowed an emotional, as well as theoretical, adjustment. In reluctantly acknowledging that the war subverted bedrock assumptions, a sense of betrayal is intriguingly implicated. Within a few years he would set out the phenomena of traumatic neurosis and death drives—the power of human violence and destructiveness—in *Beyond the Pleasure Principle* (1920). In "On Transience," however, he wasn't yet resigned to a war-ravaged world order. He argued for renewal after loss. Written by someone who was self-consciously Jewish,[98] the existence of doctrinaire beliefs—rooted in Enlightenment tenets—in the essential good will of their compatriots illustrates a strong current in modern Jewish experience. The achievements of civilization, he fervently believed, were capable of pacifying evil, but the force of reality raised troubling doubts. Preferring at this point to displace loss with "other objects instead," doubt inspired adherence to these beliefs "with greater intensity" and his regard for "what is left to us" as just as precious as, if not more precious than, what was lost. Freud's experience with loss wasn't just transient; it was fugitive. The essay, written on the foothills of total war, left the question of what was lost unexamined.

"On Transience" is an instructive example of how Freud's emotional predilections at times compromised his acclaimed commitment to psychological truth and interfered with drawing logical conclusions. In arguing that loss, including traumatic loss, is negotiable, it offers seminal insight for clarifying the dynamics of narrative transition in survivors' accounts. But, by failing to accommodate the terrible, excessive effects of massive destruction in his conception of a worldly reconnection, his nascent theory of mourning falls short of explaining the coexistence in the same text of narratives that, on the one hand, bear witness to loss and condemn those who were culpable, and, on the other, gaze forward toward "other objects." The essay didn't even identify, much less condemn, the responsible agents of destruction beyond the metonymic reference to "the war," in spite of his acknowledgment of "differences between nations" that defined the war's origins and its progress, or between "races" that once thwarted his early ambitions.[99] As important as the mourning process is for clearing a path to the future, his conception of the future, in early analytic theory, is uncomplicated: "When once the mourning is over, it will be found that our high opinion of the riches of civilization has lost nothing from our discovery of their fragility [*Gebrechlichkeit*]." Nothing is broken. "We shall build up again all that war has destroyed, and perhaps on firmer ground and more lastingly than before."[100]

The full impact of the war is apparent in *The Ego and the Id* (1923), where Freud argued that the reattachment incorporates lost objects in modified ways instead of taking the form of completely new objects.[101] Orthodox psychoanalytic theory, however, by examining a process that "works through" traumatic loss to its mitigation, regards negative emotions as unwanted because, as much as they are amenable to regulation, they are seen to retard, if not sabotage, normal development. It provides for a release from the grip of unconscious intrusions, such as the compulsion to repeat unresolved behavior.[102] Recent studies in moral philosophy offer another way of seeing the disposition of negative emotions in the process of post-traumatic resilience. As we observe in survivors' accounts, much as survivors recognized the emotional poverty of resentment and dreamt about their release from it, they never let up on the deep disquiet. Constituting their strong narratives, condemnation remained firm because survivors could not forget or resolve their traumatic injuries and even summoned memories of them to admonish their contemporaries, as they did in rallying against the enforcement of statutory limitations. The process of communicating negative emotions was, itself, important: it provided a measure of independence and self-respect, germinated a capacity for action, and brought them into contact with a world that they had forsworn and still distrusted.

Jeffrey Blustein achieved a balance between the two emotions—recrimination and resilience—in his study of non-retributive emotions after a breakdown in interpersonal relationships.[103] While he is interested in the phenomenology of forgiveness, the case he makes for the permeable properties of certain tenacious negative emotions demands our attention here. In looking at victims' reactions to wrongdoing, he distinguishes between the non-negotiable emotions of anger, vengeance, and excessive resentment and those that are flexible—disappointment, grief, and sadness. The former emotions arouse a desire to retaliate and punish the wrongdoer; they are impermeable because they seek to maintain an unbridgeable distance from the offender. In dwelling on faults that led to willful destruction and, belatedly, to willful inattention, they keep "a moral chasm … wide open." Wiesel's tirade against his neighbors was, in the end, non-negotiable:

> I have learned the true face of the Hungarians. It is the brutal face of an animal … At the end of the war, I refused to return to my hometown because I didn't want to see any more the faces they revealed behind the disguises on that day of expulsion. However, from one perspective, I am sorry I didn't return home, at least for a few days, in order to take revenge.[104]

By contrast, disappointment, the emotion I want to consider because of its kinship with betrayal, can generate emotions that permit something more dynamic after the offense. When it is not overwhelmed by anger and other retributive emotions, feeling betrayed, as a reaction to wrongdoing, enables relationships again without completely erasing the underlying pain. The important point is Blustein's insight that a victim of wrongdoing responds to an offense with a range of reactions that express acrimony while leaving just enough of an opening for renegotiating the relationship: she can blame the wrongdoer without sacrificing the relationship altogether. She may need to reorganize her beliefs and expectations after the breach, but not at the expense of banishing memories of the offense and the feelings that go with them. Indeed, the "frame of mind" she arrives at incorporates negative feelings "into the fabric of her life[105] … The one who was wronged need not even renounce her right to continue to feel them."[106]

I believe that the nuance Blustein realized responds more roundly to the narrative complexity in survivors' accounts than Freud's valuable but partial early theory of mourning. As we have seen, the accounts we have considered in this chapter recalled considerable circumstances of ascendant assault. While Wiesenthal could well have dismissed the pressures he felt at school as exceptional behavior—another sporadic outburst of anti-Jewish hostility—the Nazi-era mobilization and consolidation of hostilities into a sustained and wholly lethal campaign destroyed his and other survivors' faith in human fellowship as they had understood and anticipated it. Améry, with declarative force, condemned the enemy's sadism. Jankélévitch evoked "the full horror of the catastrophe." Their sense of loss never waned: We "cannot obliterate the hell we endured," as Wiesenthal put it, an observation Freud could not, or chose not to, accept even in the midst of an "evil" war. At the same time, survivors appeared not to have relinquished memories of their anterior attachments to their compatriots—Améry's evocations of home, "the people: the schoolmate from the same bench, the neighbor, the teacher";[107] Wiesenthal's sympathy for the offending SS officer; or Ringelblum's allusions to the presence of noble individuals. The relationship between the two memories is articulated in expressions of betrayal. Améry had come to regard his faith in mutual relationships as an "emotional fraud,"[108] the collapse of his "foolish, sham undertaking."[109] But it is noteworthy that memories of betrayal possess posterior implications. As Améry put it, in spite of its fraudulence, his former faith resurfaced after betrayal as a "longing" for home. He and Jankélévitch dreamt about a moral transformation.

Survivors' accounts are a manifestation of different remembrances: strong, assertive memories of human cruelty and reminiscent counter-narratives of shocking betrayal. If their memories were just retributive—ultimately reiterations of Améry's "retrospective grudge"[110]—we would not find dispositions to look forward or a willingness to imagine possibilities. The existence of their accounts alone suggests a renewed human connection, even if they met with resistance during and after the Frankfurt Auschwitz trial and the statutory limitations debates. There is strength bordering on intransigence in narratives that condemn and admonish. Survivors would agree with Avishai Margalit that compromised human relationships are here to stay. Like other misdeeds that harm and offend others, "betrayal, like laughter, belongs to the basic fabric of human existence."[111] Its antidote – "total transparency" – is, he noted, a fantasy, the destruction of civilization as we know it.[112]

But we have seen in their allusions to betrayal references inhabiting the narrative byways of pathos, reminiscence, and dreams. Betrayal is a transitional emotion permitting, if not fueling, a renegotiation with a world, a world survivors believed they no longer belonged to but still longed for. We are naturally confused by survivors' preoccupation with loss and their simultaneous inclination to look forward. That is a contradiction representing two truths. With painful awareness and an uncertain future, survivors left it unreconciled.

5

Critical Forgiveness

The riddle of disproportion

Our first assumption is that survivors of Nazi-era destruction avoided or evaded the term "forgiveness" in their accounts, but that is not true. They were quite willing to write about it, but only negatively, in strong, witness narratives where recrimination and condemnation were paramount. These narratives provided a record of the destruction process—the impossible indignities of physical and psychological exposure; naked brutality, sadism, and other excrements of human behavior; and sometimes, in response, an appeal to retributive justice. The voice survivors adopted was descriptive and, though the torment of their memories is apparent, their expression is more indicative than emotional, more assertive than inquisitive. Even reflective accounts exhibited little or no inclination to consider forgiveness as a legitimate response to destruction. They summoned the word only to repudiate it, sometimes summarily.

For Jean Améry, forgiveness is cheap and lazy.[1] Whenever "the peace chorus" invites survivors to look forward, not backward, it is "too difficult" for him. The "lofty ethical flights"[2] merely authorize an easy indifference to past crimes whose pastness is always present.[3] Worse, were he to forgive, he would become "the accomplice of my torturers."[4] Simon Wiesenthal felt that forgiveness, as acquiescence, was "weak."[5] Primo Levi, responding to an accusation of weakness leveled by Améry, flatly denied forgiveness as an option: "I am not inclined to forgive … because I know of no human act that can erase a crime."[6] Ruth Kluger renounced forgiveness on two counts: since it implied "closure," she wasn't ready to move on.[7] More assertively, she wrote, "Where the crime surpasses a certain magnitude, we can't handle it, not with retribution, not with forgiveness. So we throw in the towel. Genocide is off the charts, as it were."[8] For Vladimir Jankélévitch, the crimes against humanity were too "exorbitant" to heed "the call for a pardon."[9] Using the term "pardon" for forgiveness in reference to lenient acts of state, including his country France, he proclaimed that "pardoning died in the camps."[10]

Forgiveness has long been a notion in contention. In conventional parlance, it is, on the one hand, a venerable term representing ardent generosity that is semantically similar in English to a "gift," as it is in French (*don-pardon*), Spanish (*don-perdonar*), Italian (*dono-perdono*), German (*Geben-Vergeben*), and so forth. For some, in its purest form it exceeds a gift when a gift is predicated on a contractual expectation of receiving something back in exchange and therefore compromised by expedience.[11] Jankélévitch agreed. More than a gift, when it is "happy to forget the injury,"[12] forgiveness deals with the misdeed as well as the person[13] and, beyond that, creates completely new relations with the guilty person.[14] As such, forgiveness is a "gratuitous gift."[15] The gesture inspires acclamation to the point of disbelief. Indeed, to many observers who exalt it, it seems miraculous.[16]

On the other hand, it is a term of disparagement. Forgiveness is supererogatory, a standard of implausible rectitude and moral purity. Philosopher Maurice Blanchot deflated the sanctimony of this position by asserting its hypocrisy. "Giving and forgiving cease to be possible" since forgiveness is really not generous at all: By calling attention to moral offenses, "forgiveness accuses before it forgives."[17] For some, it glosses over injuries for the sake of social peace, a problem that has piqued other philosophers, notably Jankélévitch, Jacques Derrida, and Paul Ricoeur.[18] Most detractors worry about those who seem zealous to forgive: granting forgiveness, especially when it isn't strenuously earned, is soft, diffident, and self-effacing. It is also irresponsible for letting offenders off the hook and threatening the moral balance. In this case, the gesture inspires contempt if not derision. Today, in light of our troubled time's ardent security concerns and an extraordinary climate of suspicion fueled by panoptic surveillance, forgiveness is thoroughly edged out by an urgency to get tough.[19] Both interpretations—forgiveness as generous and as naïve—converge in seeing the term as quixotic. While there are concessions to the therapeutic value of moving on, concern about the perilous consequences of forgiveness is paramount. Such "lofty ethical flights" amount to an evasion of worldly complexity. According to this view, when reality occasionally manifests rank cruelty, it is better to expose and, ideally, disarm it than to give it a pass. Witnesses to destruction saw it that way, and so do most other observers.

Those who give thought to forgiveness invariably deal with the riddle of disproportion. How is it possible to reconcile the radical disparity between, in Ricoeur's terms, "the depth of the fault and the height of forgiveness?"[20] This is the question Jankélévitch dealt with when he noted the "shocking collision," the "scandalous contradiction"[21] between wrongdoing and the "immensity" of true forgiveness.[22] Although they both exalted the height of what Jankélévitch called "true forgiveness," and, hence, endorsed the disproportionality, Hannah Arendt, who teased out forgiveness's possibilities, could not recognize forgiveness as a legitimate response to limit behavior. Such extreme offenses simply "transcend the realm of human affairs," exceeding the power to punish as well as to forgive.[23] Forgiveness, in this representative view, is a grand ideal whose insubstantiality is no match for the grave offenses it feebly tries to negotiate.

Yet, in the past twenty years, successor states dealing with the aftermath of atrocity have enlisted the ideal to hasten reconciliation between victims and perpetrators. The strategy, a key element of transitional justice, has had a difficult journey. For all the praise that South Africa's Truth and Reconciliation Commission received for averting cycles of post-apartheid violence, many believe that its emphasis on forgiveness actually fell short of achieving reconciliation. As Lyn S. Graybill noted, the constant "harping on the infinite capacity of Africans to forgive" imposed pressures on victims at the expense of more promising steps toward compassion.[24] The theology that informed Desmond Tutu, the commission's chair, was surely noble based on a belief in an irreducible humanness and a redemptive *ubuntu,* or social harmony.[25] But, as Colleen Murphy observed, a categorical faith in redemption was not only naïve but, as an elision of aggressive behavior, also an instrument of complicity.[26] In this view, the price for forgiveness—impunity or denial—is too steep. The alternative postulate, retribution, or the punishment of offenders, garners support as a stronger precondition of reconciliation because it clarifies the wrongdoing, condemns the wrongdoers, and establishes an "upper limit" on punishment—all vigorous measures paving the way to an impartial and distributive rule of law.[27]

As a method for dealing with intransigent social fault lines, resentment has drawn more supporters by far than forgiveness. To begin with, it is an affirmative emotion that calls out the wrongfulness of behavior responsible for causing harm and violating common values.[28] As Jeffrie Murphy observed, in expressing anger and blaming wrongdoers, it says, "We care about ourselves and our rights."[29] Even if resentment doesn't produce results, its expression of self-worth is intrinsically valuable for reversing the circumstances of persecution in which victims were coerced into subservience, muteness, and humiliation. Thomas Brudholm, in an essay on Améry, concurred. Resentment, whose reputation for moral inferiority or pathology is notorious, demands reconsideration. Far from vengeful, as Tutu asserted,[30] resentment constitutes "a moral-political protest."[31]

It stands firm against hasty reconciliation, an accusation leveled at forgiveness and its alleged disregard for victims' standing in deference to the public good.[32]

By articulating its moral purpose, defenders have taken resentment's virtues to the next step. Nancy Wood and Arne Johan Vetlesen, citing Améry, exalted its capacity for compelling accountability for past wrongs.[33] Margaret Walker argued that the emotion is superior to forgiving and forgetting for promoting reconciliation between enemies: forgiveness, as Améry asserted, was "utterly false conciliatoriness";[34] resentment rallies a social commitment to renewed normative standards.[35] At minimum, Brudholm observed, it could establish a baseline for negotiating the terms of a stable transition by recognizing and accounting for historical injustice, for, whether or not it coaxed corrective action, it would reveal "the resentful victim's unreconcilable attitude to the inexpiable evils of the past."[36]

Survivors roundly valorized resentment's merits, though not always with Améry's relish. Améry devoted an essay to the subject, regarding resentment as the "emotional source of every genuine morality."[37] That position, the value of self-expression, seemed sufficient. Believing that his protest wouldn't make a practical difference "for the good of the German people,"[38] he concluded: "We victims must finish with our retroactive rancor." His choice of the verb "finish" (*fertigwerden*)—as in, "to regard [our rancor] as an end in itself" or "to assert a point with [our rancor]"—revealed the force of his convictions, for he said that, like the term *fertigmachen* ("finish off") used in the camps, it could also mean "to kill" (*umbringen*), or spoil, the peace of indifference.[39] In the end, "I bear my grudge for reasons of personal salvation."[40] Jankélévitch was also adamant. Among his vertiginous works on the subject of forgiveness, his essay "*Pardonner?*" is his strongest defense of moral-political protest. "The past needs us to help it, to recall it to the forgetful, the frivolous, and the indifferent."[41] For him, resentment was a moral obligation: "By invoking these days of rage, calamity, and tribulation, we protest against the work of extermination and against the forgetfulness that completed it."[42] He could not imagine forgiving the criminals, which he believed permitted his contemporaries "to forget this gigantic crime against humanity."[43] Wiesenthal, for all the scrutiny of forgiveness's possibilities, asserted the "shame" of Germany's criminal record and claimed that every German is responsible for it, even if no one in particular was responsible for the crimes.[44] Like other survivors, he apparently had little faith in the capacity of Germans for moral redress, for though he believed that Germans had an obligation "to find out who was guilty,"[45] he had already committed himself to taking on the task himself. Wiesenthal elucidated resentment's integrity: it resisted the world's advice "to keep silent." It proclaimed a refusal to "obliterate the hell we endured."[46]

I want to argue that the expression of protest acquires additional moral force for historical as well as psychological reasons. Spirited protest is surely a considerable metabolic emotion for victims: Its very expressiveness turns the tables, so to speak, against their persecutors and restores their voice. But their articulated refusal to keep silent and forget the terrible past is an expression in response to extrinsic circumstances, the social and political pressures of each moment. In stating that "I lack the desire, the talent, and the conviction … to internalize our past suffering and bear it in emotional asceticism,"[47] Améry railed against the plea that victims look calmly to the future. In fact, such advice is a paramount reason why survivors wrote their accounts. When Améry, Jankélévitch, and Wiesenthal published their accounts in the 1960s, they did so in direct response to the ascendant mobilization of public opinion against memory. The origins of survivors' collective decision to assert accounts of their ordeal in order to berate public opinion should be seen as an interruption of what appeared to them as a cultural imperative to forget.[48] If survivors rejected forgiveness as an option, they nonetheless couldn't avoid the subject. They wrote and, more important, published their stories to express moral sovereignty, which is a virtue regardless of time or place, but also to parry "the peace chorus" that Améry and other survivors so vigorously combated.

The chorus that felt like a moral threat received considerable impetus from the Auschwitz trial that took place in Frankfurt am Main, in the Federal Republic of Germany, from December 1963 to August 1965. It was a twenty-month public spectacle, one of the largest and most closely observed trials in West Germany looking at Nazi-era crimes. No other postwar German trial received as much preliminary investigation or lasted as long. There was considerable press coverage during the trial, as well. In short, the trial contributed substantially to the expansion of the national conversation about the Nazi past.[49] Technically, the proceedings were the second Auschwitz trial;[50] the first took place in Kraków, Poland, in 1947 with the prosecution and execution of senior SS officials who had served at Auschwitz. The Frankfurt trial put second- and third-tier officers, medical personnel, and one Kapo on trial. What drew the most attention was a controversy over the criteria for prosecuting Nazi-era crimes. To the dismay of many, the West German legal code governing the trial regarded criminal violations that were deemed accessory to murder as lesser crimes inviting relatively mild sentences.[51] West German national policy, proscribing retroactivity, additionally prohibited prosecuting former Nazis on internationally sanctioned grounds of crimes against humanity or the crime of genocide.[52] It therefore reserved the harshest judgment for egregious perpetrator behavior—"base motives," such as willful or impulsive sadism, hatred, or greed—rather than for violations of international jurisprudential standards. As a result, West German jurisprudence ignored the systemic dimensions of mass murder and occluded the responsibilities of "ordinary" Germans.[53]

The trial was, in fact, the culmination of a long-term campaign to erase the past starting with the founding of the sovereign West German state in 1949. Under the leadership of Konrad Adenauer, who presided as chancellor from 1949 to 1963, the nation was on track to reconstruct and unify its society rather that face its divisive Nazi past.[54] The policy, a strategy known as the *Schlussstrich* (a firm line separating past and present), included amnesty for, and the integration of, former Nazi Party and SS officers. As Adenauer declared in 1949, "The government of the Federal Republic, in the belief that many have subjectively atoned for a guilt that was not heavy, is determined where it appears acceptable to do so to put the past behind us."[55] Historian Jeffrey Herf observed that in providing no proof to support his contention that "many" atoned for their misdeeds and no explanation that the weight of the past was "not heavy," "integration" outmaneuvered "justice" as national policy.[56] A little more than a year later, Adenauer reiterated the point in a meeting with the Allied High Commissioner and requested the cessation of all war crimes trials and the commutation of all death sentences.[57] Effectively granting protection from prosecution to all but those whose behavior was extreme, including those convicted in the Allied military courts and awaiting punishment, literary scholar Jean-Paul Bier characterized the policy as "strategies of oblivion."[58] Steps taken toward ending the process of denazification (seen by many as an odious international intrusion), granting amnesty to those convicted during the postwar occupation, and halting further prosecutions for all but the relatively few perpetrators received considerable support from a wide berth of opinion, backed by political and clerical leaders as well as the media, during the first five years of the West German Federal Republic of Germany (FRG). Amnesty legislation benefited nearly 800,000 people in the first two years alone, including more than 3,000 members of the SA (the Nazi Party's and regime's auxiliary police), SS, and the Nazi Party. As historian Norbert Frei noted, "Those who had never personally been held accountable could consider themselves symbolically exonerated."[59] By 1954, between 25 and 30 percent of positions in the national government were taken by individuals who served in the Nazi regime. Over the long run, the effects of the amnesty campaign discouraged a will for national self-examination. In such an atmosphere survivors found little recognition, much less sympathy.

The timing of the Frankfurt Auschwitz trial is important for helping to explain why it provoked survivors to overt action. The West German legislature compounded executive and judicial maneuvers by preparing to exercise statutory limitations for Nazi crimes. Jankélévitch suspected that the reluctance to prosecute the trial's defendants aggressively was merely a screen for "justifying statutory limitations in advance."[60] Wiesenthal objected, stating that the world "urges that we draw a line, and close the account as if nothing had ever happened."[61] The West German penal code prescribed that after twenty years, that is, in May 1965, the crime of murder would become immune to prosecution. That would mean that the Frankfurt Auschwitz trial would be the last one of its kind. The debate (*Verjährungsdebatte*), which brought its proponents, who privileged a strict adherence to the rule of law, into conflict with those who argued for its extension for the sake of justice, revived arguments over statutory limitations that commenced in 1960. After a brief debate, the settlement in parliament that year resulted in favor of the rule of law with enforcement of the statute prescribing a fifteen-year limit on second-degree offenses (manslaughter[62]). The agreement inspired confidence among proponents five year later that the twenty-year statute would automatically lapse.[63] As statutory limitations reached a pinnacle of popularity, the movement to terminate Nazi prosecutions—against a background of anemic, postwar judicial proceedings and a foreground of imminent ratified oblivion—troubled survivors, the Socialist opposition, and others. It threatened to eviscerate the appeal for designating Nazi crimes an exception ("imprescriptibility") that would have cleared the way for an extension of the prescribed period.[64] Jankélévitch doubted that justice would prevail in any case, even though the French parliament already voted in 1964 for the imprescriptibility of crimes against humanity.[65] In fact, it did, when, in 1969—the year Wiesenthal published his account *The Sunflower*—the West German parliament again debated the question of imprescriptibility.[66]

Intensifying the justice movement was a decision by the Frankfurt Auschwitz trial's lead organizer, federal state attorney general Fritz Bauer, to call attention to wider circles of criminal complicity. His determination to use the trial as a platform for exposing ordinary Germans was prodigious and often came at the expense of prosecuting the defendants on trial. In the lead-up, he declared, "Germany was not made up only of the Nazi Hitler and the Nazi Himmler. There were hundreds of thousands, millions of others, who carried out the 'Final

Solution' not only because they had orders, but because it was their worldview as well, which they willingly admitted."[67] His argument received material justification from the Central Office for the Investigation of National Socialist Crimes, which started its work in 1958, and from the Ministry of Justice, which, in the course of the trial, reported that "acts and perpetrators" were still outstanding and "might become known."[68] Theologian Helmut Gollwitzer, articulating the view of a German majority, including a substantial right-wing nationalist minority, remarked that Germans wanted the trial to end "for the sake of a quiet conscience."[69] The weight of the past appeared heavier than Adenauer contended. As the trial drew to a close, the mood in Germany turned distinctly against pronouncements and endeavors invoking the past. Adolf Arndt, a political leader who had helped Jews escape from Nazi Germany in the 1930s, believed it was rooted in "historical and moral guilt."[70] Whatever the reason, it became clear that the trial produced unintended consequences. As historian Devin O. Pendas observed, "A substantial portion of the German public, and a number of high-ranking public officials as well, in fact used the trial to argue against holding further trials like it."[71]

In larger perspective, the zeal of the movement for advancing national interests intensified in light of a multinational specter of new groups—workers, women, and minorities—competing with elites for the nation's memory and self-understanding. An era traceable to the eighteenth century of triumphalist national allegiance was in a state of exhaustion.[72] The trial offered a stage for this conflict of memory. Victims, living with an inescapable past, felt enfranchised by a climate of plural interpretations. They drew attention to past injustices for evidence of the muscular, heroic nation's bankruptcy. Aware, like other self-styled groups, of a common destiny, they demanded a course for a mature nation that integrated its misdeeds. Partly in response, many citizens, seeking to preserve Germany's good name, pushed for an end to the trial. Typical of monumental national predilections, they wanted to break with past injustices and, echoing those asserting a *Stunde Null*, or zero hour, after the war, to start anew.

The censorious climate was a necessary but not a sufficient condition of survivors' decisions to break their public silence. The early 1960s were a period when victims, at least in courts of law, started to receive recognition as witnesses to Nazi crimes. Though the question of guilt preoccupied the Frankfurt trial's observers, what concerns us here is the exposed platform the trial provided for more than 350 survivors. The proceedings in Frankfurt occurred just two years after the Eichmann trial in Jerusalem, a watershed event that privileged victims' testimonies and augmented victims' standing. There were, however, limitations imposed on witnesses at the Frankfurt trial: the requirement to recall specific incriminating incidents was an extraordinary stipulation; and, like other FRG Nazi trials, the Frankfurt proceedings treated witnesses with skepticism, questioning whether emotions would compromise the reliability of their testimonies.[73] But the dramatic attention victims received as witnesses brandished their claim to legitimacy in the court of public opinion as well as within the limits of criminal proceedings.

In response to the trial's vigorous detractors, a number of survivors emerged en bloc from their public silence, exerting counterpressure against what they saw as obtuse as well as obstructionist behavior. Occurring at a time when victims started to assert themselves, the campaign to bury the past was, in the sense that Thomas Hobbes recognized, a blessing in disguise, "for no man is a witness to him that already believeth, and therefore needs no witness; but to them that deny or doubt, or have not heard of it."[74] Ralph Giordano, who was half-Jewish and a Nazi victim, wrote a series of remonstrative articles at the time for the *Allgemeine Wochenzeitung der Juden in Deutschland,* the main postwar newspaper written for Germany's Jews. He felt that the trial didn't make a strong enough case for the nation's moral debt: "The danger of these trials lies in the possibility that the national responsibility for that which took place between 1933 and 1945 will be reduced to that group of perpetrators who happened to be on trial today or tomorrow."[75] He believed that the trial's narrow construction "would not set [us] free," effectively sentencing Jews to "living—with Auschwitz."[76] Améry, echoing Bauer, observed larger ramifications, remarking, "I could and can say that the crimes of the regime entered my consciousness as collective deeds of the people."[77] But he regretted the world's insouciance, which "has sentenced me, not those who murdered or allowed the murder to occur,"[78] adding, "I am burdened with this knowledge in a world and a time that has proclaimed the collective innocence of the Germans."[79] Jankélévitch, writing in 1965, was more hopeful. He noted the general reluctance and "bad faith" surrounding the trial but believed it could serve some didactic purpose.[80] But survivors ultimately recognized that the trial was more about a relationship they could re-establish with their world than about anything they could do to actually influence it. The trial, wrote Améry, inspired his decision to communicate his experiences "after twenty years of silence." Referring to "the big Auschwitz trial" in the very first sentence of his original preface, it clearly made an impact on him.[81]

Resentment, under these circumstances, is surely the proper pose, the one that granted "personal salvation." But in hearing pleas to forget the past, survivors heard something else. Emmanuel Levinas, who had been interned in a German prisoner-of-war camp from 1940 to 1945, opened the 1963 *Colloque des intellectuels juifs de langue française* (the annual Colloquium of French-Speaking Jewish Intellectuals) with references to the pressures Jews felt to forgive Germans, reprising, "We are being reproached for not knowing how to forgive."[82] Jankélévitch added simply and pointedly, "Must we still forgive?"[83] Again and again he asked, "Should we be asked to forgive and forget?"[84] Améry and Wiesenthal resented the demand to forget but also the plea to forgive.[85] It turns out that the question of forgiveness played an important role in survivors' accounts during this period and can't be reduced to incidental comments. For Jankélévitch and Wiesenthal, it was a substantial preoccupation. Allusively, in counter-narratives, they even endorsed dispositions to forgive once they reworked the concept in a different register, even as they showed little patience for the term, and less for those who requested it, in stronger and declarative narratives of recrimination. Jankélévitch objected that the campaign to forget sought to make the unforgivable forgivable practically overnight. *Le Pardon* (*Forgiveness*), his 1967 philosophical tome on forgiveness, expanded on the relationship between forgetting and forgiveness as he reasoned his way to finding the nexus between the victim and the wrongdoer. Forgiveness, he argued, is possible, but when the wrongdoer is interested only in expedient self-indulgence, expressed as indifference and remorselessness—when forgetting is the "mortal loss of affection"—then forgiveness's search for a human connection, essentially for the human ("hominity"),[86] reaches an impasse[87] of insincere and "hasty reconciliation."[88] It is merely "the adagio of forgetting."[89]

Other survivors weighed in uneasily on the subject of forgiveness. At the 1963 *Colloque,* whose theme was forgiveness, Levinas made clear his concern: "It is difficult to forgive Martin Heidegger," the German existentialist philosopher who favored National Socialism and a Nietzschean "will to power." But "new attempts to clear Heidegger, to take away his responsibility—unceasing attempts" were reprehensible and "the origin of this colloquium."[90] "Germany as a whole," Jankélévitch remarked, "bypassed the most horrible tragedy in history … They feel in no way responsible, acknowledge no mistake."[91] Wiesenthal reviled the campaign's prodigious perversity: It didn't take long before "priests, philanthropists, and philosophers implored the world to forgive the Nazis." If "compassion for the murderers of innocent millions" weren't reason enough for their entreaty, then priests would provide the justification: The true judge was divine; "earthly justice" wasn't necessary.[92] For Améry, it was the "insensitive and the indifferent" who rallied for forgiveness so that "what happened" would "remain what it was."[93] Statutes of limitations merely provided the excuse, he wrote, the kind of excuse a child uses to disarm a reprimand for her indiscipline, asserting that the infraction has already past.[94] "Forgiving and forgetting induced by social pressure is immoral," he wrote.[95] Like other survivors, he asserted that he would remain irreconcilable.[96]

Semantic confusion

The discourse of forgiveness in the 1960s inspired the first aggregate of witnesses' politically engaged public accounts of Nazi-era experiences and repercussions. Survivors were determined to record what Arendt, after Kant, called "radical evil." Some, like Jankélévitch, hoped that it might force "frivolous people," inclined toward forgetting, "to learn."[97] The international debate gave rise to two of the most important survivor reflections on forgiveness—Wiesenthal's *The Sunflower* and Jankélévitch's *Forgiveness*. On the one hand, then, survivors, in mounting a campaign of their own against the "peace chorus," attended to the question of forgiveness. On the other, in pushing back against objections to the Frankfurt trial and support for statutory limitations, they refused to forgive, or, as they made clear, to forgive and forget. They resisted appeals that exhorted Améry, and other survivors, "Not backward let us look but forward, to a better, common future!"[98] Recognizing in words like these a demand to keep silent—a demand that echoed survivors' earlier experience with malevolent authority—they wrote their accounts with notable assertiveness. Indeed, the phenomenon of witnesses' reflections—the narratives themselves—signified speech, in particular, defiant speech.

While survivors insisted on remaining irreconcilable with an immoral world, then and in the 1960s, our task is to see just how irreconcilable they were. This is not to suggest that their refusal to forgive was anything but emphatic; indeed, it was bedrock. But we can't avoid inclinations that express fellow-feeling, either. The difficulty critics have with juxtaposing Jankélévitch's diatribes against forgiveness with his defense of true forgiveness in *Forgiveness* is an indication of a problem that demands a response. Jankélévitch, himself, suggested a contradiction, remarking, "I have not attempted to reconcile the irrationality of evil with the omnipotence of love."[99]

The expressions that do, indeed, look forward interrupt strong, backward-looking statements in witnesses' accounts. What is noteworthy is that they exist at all. At times, they seem like departures from the narrative. Améry noted that society is inclined to forgetfulness and, with it, to lose its moral convictions, especially when principles, like statutory limitations, rationalize it. A "time-sense," that is, the passage of time, governs the "biological and social sphere" and eludes the "moral sphere." But in what strikes me as an evocation of Emersonian self-reliance, he acknowledged exceptions—the person who refuses to blend into insensitive society is "the person who perceives himself to be morally unique."[100] He was that person; he saw himself serving as society's proxy conscience. Did he believe that others could mimic his act of moral protest? That possibility surfaced in an "extravagant moral daydream" of a redemptive German transformation that would "no longer repress or hush up" the Nazi past but, on the contrary, would "integrate it" for a grounded future.[101] It's clear that the crowd's self-indulgence motivated Améry to speak out against it, but it's less clear that his attention to rectitude in the world at large appeased his irascibility. What do we make of his allusions to moral exceptions who stand by themselves and, moreover, are preternatural and completely irrelevant, as he admitted, to the acrid thrust of his argument? He came around to recognizing that these visions were absurd and insane: Germans would never make it good. Yet, they represented interludes he momentarily "abandoned" himself to.[102] Why propose these ideas only to reject them? Something besides condemnation is stirring in the text. He wrote an entire essay devoted to suppressing fond, antediluvian memories of home—"the neighbor," "the good comrade," "trust and confidence."[103] We need only recall the wisdom of seeing wishes in suppressed memory to remind ourselves of just how much he longed for a human connection.

Jankélévitch's 1967 inquiry into true forgiveness is anything but fanciful, and, as an intricately composed treatise, it stands on its own. But he recognized that it also served as a counter-argument—he called it an intervention[104]—and, in relation to his earlier essay, "Should We Pardon Them?," it certainly seems that way. The essay's condemnation of a morally poor society represents a position that he said remains as strong as ever, "but an arbitrary and gratuitous change has intervened, a diametrical and radical inversion … inverted, overturned, and overwhelmed!" with a power that "transfigures hatred into love."[105] True forgiveness, he recognized, is not proportionate to grave misdeeds: it is "hyperbolic." He wrote that true forgiveness is "supernatural," an extraordinary feat in loving "the drunk and miserable person who betrayed you."[106] Wiesenthal's *The Sunflower* offers another rhetorical device for opening a space in narratives that are otherwise tethered to the past. The ambiguity the account expresses about the question of forgiveness conceals and reveals a desire to look forward. His interview with the SS officer, he recalled, imposed a "heavy burden" on him: It "had profoundly disturbed me."[107] After all, the story about the officer's ironclad request for "a Jew"[108] to hear his confession in anticipation of forgiveness compressed Wiesenthal's experience of abject, ghettoized powerlessness. Finally, he could not forgive him, "and without a word I left the room."[109] But he left the symbolic door open, for, as his comrade, Arthur, observed, there will be time to discuss forgiveness "if the world comes to its senses again."[110] The ending is particularly suggestive. The usual reading regards the question he asked, "Ought I to have forgiven him?,"[111] as the lead-in to a "symposium" of responses. The original German ending, written for his contemporaries, was, however, more auspicious: "Once the trials are over and the crimes of the Nazis fade away, the question of forgiveness will still demand our attention. Therefore, I appeal to people who I believe have something to say (*sie etwas zu sagen haben*). The question deserves consideration because what happened could happen again."[112] It's not that the world might or might not come to its senses. He evidently believed that it was poised to do so.

Wiesenthal was satisfied with leaving the question of forgiveness open. It is appropriate that he did so. Though he condemned transgressions and regarded them as unforgivable, his simultaneous inclination to rework worldly relationships, suggesting possibilities, suspended final judgment. Survivors did not assert forgiveness; just the opposite. But with the existence of expressions suggesting fellow-feeling, it appears that there are narrative dispositions toward forgiveness. Though the salience of backward-looking narratives prohibited dramatic narratives turns, it didn't exclude forward-looking narrative swerves. Of course, it seems overreaching to suggest anything like forgiveness in accounts that explicitly refused it. But our argument is rooted, first, in survivors' preoccupation with the question of forgiveness that made the question a matter of material concern and contention for them, and, second, in their periodic expressions of human love and longing that kept the question vivid and open-ended. Survivors did not back off from the refusal to forgive, but we believe that, alongside a rejection of the concept as they understood it, a process occurred in counter-narratives that simultaneously reconceptualized it.[113] As an organic process existing uneasily and exceptionally in accounts that plainly condemned behavior, we cannot expect settled formulations. On the other hand, the existence of occasional swerves, running against the grain of strong, resentful narratives, offers intriguing hints of forgiving dispositions that are more affirmative than we might expect, and certainly more suggestive than conclusive. The main obstacle to evaluating these narratives is, as we noted before, the word itself.

How, exactly, do we understand forgiveness as a term and an idea? One way to begin, though not the most felicitous, is to acknowledge that the term is "polysemic." That is, it is a term with many different and sometimes competing meanings. We often encounter words with multi-edged meanings. To say, for example, that Buckingham Palace denied the rumors is to enlist the predicate for double duty—as a physical place and as the seat of national leadership. Or to say that we are fixing dinner is not the same as saying we are fixing the game (although as a polysemic term itself, it could be the same if "game" were found on the menu). Forgiveness has the added problem of a preponderant preconception that often expels its other, tenable meanings. In conventional parlance, the term means forswearing anger for the sake of the victim with the unpopular implication of releasing wrongdoers from their offense and letting them off the hook.

Forgiveness, in this canonic sense, has a strong pedigree. In a formative analysis from the eighteenth century, English bishop Joseph Butler valorized forgiveness as a measure of overcoming excessive anger or resentment, especially when the offense was inadvertent. He did not argue for erasing resentment completely. In fact, he believed regulated resentment is valuable for self-preservation, the protection of others, and the pursuit of justice. But when resentment "entirely destroys our natural benevolence toward [the enemy], it is excessive, and becomes malice or revenge."[114] He believed that forgiveness and fellow-feeling play an important role "to keep clear" of hostile passions before they become excessive.[115] Forgiveness, in this iteration, by forswearing revenge, is a measure of self-renewal.

In championing forgiveness, Butler kept the offense in sight. A century later, Nietzsche argued that forgetting the offense was the key to moving on. His protagonist, here as elsewhere in his critique of moral convention, is the sturdy, noble, transcendent figure of sovereign will and triumphant self-affirmation. As an exemplification of bold action in contrast to mere reaction, "strong, full natures," whenever they are offended, are immune to the usual, toxic reactions of envy and revenge. Rising above "ressentiment"—his term for an emotional acquiescence in rumination—they are "unable for any length of time to take his enemies, his accidents, his *misdeeds* themselves seriously." The great figure is "unable to forgive because he—forgot. Such a human is simply able to shake off with a *single* shrug a collection of worms that in others would dig itself in." Butler recognized in forgiveness a "natural benevolence" toward the enemy. For Nietzsche, forgetting the offense made possible "the true '*love*' of one's enemies," though, in adding "assuming that it is possible on earth," he acknowledged its disproportionality to the crime.[116]

Something of this claim to forgetting the offense for the sake of the offended surfaced in expressions by Eva Kor, perhaps the only survivor who explicitly forgave Nazi perpetrators, and certainly the only one who received considerable attention for the assertion. Although she felt it was important to forgive before she could forget, she exemplified forgiveness as an inner and self-referential experience. To the consternation of many, she claimed that forgiving Nazis, including Mengele, is necessary for the survivor alone: "Forgiveness has nothing to do with the perpetrator. Forgiveness has everything to do with the victim taking back their [*sic*] life."[117] She even granted "amnesty" to one Nazi doctor—paradoxically, to Hans Münch, an SS officer who was a defendant at the first Auschwitz trial in 1947 (he was acquitted). In doing so, "I was finally free."[118] Kor's position is valuable as an indication of relief from the agony of merciless resentment and as an expression of self-respect, though, in Nietzschean perspective, by asserting a need to forgive, it betrays memory traces of the offense that raise questions about the "finality" of forgiveness.[119]

Other theorists consider the role of the offender as pivotal in the forgiveness process. Avishai Margalit, for example, summoned religious injunction to indicate that forgiveness begins with the offender, whose contrition restored her to the community.[120] This traditional perspective shifts the burden of responsibility for repair, displacing the forgiver from driving the process.[121] Arendt, instead, attended to the offender even as she privileged the forgiver. Her analysis, which is as controversial as it is original and scrupulous, is notable for exploring the relationships between both ends of the process. Devoting a succinct section of her 1958 work, *The Human Condition*, to the subject, she investigated the implications of releasing the wrongdoer from the consequences of his past deeds. For her, the act of forgiveness, which she valorized, simultaneously possessed the power to "undo what one had done" so that the wrongdoer would no longer be "confined to the one single deed"[122] and, therefore, defined by it. By looking at the effect of forgiveness on the offender, Arendt considered the act as a dynamic process. Butler's mission was "to beget in us a right temper of mind towards those who have offended us."[123] Nietzsche's gaze was entirely inward. The offender and the offense vanished before the dazzling ascent of strong figures. For Arendt, releasing offenders from the grip of their offenses is an act of communitarian recovery[124] that arises "directly out of the will to live with others."[125]

Arendt recognized that undoing the misdeed set an extraordinary standard. Indeed, she acknowledged that it is seen as "unrealistic"[126] and, because of its relationship to "love," "unworldly."[127] To many of us, it seems almost as impossible as Nietzsche's love of enemies. But she believed that forgiveness possessed significant worldly possibilities. It is mystical, she said, only when it is yoked to its "religious context," one reason, we note, why Nietzsche, who repudiated piety as slave morality, renounced forgiveness altogether. Though she drew upon the teachings of Jesus of Nazareth, she negotiated them in a broader, "strictly secular" context[128] and made forgiveness manageable by keeping the concept within the province of everyday, prosaic "trespassing."[129] Forgiveness belonged to the plurality of human affairs, where "respect" replaced Christian love: Respect is "quite sufficient to prompt forgiving what a person did."[130] Even if acts like forgiveness on this scale are "infinitely improbable,"[131] they only look miraculous: she believed in the "possible redemption" of undoing.[132] She did make an exception, which will demand our special attention: Like Butler, she exempted misdeeds that were done knowingly,[133] and, in particular, the "extremity of crime and willed evil"—an allusion to the annihilation of Jews.[134]

The 1990s witnessed the manifestation of forgiveness as a worldly, political, and dynamic phenomenon inspired by the paradigmatic Truth and Reconciliation Commission (TRC) in South Africa. Its aspirations were surely ambitious. Pumla Gobodo-Madikizela, the chair of the TRC's public hearings in the West Cape region, observed that some victims could forgive perpetrators of apartheid "the moment there was an opportunity to meet those who had brought them misery and pain, even before there was any indication of an apology on the part of the perpetrator."[135] But in granting amnesty to offenders for their explicit admissions, its critics reinforced the impression that the price of bringing forgiveness down to earth to deal with rank crimes in public settings for the public good was the concession it made to disproportionality. Though hardly a Nietzschean shrug and not even a condition of forgiveness, it looked to many like a misguided example of forgiving and forgetting.[136]

This conventional version of forgiveness, from Butler to the TRC and to the present day, governed survivors' conceptions during the debates in the 1960s over statutory limitations. It largely explains their refusal to forgive: They did not and could not diminish anger—though by this time some were able to control it—and certainly refused to release culpable persons from their crimes even if they committed them unknowingly—a position that seems especially defiant in light of rulings in West German courts that granted leniency for accessory crimes. As we have seen, they ruled out forgiveness because the term, as they understood it, meant erasing the crime (Levi), disposing the past (Wiesenthal), and looking only ahead (Améry). For Jankélévitch forgiveness meant forgetfulness, "a moral amnesty that is nothing but shameful amnesia."[137] No matter how generous and gratuitous he conceived it in *Forgiveness*, the concept would have to accommodate evil and would not permit its attenuation. He had defied pressures to "settle the past," responding with unconcealed impatience over the current indifference: "Was that past ever a present for them?"[138]

A corollary of the conventional conception is the one Margalit observed: If the offender initiated the process, victims were more likely to confer forgiveness. Survivors sometimes imagined the possibility of forgiveness if their contemporaries, at the time of their writing, exhibited contrition or sincere repentance. Wiesenthal wouldn't have considered forgiveness unless the dying SS officer expressed sincere remorse. The dying officer met this condition twice: in begging for forgiveness, he "showed a deep and genuine repentance,"[139] though Wiesenthal qualified the remark by noting "he did not admit it in so many words."[140] Levi also expected "certain signs of repentance" before "I declared myself ready to forgive my enemies."[141] Levinas asserted the offender's obligation to apologize: "There can be no forgiveness that the guilty party has not sought! ... No person can forgive if forgiveness has not been asked him by the offender, if the guilty party has not tried to appease the offended."[142] Jankélévitch argued that repentance was important for making forgiveness meaningful,[143] perhaps by giving it traction, but did not regard it as a condition as Wiesenthal, Levi, and Levinas did.

Two problems inhibited the likelihood of conditional forgiveness. The first, which survivors did not articulate, was the burden imposed by the precondition of repentance that granted wrongdoers authority over initiating the process and therefore reprised victims' dependence on them. Forgiveness, as conditional, is precisely what survivors didn't want and ultimately couldn't accept. Levinas, however, noted that victims could escape from the imposition by refusing forgiveness,[144] but that noteworthy alternative banished forgiveness altogether. Second, survivors, at any rate, regarded the prospect too remote for serious consideration. "Perhaps they'll find a way to 'buy us back,' to redeem us," commented Kluger, but "given past experience, the odds are against hope."[145] Levi and Jankélévitch were also skeptical about how sincere expressions of repentance were. The letters Levi received "did not satisfy me, those honest, generalized declarations of repentance and solidarity."[146] As Jankélévitch put it, "Alas! As an act of repentance, the Austrians have presented us with the shameful acquittal of torturers."[147] Extending the argument to his fellow citizens, he expressed similar exasperation: "We have waited for a word for a long time, a single word of understanding and sympathy."[148] Jankélévitch observed a third problem: forgiveness that is conditional is not true forgiveness, for as a response to repentance, as a "need of kindness in order to love," it is "mixed with reservations; and consequently this is not love."[149]

If not forgiveness, what, then, of their occasional expressions of fellow-feeling? The process in counter-narratives that involved reworking the human connection rules out the possibility that they were mere random or momentary and insignificant lapses. If conventional conceptions promoting self-renewal were anathema; if conditional forgiveness lost its potential efficacy for lack of persuasive evidence during the *Verjährungsdebatte* suggesting a trustworthy willingness to apologize, assuming survivors were predisposed to the redemptive possibilities of contrition; if the word, itself, was especially repulsive, then instead of conventional and conditional conceptions, a third conception of forgiveness—the notion that it is unconditional—is worth considering for shedding light on survivors' counter-narrative aspirations. First, a disclaimer: unconditional forgiveness suggests the kind of lofty conviction that philosophers love to game. As Jankélévitch remarked, true forgiveness, among its "absurd" characteristics,[150] is "supernatural." In the words of Jacques Derrida, who, in the late 1990s, made the ideal of unconditional forgiveness famous, if elliptical, it is "gracious, infinite, aneconomic, forgiveness granted *to the guilty as guilty* ... even to those who do not repent or ask forgiveness."[151] These views echo the other-worldly, Abrahamic conception of divine forgiveness that pictures God, in interrupting the covenantal agreement, ministering to his people in spite of their unruly disrespect and without, or at least before, its expression of repentance.[152] As we have seen, Nietzsche and Arendt, among most critical observers, endeavored to liberate forgiveness from its seductive theological moorings, replacing church with state and society. As asymmetrical ("aneconomic"), or as an idea that Derrida regarded as "excessive, hyperbolic, mad,"[153] unconditional forgiveness doesn't seem bearable in everyday human interaction. Charles Griswold regarded it as plainly and "irremediably imperfect";[154] Paul Ricoeur, who affirmed it, believed it was flatly "difficult,"[155] as in, beyond our reach. It is our argument, however, that survivors, in imagining and dreaming about "the neighbor," "the good comrade," and "trust and confidence," are not veering toward abstract, spirited hyperbole. Their accounts are too grounded in narrative witnessing, in rumination about traumatic loss and shame in their own inadvertent and historically bounded entanglement, and in emotions decrying the world's abandonment and seeking relief to idealize their conceptions of their enemies.

In Wiesenthal's view, the question of forgiveness is open-ended. It invites our attention. It demands consideration.

To begin with, there are elements of unconditional forgiveness that are apparent in survivors' accounts. Unlike criminal court proceedings or truth commissions, the act of writing is unilateral. There are no cross-examinations to interrupt it or rules of procedure to constrain it. It is not dependent, or conditioned, on another's terms, such as the state or for the sake of the public good. This is a key point, and not only because the form of expression is permissive. Accounts serve their writers because it escorts them on their emotional journey from victims to survivors. They *chose* to write to achieve narrative clout, among other reasons—a condition that transformed their former disfranchisement and experience of helplessness into what we may appropriately call a transitional sense of agency. Becoming authors was salvific. Writing, Améry observed, broke his "gloomy spell" of silence: "Suddenly everything demanded telling." If *At the Mind's Limits* had a stated purpose—to disquiet consciences—it was also a process, "a process of writing," that granted survivors as authors authority. This, he reflected in his original preface, is "how this book came about."[156] If there is something extensive in his search for a human connection, it is an expression without predicates, qualifications, or conditions.

The act of writing inspires many writers' desire for a legacy and, more generously, to benefit posterity, but for Wiesenthal, as for Améry, its immediate benefit is discernible in historical perspective. He observed that it gave him a chance to break not just the silence as insularity, but also the silence as indignity. Writing, as he made clear, gave him the opportunity to speak out against the demand, then and in the present, to remain silent and inconspicuous. That demand recalled the silence he wrote about in describing his unwilling role as the SS officer's confessor. Writing also constituted an act of protest against onlookers who kept silent while prisoners were "led to the slaughterhouses of Europe."[157] Yet, for all its insufferable associations, he regarded silence, at the end of the English version of his account, as an opportunity that paradoxically granted silence, in a witnessing context, a voice: "Silence can be more eloquent than words."[158] For him, there was no apparent answer to the question of whether and on what basis to forgive. But as a question, only silence could keep the question vivid. Official deliberations in legal proceedings, in truth commissions, or in positions staked out in the *Verjährungsdebatte* require finite decisions. Writing permitted Wiesenthal to ask questions, to sound the silence, and to inspire debate and discovery. "I believe [people] have something to say."

Volition is Jankélévitch's main concern as well. "It is indeed necessary that someone begin, is it not?"[159] Forgiveness is nothing, he claimed, if not an impulse—each "instant" of forgiveness is entirely spontaneous, "the absence of every reservation":[160] Forgiveness "forgives in one fell swoop and in a single, indivisible élan."[161] Action was the cornerstone of Arendt's discussion of forgiveness, as it was of her philosophical investigations in general. Her argument for forgiveness is therefore instructive for evaluating survivors' worldly negotiations. She did impose limits, however. "Willed evil," she asserted, disqualified the offense from legitimate forgiveness, though it is arguable based on her reasoning that Eichmann, for one, contrary to her judgment, was someone who warranted consideration since, as she claimed, he acted "unknowingly"—an argument based on her claim, since disputed, that he was merely a cog in the machine of destruction. Though she affirmed Eichmann's thorough repugnance, she felt that the absence of control over his actions would make him both culpable and as someone who "may be more than anything he ever did."[162] Arendt argued that the act of forgiveness begins with a Nietzschean "capacity to act":[163] Forgiving, in one of her memorable refrains, "is the only reaction which does not merely re-act but acts anew and unexpectedly, unconditioned by the act which provoked it."[164] Action, she wrote, derived from the Greek word for "to begin." It "set something into motion."[165] As spontaneous and entirely unconditioned, it seems improbable, a matter of "startling unexpectedness."[166] But, because it is innate, it is possible "by virtue of being born,"[167] or, in her native locution, by virtue of "the human condition of natality."[168] More than possible, action, and its embodiment as forgiveness, rises up against "overwhelming odds":[169] "it interrupts the inexorable course of daily life,"[170] including "the darkness of the human heart."[171] "Darkness" is a matter of degree, but, since it is implicated in the condition of living with others, as she said, and since "others," as survivors regarded it, constituted an immoral world that included the longed-for morally unique, forgiveness as she meant it—forgiveness as volitional and surprising—serves as a paradigm for how survivors also meant it.

Non-ideal forgiveness

The idea of what Arendt called the "greatness of human power"[172] found a receptive, if not enthusiastic, audience among her intellectual descendants. Julia Kristeva observed that forgiveness "stops time, which proceeds toward vengeance, and allows the person who committed the reprehensible act to begin anew, to take up another life and another activity."[173] Derrida, as always, was theatrical: Unconditional forgiveness is "a madness of the impossible."[174] Arendt, however, was committed to the possible. Forgiveness, for Derrida, was "exceptional and extraordinary";[175] its "radical purity" was "heterogeneous" and completely alien to the ordinary course of events.[176] But what truly distinguished Arendt as a theorist of unconditional forgiveness was her inclusion of the offense in the process. In this, she takes our exploration of survivors' accounts one step farther.

Arendt's interest in the career of the offense was seminal if undeveloped. She certainly didn't go as far as Derrida did, who claimed that one must "forgive both the fault and the guilty *as such?*,"[177] or as Jankélévitch did, who observed that gratuitous forgiveness not only forgives "the being" but also "the doing, or rather the having-done."[178] The fault, for her, didn't end with the conferral of forgiveness. She recognized that misdeeds endured, along with whatever else the offender represented—"his qualities and shortcomings, no less than with his achievements, failings, and transgressions."[179] This is a significant observation, with considerable implications for interpreting survivors' accounts, for if there is evidence in their work of forward-looking narratives exploring possibilities for renewed worldly relationships, there is stronger evidence of irreconcilable, backward-looking recrimination. Neither Butler, who essentially ignored wrongdoing beyond the victims' response to it, nor Nietzsche, who shrugged it off altogether, acknowledged the steady existence of the offense after forgiveness. But ultimately, Arendt remained true to how the release influences the offender as he rejoins the community: "*What* was done is forgiven for the sake of *who* did it."[180] It is the "who" that primarily concerned her because he "may be more than anything he ever did" (presuming that, unlike Eichmann in her explicit estimation, there was something to salvage). This, too, is an important contribution to interpreting survivors' accounts. As she wrote, it is "the person" in the criminal who counts above all. Forgiveness is important "for the sake of the person."[181] This perspective alerts us not just to survivors' narratives of fellow-feeling but to their emotional underpinnings discernible in Améry's "longing" and Jankélévitch's "omnipotence of love." It requires close attention to the kind of immeasurable connection they appeared to yearn for. In valorizing the person, however, Arendt did not elaborate on the role or the memory of the offense in human affairs once forgiveness sets the process in motion. In fact, she was "unconcerned"[182] with the misdeed beyond acknowledging its legacy and considered it "independent" of the blinding regard for the person.[183] It was sufficient for her to observe that misdeeds linger rather than expire, implying, importantly, that forgiveness is not the same thing as exoneration.

Arendt's acknowledgment of immutable misdeeds clarifies a dimension of survivors' predilections toward unconditional forgiveness and discloses something "non-ideal in their accounts"; that is, the recognition, in contrast to "ideal" conceptions of transcendent forgiveness, that nasty realities live on.[184] But her regard for wrongdoing is closer to statutory prescriptibility than to forgiveness that actively remembers, for the code, by proscribing further interrogation of misdeeds, failed to comment on them.[185] Since her unconcern with the trajectory of an offense borders on neglect, though not on wholesale forgetfulness—in either case, inconsistent with survivors' commitment to memory—we need to consider the contributions of other philosophers for further elaboration.

In his discussion of "difficult" forgiveness, Ricoeur reversed Arendt's unconcern for the persistence of the offense by integrating it into the process of forgiveness. Forgiveness, Ricoeur agreed, aspired to the offender, just as Arendt posited forgiveness "for the sake of the person." But he showed no mercy for the offense even if its commission was inadvertent. In contrast to dissecting misdeeds for their eligibility for forgiveness, as Arendt did, he drew a distinction instead between the act and the actor, the offense and the offender. Forgiveness, in this conception, preserved the act of caring for the person responsible for the offense while simultaneously attending vigorously to the offense—"forgiving the guilty person while condemning his action."[186] It's hard, indeed "difficult," to imagine that an offender, who is accountable for his actions, still merits release from his actions, but here, like Arendt, Ricoeur made a further cut between the person who committed the act and the same person who, as Arendt put it, "may be more than anything he ever did." In other words, forgiveness applied not only to the person but also to "a subject other than the one who committed the act."[187] Derrida, in justifying his much-cited imperative to forgive the unforgivable, came to the same conclusion about the offender, though without concern for the act: "It is no longer the guilty person as such whom one forgives."[188] In the same spirit, Kristeva asserted the possibility of forgiving the murderer but not the murder, but only, she added, in confidential circumstances, notably in analysis (her field), that presumably permitted observations of something pure. It involves a belief that "humanity is perfectible"[189] and, following Arendt, can involve an "act of love" or, at least, a consideration of "the person."[190]

These formulations, though daring, are significant for two reasons: forgiveness can accommodate condemnation of the crime. This is an especially important point in relation to traumatic memories, for survivors cleaved to these memories even as they sought to recall criminals in a new light. Severe injuries that once mattered still mattered to them, as their strong narratives of condemnation make unavoidably clear.[191] Second, forgiveness does, indeed, cast the criminal in a strikingly new light. It can accommodate condemnation of the crime without categorically condemning the criminal as hopeless. But to say that the criminal is not hopeless severely understates the implications of the argument and, indeed, of survivors' counter-narratives. There is a leap from the fault to what Ricoeur calls the hymn to forgiveness. Survivors do not just see the person in the criminal; they yearn for that person. They are drawn to, or back to, the person beside the commission of the crime. Even if the criminal's inclinations were conditioned by influential circumstances that robbed his agency and therefore compromised his humanity, for them he is no less a "person" for that, a subject distinct from the one responsible for the crime. This argument presumes what Jankélévitch called a "naked" human "essence," or what Wiesenthal called a human "good," or Améry's notion of self that a criminal doesn't "lose."[192] If "love" for the enemy sounds utopian, we need to remember that, for survivors, it expresses an emotionally profound, if elusive, desire for human fellowship, a "bond," as Kristeva put it.[193] Engaging an act of forgiveness, noted Ricoeur, springs from a belief in the offender that "you are better than your actions,"[194] and, as Derrida observed, "better than the guilty person."[195] Forgiveness as love, in this iteration, is less "unworldly," as Arendt observed. It is an emotionally strong articulation of a human connection, stronger than a mere acceptance or acknowledgment of the person, stronger than conceptions, found in theories of distributive and transitional justice theories, of utilitarian social arrangements based on calculated rights and agreements. Difficult forgiveness, as a human attachment, is, perhaps, closer to Kant's notion of *reverentia*, an implicit sense of human relatedness.[196] These formulations constitute forgiveness as a repository of condemnation and irreducible and deeply expressive human attachment.[197]

Still, the notion that attachment, even if apparent in counter-narratives and in historical experiences in Jewish history since the Enlightenment, seems irreparably compromised by the confluence of traumatic injury, the shock of betrayal, and belated disregard. The leap seems too considerable for implementation. Theorizers, in addition to Arendt, did, however, weigh forgiveness's practical chances. Derrida launched an argument with Hegelian overtones: Pure forgiveness, if it "wants to *arrive*, to happen by changing things," can enter "history, law, politics, existence itself," inhabited by "decisions and responsibilities," and become "effective, concrete, historic."[198] Kristeva similarly argued that it must make "cuts" in historical "continuity and linearity."[199] But what, exactly, is the worldly effect of forgiveness? Derrida imagined its influence on "the evolution of the law."[200] Kristeva envisaged a time when forgiveness could succeed at "modifying" history."[201] These considerations, however, are not satisfying. Besides imprecision, arguments for applied forgiveness—whether or not they renounced the offense—forfeit their potential for persuasion when tested against the highest stakes, the radical evil, that interminably tormented survivors. Ricoeur believed that difficult forgiveness involves an "ultimate act of trust,"[202] which is exactly what survivors lost. Referring to Nazi crimes, Kristeva asserted that forgiving assailants required expressions of repentance and, even then, not before judicial judgment and punishment.[203] For survivors, these conditions were immaterial and unacceptable.

Yet formulations that bring condemnation of crimes together with recognition of the person beside the criminal provide an important framework for evaluating contrary narratives in survivors' reflections. Clear statements of moral protest meet the first condition. Expressions of presumptive fellow-feeling—Améry's moral daydream, Wiesenthal's sympathetic address, and Jankélévitch's "essential similarity with the guilty person"[204]—appear to satisfy the second condition with implications for seeding dispositions to forgive.[205] More dynamically, survivors' reflections involve a process of negotiation not only against a background of extreme assault but also within a force field of vital possibility—a process disposed to "critical forgiveness." Indeed, their counter-narratives represent a study in renegotiating or reworking deeply violated relationships without necessarily working through them. The dispositions we observe, if they are forgiving and simultaneously condemning, are "critical," polysemically. They constitute an exigent process in deep search for, in Améry's terms, freedom from the trap of resentment.[206] They also, Janus-like, look backward accusingly, clinging inescapably to traumatic and post-traumatic realities, while gazing forward to qualified human fellowship.

For illustration, let us pay particular attention to survivors' expressions in juxtaposition—static narratives of condemnation alongside countervailing narratives that opened up possibilities. Wiesenthal manifestly recounted the SS officer's "gruesome" confession of his participation in an assault on some 200 Jews in a Polish village that included tossing grenades at a burning two-story structure where they were concentrated and shooting those who jumped desperately from windows in futile flight from the blaze.[207] In this account, he was clear, if not explicit, about what was unforgivable: it was the crime (*das Verbrechen*) that was reprehensible, not the criminal.[208] That's how he also depicted bystanders "gawking at doomed men so callously,"[209] a reference to ghetto inmates returning from assignment: What distressed him was their heartless behavior as they looked on "quietly and without protest at human beings enduring such shocking humiliation."[210] It was the deed that inspired him to blame—in Ricoeur's words, he was "condemning the action." Deeds, he remarked, were "wicked" (*schrecklich*).[211]

But when it came to the SS officer, his remarks were extensive. Wiesenthal made a point of noting that the officer, recalling the scene at the decimated structure, remembered one family he couldn't forget, especially a child with "black hair and dark eyes."[212] That impression, Wiesenthal further recounted, prevented the officer, during another campaign, from shooting "a second time."[213] He was surely a murderer, but he wasn't only a murderer: "He was a murderer who did not want to be a murderer but who had been made into a murderer by a murderous ideology."[214] He asserted the point three times. The officer's behavior was inexcusable, but the officer, himself, was more than a criminal defined by his commission of crime: "He was not born a murderer nor did he want to be a murderer."[215] What accounted for the evil was not "the person" but his ideological indoctrination.[216] In this, by leaving open the question of forgiveness, he allowed for the possibility, to invoke Ricoeur again, of "forgiving the guilty." The fact that the officer clung to racial convictions, even as he sought forgiveness, didn't make it any easier for Wiesenthal "to forgive a subject other than the one who committed the act" (Ricoeur). But then again, even as the officer implied that Jews were nothing more than "a single condemned community," a remark Wiesenthal didn't refute,[217] and attributed a measure of guilt to Jews, including those who perished during the siege on the Polish village,[218] Wiesenthal made a note earlier in the story of the officer's response to disparaging antisemitic propaganda: "that was not the sort of thing I cared for."[219]

Jankélévitch divided his attention to crimes and criminals in the two main works that constitute his reflections on the Nazi era and its legacy, "Should We Pardon Them?" (1965) and *Forgiveness* (1967); the book also explores their relationships. He showed little of his acclaimed generosity when he wrote "Should We Pardon Them?," for he felt Germans' silence was not much different from the "complacent silence"[220] exhibited during the period of Nazi rule that they preferred to forget. Germans, and not only Germans, were "more or less guilty"[221] because of their misdeeds: "millions" were "mute or complicit."[222] Observing their impatience with trials dredging up the Nazi past as the enforcement of statutory limitations approached—the May 1965 deadline that, to their dismay, the West German parliament extended at first temporarily and, eventually, indefinitely—he declared how easy it would be for them to "recognize themselves" in the criminals.[223] In order to awaken them from "shameful amnesia,"[224] he called attention to "racial genocide"[225]—crimes against humanity—which, for him was "the most monstrous crime in history"[226] but also the most likely to fade from memory since West German courts specifically invalidated the crime of genocide and crimes against humanity as grounds for prosecution. He would not permit Germans to forget them: they were "inexpiable," he insisted.[227] In *Forgiveness*, he observed that nothing could erase the stain, stating that even forgiveness cannot make it so "the action that occurred did not occur."[228] But what forgiveness could accomplish is the exemplification of the person, or what he liked to call the "hominity of the person"[229]—"the human as *human being*."[230] That, he said, is why crimes against humanity are inordinate and "exorbitant."[231] So strongly did he burnish the person beyond his crime that sometimes it wasn't possible to see him as anything but a person, declaring that "the wicked person is a poor person just like each of us"[232]—a remark similar to one we find in Wiesenthal's account, where he asserted rhetorically that murderers and victims were "made of the same stuff."[233] Here, then, is the foundation of forgiveness: Everyone is, at bottom, like everyone else. It is an Enlightenment conception whose extraordinary violation transformed a rational worldview into unstable, emotionally riven worldviews for those who continued to believe in it. Jankélévitch pleaded with Germans for an apology, for even though he didn't expect it, he "wished for it, this fraternal word!"[234]—"a single word of understanding and sympathy"—"with tears in our eyes."[235] Expressive statements like these, a willingness to say, "He will not abandon the wicked person, his brother"[236]—exalted a love for the person other than the one who was guilty: "The lover loves his beloved because it is he and because it is she."[237]

Jankélévitch instructs us about the sovereign irreducibility of each narrative. "Forgiveness is as strong as evil," he wrote in a foreword to "Should We Pardon Them?," "but evil is as strong as forgiveness."[238] Evil is, moreover, constant, just as love for the person is, which, as for Jankélévitch, was an articulation of forgiveness. But Jankélévitch complicated the argument by asserting a forgiveness so "infinite"[239] that it was capable of forgiving misdeeds, "even the inexpiable ones."[240] This is, as we have noted, his signature philosophy of "true forgiveness." It is the reason why critics cannot quite reconcile his views on the subject. Are misdeeds inexpiable or not? How irreducible are they? But the starkness of the distinction between backward- and forward-looking narratives is not apparent in the same text, as it is in Wiesenthal's and Améry's. Jankélévitch devoted separate works to each narrative—recrimination is the main conceit in his 1965 article, with the *Verjährungsdebatte* as background; brotherhood, abstractly considered, is thematic in his book two years later. As alternate arguments, so, too, his narrative paradigm: True forgiveness is gratuitous because it occurs in an "instant," only to succumb the next moment to the conquest of misdeeds, the dominion of evil. True forgiveness is extravagant, but only in the remarkable flash-instant of its immensity. Forgiveness and evil mirror each other, oscillating energetically and continuously, moment to moment, with evil and love intermittently overwhelming each other.[241] Neither disappears; each one just seems to from moment to dormant moment. In one instance, victims abjure misdeeds—"In no way is [forgiveness] a matter of approving or admiring the evil guilt";[242] then, all of a sudden, they see the person and, in his radiance, can even forgive a misdeed "*despite* his misdeed"[243] until they again condemn them as inexpiable, and so forth. Forgiveness appears in "scandalous contradiction" to wrongdoing and is certainly disproportionate to it, but over the course of human affairs, they in fact spar for supremacy. Jankélévitch's argument for the "reciprocity" of forgivability and unforgivability,[244] where compassion relents to resentment before and after resentment relents to compassion, converted a worldview into an unending negotiation: "The debate between forgiveness and the unforgivable will never have an end."[245]

Améry, of course, adopted a different, less charitable attitude toward the criminals than Wiesenthal and Jankélévitch did. Even if forgiving dispositions besides bitterly admonishing tirades is, at best, "difficult," as Ricoeur would have it, Améry is surely a test case. To honor what Thomas Brudholm called the "virtue" of his resentments in their role of disrupting his contemporaries' complacent indifference, we must underscore the distinction and tension between manifest and counter-narratives. Admonishment governed the former; swerves toward forgiveness persevere in the latter. In titling one of his essays "Torture," Améry announced that "the radical negation of the other"[246] inspired a vigorous response. Torture, he asserted, was the "essence" of the Third Reich,[247] exerting power for the sake of power.[248] The "first blow" confirmed his helplessness[249] and destroyed his faith in the world.[250] It represented a violation distinguished by its permanence: "Torture has an indelible character. Whoever was tortured, stays tortured. Torture is ineradicably burned into him, even when no clinically objective traces can be detected."[251] He considered the actor, the torturer, as well, but he didn't do so manifestly. The small segments of the essay he devoted to the person behind the act are where the work of transition is apparent and swerves away from condemnation and acrimony. He began with the kind of references to his tormentors we have come to expect: they were "sadists" who reveled in an "orgy of unchecked self-expansion."[252] But then, allusively, he suggested that circumstances accounted for destructive behavior: The sadist was the archetype of a world conditioned by brutality and death; so conditioned, he "does not care" about the world beyond.[253] But maybe he did care, or at least knew a world beyond the pale of negation, since he doesn't "lose himself" entirely in dystopia: "He can, after all, cease the torture when it suits him," returning to life as usual.[254]

From these observations, Améry occasionally reflected on what Jankélévitch called the "mixed zone of existence," where the sadist's "destructive being"[255] and his double—the sadist as "fellow man"—traded places.[256] The torturer is not only a torturer. His overpowering behavior prevailed, but Améry discerned a dormant humanity—his tormentors' "faces" beyond their "leather coats and pistols," and not just "Gestapo faces" but, echoing Jankélévitch and Wiesenthal, ordinary faces "like anyone else's."[257] For him, the "horror," his nightmare, was not only the ineradicable injuries he sustained but also the shocking behavior of his putative fellow man.[258] By comparison, the elation he sometimes permitted for himself occurred in a moment of recognition. He recounted one story of a torturer who, in facing down the firing squad at his execution, "experienced the moral truth of his crimes," adding, "I would like to believe that at the instant of his execution he wanted exactly as much as I to turn back time, to undo what had been done."[259] Evoking Jankélévitch's intuitive flash-instance, here was a moment of emotional truth for him, for he felt that, at last, "the antiman had once again become my fellow man."[260] Of course, this episode, beyond the evident facts, was strictly an emanation of Améry's imagination: The SS man was more likely reviewing his stormy life or ruing his capture, or just frozen in mortal fright. But Améry yearned for the opportunity to dispel what he called in the same story his "extreme *loneliness*."[261] Taking his thoughts further, to a place where he could imagine the moment when "he was with *me*,"[262] he felt he could die "calmly" and "appeased." It was the place whose pull he simply could not entirely resist.

Améry's belief that the origins of the criminal's brutality resided in external circumstances, like Wiesenthal's belief that the SS officer he wrote about was indoctrinated with brutality, created a space for critical forgiveness. The presumption made it possible for them to distinguish misdeeds from the "whole person" and to sympathize with the criminal beyond his crimes, just as Jankélévitch, with precision, asserted: "In reality, forgiveness does not forgive the misdeed as much as it forgives the guilty person."[263] Conditional forgiveness, by contrast, draws a radically different conclusion about the offender. Predicated on the offender's repentance, it presumes that wrongdoing, especially when it is willed, represents something deficient about the wrongdoer. The wrongdoer adopts a confessional perspective—the fault is her responsibility—and begins the process leading to forgiveness with an act of exorcism, an apology. On this conception, a victim of wrongdoing must receive evidence of an offender's "coming clean" before she could forgive. For her, forgiveness is a reaction, whereas a victim, who recognizes the role of circumstances, does not require signals or prompts from the offender. Recognizing that the fault is not the wrongdoer's alone but is rather overdetermined, she could begin the process de novo (although historical antecedents—Améry's and other Jews' memories of home—played an important preliminary role). The distinction, a species of the nature-versus-nurture debate over the origins of human capacity, involves the question of responsibility. Both conditional and critical forgiveness require accountability for wrongdoing—in the first instance based on an acknowledgment of wrongdoing, but in the second instance as well, even when victims, noting that circumstances have given rise to transgression, are inclined to forgive offenders unconditionally, without prior expressions of contrition. Critical forgiveness, as we have seen, is not an absolution. The SS officer in Wiesenthal's story, like Améry's tormentor, acted knowingly and destructively. In Wiesenthal's construction, the officer elected to join the Hitler Youth and the SS; he recalled his enthusiasm for the "genius" of the Führer, who needed "real men" for Germany's future.[264] Although it is important for the story that he expressed regret, recognizing even at the time of the criminal commission that the "fighting was inhuman," Wiesenthal made a point of noting that the officer joined other assailants in persisting with misdeeds; in words Wiesenthal recorded, "We [Nazis] continued to make history."[265] In Améry's account, the torturer "has control of the other's scream of pain and death; he is master over flesh and spirit, life and death."[266] He also could have stopped torturing whenever he wanted to. Misdeeds demanded admonishment, but in relating the offenders' responsibility for them to situations that distorted or hijacked their "better origins," as Améry observed,[267] they could see the offender separately, wholly, from circumstances that implicated them. What they saw was Jankélévitch's "pure" humanity,[268] which was vulnerable to seduction but which they wanted to affirm and preserve.

Améry's indulgence in the fantasy of the SS man's alertness to moral truth, something "I would like to believe";[269] Jankélévitch's wish for just "a single word of understanding and sympathy"; or Wiesenthal's "appeal to people who I believe have something to say" might sound like conditional forgiveness, a readiness to reach for the extended hand of awakened sympathy. But having resigned for the indefinite future to an indifference that seemed endemic, which, in Améry's words, "places the incomprehensible in the cold storage of history,"[270] their worldly orientation was, instead, emphatically asymmetrical. The wish expressed a longing without expecting a response: "I am not at all speaking with the intention to convince; I just blindly throw my word onto the scale, whatever it may weigh."[271] Améry knew that it was absurd to think of resentment as inspiring ripples of remorseful self-correction followed by forgiveness, but as an emotion that "demands that the irreversible be turned around, that the event be undone,"[272] it expressed nonetheless a yearning for correction, a true understanding. It was enough for him to imagine "hypothetically … two groups of people, the overpowered and those who overpowered them, would be joined in the desire that time be turned back and with it, that history become moral."[273] The tone of their appeal was less an "if-then" proposition, implying an anticipated response, than a subjunctive "if-only" hypothesis that resided in dreams.[274]

It never took Améry long to return to his senses, and so he explicitly ruled out forgiveness. Like Wiesenthal and Jankélévitch, he couldn't seriously consider the term that his contemporaries, in exhorting enforceable statutory prescription, used in tandem with appeals to forgetting the past and moving on; hence, "my scant inclination to be conciliatory."[275] But in terms we are exploring, there are narrative thrusts escorting a search for a human connection that expressed an inclination to forgive in a different register. Like Jankélévitch and Wiesenthal, Améry crafted his reflections to permit both condemnation and the "continued existence of the world."[276] Misdeeds—Améry's reference to the historical "triumph" of "torture, destruction, and death"[277]—were unforgivable. Yet, against the stark grain of resentment, all three survivors, by considering the subject other than the "destructive being" implicated in crime, made room for forgiveness. Time and again, we see a deep longing for a human connection that critical forgiveness permitted without diminishing memories of destruction or the standing they and other survivors achieved by expressing resentful protest. What I find compelling is the discordant coexistence of the two narratives: both, independently, demanded a hearing. Looking backward promoted an outlook of distrust and suspicion; looking forward reflected a homesickness for human fellowship. Brokenness was the paramount voice, but fellow-feeling and dispositions to forgive were sufficiently vital to acquire expression and occasionally interrupt the gloom. Survivors' accounts articulated an extraordinary aesthetic: two narratives in conflict, each satisfying separate emotional requirements without regard for the other, thesis and antithesis without regard for synthesis, neither one truer or more radiant than the other. We look for reconciliation where it doesn't exist.

But there is balance in the architecture of critical forgiveness: Améry's distrust and fellow-feeling, Jankélévitch's "immense" forgiveness and recognition of overwhelming human evil, and Wiesenthal's "person" in the "wicked" each served as countervailing forces. For them, the balance was clearly important, for the triumph of destruction was as unbearable as an achievement of common humanity was unattainable. But over time and to varying degrees, what would keep them in balance? In recalling his experience with torture, Améry lamented the absence of his fellow man, which he defined as offering assistance to anyone in distress: Under circumstances of torture, he concluded, "No help can be expected."[278] The observation was prescient. The conclusion did not rule out the longed-for human response. It only declared that a helping hand or spontaneous respect was no longer normative. Because it was no longer certain, it was reckless to expect it.[279] Survivors, in nurturing a desire for a human connection, realized that, if it were ever to come into view, the responsibility rested in the end with them. Wiesenthal recognized that it was up to him to "help" the dying SS officer. Even if he weren't yet willing,[280] the realization that moving forward was locomotive was, itself, transitional: it displaced an unpromising expectation of help as well as the static helplessness of the victim with a new stage for negotiating, on their terms, a dangerous world fraught with misdeeds and bloodlust. As the fact of their accounts for public consideration attests, it was a world they believed was worth negotiating. The burden of abandonment and loneliness was otherwise impossible to endure. Imagining an imperfect humanity and dreaming about joining it in a spirit of critical forgiveness cast their reflections as intriguing conceptions of the transitional society.

6

Deep Transitions: A Conclusion Resisting Finality

Future imperfect

In a passage of his essay on torture, survivor Jean Améry raged about the sadist: He is an embodiment of "the radical negation of the other ... He wants to nullify this world." But thoughts lurked in the back of his mind. The first hint was his repetition of the term "fellow man" (*Mitmensch*)—four times—weaving it into relentless observations about death and destruction. The references suggested that, for all his acrimony, he was clinging to a tenuous human bond, determined to save the notion from extinction: "Torture becomes the total inversion of the social world, in which we can live only if we grant our fellow man life." Preferring to condemn, he continued: His torturer inflicted menacing pain—"a slight pressure by the tool-wielding hand"—ruining the victim before him. Yet he didn't leave it there: Such a world "obviously cannot exist." In this account, like so many others, dread is shadowed by allusions to the "continued existence of the world," a world, he believed, that eases suffering, honors humility, and enjoys the life of the mind—"Kant and Hegel, and all nine symphonies, and [Schopenhauer's] World as Will and Representation."[1]

Survivors of the Nazi era, actively importuning their contemporaries with their tribulations in the 1960s as never before, published their accounts in two time frames: backward-looking condemnation, which is predominant, and forward-looking interruptions, which are recessive swerves toward negotiating a relationship with a world they have come to distrust. It is commonplace to read survivors' accounts for their narrative condemnation and desolation. "The reactions that [atrocity] inspires are above all despair and a feeling of powerlessness before the irreparable," Vladimir Jankélévitch wrote. "One can do nothing. One cannot give life back."[2] But not long after that statement, he surprises us with a remark like this: "Forgiveness [reveals] itself capable of instituting a new order," adding, "One understands, consequently, why forgiveness can be the founder of a future."[3] In arguing that survivors' accounts expressed forward-looking aspirations, we are foregrounding what is incidental in the text. But doing so exposes an intriguing, emotional process of reworking worldly relationships against the manifest narrative grain of resentment and loss. Memoirs, as these accounts are often labeled, possess a future-imperfect dimension.

A considerable influence on counter-narrative swerves is rooted in the past, specifically, in the pre-traumatic, ancestral past. Améry didn't just believe in the "continued existence of the world," a world that granted human fellowship. He and other Jewish survivors recalled it. As a people driven to integration with their compatriots for a century and a half, coaxed by political promises and convinced by a substantial measure of progress, post-emancipation European Jews became emotionally attached to their neighbors and compatriots. They wanted to belong even when they were sometimes overtly not welcome, a reminder that convictions based on subjective beliefs usually triumph over evaluations based on objective realities. Simon Wiesenthal acknowledged his ancestors' aspirations: They "had worked hard and done all they could to be recognized by their fellow creatures";[4] Améry evoked memories of his own pre-war longing for home among his German neighbors, doing everything he could to parrot their observable existence. For him, these memories were ineradicable. "Mother tongue and native world grow with us, grow into us," Améry maintained,[5] and, indeed, ancestral traces of aspirations to belong resurfaced in survivors' counter-narratives. The campaign in the meantime to destroy European Jewry transformed pre-war hopes and expectations into episodic and cautionary distant dreams, but it is important to note that the ideal of *Mitmensch* lived on.

Two dispositions are particularly noteworthy in survivors' forward-looking counter-narratives—expressions of betrayal and nuanced inclinations toward forgiveness. With the rupture in Jews' relationships with their neighbors, survivors sometimes veered away from recounting past crimes to recall their neighbors who, they believed, violated an unspoken social contract: a mutual commitment to care for each other, especially under conditions of vulnerability and distress. Betrayal is the historical source of their manifest resentments. As witnesses to unleashed tribalism, they had come to believe that expectations of help were bankrupt. Tadeusz Obręski, a Polish Jew in hiding during the Nazi occupation, expressed what so many Jews felt as their people were decimated: "Where was it [the Polish government-in-exile] … during the four and a half years of occupation? Why … didn't it order the Poles, back in 1939, to help Jews hide from the German murderers? Why did they keep silent? Why did they let, and why are they still letting, us be destroyed, here on the Aryan side?" Scholars have observed expressions of betrayal in survivors' accounts; in Obręski's accounts, it is impossible to miss: "All of Polish society helped exterminate Jews … The Polish people betrayed three and a half million Jews. This is a fact that will be discussed in [future] history."[6]

As a serial phenomenon recounted in survivors' accounts, betrayal deserves more than passing notice. Omer Bartov, in a significant study of the destruction of Ukrainian Jews "from below," reproduced testimonies replete with expressions of betrayal.[7] But there is more to say. Under-theorized, feeling betrayed is typically understood as a disruption of human relationships. It is surely a severe emotion, but it is not always non-negotiable. It fact, it serves significant purposes. Mainly it recalls the criminals as well as their crimes; that is, who was responsible for the misdeed and not only the misdeed itself. In his torture essay dedicated to describing unbearable anguish, Améry digressed to consider the torturer, a sadist who, he imagined, "realizes his own destructive being."[8] A consideration of betrayal acts compelled memories of relationships and, in the case of survivors who were entrenched, as modern Jewry was, in an interethnic social milieu, relationships specifically with enemies who they believed were, in essence, *Mitmenschen*. Wiesenthal's *The Sunflower* is an encounter between two individuals, a murderer on his deathbed and a victim summoned to it, but more than that, it is an inquiry by a victim into the person who became a murderer. Stories about betrayal, in other words, usher memories to perpetrators who, in the end, as Améry remarked, had "faces like anyone else's. Plain, ordinary faces."[9]

As survivors ruminated about transgressors, a process of negotiation was under way. Murderers were, after all, formerly their compatriots. Rather than fixate on their crimes, they enlisted their ancestral beliefs in common humanity: "Was there in fact any personal relationship between us," Wiesenthal reflected, "between the murderers and their victims?"[10] Occasionally, survivors abandoned themselves to dreams where they imagined their enemies' moral transformation. Améry dreamt that the Nazi criminal would take responsibility for his crimes and would "once again become a fellow man."[11] Jankélévitch, like Wiesenthal, conjured a sympathetic conception of "the wicked person [who] is a poor person just like each one of us."[12] If the criminal was really no different from anyone else, the "whole orientation of our relations" with the guilty is "overturned," transfiguring hatred into love."[13]

The plural narratives in survivors' accounts offer layered reasons why survivors elected to publish their accounts in the 1960s. Manifestly, it was an act of public protest against contemporaries for insisting on moving on, specifically away from further prosecution of former Nazis, once the incendiary 1963–5 Frankfurt Auschwitz trial concluded, buttressed by the imminent lapse in May 1965 of West Germany's statute of limitations for heinous crimes. But the decision to publish their accounts at all is, itself, significant. As an act of direct communication, it expressed a desire to connect with their contemporaries who, as Améry wrote, did not live up to their "better origins."[14] The reader, Améry hoped, "would have no choice but to accompany me, in the same tempo, through the darkness that I illuminated step by step."[15] Even as Germans and other Europeans insisted on silence about the past—an insistence that sounded all too familiar to those who had endured dehumanizing repression—survivors, in making their stories heard, were reaching out, suggesting that their adversaries inhabited, or could inhabit, the same moral universe. Though Wiesenthal recalled his "silence" at the bedside of his interlocutor, a dying SS officer, the publication of *The Sunflower* was an "appeal to people who I believe have something to say,"[16] an attempt to reorient his relations with an inimical world. Feeling betrayed is a negotiable emotion.

If nothing else, survivors' concern in the 1960s with the question for forgiveness suggests an interrogation of the concept and, in the train of multiple swerves, its possibilities. Survivors explicitly refused to forgive, but that's the vocation of manifest narratives. Denotatively, they adopted and then rejected a conventional conception that exhorted victims to erase excessive feelings of anger. Observing a demand to "forgive and forget," they could hardly comply and felt that they had no choice but to demur. Connotatively, however, dreams and other allusions to a human connection and the imagined prospects of common fellowship started a process of transition. In the stark light of narrative condemnation, they were inclined in their counter-narratives to re-evaluate the offenders beyond what they did. Like their reactions to betrayal, an inclination to forgive the person in offenders dynamically emerged from and also reawakened historical emotions of attachment. Side by lopsided side, they emphatically denounced misdeeds (though not always in Jankélévitch's radical reformulation) but occasionally gave vent to generous predilections. Rather than reject forgiveness as an option, survivors reconceptualized it to demand accountability and simultaneously permit possibilities for "a continued existence of the world."

Witnesses and transitions

In their accounts, survivors' transitional dispositions alongside inescapable memories of atrocity invite their accounts' inclusion in current, and vigorous, debates about strategies for reconstructing broken societies. Recent proposals—especially those arising from the human rights and transitional justice movements—are drawing attention not only because of the global proliferation of post–Second World War, large-scale, collective violence and atrocity crimes but also because their paradigms, which are incommensurate to the scale of human destruction, constantly demand revision. Indeed, the charter, 1948 United Nations Genocide Convention, is silent on the aftermath of genocide. It defined what genocide means and provided for punishment of guilty parties. It also referred to actions "appropriate for the prevention and suppression of acts of genocide" (Article 8), but prevention skirts the question of negotiating the crime's considerable legacies in the meantime. In the end, the convention presumed that a statement by world leaders, backed by member nations, would "liberate mankind from such an odious scourge." Clearly, the liberation hasn't yet occurred, nor has regional conflict since the Second World War subsided, much less withered, and it is likely that it never will.

By contrast, the human rights movement, which involves some 20,000 nongovernmental organizations (NGOs) worldwide, exposes and seeks to curb egregious violations. Fortify Rights, for example, supports investigations into the mistreatment of Myanmar's Muslim Rohingya (known by many in Myanmar as illegal Bengali immigrants), exerts pressure to grant them citizenship and free movement, and seeks to open channels of humanitarian aid. The International Organization for Migration, as another example, has helped the government of the Dominican Republic register and document more than half of Haitian immigrants residing in the country illegally. The exposure has contributed to an unwillingness to expel Dominicans of Haitian descent, at least in the short run, though police work with street gangs to exert pressure on immigrants in the big cities by threatening to burn down their homes, among other tactics, and bureaucratic and financial hurdles have slowed down the registration process. It is significant that immigrants who flee the Dominican Republic cross the paradoxically named Friendship Bridge to Haiti: As the scene of carnage in 1937 when the Dominican dictator, Rafael Trujillo, ordered the massacres of more than 10,000 Haitians, it represents an axiom of the human rights movement: Conflict is an endemic political condition. It eludes mankind's liberation.

The same conception of conflict cannot be said of the classical transitional justice movement. Though it is sometimes criticized for its western, neoliberal, and legalistic presumptions of justice, it has no peer in aspiring to the summary transformation of successor societies. Recognized most conspicuously for promoting truth commissions in the global south, the transitional justice (TJ) movement—like its human rights companion, in full throttle over the past quarter century—notably parts ways from the human rights movement's surgical exposure and mitigation of wrongdoing.[17] TJ is an umbrella term for a variety of forward-looking practices with the common purpose of achieving an open society or at least a less repressive political order. As it evolved, its grounded mechanisms included state apologies, education mandates, and a range of justice schemes—restorative, as exemplified by truth commissions; corrective or reparatory; compensatory; restitutive; and criminal justice, which, in the context of repair, plays a complementary role and, from the Eichmann trial on, provided a platform for victims' perspectives. Successor state actors—government leaders, vetted civil servants, prosecutors, state-mandated truth commissions, restorative justice panels under state guidance, official apologies, and so forth—have dominated the practice of conventional transitional justice, an appeal to "positive" rights in adjudicating differences between parties in or emerging from conflict. Recently, initiatives in civil society—an appeal to "negative" rights in downplaying if not side-stepping the state's involvement—have started to make a dramatic difference. These include museums of conscience; public commemorations; naming of public places, streets, and plazas; citizen activism from the 1990s on in U.N. conferences on the environment, women, social policy, and so forth; and "counter-memorials." Counter-memorials, like other civil society undertakings, challenge self-serving statist accounts of historical injustice. Noteworthy installations in Germany are *Neue Wache,* the central memorial to the victims of war and tyranny, with its large interior sculpture *Mother with Her Dead Son* by Käthe Kollwitz; *Bibliothek,* an installation commemorating the Nazis' incineration of books in 1933; the widely celebrated Memorial to the Murdered Jews of Europe; and the *Stolpersteine,* or brass-topped sidewalk "stumbling" cobblestones, marking residences where Jews lived before their deportation to fatal destinations.[18] Citizen activism in transitional justice enterprises seeks to set in place a common foundation for shared memories, or "co-remembering." As Edward Casey observed, "Not only is something communal being honored, but the honoring itself is a communal event, a collective engagement."[19]

Surprisingly, however, little attention has been paid to the role witnesses' accounts can play in articulating transitional prospects for post-conflict conditions.[20] One reason, perhaps, is the belief that survivors possess a rarefied, esoteric perspective whose merit as guidance for general observers is limited to inferential, sweeping "values clarification"—the misdeeds of ordinary people, seductive crowd behavior, the differences one person can make in saving a life, early warning signals, and so forth. Another likely reason for inattention is a tendency to devalue emotional and contingent expression at the heart of survivors' accounts, the subject of our concern. Their reactive attitudes—resentment, forgiveness, and other dispositions—seem existential and "post-traumatic," dramaturgy that stimulates interest but can seem solipsistic and often invites skepticism, diminishing if not subverting their historical credibility.[21] Our contention is that they warrant reconsideration for the significant information they offer about relationships before, during, and after calamity. Améry, a survivor of Auschwitz who wrote reflectively about his experiences a generation afterward, elaborated on the historical value of witnesses' accounts, deliberations that suggest their importance for evaluating transitional conditions. He recognized how easily others dismissed survivors as a "traumatized,"[22] but, even if he did "go through life like a sick man,"[23] he believed witnesses had something exceptional to offer. Experiencing the ordeal, he wrote, was the precondition for exemplifying the "historical reality of my epoch,"[24] asserting a relationship between deep, emotional experiences and lucid exposure.[25] What survivors observed and could communicate was the sheer affective power of historical experience that others miss. In documentary analysis, visual or literal references to brutality are objectified and detached—"like a blind man talking about color"[26]—that fail to touch the "crushing force," the "entire overwhelming might" of antisemitism.[27] Formulations for making amends to redress past wrongdoing weakly approximate post-conflict aspirations, the "craving to assimilate"[28] that not only articulates a preoccupation in much of modern Jewish history but also identifies a source of inspiration that fueled an urgent, post-conflict search for recovery. From within history, or from below, their grasp of hostilities' profound "elemental force"[29] and victims' truculent ensuing worldly distrust explains why transitions to successor polities are difficult to implement and harder to sustain. "Humane pronouncements" can't offer guidance,[30] he said. Worse, they could "again lull" society—not only Jews, but the wider society as well[31]—dangerously into "the slumber of security"[32] and once more to the precipice of catastrophe.[33] Améry believed that survivors were "better equipped" to recognize and affirm the intractability of realities"[34] and "be more sensitive to injustice of every kind than his fellow man."[35] Having experienced them and knowing them emotionally, they are in a prescient position, we believe, to tell us a great deal about the unsettled and unreconciled ecology of transitional circumstances.

To be sure, witnesses to calamity have been visible in transitional circumstances, notably Nelson Mandela in post-apartheid South Africa and the Mothers of the Plaza de Mayo in the aftermath of Argentina's Dirty War who alerted the world to "disappeared" children. But in addition to engaging in and emerging from conflict, witnesses are in a special position to provide an uncompromised and realistic evaluation of conflict's tremors and aftershocks. There are instructive analogies in indigenous cultures—such as Rwanda's post-genocide gacaca proceedings that centered on shaming practices—as well as in social media. The "Bondy Blog" that emerged from the 2005 upheaval in France remains a platform for "citizen journalists" who provide an unvarnished perspective from inside the 93—Department 93, a *banlieue* (suburb) northeast of Paris recognized pejoratively as a *slum*—that is commonly under-represented in mainstream media. They are often unapologetic about the emotional and tendentious nature of their posts. It is noteworthy for our argument that established media are hosting the blog on their websites,[36] a development that suggests the influence witnesses' accounts exert on orthodox opinion and could exert on transitional developments.

Survivors as witnesses articulate a worldview of what comes after atrocity that anticipates the aspirations of transitional justice theory. While their differences are profound, it is worth noting their convergence, for both are forward-looking and refer to an aftermath that is transformative, indeed, a new configuration responsive to social and moral collapse. Basic to formative TJ's conception of an aftermath is its paramount ideal of political reconciliation between adversaries emerging from conflict.[37] Responding exhaustively to massive, endemic wrongdoing, the concept represents a sea change in dealing with past conflict by comprehensively revising human rights' piecemeal remediation and criminal justice's limited sanction of exemplary, high-level wrongdoers. Transitional justice eludes a canonical interpretation, but, essentially, it is distinguished from retributive justice by its forward-looking commitment to forming viable relationships for the sake of the public good. Ernesto Verdeja presented a middle-of-the-road, workable formulation: "Reconciliation is, in it final calculus, about reintroducing former antagonists back into the same moral sphere."[38] The goal, as P. E. Digeser observed, is the condition of "peace" where civility and "civic friendship" replace "past wrongs."[39] This position is sometimes referred to as "democratic reciprocity."[40] David A. Crocker characteristically observed the nature of reconciled relationships: "Former enemies or former perpetrators, victims, and bystanders are reconciled insofar as they respect each other as fellow citizens."[41] This view exists between a basic "minimalist" conception of nonlethal, arms-length coexistence and an ambitious, "maximalist" interpretation that promotes social harmony, community solidarity, and mutual compassion. It is a sentiment that is intrinsic to renewed relationships among adversaries, what Stephen Darwall called "recognition respect." It is a respect for the other as a person without reference to an external, normative standard or authority (which Darwall designated, by contrast, "appraisal respect"). According to Darwall, the nature of the encounter—whether the antagonism is "former" or still coarse—requires a mutual response to appeals for claims or demands—in a word, answerability. In place of what Kant labeled "arrogantia"—a self-indulgent desire to make one's claims primary—individuals in the reconciled society achieve equal standing "to demand, remonstrate, resist, charge, blame, resent, feel indignant, excuse, forgive, and so on."[42]

Underlying the ideal of recognition respect is the TJ concern for the victim and her "standing" or "voice." Unlike conclusions to conflicts that condemn and prosecute offenders, TJ regards victims and their elevation to a common "moral sphere" as a critical component of repair. In this, survivors' decisions to communicate their stories is a prototypical articulation. Recognizing victims' accounts of assault as truth-telling and heeding their emotional expressions confirm victims' standing. Margaret Urban Walker argued that truth-telling, or bearing witness, grants them "epistemic" repair by combating wrongdoers' "outright denial, defensive reinterpretations, 'double discourses' that simultaneously deny facts and provide justifying or minimizing explanations and euphemisms for the very thing denied, and [their] safe incuriosity protected by tacit agreements not to know more or not to say publicly what some or many know."[43] A victim, as a "self-accounting actor," achieves the power "to speak with basic credibility."[44] Whether or not victims as witnesses present common and conclusive truths, dispel disbelief, or make a difference in subsequent behavior,[45] just acknowledging their presentation, as Pablo de Greiff observed, "constitutes a form of recognizing the significance and value of persons as individuals, as citizens, and as victims."[46]

To these viewpoints Walker added an element of moral responsibility and accountability in order to regulate reconciled relationships and keep them reciprocal. There must be "expectations" and "confidence" that standards are "mutually recognized" as "authoritative" and "shared."[47] Expectations constitute the presumption that others will play by the rules or will "rise to the reiteration and enforcement of those rules when someone goes out of bounds."[48] Formulating "reliable and stable expectations," Colleen Murphy remarked, makes it possible for citizens "to pursue their goals and plans."[49] As Richard Wallace observed, expectations are an important postulate of reconciled relationships, for they tether individuals to normative standards as a requirement (keeping promises) or as a prohibition (not breaking promises).[50] A common commitment to observing normative standards is necessary if citizens of the new order were to reasonably expect a successful transition. Citizens, wrote de Greiff, "are sufficiently committed to the norms and values that motivate their ruling institutions, sufficiently confident that those who operate those institutions do so also on the basis of those norms and values, and sufficiently secure about their fellow citizens' commitment to abide by and uphold these basic norms and values."[51] The state demonstrates its commitment by exercising the rule of law and protecting the inviolability of civil and human rights. The conditions of moral worth, mutual respect, shared standards, and common expectations all presume that negative emotions, such as resentment, threaten the stability of the new order. This is not a simple matter, however, because transitional justice theorists also recognize a role for resentment in the reconciled society. It is, indeed, an appropriate, if not requisite, response to the violations of expectations. But resentment requires restraint. If there is one feature of the reconciled society about which theorists are in agreement, it is the wisdom of managing resentment for the sake of stable relationships and the security of the community. The emotion, were it to linger and hector, would defeat the transition.

The foundation of reconciliation that transitional justice postulates, then, is twofold: achieve the conditions of respect for the other's standing, and modulate expressions of resentment to assure a commitment to, and confidence in, shared normative standards. TJ postulates are readily discernible in repair endeavors. John Hope Franklin, the historian–activist who peerlessly delineated the legacy of slavery and race in the United States, offered eloquent articulation. Once "racial brutality" is observed and confronted,

> We should make a good-faith effort to turn our history around so we can see in front of us, so that we can avoid doing what we have done for so long. If we do that whites will discover that African-Americans possess the same human qualities that other Americans possess, and African-Americans will discover that white Americans are capable of the most sublime expressions of human conduct of which all human beings are capable.[52]

This perspective firmly inflects civil rights aspirations, which Bryan Stevenson, director of the Equal Justice Initiative in Montgomery, Alabama, starkly referred to as a commitment "to a process of truth and reconciliation."[53] The notion that we should "turn our history around … [and] avoid doing what we have done for so long," or the confidence that, inevitably, the "moral arc of history … bends toward justice," famously intoned by Martin Luther King, Jr., from words expressed by the nineteenth-century abolitionist Theodore Parker, shows the appeal in civil rights discourse of a post-conflict picture exhibiting regulated, reconciled relationships.[54]

In what respects do witnesses confirm TJ's foundational tenets? Améry, Jankélévitch, and Wiesenthal—three survivors of Nazi-era destruction who published their accounts in the 1960s as part of an emerging cohort committed to communicating their stories fiercely—serve as commentary. (For brevity, we will refer to them as "survivors," though there is no presumption that they stand for all survivors.) They started to write openly and boldly about the Nazi past and its legacy in response to an unfriendly climate of German opinion coalescing around the imminent lapse of statutory limitations for egregious Nazi-era crimes and a preoccupation with the Frankfurt Auschwitz trial, which lasted for twenty months (1963–5). Both events clarified Germany's impatience with unpleasant historical reminders of and questions about accountability. In principle, survivors and TJ theorists agree on the potential merits of criminal justice. Indeed, Améry expressed hope that Germany, or the world, "was already on the point of healing in 1964."[55] According to the TJ model, when the commission of crimes is the rule and not the exception, criminal justice jurisprudence required blanket revision: its laudable goals—the punishment and prosecution of proven offenders to correct the moral imbalance and restore the pre-existing order and rule of law—were otherwise untenable. According to John Locke's classical social contract theory from the seventeenth century, conventional jurisprudence privileged the state's authority, granted by citizens, to resolve grievances peaceably and protect citizens from fear and distrust. It also served to maintain order by deterring crime just by threatening certain and swift punishment, as Cesare Beccaria famously argued in his 1764 tract, "On Crimes and Punishment." As such, fair trials provided closure.[56] But when massive violence saturates political life, the requirement to prosecute all those who were implicated is unsustainable, or, as Argentine political adviser Jaime Malamud-Goti observed, even within the military during the country's preceding period of repression, "the thought of trying all military personnel responsible for every sort of offense … was untenable … It simply was not feasible to try them all."[57] It certainly was unfeasible when, in Jankélévitch's view, just about every German was complicit in "what happened," including the "passive who accepted it and the indifferent who have already forgotten it."[58] Ordinary proceedings under extraordinary circumstances are incompetent and prohibitively expensive, especially for strapped successor states.[59] TJ theorists, by placing criminal justice in a larger perspective of shared norms, glean its forward-looking predilections. In this perspective the Nuremberg trial of former Nazis represented a normative shift: it made clear that fair justice in the aftermath of gross wrongdoing could be effective when it is exemplary and "consequentialist"; that is, when it not only asserts the successor society's rule-of-law political identity but also elevates and privileges a culture of disinterested, just violence over a perpetrator culture of domination, intimidation, and unjust violence.[60]

Survivors endorsed criminal justice's potential. By denouncing the cry in Germany for ending legal proceedings against former Nazis and condemning belated generations for resisting a formal process of self-examination, they recognized the Frankfurt trial's role in authorizing the transitional credentials of Nazi Germany's post-occupation succession to a Federal Republic. Jankélévitch discerned "some purpose" in the Frankfurt trial and other trials: they "forced" people to grasp what occurred.[61] In addition, the nascent publication of their aggregate accounts complemented the ascendant jurisprudential practice of leveraging victims' testimonies. The prosecution of the Eichmann trial as well as the platform the Frankfurt trial provided for more than 200 victims satisfied an urgent requirement for sanctioned self-expression. The Frankfurt trial also promised just accountability for misdeeds by confirming the Nuremberg standard of individual rather than state liability, even for state wrongs. This principle discredited the "head of state" defense that sought to grant immunity from criminal responsibility to individuals who acted on behalf of the state.[62] Eventually, however, whatever hope survivors secreted for a successful trial at Frankfurt and however much they believed in its potential for healing and reconciliation, they demurred, giving little thought in their accounts to deliberative accountability even as they provided evidence of wrongdoing. Like TJ observers, but more so, they came to recognize how much the problems compromised the potential. The Frankfurt trial convinced survivors that the institution of criminal justice is deficient as a path to healing and therefore couldn't offer consolation as an instrument for the social good. In Austria and Germany, wrote Améry, in "core countries" where antisemitism persisted, "Nazi war criminals either are not convicted or receive ridiculously mild prison sentences."[63] In contrast to trials guided by international judicial policies, as the Allies established at Nuremberg's International Military Tribunal, national trials were prone to political influence. Defying the Nuremberg paradigm, the West German legal code proscribed legislative attempts at exempting retroactivity constraints that would have made it possible to prosecute former Nazis for crimes against humanity. As a result, the state prosecuted behavior on grounds of criminal "base motives," circumventing the crime of genocide. In addition, regnant skepticism about the credibility of victims' courtroom testimonies produced lenient verdicts. The four-year extension of time limits for prosecuting criminals to 1969, based on the crimes' transcendent magnitude and severity, might have heartened survivors were proceedings fairer, but even that measure fell short of the doctrine of timelessness, or imprescriptibility, for crimes against humanity.[64]

Jankélévitch came around to recognizing the disingenuous conduct of the Frankfurt trial "with the intention of hypocritically justifying statutory limitations in advance."[65] He opposed the "penal logic" altogether in his 1967 tome *Forgiveness*.[66] For him, "justice" was incapable of anything more than a "narrow morality," a likely reference to the Frankfurt trial's prosecution of criminals for their personal defects rather than for rupturing inviolable social bonds. But survivors didn't give up altogether on the question of justice: they directed their concern toward the intransigence of historical injustices and considered forward-looking alternatives to state-sponsored criminal justice. It was this frame of mind that gave shape to their accounts and, emerging as a corpus of conscience, lent a genre to a vast cultural enterprise of post-atrocity memory. They took justice into their own hands and framed their accounts as depositions. Bearing witness constituted their primary narratives: Améry identified wrongdoers by name; Jankélévitch reviled Germans' "exceptional" crimes.[67] Often they were preoccupied with the enormity of injustice. In notable departure from TJ's presumption of a common commitment to normative standards, Améry derided "written or unwritten social contracts" intended to assure reliable social relationships and inspiring "the certainty of help." He lost faith that, when faced with adversity, "the other person will spare me,"[68] and devoted his attention not to repair but to rupture. Wiesenthal, too, wrote about his experiences of betrayal, the violated expectation of mutual respect with the outbreak of antisemitism at school and the heartless indifference of bystanders to the mistreatment of ghetto inmates: "In their eyes were we human beings at all?"[69] Though he devoted his postwar life to finding and bringing former Nazis to trial, in his accounts he expressed concern about the moral implications of broken humanity. Where is the evidence of a "common link"?, he asked searchingly.[70] Why didn't "Poles" and "Jews" recognize their "common misery," he rued; "there were still barriers between us."[71] Indeed, the implication in this phrase that Jews weren't Poles is itself revealing. His worldview is, perhaps, exemplified in a particularly melancholy momentary reflection: "I realized that the break with the world around us was now complete."[72]

What rescued these observations from stark nihilism were considerations of a moral sphere of interrelationships embedded in counter-narrative departures. Two of perhaps the most eloquent meditations on forgiveness after atrocity materialized when survivors like Jankélévitch challenged "the duty to punish":[73] Jankélévitch's *Forgiveness* and Wiesenthal's *The Sunflower,* written two years later in 1969. Though the disposition of forgiveness is clearly and widely suspect, and not only because it seems outrageously quixotic—even Wiesenthal balked at authorizing it and, indeed, most survivors refused to defend it—it is seriously considered by TJ adherents and survivors alike because it represents a significant alternative not only to backward-looking punishment but also to criminal justice's inability to deal comprehensively with the blighted and enduring legacy of rank social violence. Perhaps the most prominent articulation of political forgiveness in transitional justice perspective is South Africa's Truth and Reconciliation Commission (TRC). Archbishop Desmond Mpilo Tutu, its chair and primary proponent, rejected the "Nuremberg trial paradigm" as a measure for dealing with extreme mass crimes.[74] TJ advocates in general give several reasons for the drawbacks of criminal justice in these circumstances. First, the requisite recourse to exemplary, or selective, prosecution policy runs the risk of subverting the rule of law's fairness principle that it claims to defend.[75] Indeed, amnesty protection provided by the two sovereign Germanys, once the Allied occupation period ended in 1949, demonstrated the shortcomings of selective punishment. The West German legal code, itself, exempted from the harshest punishment those who were accused of accessory crimes, since actions, no matter how brutal, were deemed irrelevant to a determination predicated on "base motives."[76] Second, retroactivity policy invites arguments against the imposition of new standards of justice, in response to unprecedented prevalent mass violence, about what constitutes a crime. The counterargument, asserting a transcendent criterion for crimes against humanity—a presumption at the heart of the imprescriptibility principle—is persuasive and would have concentrated German attention to the ubiquity of criminal collaboration, but the policy nonetheless casts doubt on the credibility of political justice.

The third problem with justice proceedings is the risk of harming victims, a risk that can outweigh the benefits of self-expression and self-respect for victims serving as witnesses. The testimony of K-Zetnik 135633 (aka Ka-Tzetnik) during the Eichmann trial is frequently summoned to illustrate this point, in part because of dramatic extant documentary footage.[77] Yehiel Dinur adopted a name whose initials, K-Z—letters referring to the German word for concentration camp (*Konzentrationslager*)—would indicate how traumatized he was after spending two years in German captivity. At one moment during his testimony, a judge interrupted him with instructions: "Please listen to Mr. Hausner [the chief prosecutor] and to me," at which he succumbed and fell from the witness stand to the floor. This episode exhibits emotions victims often feel during adversarial cross-examination. Hearing a command from the bench, Dinur, it seems, re-experienced what he endured at Auschwitz. Victims also report feeling alienated and demoted when they recognize that their testimonies are in service to the interests of the state, for the social good, and not in recognition of their personal need for expression, often to condemn wrongdoing.[78] Efforts at reforming the process to preserve victims' rights and interests make clear the perils of victim participation in criminal justice proceedings.[79] Finally, as an instrument of transition, criminal trials also risk provoking a backlash from stakeholders in predecessor regimes. This was a concern in Argentina with the transition from the 1976–83 military dictatorship to the presidency of Raúl Alfonsín. As an adviser to the president, Malamud-Goti opposed the consequentialist argument for punishing state criminals, asserting that prosecutions of military commanders in chief, who were responsible for masterminding repression, could destabilize the new order by provoking military coups and noncooperation.[80]

Not only survivors' defeated expectations, but also the practical limitations of criminal-justice procedures that are hard-put to evaluate crimes when they are normative, give rise to alternative, forward-looking measures, including forgiveness. A body of thought confirms forgiveness as a more appropriate response to massive wrongdoing than criminal justice, though definitions of forgiveness vary considerably. Jacques Derrida observed that "the order of politics or of the juridical as they are ordinarily understood" cannot fully deal with extraordinary crimes and criminals.[81] Paul Ricoeur believed that forgiveness provides a "consideration due to every human being" that "institutions responsible for punishment" cannot.[82] Julia Kristeva argued that forgiving the unforgivable, though "utopian," permits an opening to seeing extraordinary criminals "without judgment and punishment."[83]

As an essential and promising part of the TRC's amnesty–forgiveness framework, the commission encouraged victims to grant forgiveness without the precondition of perpetrators' remorse or moral correction not only to help smooth the transition to a reconciled order but also to exhibit, as Tutu commended, a "remarkable generosity of spirit."[84] The TRC was an archetype of maximalism: "In the act of forgiveness," Tutu implored, "we are declaring our faith in the future of a relationship … [W]e are saying here is a chance to make a new beginning. It is an act of faith the wrongdoer can change."[85] But for all the consideration it has received, forgiveness is a hazardous measure. Survivors and TJ critics acknowledge this without, however, jettisoning it. The defining concern is not the act of forgiveness itself but the pressure behind it to hasten reconciliation. Several TRC critics observed the coercive constraints on victims to forgive, since the state's security depended on them to surrender negative reactive attitudes and their potential for reigniting conflict. Mainly for this reason, detractors pointed to the confusion of personal and political forgiveness, granting only the former plausibility.[86] Verdeja concluded that "the institutionalization [of forgiveness] as a prime mechanism for reconciliation is deeply problematic."[87] Sisonke Msimang, a former executive director of the Open Society Initiative for Southern Africa, articulated citizens' disenchantment with the TRC framework for the post-apartheid succession: "We have lived with choreographed unity for long enough to know that we now prefer acrimonious and robust disharmony." Referring to the background of heightened concern leading to the state's ratification of the commission, he continued: "We see reconciliation as part of a narrative that was constructed on the basis of anxieties that are no longer relevant: Democracy has taught us that raised voices don't have to lead to war."[88]

Survivors, who weighed in on the prospects of forgiveness, were also skeptical that the disposition could accomplish anything more than a reckless reconciliation. They regarded it as naïve and dangerously permissive, if not complicit, in the tenuous aftermath of civil conflict, a position that Améry articulated. How, he asked, could he comply with the wishes of his contemporaries and "internalize our past suffering" in order to clear the way forward? For him and other survivors, "a fresh, calm look toward the future is too difficult."[89] Cultural pressures rather than institutional were survivors' concern and a source of their resentment. According to this view, when injuries are great, forgiveness pales as an abstraction. How is forgiveness virtuous when offenders, habituated to wrongdoing, remain prone to injustice while victims, traumatized by exposure to violence, are irredeemably scarred? By making it easier to forget past wrongs, doesn't forgiveness give offenders a pass and defeat transitional aspirations to moral order?[90] Corroborating this position, many argue that forgiveness's appeal to victims' magnanimity would actually hurt them, for it is ultimately a capitulation and would rob them of retributive emotions that articulate a sense of self-worth.[91] It would also deny them the opportunity to mourn and parley losses into new configurations.[92] From this rigorous perspective, the onus properly falls on institutional reform, not on victims' generosity (or on criminal justice), for assuring a promising transition: "A primary emphasis of political reconciliation," wrote Murphy, "should be on ending violence and addressing the institutional and social conditions that make violence possible."[93] Malamud-Goti, the Argentine adviser, argued for institutional and military reform as the key to transition.[94] Forgiveness is set back considerably in this perspective and disappears entirely from reconciliation schemes. For victims, the transition can proceed without forgiveness by achieving understanding, working toward stable relations, and expressing condemnation, though not necessarily the divisive demand for punishment.[95]

TJ proponents and survivors give forgiveness a second chance as a transitional measure by qualifying the notion in order to permit an unhurried evaluation of the offender and the offense. In TJ theory, restorative justice practices elucidate this approach. If not for its key amnesty provision, the TRC, itself, is the classic articulation of restorative justice. This practice brings victims and offenders together to deal with the aftermath of an offense. As an interpersonal mechanism, restorative justuce procedures convene mediation or group conferences centered on victims' expectations that offenders will make voluntary reparation. Elective recourse to the state, including judicial procedure, for enforcing the terms of an agreement confers credibility on the process as "whole" justice.[96] Reparations commonly include a review of the offense, a willingness to hear the victim's account, and offenders' expressions of sincere remorse as measured by acknowledging responsibility for wrongdoing, recognizing harm, and committing to rightful behavior as well as compensatory service or material restitution.[97] In satisfaction of these conditions, victims are likely to be assured and, accordingly, express forgiveness.[98] In civic and political context, citizens' and state institutions' expressive affirmation of apology for wrongdoing, backed by reparations and other TJ measures, can have the effect of attenuating victims' resentment, earning back their trust, and inspiring forgiveness.[99] Janna Thompson argued that citizens, by virtue of their membership in an "intergenerational" polity, are collectively responsible for apologizing for past injustices as a national and transitional undertaking.[100]

It is worth asking if the TRC could have avoided some of its harshest criticism had it observed the recommendations, issued a decade earlier by South African theologians, for mandating the practice of conditional forgiveness; that is, requiring offenders to express remorse before inviting victims to forgive. The statement, known as the Kairos Document,[101] was drafted in the black townships of Soweto after the apartheid government's declaration of a state of emergency. It challenged the "Church Theology" of English-speaking South African churches for proposing a "counterfeit reconciliation," arguing that the proposal would merely bring two sides together without acknowledging that "one side is right and the other is wrong." In conflicts between justice and injustice, "No reconciliation, no forgiveness and no negotiations are possible *without repentance*." The Promotion of National Unity and Reconciliation Act, the 1995 law empowering the TRC to provide for amnesty, stipulated the condition of full disclosure but not contrition. All that offenders were required to do for amnesty protection was to provide an accurate accounting of their misdeeds. To be fair, the amnesty provision helped ensure the cooperation of privileged whites in possession of power to negotiate the terms of peace. Even in its limited mandate, it shamed those confessing to their political crimes through interrogation in a public setting by the Amnesty Committee as well as by victims or victims' counsel.[102] It also exposed a breadth of complicity, which eludes criminal justice prosecution, while culling a verifiable documentary record.[103] But apologies were off the table, as state president P. W. Botha made clear: "I do not apologize for the struggle against the Marxist revolutionaries."[104]

There is considerable reworking in survivors' counter-narratives that suggests inclinations to forgive offenders even as they declared their refusal to so. Améry and Wiesenthal discerned the humanity in their enemies, Wiesenthal more extensively than Améry; Jankélévitch, in his idiosyncratic parlance, addressed "the pure hominity of the man"; that is, the "essence."[105] They did so intimately with expressions inflected with emotion that bent the conceptual arc of their counter-narratives toward forming new relationships. Not only did Améry recognize the fellow man in the antiman, his torturer. In recalling an encounter with a member of the Gestapo, he also confessed to an "intimate cordiality," detecting in his opponent a "potential friend."[106] Wiesenthal perceived something "good" in the dying SS officer who requested his audience, and in exploring the relationship he found the prospect magnetic. Twice he admitted to feeling "sympathy" for the officer, who, as Wiesenthal observed, had participated in killing defenseless Jews:[107] "I noticed that the dying man had a warm undertone in his voice as he spoke about Jews."[108] The officer never said he was repentant, but Wiesenthal believed he was.[109] These were swerves in his account of earnest condemnation that germinated a process to "help me regain my faith in humanity."[110] Jankélévitch limned the "truth" of "brotherhood,"[111] but, more than an idea or an abstraction, it implied "an effort and relates to the future."[112] Terms like "hominity" ("humanness") and "ipseity" ("essence") intellectualized his argument for forgiveness, but forgiveness for him, like other survivors, was sentiment-based: his "love for humans" was "most sacred."[113] In light of these narrative tendencies, it appears that survivors were disposed to forgiveness, the type of forgiveness that is transitional. Their transitional predilections are discernible in their accounts' counter-narratives that look outward to a world they have learned to distrust and forward to a world they seek to negotiate. They comprise distinctive, if inarticulate or impermanent, passages that interrupt backward-looking, salient narratives—strong narratives that bear witness to crimes and condemn historical bloodlust as well as contemptuous contemporary indifference—with dreams and digressions in search for an opening to human fellowship—Améry's longing for home; Jankélévitch's generous, though partial and volatile, conception of forgiveness; and Wiesenthal's searching references to a human connection. This is fertile, tactile material promising successor societies a blueprint unencumbered by an impatience for resolution—what Jacques Derrida called staging—"in the service of a finality" (*à chaque fois que le pardon est au service d'une finalité*).[114] Customarily impervious to external pressures or ulterior motives, it avoids what Jankélévitch called a "hasty reconciliation"[115] and instead produces a more pliable and necessarily elastic basis for transition. Witnesses' accounts offer a demanding conceptual alternative to transitional justice theories for a deep and promising aftermath.

Conceptual divergence

The similarities between transitional justice theories and survivors' accounts are strong, though the closer we look, the clearer do procedural differences and other important qualifications appear. Survivors' conceptions, and in part TJ's—Thompson's intergenerational imperatives—are both expressions in the domain of civil society. Their endeavors not only play out in public settings but also play to an attentive public. This was both the bane and boon of the TRC, for it could be seen as play-acting in scripted roles,[116] while others have noted its importance as a ritual of reflection, public engagement, and shared community identity,[117] even if the latter in transitional procedures, by bringing adversaries together, is difficult to achieve and may reignite antagonisms.[118] On the smaller scale of "group conferencing," restorative justice advocates regard the involvement of community members—family members, a teacher or an employer, neighbors, etc.—as beneficial for supporting an offender's reform.[119] Survivors' accounts are also expressions "from below." Their intimate expressions are located in counter-narratives where the relationship with an inhospitable and untrustworthy world is subject to interrogation. Counter-narratives, like transitional justice, are forward-looking.

But at this point, survivors' accounts diverge from the principles of transitional justice. Unlike TJ's involvement and dialogue with other parties, especially the state, survivors' accounts postulated a society in transition on their own terms, as independent agents. Though committed to renegotiating difficult relationships and responding to exigent concerns—in the 1960s, they spoke out against impending statutory limitations and other political machinations that defied accountable memory in postwar Germany—their accounts were asymmetrical expressions, essentially monologues in the heat of a national debate. Their freedom from functional relations with the state—indeed, the state seemed to them hopelessly inept—conferred not only unfettered expression but also the license to posit forgiveness as unconditional. Victims, not offenders by expressing remorse, were to begin the process. (This, of course, was a TRC premise as well, but its consequentialist thrust compromised victims' free expressions.) By the time they elected to publish their accounts, they had relinquished whatever hope they invested in conditional forgiveness: Améry and Jankélévitch looked in vain for pronouncements of apology or at least national self-understanding, concluding that they would never materialize;[120] Wiesenthal appealed to Germans for understanding,[121] though he came to feel unsure who, if anyone, would listen. In fact, survivors were not confident in their accounts' potential to influence their readers. "I am not at all speaking with the intention to convince," Améry wrote.[122]

Their retreat from expecting apologies illuminates a larger significance: It represents a worldview. They came to a point of not expecting anything. This perspective is one of the major critiques of transitional justice that witnesses to catastrophe are inclined to offer, for the reconciled society aspires to a reconstruction based on expectations that members will share and support justly regnant norms for "common life." De Greiff's normative conception of transitional justice is a conception witnesses did not accept. Having fatally misplaced their trust in institutions that promised protection and in neighbors who were their compatriots, why would they ever again come "to expect a certain pattern of behavior"?[123] After witnessing the collapse of civil order, how likely would citizens feel "sufficiently confident" in their ruling institutions, and how "sufficiently secure" would they feel in their fellow citizens' "commitment to abide by and uphold" basic norms and values?[124] Reconciliation is a worthy ambition, but if "we always risk having our expectations defeated,"[125] does it promise too much?

Expecting mutuality was a presumption Jews embraced before their devastating experiences with betrayal. It was at the heart of the emotional relationships they had with their neighbors, relationships woven from the material of Enlightenment and emancipation credo that promised a new order of social integration for pariah Jews. Embarking on this hopeful journey, they didn't just assimilate to native dress, language, and customs; they were fundamentally and interminably attached to European society. "With tears in our eyes," Jankélévitch implored his contemporaries for even "a single word of understanding and sympathy."[126] Here was an echo of Herzl's loyal Jewish patriots, "sometimes superloyal";[127] memoirist Freddie Knoller's "sense of belonging";[128] as well as Améry's "first love" for his homeland[129] and Wiesenthal's forebears' aspirations "to be recognized by their fellow creatures."[130] Acts of betrayal literally split their memories into two dichotomous narratives. Vestiges of an emotional connection lingered in counter-narratives as recognition in their assailants of the compatriots they once knew, or as a longing for human fellowship; negative, reactive emotions of resentment and recrimination, as a result of violated promises, governed their accounts' main conceit. Betrayal ended the regime of expectation. Jews who survived systematic and merciless assault articulated brokenness in their post-conflict lives. "We dwell indefinitely on the litanies of bitterness," wrote Jankélévitch. "This matter will not be easily settled,"[131] a view shared by Améry who asserted that "no conflict is settled."[132] They declared their loss of trust—a manifest assertion in Améry's account: "Whoever has succumbed to torture can no longer feel at home in the world"[133]—and berated themselves for their shameful credulity, Wiesenthal's "incorrigible" optimism.[134] Simultaneously, they evoked enduring ancestral memories that activated dreams of a human connection. In narrative tandem, they imagined a world pieced together from the fragments, but not, as before, in covenantal partnership. Liberated once from the camps and ghettos and hiding places and fugitive desperation, survivors sought a second liberation to a world in transition that they would negotiate without any expectation of help whatsoever. "If I am to have trust," wrote Améry, "I must feel on it only what I *want* to feel."[135]

So how do survivors imagine relationships between victims and victimizers in post-conflict societies? In this, too, survivors' accounts depart from transitional justice theory, forming an alternative witness paradigm. The two transitional conceptions branch off in their answers to the questions, How far should societies in transition go toward reintegrating offenders? To what extent should victims shed their reactive emotions for the sake of the public good? How do witnesses' preconceptions of negotiation compare with transitional theories of reconciliation? Reintegrating offenders became an especially important concern in societies transitioning from periods of massive wrongdoing since most of them escaped or were exempted from interrogation. Recognition of this limitation compelled TJ theorists and survivors to re-examine the proper course for dealing with countless wrongdoers at large. In order to move forward, TJ theorists and practitioners assert that it is important to restore offenders to the community by reaching a "settlement" with the past, as P. E. Digeser argued. Settlement meant that the effects of the past "should no longer reverberate into the future."[136] In the process, the community releases transgressors from obligations and restores their place in civil society. This alternative to punishment skirts criminal accountability, as Digeser and others acknowledged,[137] but he offered several remedies: offenders must be prepared to apologize, express remorse, and provide reparations; the state must seek at least a minimum of justice; and the community must be wary of backsliding. In other words, reintegration is probationary: the community is "committed to sustaining an ongoing" political relationship.[138] Digeser's argument is committed to "opening the future and settling the past,"[139] to reaching "closure" with the history of wrongdoing.[140] Reintegrating offenders in the reconciled society "provides a way to start anew."[141]

This and more was the objective of the TRC. It aspired not only to offenders' reintegration but also to their moral renewal. Though susceptible to accusations of impunity and a "hasty reconciliation," the commission regarded its role as cautionary, using the threat of prosecution and punishment to coax offenders toward confession in exchange for amnesty. But in practice most offenders, including political leaders and military personnel, avoided both the hearings and prosecution.[142] In spite of the imperfections, defenders consider its accomplishments and, indeed, the process itself as transitional and transformative. In addition to exposing crimes and criminals through shaming and for the record, the TRC confirmed the successor state's moral legitimacy by exhibiting its political sovereignty and influence in commissioning the hearings and establishing regular and fair procedures, such as equal treatment of similar cases.[143]

But whether the state's transitional construct was a rite of passage for a transgressive society, whether, as Tony F. Marshall presumed, there was a "change of heart,"[144] is open to question. Raquel Adana argued that "lesser sanctions," such as confessions or unsolicited apology, do not satisfy customary standards of accountability and fail to inspire trust in the state's administration of justice.[145] Nor was there any program for incorporating, beyond restoring, offenders into the reconciled South African society. Though the amnesty provision was neither hasty nor a "counterfeit" reconciliation, it didn't possess the probationary rigor recommended in schemes outlined by Digeser. It looked vigorously forward but, as Tutu observed, it regarded reconciliation as a matter of faith—"faith in the future of a relationship … faith [that] the wrongdoer can change."

In light of the Frankfurt trial's shortcomings as fair justice, much less exemplary justice, survivors also contemplated the prospects of reintegrated offenders, but they didn't rely on faith in the future or in the state, nor did they expect a change of heart. They weren't even prepared to settle the past. This perspective signals another key difference between victims in witnessing roles and the transitional justice model. Survivors were prepared to consider positive relationships with offenders even as they condemned them, a noteworthy nuance in their accounts. Indeed, they expressed a desire and a search for relationships with the unreconstructed—Jankélévitch's "love for the wicked person,"[146] or Améry's and Wiesenthal's "potential friend" and "sympathy" with the enemy. They sometimes gave themselves momentary permission to imagine a change of heart and indulged the fantasy that they could influence it. When Wiesenthal claimed to detect repentance in the SS officer's confession, it is just as likely as not that he thought or hoped his close, sympathetic attention had an effect on fulfilling the prophecy. Améry dreamt that his expressions of resentment would serve the purpose of transforming Nazi crimes into "a moral reality for the criminal, in order that he be swept into the truth of his atrocity."[147] For Jankélévitch, forgiveness possessed a potential for inducing change: The wicked person "has much need of our help"[148] and forgiving unconditionally could provide it: it seeks to "transfigure the guilty person"[149] and is "capable of regenerating the sinner."[150] Even if they recognized the grandiosity of their dreams, the wish expressed a longing, an irrepressible urge for reconnecting with their betrayers. How much more luminous is this urge to see a "human essence" in their enemies than conceptions of reintegration based on notions of morally adequate relationships and "recognition respect." In the end forgiveness, for Jankélévitch, is a spontaneous and gratuitous gesture that exceeds "meaning"[151] and anything instrumental: That the father "welcomes the repentant son into the house is just and understandable. But to embrace him, … this constitutes the inexplicable, the unjust, the mysterious great feast of Forgiveness."[152] Behind this passage lurked vestiges of ancestral memory recalling an archaic attachment to their neighbors before the collapse in relationships. Indeed, Jankélévitch's "mysterious great feast of Forgiveness" (*La mystérieuse grande fête du Pardon*) recalled the Jewish Day of Atonement (*fête du Grand Pardon*), a reference localizing the wish for renewal as a historically Jewish quest. His wish for a word of sympathy signaling a change of heart was, indeed, a deeply felt yearning. "We have wished for it," Jankélévitch asserted, "this fraternal word!"[153] The transformation would surely never occur, but their counterfactual assertions constituted an emotional consummation. "Hypothetically," Améry proclaimed, "two groups of people, the overpowered and those who overpowered them, would be joined in the desire that time be turned back and, with it, that history become moral." It would amount to "the eradication of ignominy."[154]

These dreams ultimately collided with what Améry called "an enormous perception at a later stage."[155] He would "sometimes hope" that writing about Auschwitz and torture "could concern all those who wish to live together as fellow human beings."[156] It is a grand articulation of reconciliation. The sentence just before, however, diminishes the indulgence: The Germans, "in their overwhelming majority do not, or no longer, feel affected by the darkest and at the same time most characteristic deeds of the Third Reich." Turning a new page, much as he wanted to, wasn't possible. Too much history and too few signs of reconciliation—either for a world in a hurry to forget or for victims who could not forget—complicated survivors' search for a basis of life in synchrony with offenders. Too much knowledge, as well. In recalling what seemed like unbroken homeland kinship before the unanticipated breakdown, Améry recognized just how complacent he had been. "Home is security … . At home we are in full command of the dialectics of knowledge and recognition, trust and confidence."[157] But he came to grasp the illusion: "We, however, had not lost our country, but had to realize that it had never been ours. For us, whatever was linked with this land and its people was an existential misunderstanding."[158] A realistic evaluation of a tarnished world required less faith and more suspicion.[159]

Jankélévitch recognized that a propensity to misdeeds was integral to the human condition. "Incessantly the wall [of wickedness] reappears ahead of this goodness" of forgiveness.[160] In his conception of an "oscillation" between moral polarities elaborated at the end of *Forgiveness*—gratuitous forgiveness and interminable misdeeds—he made clear that a society that readmits offenders would have to concede that malevolence is "infinite." Forgiveness, yes; but also evil: "Love is strong like death, but death is strong like love."[161] That German people avoided self-examination only confirmed survivors' cautionary skepticism. Améry yielded to fleeting thoughts of Germans' swearing off their "past acquiescence in the Third Reich"[162] but declared, "Nothing of the sort will happen." Instead, they will regard the Nazi past as merely a historical aberration—a popular excuse and evasion—and "reject the moral demands of our resentment."[163] Jankélévitch's observations were similarly unsparing: "The Germans are an unrepentant people."[164] Reconciliation was unlikely, he believed, because any pretense to making amends was merely face-saving, a response to the pressures of the moment, and therefore specious. Austrians staged their pursuit of criminals "reluctantly and without conviction," a result, he said, of recognizing themselves in them.[165] Wiesenthal refrained from fulfilling the dying SS officer's final wish for forgiveness, in spite of his belief in humanity's grounded nexus: "There are requests that one simply cannot grant."[166] His account opened up possibilities, but prodigious memories of what he had experienced sullied the journey—the authorities who threw their prey "into the death chamber";[167] a guard who "passed the time by beating up the prisoners";[168] behavior, overall, characteristic of "beasts"[169] or a "monster"[170] that made clear who the real subhumans were. His faith was not Tutu's: if he reserved a belief in a future of relationships, it didn't include a "faith [that] the wrongdoer can change." The world that he witnessed and now inherited would never look the same as it did under the sign of Enlightenment ideals. Putting the lie to the watchwords "never again," he insisted that what had happened could, indeed, happen again.[171]

The difference between survivors' estimation of historical injustice and TJ theorists' is a matter of degree, not kind, but the difference is significant. It amounts to disagreements over whether societies in conflict can achieve reconciliation or would remain unreconciled. For survivors, the past couldn't be settled; the salient emotions that inhabited it still live on—and this is true for ancestral attachments as well as for broken expectations. Their reactive emotions, expressed so strongly in primary narratives of condemnation, are uncompromising, if disciplined by the task of legible communication. TJ proponents, on the other hand, maintain that the past "should no longer reverberate into the future." This doesn't mean that the TJ model abjures reactive emotions in transitional societies. Indeed, it validates the existence of victims' great bitterness; erasing resentment, especially in transitional contexts where wrongdoing remains formidable, would be naïve and dangerous.[172] In fact, the model regards resentment as emotionally expressive and salutary: as moral protest, it enfranchises victims with a sense of self-respect. As Murphy argued, it "communicates the belief that one has been wronged."[173] Resentment, as Walker noted, also serves a significant transitional purpose by seeking to check the resurgence of wrongdoing for the sake of "mending" in society "what a wrong has damaged,"[174] and is especially important when wrongdoers attempt to suppress others' sense of justice. It rallies a counterforce to the harmful accretions of recognizable faults "out of a sense of necessity to participate in the repair the community itself needs."[175] To this extent, survivors confirm the model. Even if Améry realized that his expression of resentment was futile, he, too, championed resentment as a counterforce and devoted an essay to the subject.[176] It was an "emotional source of every genuine morality" but parts ways from TJ's instrumentalism in observing that it offered "little or no chance at all to make the evil work of the overwhelmers bitter for them."[177] He refused "to become the accomplice of my torturers" by relenting, which, if resentful emotions subside too much, Murphy characterized as a "form of complicity in the maintenance of oppression and injustice" during periods of perilous transition.[178] Jankélévitch, too, asserted the indispensability of bitter memory: "Only one source remains: to remember, to gather one's thoughts. Here where we can 'do' nothing we can at least *feel*, inexhaustibly." Moral protest confirmed the need for self-expression, for expressing resentment "maintains the sacred flame of disquiet."[179]

But the TJ model is decisively forward-looking whereas survivors are both forward- and backward-looking, a double narrative that essentially distinguishes their worldview. Theorists are dedicated to easing relationships between former adversaries and therefore regard resentment ultimately, or at least potentially, as an impediment. This was patently Tutu's concern in framing the discourse of South Africa's transition to a reconciled, post-apartheid order. He believed that negative emotions were altogether counterproductive: "Harmony, friendliness, community are great goods. Social harmony is for us the *Summum Bonum*—the greatest good. Anything that subverts, that undermines this sought-after good, is to be avoided like the plague. Anger, resentment, lust for revenge, even success through aggressive competitiveness, are corrosive of this good."[180] Remembering the past, as long as it was "respectful"[181] and didn't interfere with "healing, harmony, and reconciliation,"[182] was legitimate; it was, after all, necessary for establishing a truthful record. But resentment was another matter: forgiveness, as a measure of "restoring broken relationships,"[183] involved "seeking to forego [*sic*] bitterness, renouncing resentment, moving past old hurt, and becoming a survivor rather than a passive victim."[184] The transition from victim to survivor is an important observation. It involves a process of acquiring agency and gaining perspective, a measure of emotional control, by means of retrospection and prospection. But it doesn't necessarily include "renouncing resentment."

Keeping to more moderate ambitions—the ideal of democratic reciprocity—TJ adherents confirm the risks of indulging resentment. De Greiff argued that resentment interfered with reconciliation, making clear that a "normative conception of transitional justice," the title of an article he wrote, has a hard time accommodating the emotion. As he wrote, "An 'unreconciled' society, then, would be one in which resentment characterizes the relations between citizens and between citizens and their institutions."[185] As we have seen, not all theorists regard resentment as toxic, though de Greiff misread Walker to make his case. He suggested that she, too, regarded the sentiment as an obstruction responsible, in his words, for "the defeat, or the threat of defeat," of normative expectations that regulate reconciled relationships.[186] Surely resentment would defeat reconciliation if it were uncontrollable. In truth, they are in agreement: resentment is compatible with reconciliation as a pre-emptive response to wrongdoing for the sake of a higher cause when it reiterates and enforces shared standards. Yet her more tolerant regard for resentment still casts resentment as an emotion to manage. Whenever the "trust we place in each other ... is disappointed," she argued, citizens would have to be "disposed" toward maintaining shared standards and relying on others for restoring them in order for moral relations to function. In other words, the "right relationship" doesn't allow for persistent resentment. "Repair" is the objective.[187]

As theories of reconciliation, there is, of course, something pure in their conceptions, what Christopher Kutz called "a dream" of equality and the common good.[188] Murphy persuasively argued that ideals, such as reconciliation, are not, however, as "remote" as they seem: they "provide guidance on the social conditions that need to be fostered so that the ideal becomes more practically feasible in the future."[189] Repair is, then, an accessible state of affairs. But in the end, the model transitional justice asserts structurally neglects and glosses over the tenacious nature of victims' resentful emotions after atrocity. From their perspective "from below," their granular emotions remain nonideal. What guides their transitions are their lived resentments, not some ideal, which, to them, remains remote or, for Améry, "abstractive." Victims remind us again and again that resentment is a *conditio sine qua non* of transitions. It is a point TJ theorists tend to elide. Creating a new political community and an "entirely new national consciousness," Kutz wrote, means "erasing ... festering resentments" resulting from historical injustice.[190] Marshall argued that unresolved differences between victims and perpetrators could be "settled" in restorative justice proceedings: "After a successful meeting both parties can effectively draw a line under the experience," including "any remaining bad feelings or fears."[191] The argument recalls Digeser's, which equated "opening the future" with "settling the past."[192] To underscore the point, Digeser observed, "Not only is the past settled but also the expectation is created that the settlement will be durable."[193] Some theorists believe that reconciliation is a matter of institutional reform and shouldn't depend on the evolution of victims' emotions. "In the context of political reconciliation, such external changes should be of central interest," Murphy observed.[194] But even here, when the process of transition is structural, internal changes are anticipated, for the goal is "the prevention of future conflict."[195] Teitel, in a moment of exuberance, proclaimed transition's dedicated gaze to the future: "Societies move in a liberal direction, through processes that allow transformation and the possibility of redemptive return."[196]

After witnessing "normative" brutality and reflecting on violated promises, survivors could no more imagine their own "internal changes" than they could imagine an offender "swept into the truth of his atrocity." Jankélévitch recognized the great, general desire to move forward. But for him the "nightmare" was just as great: "We think about it during the day; we dream about it at night." He knew these thoughts would distress his contemporaries: "This is doubtless what the brilliant advocates of statutory limitations will call our resentment, our inability to settle the past." But they, not him, impeded understanding: "Was that past ever a present for them?" For him, settling the past was impossible. The resentment he felt was simply inexhaustible.[197] For Améry, the past was destiny. Germans might believe that history discredited malicious behavior and that it was an "operational mishap … in which the broad masses of German people had no part" anyway.[198] But that viewpoint merely rekindled a new conflict, this time over evaluating the past. Germans already indulged "the industrial paradise of the new Europe." Améry, on the other hand, was in no mood for "reconciliation … with my enemies, who had just been converted to tolerance."[199] As an instance of *Vergangenheitspolitik*—of defining the relationship with the past—he was resolute in preserving his resentment, "my personal protest against the antimoral process of healing that time brings about."[200] Indeed, the more Germans moved toward "overcoming" the past, the more his resentments increased.[201] Wiesenthal recognized the lust for power as a human condition: Those who supported Nazism "expressed the contempt of the strong for the weak, the superman's scorn for the subhuman."[202] For him, past and present, like murderers and victims who were "made of the same stuff,"[203] were ultimately indistinguishable. Like Jankélévitch and Améry, he believed that any inclination to the future was inexorably freighted with an awareness borne of history. The dying officer, who confessed to his crimes against Jews, appealed to him, but he couldn't be sure "if he would have committed further crimes had he survived."[204] Nor could he be sure if his contemporaries were prepared to build a solid future. Most Germans "had probably never even had their ears boxed" and yet were eager to put the past to rest.[205] Tenacious doubts like these obstructed healing and repair; for survivors, that was the way it must be.

The negotiable society

Survivors tantalize us about an imagined future addled with contradictions. For them, the future could somehow accommodate a longing for fellowship along with deep suspicions about human behavior. Transitional justice presumes a different outcome after political conflict. In proposing renewed relationships, it requires practical compromises, like sharing values and exercising common, mutual respect. Whether survivors' forward-looking conceptions of gratuitous forgiveness and infinite malevolence are impractical, however, is debatable. Indeed, they are arguably less elusive than the TJ model of reconciliation, if only because they sound emotional disquiet that responds to extreme situations and account for extraordinary emotional intensity that these situations inherently arouse and relentlessly sustain.

In TJ perspective, the reconciled society places a premium on achieving a working equilibrium between former adversaries who could at any time return to the cycle of violence. For minimalists, the requirement is mere coexistence, a civil arrangement to avoid a resumption of conflict. There is little effort at representing the interests of victims, such as retribution or restitution for wrongdoing, or, symbolically, their enfranchisement as citizens with standing. Doing so runs the risk of reigniting offenders' hostilities and repressive passions as well as victims' desire for revenge. Hard feelings remain dormant. For some theorists, the bar set by minimalists is too low to merit recognition as reconciliation.[206] For maximalists, the requirement is social harmony. In Tutu's words, "You are generous, you are hospitable, you are friendly and caring and compassionate. You share what you have. It is to say, 'My humanity is caught up, is inextricably bound up, in yours.'"[207] The aim of the TRC was to establish the foundation of interdependent relationships. As consequentialist, it didn't always honor victims' lingering emotions of anger and resentment or the freedom to disagree or protest. The public good was paramount: "He or she has a proper self-assurance that comes from knowing that he or she belongs in a greater whole."[208]

Charting a different path to succession, democratic reciprocity has managed to augment the victim's "voice" in the process of mending relationships and achieving reconciliation. In this articulation, transitional justice is distinguished as victim-centered, providing material and moral satisfaction from the 1980s on by means of truth commissions, reparations, official apologies, commemorations and memorials, and education mandates. In the 1990s and 2000s, the United Nations codified a series of reports and principles addressing victims' rights, including the right to know and the right to justice.[209] Unlike maximalists' presumptions, arguments for reciprocity or mutual respect, which reside at the core of a broadly posited and, in Crocker's view, a "more demanding" TJ reconciliation theory,[210] permit and encourage a recognition of victims' expressions of dissent, outrage, condemnation, and moral protest as intrinsically worthy, so long as they are reasoned and deliberative.[211] As Darwall and Walker noted, respect for victims grants them authority, or standing, to make claims, which, moreover, in Walker's words, "reasonably require consideration of others."[212] Respect for offenders also applies. As Linda Radzik observed, restorative-justice encounters "seem to show respect for offenders' agency. They are treated as people who are capable of both understanding and being motivated by their moral obligations to others."[213] Darwall described the relationship as "person to other persons," or "second-personal standing" that require mutual respect for a "community of mutually accountable equals."[214]

Mutual respect, however, is a "thin," if virtuous, conception of reconciled relationships. Hannah Arendt importantly noted that respect "is a kind of 'friendship' without intimacy and without closeness. It is a regard for the person from the distance which the space of the world puts between us."[215] If we examine what TJ theorists mean by respect, we will note the thinness of reconciled arrangements, a considerable aspiration toward political stability but with little feeling for the limit experiences of brutal repression and its emotional consequences. Both Crocker and Walker, for example, refer to the reasonableness of reconciled relationships as a means of inhibiting risky expression.[216] How notably distant their positions are from Jankélévitch's affective dream of "brotherhood" and Améry's kind of friendship with his enemies that actually felt "intimate." When Walker outlined the process of achieving reconciliation, the language she used to describe it is clinical: it constitutes "repairs that move relationships in the direction of *becoming morally adequate*."[217] We get the sense that reconciliation is a matter of triage, as Judy Barsalou and Victoria Baxter observed: "Reconciliation should be aimed conservatively, with the goal of finding ways to peacefully manage rather than to eliminate conflict."[218] Under hazardous transitional circumstances, achieving a "working moral order,"[219] as Walker wrote, is surely fundamental and might well lay the foundation for a new synthesis. But the foundation TJ theorists are committed to constitutes a deficient basis for stable social relationships since it ignores primal, irrepressible emotions. Reconciliation, as Verdeja argued, is a process in which enemies come to respect each other "and eventually form alliances with one another."[220] As Digeser observed, a "durable" reconciliation amounts to putting the past's volatility to rest so that a "civic friendship" and equal relations can ensue.[221] De Greiff homes in on the thinness of these "civic" relationships in discussing the imperatives of trust. "Civic trust" is opposed to the "thick form of trust characteristic of relations between intimates."[222] It is a "significantly thinner" disposition suitable to reconciliation among "fellow members of the same political community."[223] In the final analysis, the reconciled society is a matrix—a "calculus," as Verdeja put it—of serviceable relations. Even the term favored by theorists for maneuvering and facilitating shared standards—"mechanisms"—articulates a synchronized, mechanical conception of successor societies. With its emphasis on achieving an equilibrium comprising commitments that are common, respect that is mutual, and norms and values that are shared, reconciliation this thin is, according to de Greiff, quantifiable, amenable to "impact measurement" and "assessment." As he observed, "The normative model I offer here would lead to the articulation of indices of success."[224] The ideal of democratic reciprocity is a long way from Wiesenthal's search for a "warm undertone" in the voice of his enemy.

Survivors' experiences with atrocity cast doubt on TJ's confidence in a common moral sphere, a confidence survivors themselves once presumed but displaced after the deluge with a yearning for fellowship. As a result, their worldview of post-atrocity humanity—a compound of desire and despair—and that of transitional justice are notably discordant. Transitional justice directly engages adversaries in a process of succession, usually in collaboration with the state. Restorative justice conferences and truth commissions, which are empaneled or supervised by the state and bring victims and perpetrators together, resorting, or threatening to resort, to the criminal justice system if necessary, are primary examples. Seeking results—a transformation of relationships—the process across the board is consequentialist aspiring to what Tutu called a "greater whole." Survivors also address a difficult audience with ardent concern about relationships, either broken or in cautionary search of renewal. The act of writing, itself, established a worldly connection, indeed, a connection with anonymous others, though, as their compatriots, not with complete strangers. But they presented their stories unilaterally, maintaining a distance even as they reached out. Améry believed that whatever he wrote, he could hardly expect an echo. Nor could they count on the state or the criminal justice system for support or protection, certainly not after the fascist eclipse of political order, and not after observing the failure of postwar West German authorities to demand accountability, including a swift and complete abolition of statutory limitations. More than classical TJ mechanisms, with their typical, though not exclusive, official endorsements, their accounts, when not enlisted for depositions in a court of law, are anchored in civil society.[225] From their perch, they were free to interrogate their emotions, indulge reactive attitudes of resentment, dream extravagantly, and forgive unconditionally. By being expansive, their accounts give scope to transitions and help keep their procedures honest.

Their subjective accounts, and the wide, expressive scope their severe experiences required for them, arrived at observations that significantly diverge from transitional justice theories. Survivors' emotional expressions, regulated only by expository conventions that channel desultory traumatic memory, make clear that transition is a freighted process colonized irrevocably by the past. Jankélévitch's insistence that the fraught past is never past for those who experienced it, is at odds not only with his contemporaries' indifference—"Was that past ever a present for them?," he asked—but also with the TJ contention, in Digeser's view, that the past "should no longer reverberate into the future." Misdeeds are ineradicable. Perhaps wrongdoers can change, as Tutu maintained, but for survivors, wrongdoing is the main concern: it is here to stay. As Wiesenthal observed, what happened then could happen again. Having witnessed and experienced the nightmare of human behavior, they had come to know just how combustible relationships are. For them, transitional circumstances didn't warrant confidence and hopefulness that, for Walker, were constituent attributes. Myriad acts of ruthless betrayal made sure of that. Jews in pre-war Europe, who relied on their neighbors, trusted them, and believed in them not only as equal citizens before the law and the state but, in their hearts, as members of communities bonded together by mutual obligations, recalled the aggression against them as traumatic abandonment. "It is impossible to believe anything in a world that has ceased to regard man as man," Wiesenthal mourned.[226] Walker asserted the importance of hopefulness for "functioning moral relations." It constituted a "motivating belief that there is a possibility, even if slight, that defensible standards are shared and that individuals are disposed to respond to what the standards require."[227] For survivors, the argument is vacuous. It applied only to their beliefs before the carnage, not to conditions of transition. "Normative" malevolence was the reason for that. For Améry, faith in mutual relationships turned out to be an "emotional fraud."[228] Reflections like this, manufactured in the crucible of covenantal violations as well as corporeal violence, repudiate the transitional premise of repair. The experience of carnage makes clear that mutual skepticism, not mutual respect, is the appropriate attitude for societies in the process of unsteady and uncertain readjustment. As survivors recalled broken promises and commitments and came to recognize the disingenuous presumption of mutuality and the state's duty to protect, could it be otherwise? Jankélévitch and other survivors didn't relent. Against the wishes of those who wanted to bury the past—the "brilliant advocates of statutory limitations"—they held tight to resentment, "our inability to settle the past." Having firsthand knowledge of what neighbors are capable of, the disposition that would more effectively undergird societies in transition than civic trust is suspicion. De Greiff makes a persuasive point that trust is really trustworthiness, behavior and measures that give citizens reasons to trust. The logic implies that, had Jews ultimately grounded their trust in evidence rather than in expectations of their neighbors' and the state's steadfast allegiance to the principle of citizens' equal standing, there would have been diminishing opportunities for an escalation of hostilities that were particularly predatory. To inspire trust and confidence in the state, the reconciled society would get it right with measures like official and assertive apologies.[229] There would be no need for "vigilance," for "constant watching to see what one can and cannot get away with."[230] As Jankélévitch made clear, however, official apologies cannot restore faith or salve resentment. Perhaps "the distress" of the guilty would help, but in the end, German apologies were merely "pretended."[231] They were, in fact, self-serving: repentance for moral advantage after military defeat, "commercial repentance for business purposes, diplomatic repentance for reasons of state; their contrition is worth nothing."[232] Constant watching is precisely what transition requires for durability. Succession requires negotiation, not reconciliation, and a disposition of unrelenting, panoptic, and probationary suspicion.[233]

To rescue this conception of transition from stark nihilism, survivors' forward-looking counter-narratives—informed, like backward-looking contempt, by the past—introduced a second TJ revision. In his essay "Resentments," Améry referred, briefly, to Max Scheler, the German phenomenologist from the early twentieth century.[234] Scheler had written about resentment, disparaging it as perpetual and self-destructive malice. Améry agreed: it was the "slave morality" of the meek. But Améry manifestly objected, claiming that it was the victim's entitlement and served to leverage "the overwhelmers." Even though they both recognized resentment's futility—in the end, Améry declared his "retroactive rancor"—it's tempting to see here a recessive reference to Scheler that complements his other counter-narrative aspirations to intimate human relationships.[235] Scheler, whose legacy the Nazis buried and is only recently emerging from the shadows, wrote prodigiously about the capacity of human feelings for others. In a major work, *The Nature of Sympathy* (*Zur Phänomenologie der Sympathiegefühle und von Liebe und Hass*, 1913), Scheler argued against Freud and others that sympathetic emotions are other-directed, not self-serving. A vital urge, a craving for satisfaction, draws us to others, he argued, inspiring us to take part in others' feelings and lives. The logic of the heart, including love, is the capacity for knowing others by grasping them as kindred persons behind and beneath observable features: "If the multitude of individual spiritual persons comprising mankind as a whole are to stand revealed, and even their existence brought to light, without culpable or wanton omission of anyone, as capable of being loved as persons, a general love of humanity is requisite, and indeed indispensable."[236]

In *Forgiveness*, Jankélévitch cites a passage from *The Nature of Sympathy* about Jesus's generosity. For both observers, forgiveness was unconditional, as Jankélévitch asserted: "But *first* he forgives." Scheler's point concerned love's purity: we love others "as they are," while Jankélévitch emphasized true forgiveness: "In order to forgive, forgiveness itself did not set conditions, did not have reservations, required neither promises nor guarantees!"[237] Jankélévitch consulted Scheler as an authority on "the phenomenal aspect of love"[238] and fellow-feeling, a measure of what Jankélévitch called a sacred "love for humans."[239] Given Scheler's reputation, reinforced by his respect for him, Améry plausibly made note of his ideas as they related to magnetic human love. We find evidence of Améry's swerves to humanity in narrative asides in an essay on resentment where we would not expect it. After expounding on the collective German involvement in Nazi crimes, either by recognizing, approving, or committing them, he shifted course and reflected on those "who, in the Third Reich, broke out of the Third Reich." Revealingly, the observation, in the spirit of Scheler's worldview, was anything but thin or distant: He said he would never forget "the few brave people I encountered," adding intimately, "They are with me." A Catholic worker in Auschwitz III who "addressed me by my already forgotten first name [Hans] and gave me bread"[240] was "My Willy Schneider."[241] There is evidence, too, of Wiesenthal's wish for human fellowship. Whether or not he believed he could someday regain his "faith in humanity"—a question he left open in his accounts in light of what he wrote just before about how "years of suffering had inflicted deep wounds on my faith that justice existed in the world"[242]—what he meant by humanity, and what he wanted from it, shows a desire for something thicker than adequate and manageable social arrangements under conditions of transition, for he looked for "things which mankind needs in life besides the material."[243] Recognizing the importance of "sympathy" in his relations with the dying SS officer, we can presume that what he yearned for was the kind of relationship articulated by Scheler as "a general love for humanity." In a coda to his story about his encounter with the officer, Wiesenthal wrote about his efforts after liberation at finding the officer's mother in order to learn something more about the officer's "personality" (*Persönlichkeit*).[244] This is important, too. It suggests a desire to grasp "the person" in his enemy—no one, said Scheler, should be omitted. The world is hopelessly imperfect, survivors believed, but a connection with the persons who inhabit it remained urgent.

We have argued that that urgency was an existential response to imposed and self-imposed loneliness and an emotion conditioned by the historical circumstances of modern Jewry. We observed evidence of an attachment to their neighbors and compatriots, a sense of common fellowship, galvanized by the governing premise and promise of emancipation and by centripetal pressures of the unitary nation-state. These social ties were strong enough to withstand anti-Jewish disruptions for a century and a half. Similarly, resilient dynamics are discernible in other world regions distinguished by conditions of interethnic integration in the former Yugoslavia, Chile, and elsewhere. Even after disruptions in relations, Jewish survivors summoned residual ancestral memories of interethnic comity—real or perceived—and believed they charted a promising course to the future. Like the final calamity that fueled and sustained emotions of resentment and recrimination, memories of the past that predated it lived on. "Brotherhood," Jankélévitch's anthem, was modernity's anthem as well. Its grand appeal energized Améry and Wiesenthal's search for what is good even in adversaries. Here, too, the past was present that also "relates to the future" (Jankélévitch), awakening a longing for a significant—for Jankélévitch, an intimate[245]—human bond. To suggest, as TJ theorists do, that "mutual respect" is sufficient for reconciliation neglects the logic of the heart.

Transitional justice is an exciting work in progress and is still a large tent, but it is a movement characteristically allied with canonic, western conceptions of order—from Augustine, who counseled against the private good in favor of living "harmoniously in your house,"[246] to Hegel, who submerged disharmony to harmony; sin, as "something past, as a fragment, as a corpse," to wholeness and reconciliation.[247] The material challenges of repair demand functional theories.

Though minimalist and maximalist theories of transitional justice acknowledge limit emotions—the former in recognition of predilections toward excessive resentment, which is why nonlethal coexistence is the most minimalists can hope for; the latter in praise of an ethos of caring—TJ theories gravitate to the center, proposing an ideal of reciprocity. The legitimate role they assign to emotions ultimately defers to their restraint, for nothing should threaten the common good. Reconciliation cannot accommodate emotions when they are extreme or volatile. Like Jankélévitch, who wrote that the mature "infinite 'forgivability' of the misdeed does not in the least imply the nonexistence of evil,"[248] they concede that past conflicts are never concluded. But they are no more interested in unsettling the past than Jankélévitch was in settling it. Indeed, survivors have little choice but to live unsettled lives; in post-atrocity circumstances, achieving an equilibrium is impossible. Améry called himself a "catastrophe Jew,"[249] someone whose "disturbance" precluded his "existential balance."[250] As Wiesenthal observed, we "cannot obliterate the hell we endured."[251] A "working order," even as survivors imagined their worldly re-engagement, was, like Msimang's "choreographed unity," as illusion. As Améry noted, "I was a person who could no longer say 'we.'" The new normative posited instead an "I" representing an alienated reality he became accustomed to even if he didn't like it.[252] Along with considering possibilities, survivors came to realize what Primo Levi identified as a new moral code of "selfishness," an unavoidable reality that eclipsed presumptions of mutuality.[253] Having disclosed the full force of brutality and a contemporary indifference to right or righting relationships, the world survivors experienced and inherited exhausted their faith in repair.

Conversely, TJ proponents do not expect the kind of thick, intimate relations survivors longed for, unless it's Tutu's state of existence where "You are friendly and caring and compassionate" and, we should note, intolerant of expressive emotions that threaten disruption. Even when TJ proponent Charles Villa-Vicencio postulated an "anthropological if not primordial longing for wholeness,"[254] he cautioned restraint. "The will to be human is often a deeper ingredient" than strategic concerns in the process of reconciliation,[255] he wrote, but concluded that the human ingredient in the reconciliation process is, in fact, no deeper than living peacefully together in common pursuit of a higher cause.[256]

By giving rein to emotional extremes, our trio of survivors defied the tenets of Enlightenment rationalism. For Améry, "Enlightenment can properly fulfill its task [but] only if it sets to work with passion."[257] Even more defiant, however, was the irreconcilability of their worldviews, a tragic condition of their uneasy quest for emotional satisfaction. Two incompatible impulses motivated their decision to join the public debate in the 1960s over statutes of limitations: a refusal and a desire to move forward. Their conviction that malevolence was endemic and required, as a true measure of civic obligation, a resolute suspicion of behavior rather than trust and confidence, aroused little appetite for peace. For some observers, it is the way of a chastened world, a point Edna O'Brien poignantly observed in her novel *The Little Red Chairs*. Innocent trust in strangers is self-destructive, she observed. The villagers in her story who greeted a stranger promising so much suffered greatly because they were not distrustful enough. Skepticism is the appropriate pose.[258] Yet a desire for a connection—which survivors variously called love, fellowship, or sympathy—sought urgent expression. Enlightenment ideals of humanity continued to inspire them, but disruptive experiences of destruction discouraged anticipation.[259] Rather than veer toward hopelessness, their bifocal evaluation of transition offers a conception that suggests new terms of post-atrocity engagement. It involved a skeptical glance backward toward behavior that required vigilance and, simultaneously, a wishful glance forward that inspired a worldly engagement. For Jankélévitch, the human will to evil and deep human love, like death and life, is a condition of existence. For them, succession was post-rational, a working disorder arising from emotional disparities and a worldview of disharmony. It demanded an orientation that Leo Strauss epitomized as to "live that conflict." The secret of western civilization's vitality, he asserted, is rooted in unresolved tensions.[260]

A tragic worldview like this might offer some realism but not any apparent guideposts for navigating uncertain stages of transition. Survivors generally are not adverse to providing instruction: Their accounts are often explicit about defeating tendencies to deny their truthfulness, demanding justice, or serving as "a Warning Monument,"[261] as Levi put it. And, indeed, their dissonant narratives also chart a transitional orientation. The key is located in counter-narratives of betrayal. Their defeated pre-war expectations of a steadfast neighborly nexus under duress compelled a re-evaluation of everyday human relationships. Confident expectations of renewal are a pivotal disposition for progress toward reconciliation. For survivors, such expectations represent an extravagant, perverse mirage. The idea that citizens' confidence in a mutual commitment to just norms toward common life was a premise Jews presumed before the war, not afterward. It signified Améry's atavistic "written and unwritten social contracts," Wiesenthal's "eternal and incorrigible" optimism,[262] and Jankélévitch's faith in "mutual" relationships.[263] As survivors, they had come to see that their neighbors were not committed to common life. It was "an enormous perception at a later stage" that led Améry to assert "no help can be expected."[264] It led Wiesenthal to lament that his estimation of others, including his opponents, "was kinder than the reality,"[265] and Jankélévitch to conclude that "all men would be brothers" was frankly "naïve."[266] Their experiences with betrayal dramatically altered the axis of relatedness.

Instead of what Améry characterized as a "sham undertaking," survivors—indeed, victims who became survivors in the process—knew that if they were to move forward, as they longed to do, it would have to mean "awaiting no help."[267] If they were to find a way to their world, they would have to negotiate the terms of engagement themselves. To achieve dignity, Améry proclaimed, required a commitment "through my own effort."[268] It was an ethic Wiesel sounded a few years before in a Hebrew edition of *Night,* which he never published: "This time we are the judges [of God] and he [is] the accused. We are ready."[269] The new world of self-reliance and self-assertion would come at a considerable expense, for it would nullify the once-appealing, seductive belief in mutuality. Since "there was no order for me in this world,"[270] moving forward would require puzzling out the terms of brotherhood and a common link. As long as human fellowship remained a dream or a narrative digression, the way forward would remain inchoate and undeveloped. Moving forward would involve the high price of unsparing alertness, for they could neither trust their peers nor feel confident in their trustworthiness—in what Murphy termed a "trust-responsiveness."[271] Indeed, if they expected anything, it was some hostile threat around the next corner. Already, during his first days of exile in Belgium, Améry believed he looked at the world differently: "I was having a beer with a big, coarse-boned, squared-skulled man, who may have been a respectable Flemish citizen, perhaps even a patrician, but could just as well have been a suspicious harbor tough about to punch me in the face and lay hands on my wife."[272] This was a world that demanded negotiation, not reconciliation. It required vigilant navigation between Levi's moral code of selfishness and an ethic of care that exalts, according to Virginia Held, "the relation itself," the "self-and-other together."[273] However that relation evolves, it would begin with action in search of negotiation, not with an implicit preordained social contract delineating mutual obligations. Help, in other words, would be possible, even necessary, just not certain. Love, for Jankélévitch, would be an act, not a reaction—"unreciprocal," "asymmetrical" love.[274] This, it seems clear, is the significance of the decision many survivors made in the 1960s to publish their accounts for a general public. More than an act of writing, itself noteworthy, exposing their stories in full public view, at great risk to cynical interrogation and distortion, represented an incipient act of assertion and the will to participate, however warily, in the conversation. In considerable contrast to their muteness during the Nazi years, taking their experiences to the threshold of broad public opinion in itself charted a new beginning into uncharted territory.

Territory this uncertain is better left unfinished. It is *non-finito,* a perpetual present in constant but negotiable flux in search of elusive futures. There is no finality, not because of an unexpected disruption, like an illness or exhaustion; or unwanted interference, like war or death, but because it must be so.[275] Combining implacable suspicion with an urgent wish for consummate human fellowship is possible only if the unexpected is anticipated and the combination, itself, is variously re-created. This is surely a world of "riddles,"[276] no longer presumed or seductively secure. But beyond survivors' physical liberation from captivity, it was one that energized their second liberation with executive responsibilities and with a longing for thick, emotional human connections.

Notes

Introduction: Unseen

1 Hannah Arendt, *Eichmann in Jerusalem: A Report on the Banality of Evil* (New York: Penguin Books, 2006), 229.

2 Annette Wieviorka, *The Era of the Witness* (Ithaca, NY: Cornell University Press, 2006).

3 Primo Levi, *The Drowned and the Saved*, trans. Raymond Rosenthal (New York: Summit Books, 1988), 82.

4 Jürgen Zimmerer, "The Birth of the Ostland out of the Spirit of Colonialism: A Postcolonial Perspective on the Nazi Policy of Conquest and Extermination," *Patterns of Prejudice* 39 (2005): 218. See also Jürgen Zimmerer, "Colonialism and the Holocaust: Towards an Archeology of Genocide," in *Genocide and Settler Society*, ed. A. Dirk Moses (Oxford: Berghahn Books, 2004), 49–76; Jürgen Zimmerer and Joachim Zeller, eds, "Völkermord in Deutsch-Südwest-Afrika: Der Kolonialkrieg (1904–1908)," in *Namibia und seine Folgen* (Berlin: Christoph Links, 2003).

5 A. Dirk Moses, "Empire, Colony, Genocide: Keywords and the Philosophy of History," in *Empire, Colony, Genocide: Conquest, Occupation and Subaltern Resistance in World History* (New York: Berghahn Books, 2008), 36, 39–40; see also A. Dirk Moses, "Revisiting a Founding Assumption of Genocide Studies," *Genocide Studies and Prevention* 6 (2011): 287–300.

6 Donald Bloxham, *The Final Solution: A Genocide* (New York: Oxford University Press, 2009), 1.

7 Ibid., 315.

8 Zimmerer, "The Birth of the Ostland out of the Spirit of Colonialism," 218.

9 Marianne Hirsch and Leo Spitzer, "The Witness in the Archives," *Holocaust Studies/Memory Studies* 2 (2009): 165.

10 Daniel Levy and Natan Sznaider, "Memory Unbound: The Holocaust and the Formation of Cosmopolitan Memory," *European Journal of Social Theory* 5 (2002): 87–106.

11 Ibid., 164.

12 Ibid., 165.

13 Ibid., 92.

14 Ibid., 165.

15 See Debarati Sanyal, *Memory and Complicity: Migrations of Holocaust Remembrance* (New York: Fordham University Press, 2015) for a discussion of

French and Francophone literary and cinematic representations of transhistorical memories of violence.

16 Hirsch and Spitzer, "The Witness in the Archives," 165; Levy and Sznaider: "Can we imagine collective memories that transcend national and ethnic boundaries?" Levy and Sznaider, "Memory Unbound," 88.

17 See, for example, Natalia Aleksiun, "The Central Jewish Historical Commission in Poland, 1944–1947," *Polin: Studies in Polish Jewry* 20 (2007): 74–97; François Azouvi, *Le mythe du grand silence: Auschwitz, les français, la mémoire* (Paris: Fayard, 2012); David Cesarani and Eric J Sundquist, eds, *After the Holocaust: Challenging the Myth of Silence* (New York: Routledge, 2012); Hasia Diner, *We Remember with Reverence and Love. American Jews and the Myth of Silence After the Holocaust, 1945–1962* (New York: New York University Press, 2009); Laura Jockusch, *Collect and Record!: Jewish Holocaust Documentation in Early Postwar Europe* (New York: Oxford University Press, 2012); and Zoë Vania Waxman, *Writing the Holocaust: Identity, Testimony, Representation* (New York: Oxford University Press, 2006).

18 Diner, *We Remember with Reverence and Love,* 150–215.

19 David P. Boder, *I Did Not Interview the Dead* (Urbana: University of Illinois Press, 1949); David P. Boder, *Topical Autobiographies of Displaced People Recorded Verbatim in Displaced Persons Camps, with a Psychological and Anthropological Analysis* (Chicago: David Boder, 1950–7).

20 Laura Jockusch, "Historiography in Transit: Survivor Historians and the Writing of Holocaust History in the Late 1940s," *Leo Baeck Institute Year Book* 58 (2013): 76.

21 Ibid., 94; Jockusch, *Collect and Record!,* 4.

22 Simon Wiesenthal, *The Sunflower: On the Possibilities and Limits of Forgiveness* (New York: Schocken Books, 1998), 97.

23 Jean Améry, *At the Mind's Limits: Contemplations by a Survivor on Auschwitz and Its Realities* (Bloomington: Indiana University Press, 1980), xiii–xiv.

24 Jockusch, *Collect and Record!,* 191.

25 The phrase is the subject of an article by Jean-Paul Bier, "The Holocaust and West Germany: Strategies of Oblivion, 1947–1979," *New German Critique* 19 (1980): 9–29.

26 Wiesenthal, *The Sunflower,* 97.

27 John R. Gillis, "Memory and Identity: The History of a Relationship," *Commemorations: The Politics of National Identity*, ed. John R. Gillis (Princeton, NJ: Princeton University Press, 1994), 3–24.

28 Améry, *At the Mind's Limits,* 99.

29 Ibid., 20.

30 Testimony of "Rabbi Baruch G.," Joshua M. Greene and Shiva Kumar, eds, *Witness: Voices from the Holocaust* (New York: The Free Press, 2000), 214–15.

31 Hadassah Rosensaft, *Yesterday: My Story* (New York: Yad Vashem, 2005), 51–2.

32 Freddie Knoller and John Landaw, *Living with the Enemy: My Secret Life on the Run from the Nazis* (London: Metro Publishing, 2005), 209.

33 Améry, *At the Mind's Limits,* 9.

34 Ibid., 90. Recent research explores liberation as an ongoing process, not only as a historical moment. This was the subject of the Mauthausen Memorial Dialogue Forum (2015), https://eventmaker.at/mauthausen_memorial/7th_mauthausen_memorial_dialogue_forum (accessed June 11, 2016).

35 For a discussion of assimilation's external appropriations, see, for example, Ritchie Robertson, *The German-Jewish Dialogue: An Anthology of Literary Texts, 1749–1993* (New York: Oxford University Press, 1999), vii–xxviii.

36 See, for example, Shmuel Feiner, *The Jewish Enlightenment*, trans. Chaya Naor (Philadelphia: University of Pennsylvania Press, 2004), in which he illuminated Jews' struggle, mostly uneasily, for their place in public life; and Todd Endelman, *Leaving the Jewish Fold: Conversion and Radical Assimilation in Modern Jewish History* (Princeton, NJ: Princeton University Press, 2015): "Driven by hunger or ambition, in search of fame or status, peace of mind or even a roof over their heads, they sought relief in *radical* assimilation." (6)

37 Vladimir Jankélévitch, "Should We Pardon Them?," *Critical Inquiry* 22 (1996): 567–8. This article originated as a letter to *Le Monde,* January 3, 1965.

38 Maurice Halbwachs, "*The Social Frameworks of Memory*," in *On Collective Memory* ed. and trans. Lewis A. Coser (Chicago: University of Chicago Press, 1992), 38.

39 Paula E. Hyman, *Gender and Assimilation in Modern Jewish History: The Roles and Representation of Women* (Seattle: University of Washington Press, 1997), 10–49.

40 Améry, *At the Mind's Limits,* 17–18.

41 Ibid., 53.

42 Ibid., 84.

43 Ibid., 97.

44 Ibid.

45 Ibid., 83.

46 Ibid., 84.

47 Ibid.

48 Ibid., 82.

49 Ibid., 53.

50 Sidney Rosenfeld, "Afterword: Jean Améry: The Writer in Revolt," in *At the Mind's Limits*, trans. Sidney Rosenfeld and Stella P. Rosenfeld (Bloomsington: Indiana University Press, 1980), 106–7; Irene Heidelberger-Leonard, *The Philosopher of Auschwitz: Jean Améry and Living with the Holocaust* (London: I.B. Tauris, 2010), 49–54.

51 See Améry, *At the Mind's Limits*, 42.
52 Ibid., 43.
53 Rosenfeld, "Afterword," 106.
54 Améry, *At the Mind's Limits*, 55–7.
55 Much of the following outline highlighting Jankélévitch's accomplishments is adapted from Andrew Kelley's introduction to Vladimir Jankélévitch, *Forgiveness*, trans. Andrew Kelley (Chicago: University of Chicago Press, 2005), vii–xxvii.
56 Vladimir Jankélévitch, "Le judaïsme, problème intérieur," *La conscience juive: Données et débats*, ed. Éliane Amado Lévy-Valensi and Jean Halperin (Paris: Presses Universitaires de France, 1963), 54–79; see Jonathan Judaken, "Vladimir Jankélévitch at the Colloques des intellectuels juifs de langue française." *Vladimir Jankélévitch and the Question of Forgiveness*, ed. Alan Udoff (Lanham, MD: Lexington Books, 2013), 7–9, 12–13.
57 Ernst Falzeder and Eva Brabant, eds, *The Correspondence of Sigmund Freud and Sándor Ferenczi, Volume 3, 1920–1933*, trans. Peter T. Hoffer (Cambridge, MA: Harvard University Press, 2000), 45 n.2.
58 For a succinct summary of Jankélévitch's philosophy, see Jean-Christophe Goddard, "Vladimir Jankélévitch (1903–85)," in *The Columbia History of Twentieth-Century Thought*, ed. Lawrence D. Kritzman (New York: Columbia University Press, 2006), 551–3.
59 Jankélévitch, *La conscience juive*, 61; see Judaken, "Vladimir Jankélévitch," 13.
60 Vladimir Jankélévitch, "Introduction au thème du pardon" in *La conscience juive face à l'histoire: le pardon*, ed. Éliane Amado Lévy-Valensi and Jean Halperin (Paris: Presses Universitaires de France, 1965), 247; see Judaken, "Vladimir Jankélévitch," 15.
61 Vladimir Jankélévitch, *Forgiveness*, trans. Andrew Kelley (Chicago: University of Chicago Press, 2005), 35.
62 Hella Pick, *Simon Wiesenthal: A Life in Search of Justice* (Boston: Northeastern University Press, 1996), 78.
63 Tom Segev, *Simon Wiesenthal: The Life and Legends* (New York: Doubleday, 2010), 122.
64 For an examination of Lauterpacht and Lemkin, see Philippe Sands, *East West Street: On the Origins of "Genocide" and "Crimes Against Humanity"* (New York: Alfred A. Knopf, 2016). For context, see Samuel Moyn, *The Last Utopia: Human Rights in History* (Cambridge, MA: Harvard University Press, 2010).
65 Segev, *Simon Wiesenthal: The Life and Legends*, 32.
66 Ibid., 38.
67 Pick, *Simon Wiesenthal: A Life in Search of Justice*, 44.
68 See Segev, *Simon Wiesenthal: The Life and Legends*, 85.
69 Wiesenthal, *The Sunflower*, 65.

70 Paulina Kreisberg, Wiesenthal's daughter, 2008, as cited by Segev, *Simon Wiesenthal: The Life and Legends,* 33.
71 Pick, *Simon Wiesenthal: A Life in Search of Justice,* 44.
72 Ibid., 46.
73 Ibid.; Segev, *Simon Wiesenthal: The Life and Legends,* 40.
74 Wiesenthal, *The Sunflower,* 56–7, 18–20.
75 Segev, *Simon Wiesenthal: The Life and Legends,* 51.
76 See Eliyahu Yones, *Smoke in the Sand: The Jews of Lvov in the War Years, 1939–1944* (Jerusalem: Gefen, 2004), 180.
77 Segev, *Simon Wiesenthal: The Life and Legends,* 7. As an example, he magnified his role in alerting Israelis in 1953 to Eichmann's whereabouts in Argentina into claiming that "I hunted Eichmann," the title of his 1961 book *Ich jagte Eichmann.*
78 Wiesenthal, *The Sunflower,* 84; Simon Wiesenthal, *Die Sonnenblume: Eine Erzählung von Schuld und Vergebung* (Frankfurt: Ullstein, 1998), 93.
79 Ruth A. Kok, *Statutory Limitations in International Criminal Court* (The Hague: T. M. C. Asser Press, 2007), 39.
80 Segev, *Simon Wiesenthal: The Life and Legends,* 7; Pick was more generous: She believed Wiesenthal "understood the importance of generating political pressure and publicity through judicious use of the media … so that his frequent press conferences would score maximum impact." Pick, *Simon Wiesenthal: A Life in Search of Justice,* 166–7.
81 Segev, *Simon Wiesenthal: The Life and Legends,* 305.
82 Jankélévitch, *Forgiveness,* 144.
83 Améry, *At the Mind's Limits,* 35.
84 Primo Levi, *Moments of Reprieve* (New York: Penguin Books, 1995), ix.
85 See Jankélévitch, "Should We Pardon Them?," 554.
86 Améry, *At the Mind's Limits,* 13.
87 Ibid., 14.
88 Ruth R. Wisse, *The Modern Jewish Canon: A Journey Through Language and Culture* (New York: The Free Press, 2000), 197.
89 Améry, *At the Mind's Limits,* 24, 38.
90 Jankélévitch, *Forgiveness,* 152.
91 Wiesenthal, *The Sunflower,* 97.
92 Améry, *At the Mind's Limits,* xi.

Chapter 1: Traumatic Memories and Historical Memories

1 On the process of projection in interpreting the Holocaust, see Dominick LaCapra, "Representing the Holocaust: Reflections on the Historians' Debate,"

Probing the Limits of Representation: Nazism and the "Final Solution," ed. Saul Friedländer (Cambridge, MA: Harvard University Press, 1992), 110; Marianne Hirsch and Leo Spitzer argued that "the figure of the muted, traumatized survivor … can become a screen on which the listener/interpreter can project various meanings." Marianne Hirsch and Leo Spitzer, "The Witness in the Archives," *Holocaust Studies/Memory Studies* 2 (2009): 164.

2 The classic example of this methodological debate is an exchange of letters in 1987 between Martin Broszat and Saul Friedländer over the capacity of memory to compete with "rational" historical scholarship. The letters were published as "Martin Broszat/Saul Friedländer: A Controversy about the Historicization of National Socialism," *Yad Vashem Studies* 19 (1988): 1–47.

3 See Samuel D. Kassow, *Who Will Write Our History? Rediscovering the Hidden Archive from the Warsaw Ghetto* (New York: Vintage Books, 2009).

4 Raphael Lemkin, *Axis Rule in Occupied Europe: Laws of Occupation, Analysis of Government, Proposals for Redress* (Washington, DC: Carnegie Endowment for International Peace, 1944), 94.

5 Hannah Arendt, *Eichmann in Jerusalem: A Report on the Banality of Evil* (New York: Penguin Books, 2006), 253–79.

6 Cited in Shoshana Felman, *The Juridical Unconscious: Trials and Traumas in the Twentieth Century* (Cambridge, MA: Harvard University Press, 2002), 132–3.

7 Arendt, *Eichmann in Jerusalem,* 223.

8 Ibid., 260.

9 Gideon Hausner, *Justice in Jerusalem* (New York: Harper and Row, 1966), 291.

10 Ibid., 292.

11 Elie Wiesel, "The Holocaust as Literary Inspiration," *Dimensions of the Holocaust,* ed. Elliot Lefkowitz (Evanston, IL: Northwestern University Press, 1990), 9.

12 Annette Wieviorka, *The Era of the Witness* (Ithaca, NY: Cornell University Press, 2006), 143.

13 Hausner, *Justice in Jerusalem,* 291.

14 Wieviorka, *The Era of the Witness,* 66.

15 Arendt, *Eichmann in Jerusalem,* 253–79.

16 Wieviorka, *The Era of the Witness,* 68.

17 Maurice Halbwachs, "*The Social Frameworks of Memory,*" *in On Collective Memeory,* ed. and trans. Lewis A. Coser (Chicago: University of Chicago Press, 1992), 38.

18 Ibid., 52.

19 Ibid., 38.

20 Jean Améry, *At the Mind's Limits: Contemplations by a Survivor on Auschwitz and Its Realities* (Bloomington: Indiana University Press, 1980), 22.

21 Ibid.

22 Ibid., 22–3.

23 Ibid., 100.
24 Vladimir Jankélévitch, "Should We Pardon Them?" *Critical Inquiry* 22 (1996): 562.
25 Ibid., 562.
26 Albert Memmi, *Portrait of a Jew*, trans. Elisabeth Abbott (New York: Orion Press, 1962). Michael Rothberg noted the cross-sections of colonization and genocide in André Schwarz-Bart's 1959 novel, *The Last of the Just*, in Charlotte Delbo's work about her Nazi-era past, and in many other contemporary French–Jewish accounts. Schwarz-Bart also compared genocide with U.S. slavery. See Michael Rothberg, *Multidirectional Memory: Remembering the Holocaust in the Age of Decolonization* (Stanford, CA: Stanford University Press, 2009).
27 Ibid., 195. See also Michael Rothberg, "The Work of Testimony in the Age of Decolonization: *Chronicle of a Summer*, Cinéma Verité, and the Emergence of the Holocaust Survivor," *PMLA* 119 (2004): 1235.
28 Halbwachs, "*The Social Frameworks of Memory*," 38.
29 Wieviorka, *The Era of the Witness*, 73.
30 Jeffrey C. Alexander, "Toward a Theory of Cultural Trauma," *Cultural Trauma and Collective Identity*, ed. Jeffrey C. Alexander (Berkeley: University of California Press, 2004), 14–15.
31 Ruth Wisse, *The Modern Jewish Canon: A Journey Through Language and Culture* (New York: The Free Press, 2000), 191–236.
32 On "active memory" and its "engagement of memories of a past long gone, with the ever emerging present," see Mary Louise Seeberg, Irene Levin, and Claudia Lenz, *The Holocaust as Active Memory: The Past in the Present* (New York: Routledge, 2013), 4.
33 Améry, *At the Mind's Limits*, 23.
34 Ibid., 24.
35 Ibid., 23.
36 Jankélévitch, "Should We Pardon Them?," 562.
37 Ibid.
38 Ibid., 566.
39 Ibid., 571.
40 Simon Wiesenthal, *The Sunflower: On the Possibilities and Limits of Forgiveness* (New York: Schocken Books, 1998), 84.
41 Ibid., 91.
42 Ibid., 92.
43 Ibid., 93.
44 Ibid.
45 Ibid., 92.
46 Ibid., 93.

47 Michel Foucault, *Language, Counter-Memory, Practice: Selected Essays and Interviews,* ed. Donald F. Bouchard, trans. Donald F. Bouchard and Sherry Simon (Ithaca, NY: Cornell University Press, 1977).

48 Pierre Nora, "Between Memory and History: Les Lieux de Mémoire," *Representations* 26 (1989): 12.

49 Ibid., 7.

50 Ibid., 8.

51 Ibid.

52 For an analysis of the reflective method, see Jean Nabert, *Éléments pour une éthique* (Paris: Aubier, 1962). The work was first published in 1943.

53 Améry, *At the Mind's Limits,* 76.

54 Ibid., 67. Primo Levi explained his need for distance as the persistence of the "old trauma, the scar of remembrance." Primo Levi, "Revisiting the Camps," *The Art of Memory: Holocaust Memorials in History*, ed. James Young (New York: Prestel-Verlag, 1994), 185.

55 Jankélévitch, "Should We Pardon Them?," 558.

56 Améry, *At the Mind's Limits,* 57.

57 Nora, "Between Memory and History," 8.

58 Ibid.

59 Ibid., 9.

60 Lawrence L. Langer, *Holocaust Testimonies: The Ruins of Memory* (New Haven, CT: Yale University Press, 1991), 5.

61 Charlotte Delbo, *Days and Memory*, trans. Rosette C. Lamont (Evanston, IL: The Marlboro Press/Northwestern, 2001), 3.

62 Charlotte Delbo, *Auschwitz and After,* trans. Rosette C. Lamont (New Haven, CT: Yale University Press, 1995), 16.

63 Ibid., 11.

64 Lawrence L. Langer, "Remembering Survival," in *Holocaust Remembrance: The Shapes of Memory,* ed. Geoffrey H. Hartman (Cambridge, MA: Blackwell Publishers, 1994), 79.

65 Langer, *Holocaust Testimonies,* 16.

66 Ibid.

67 Ibid., 204–5.

68 W. G. Sebald, *On The Natural History of Destruction,* trans. Anthea Bell (New York: Random House, 2003).

69 Ibid., 25.

70 Ibid.

71 Langer, *Holocaust Testimonies,* 13.

72 Sebald, *On The Natural History of Destruction*, 25.

73 Ibid.

74 Ibid., 25, 85.
75 Ibid., 85.
76 Ibid., 96.
77 Primo Levi, *Survival in Auschwitz: The Nazi Assault on Humanity* (New York: Collier Books, 1993), 183.
78 Primo Levi, *Moments of Reprieve* (New York: Penguin Books, 1995), viii.
79 Ibid., ix.
80 Ibid., viii.
81 Ibid., vii.
82 Saul Friedländer, "Trauma, Transference, and 'Working Through' in Writing the History of the Shoah," *History and Memory* 4 (1992): 51–2.
83 Ibid., 51.
84 Ibid., 53.
85 Ibid.
86 Felman, *The Juridical Unconscious,* 133.
87 Ibid., 152.
88 Ibid., 153.
89 Sebald, *On The Natural History of Destruction,* 94–5.
90 Hirsch and Spitzer, "The Witness in the Archives," 156.
91 Ibid., 152.
92 Ibid.
93 Jorge Semprun, *Literature or Life,* trans. Linda Coverdale (New York: Viking Penguin, 1997), 14.
94 Sidra DeKoven Ezrahi, "Representing Auschwitz," *History and Memory* 7 (1996): 122.
95 Susan Rubin Suleiman, *Crises of Memory and the Second World War* (Cambridge, MA: Harvard University Press, 2006), 155–6.
96 Dominick LaCapra, *Writing History, Writing Trauma* (Baltimore: The Johns Hopkins Press, 2001), 66.
97 Langer, *Holocaust Testimonies,* 39–76.
98 Ezrahi, "Representing Auschwitz," 139.
99 LaCapra, *Writing History, Writing Trauma,* 90.
100 Susanne Langer, *Philosophy in a New Key* (Cambridge, MA: Harvard University Press, 1951), 152–3. See also Jeffrey M. Blustein, *Forgiveness and Remembrance: Remembering Wrongdoing in Personal and Public Life* (New York: Oxford University Press, 2014), 209–10.
101 Vladimir Jankélévitch, *Forgiveness,* trans. Andrew Kelley (Chicago: University of Chicago Press, 2013), 69–70.
102 Imre Kertész, "Nobel Lecture," 2002, trans. Ivan Sanders, http://www.nobelprize.org/nobel_prizes/literature/laureates/2002/kertesz-lecture-e.html (accessed May 11, 2015). Susan J. Brison, a rape victim, similarly argued that retelling the story

as "a coherent narrative" leads to "working through, or remastering, traumatic memory." She believed the "performative role of speech acts" was salutary: "Under the right conditions, *saying* something about traumatic memory *does* something to it." Her thesis, however, differs from my argument. Narratives are not only intertextual. Nor do survivors agree with Brison that they require a response for effect. Brison observed that "One can become a human subject again through telling one's narrative to caring others who are able to listen." Susan J. Brison, "Traumatic Narratives and the Remaking of the Self," in *Acts of Memory: Cultural Recall in the Present* (Hanover, NH: University Press of New England, 1999), 48. Kertész asserted that the sovereign act of writing is sufficient.

103 Ezrahi, "Representing Auschwitz," 142.

104 Suleiman, *Crises of Memory and the Second World War,* 140.

105 LaCapra, *Writing History, Writing Trauma,* 71.

106 Suleiman, *Crises of Memory and the Second World War,* 140.

107 Ezrahi, "Representing Auschwitz," 122.

108 Jankélévitch, *Forgiveness,* 143.

109 Ibid., 162.

110 Ibid., 152–3.

111 Ibid., 162.

112 Jankélévitch, "Should We Pardon Them?," 555.

113 Améry, *At the Mind's Limits,* 43.

114 Ibid., 46.

115 Ibid., 34.

116 Wiesenthal, *The Sunflower,* 53.

117 Ibid., 9.

118 Langer, *Holocaust Testimonies,* 9.

119 See Sigmund Freud, "Mourning and Melancholia," *The Standard Edition of the Complete Psychological Works of Sigmund Freud,* Vol. 14, ed. and trans. James Strachey (London: The Hogarth Press, 1957): 243–57.

120 Sigmund Freud, "Remembering, Repeating, and Working-Through," *The Standard Edition of the Complete Psychological Works of Sigmund Freud,* Vol. 12, ed. and trans. James Strachey (London: The Hogarth Press, 1958): 145–56. In "Inhibitions, Symptoms, and Anxiety" (1926), he revisited the idea of working through, though he acknowledged "the power of the compulsion to repeat." Sigmund Freud, "Inhibitions, Symptoms, and Anxiety," *The Standard Edition of the Complete Psychological Works of Sigmund Freud,* Vol. 20, ed. and trans. James Strachey (London: The Hogarth Press, 1959): 159–60. Bessel A. van der Kolk and Onno van der Hart argued that repression as a dynamic phenomenon applies to primitive Id-impulses, not to traumatic memories, which, he asserted, are dissociative. Bessel A. van der Kolk and Onno van der Hart, "The Intrusive Past:

The Inflexibility of Memory and the Engraving of Trauma," *Trauma: Explorations in Memory*, ed. Cathy Caruth (Baltimore: The Johns Hopkins University Press, 1995), 168.

121 Dennis Klein, "Forgiveness and History: A Reinterpretation of Post-Conflict Testimony," in *Memory, Narrative, and Forgiveness: Perspectives on the Unfinished Journey of the Past,* ed. Pumla Gobodo-Madikizela (Newcastle upon Tyne: Cambridge Scholars Publishing, 2009), 113–29.

122 See van der Kolk and van der Hart, "The Intrusive Past," 158–82.

123 Langer, *Holocaust Testimonies,* 95.

124 Ibid., 175.

125 "An important element in the theory of repression is the view that repression is not an event that occurs once but that it requires a permanent expenditure." Freud, "Inhibitions, Symptoms, and Anxiety," *The Standard Edition*, Vol. 20, 157.

126 LaCapra, *Writing History, Writing Trauma,* 108.

127 Ibid., 55.

128 Ezrahi, "Representing Auschwitz," 144.

129 See Améry, *At the Mind's Limits,* 39, 40, 70, 95, 96; his essay, "How Much Home Does a Person Need?" (41–61) is a requiem to psychological loneliness.

130 See, for example, Bessel A. van der Kolk, "Dissociation and the Fragmentary Nature of Traumatic Memories: Overview and Exploratory Study," *Journal of Trauma Stress* 8 (1995): 505–25.

131 Friedrich Nietzsche, *The Birth of Tragedy from the Spirit of Music* in Friedrich Nietzsche, *The Birth of Tragedy and the Genealogy of Morals,* trans. Francis Golffing (Garden City: Doubleday & Co. Inc., 1956), 19–146.

132 Jankélévitch, *Forgiveness,* 130.

133 Ibid., 153.

134 Ibid., 162.

135 Ibid.

136 Ibid., 163.

137 From Henri Bergson, *TK* (Paris: Presses universitaires de France, 1989), 34. Quoted in Joëlle Hansel, "Forgiveness and 'Should We Pardon Them?': The Pardon and the Imprescriptible," *Vladimir Jankélévitch and the Question of Forgiveness*, ed. Alan Udoff (Lanham, MD: Lexington Books, 2013), 123 n.9.

138 Semprun, *Literature or Life,* 299.

139 Jankélévitch, *Forgiveness,* 162.

140 Ibid., 62.

141 Ibid., 163.

142 Terence Des Pres, *The Survivor: An Anatomy of Life in the Death Camps* (New York: Oxford University Press, 1976), 30.

143 Améry, *At the Mind's Limits,* 64.

144 Suleiman, *Crises of Memory and the Second World War,* 158.

145 Ibid., 157.

146 Heinrich Böll, handwritten note to Wiesenthal, August 15, 1969, in the Wiesenthal Private Papers, Vienna, as cited in Tom Segev, *Simon Wiesenthal: The Life and Legends* (New York: Doubleday, 2010), 238. According to Segev, Böll was the first to question the authenticity of Wiesenthal's story.

147 Wiesenthal, *The Sunflower,* 41.

148 Ibid., 35.

149 Bruno Bettelheim, *The Informed Heart: Autonomy in a Mass Age* (New York: Avon, 1971), 150.

150 Ibid.

151 Ibid. Similar expressions are replete in survivors' accounts. Primo Levi's work is exemplary. He often wrote about the importance of just "keeping busy—finding a bit of bread, avoiding exhausting work, patching my shoes, stealing a broom, or interpreting the signs and faces around me. The aims of life are the best defense against death: and not only in the Lager." Primo Levi, *The Drowned and the Saved* (New York: Summit Books, 1988), 148.

152 Lucy S. Dawidowicz, *The Holocaust and the Historian* (Cambridge, MA: Harvard University Press, 1981), 177.

153 Debórah Dwork and Robert van Pelt, *The Holocaust: A History* (New York: W. W. Norton and Co., 2002), 213.

154 Améry, *At the Mind's Limits,* 64.

155 Dori Laub, "Bearing Witness, or the Vicissitudes of Listening," in *Testimony: Crises of Witnessing in Literature, Psychoanalysis, and History,* ed. Shoshana Felman and Dori Laub (New York: Routledge, 1992), 69.

156 Ibid., 61.

157 Ibid., 68.

158 Jorge Semprun and Elie Wiesel, *Se taire est impossible* (Paris: Mille et une nuits, 1995). My thanks to Kitty J. Millet for this reference.

159 Wieviorka, *The Era of the Witness*, 109.

160 Ibid., 115.

161 Ibid., 116.

162 Ibid., 144.

163 Ibid., 88.

164 Ibid., 144.

165 Ibid., 132.

166 Ibid.

167 Ibid., 144.

168 Améry, *At the Mind's Limits,*78.

169 Jankélévitch, "Should We Pardon Them?," 572; Wiesenthal, *The Sunflower,* 93.

170 Ibid., 41.

171 Bettelheim, *The Informed Heart*, 108.

172 Primo Levi, *Survival in Auschwitz*, 41.

173 Alvin H. Rosenfeld, *Thinking About the Holocaust: After Half a Century* (Bloomington: Indiana University Press, 1997), 147.

174 For a philosophical inquiry into truth-telling in bearing witness, see Jeffrey M. Blustein, *The Moral Demands of Memory* (New York: Cambridge University Press, 2008), 342–5.

175 Langer, *Holocaust Testimonies*, 46.

176 Levi expressed his limitations as a witness bearer, writing that those who "did not touch bottom" spoke "in their stead, by proxy." He did not count himself as among the "complete witnesses." Levi, *The Drowned and the Saved*, 83–4.

177 Alvin H. Rosenfeld, *A Double Dying: Reflections on Holocaust Literature* (Bloomington: Indiana University Press, 1980), 27.

178 Ibid., 21.

179 Ibid., 29.

180 Ibid., 32.

181 Kassow, *Who Will Write Our History?*, 154. For examples of passages seeking revenge, see Yehuda Nir, *The Lost Childhood* (New York: Harcourt Brace Jovanovich, 1989), 105: "I wished a bomb would explode on the lovely street [in a German section of Warsaw] and tear the playing children to pieces. All of them!" Norman Salsitz recalled an incident he witnessed when a comrade killed Polish villagers in retaliation for killing three Jews. Norman Salsitz and Amalie Petranker Salsitz, *Against All Odds: A Tale of Two Survivors* (New York: Holocaust Library, 1990), 41.

182 Améry, *At the Mind's Limits*, 26.

183 Jankélévitch, "Should We Pardon Them?," 556.

184 Ibid., 555.

185 "They teach better than any treatise or memorial how inhuman the Hitlerite regime was." Levi, "Revisiting the Camps," 185. The demand for justice is also a familiar refrain, an imperative that fueled Wiesenthal's life mission. Even as Levi explored moral ambiguity in the "gray zone," he was uncompromising about the murderers: they were the prime movers behind the "sinister ritual" of destruction and deserved punishment. Levi, *The Drowned and the Saved*, 39, see also 25, 49.

186 Elie Wiesel, *All Rivers Run to the Sea: Memoirs* (New York: Schocken Books, 1995), 79.

187 Améry, *At the Mind's Limits*, 79.

188 Jankélévitch, "Should We Pardon Them?," 572.

189 Levi, *The Drowned and the Saved*, 85.

190 Geoffrey Hartman, *The Longest Shadow: In the Aftermath of the Holocaust* (Bloomington: Indiana University Press, 1996), 142.

191 LaCapra, *Writing History, Writing Trauma,* 100. For comparison, see an account by the sixteenth-century Congolese king Nzinga Mbemba, whose mediation between natives and Portuguese colonial authorities sought to protect free Congolese noblemen and "our relatives" from captivity and enslavement in the name of "justice" by recommending a local screening committee comprising "our noblemen and officials of our court." Basil Davidson, *The African Past* (Boston: Little, Brown & Co., 1964), 191–4.

192 Omer Bartov, "Communal Genocide: Personal Accounts of Destruction of Buczacz, Eastern Galicia, 1941–1944," in *Shatterzone of Empires: Coexistence and Violence in the German, Habsburg, Russian and Ottoman Borderlands* (Bloomington: Indiana University Press, 2013), 403.

193 Ibid., 407.

194 Ibid., 403.

195 Ibid., 417.

196 Levi, *The Drowned and the Saved,* 82.

197 Ibid., 36–69.

198 Ibid., 78–9.

199 Ibid., 78.

200 Ibid., 86–7.

201 Bartov, "Communal Genocide," 407.

202 Omer Bartov, "Eastern Europe as the Site of Genocide," *Journal of Modern History* 80 (2008): 561–2.

203 Jean Améry, *At the Mind's Limits,* ix.

204 Jankélévitch, *Forgiveness,* 161.

205 Ibid., 66.

206 Ibid., 70.

207 Ibid., 68.

208 Wiesenthal, *The Sunflower,* 45–6.

209 Eliezer Wiesel, Unpublished ms. [*Night,* Hebrew version], n.d. as reported in Ofer Aderet, "Newly Unearthed Version of Elie Wiesel's Seminal Work Is a Scathing Indictment of God, Jewish World," *Haaretz,* May 1, 2016, http://www.haaretz.com/jewish/news/.premium-1.717093http://www.haaretz.com/jewish/news/.premium-1.717093 (accessed June 28, 2016).

210 Wiesenthal, *The Sunflower,* 96.

211 Améry, *At the Mind's Limits,* 24.

212 Ibid.

213 Ibid., 25.

214 Ibid., 24.

215 Ibid.
216 Jankélévitch, *Forgiveness,* 141.
217 Ibid., 163.
218 Ibid., 141.
219 Ibid., 163.
220 See Anthony Polonsky and Joanna B. Michlic, *The Neighbors Respond: The Controversy over the Jedwabne Massacre in Poland* (Princeton, NJ: Princeton University Press, 2004).
221 See Jan T. Gross, *Neighbors: The Destruction of the Jewish Community of Jedwabne, Poland* (New York: Penguin Books, 2002), 42.
222 Elie Wiesel, *Un di velt hot geshvign* [*And the World Was Silent*] (Buenos Aires: Tsentral-Farband fun Poylische Yidn in Argentine, 1956), 7. Translation by the author in *Night* (New York: Hill and Wang, 2006), x–xi. Wisse observed similar criticism of fellow Jews in ghetto diaries. Ruth Wisse, *The Modern Jewish Canon,* 214. Arendt, in looking at Jewish Council members, stirred considerable disquiet for arguing that the claim of innocence was disingenuous and concealed their deliberate collaboration, though, like Levi's comments on "gray," ambiguous behavior, we can consider predispositions toward an affinity with their enemies without resorting to incendiary accusations. See Hannah Arendt, *The Origins of Totalitarianism* (New York: Harcourt Brace Jovanovich, 1973); Levi, *The Drowned and the Saved,* 36–69.
223 Wiesel, Unpublished ms., n.d. as reported in Ofer Aderet, "Newly Unearthed Version of Elie Wiesel's Seminal Work."
224 Primo Levi, *The Drowned and the Saved,* 42–3.
225 See Arendt, *The Origins of Totalitarianism,* 13–57.

Chapter 2: Historical Emotions

1 Simon Wiesenthal, *The Sunflower: On the Possibilities and Limits of Forgiveness* (New York: Schocken Books, 1998), 22.
2 Ibid., 23.
3 Ibid., 24.
4 Ibid., 24–5.
5 Ibid., 23.
6 Ibid., 24.
7 Ibid., 25.
8 Ibid.
9 Ibid.
10 Maurice Halbwachs, "*The Social Frameworks of Memory,*" in *On Collective*

Memory, ed. and trans. Lewis A. Coser (Chicago: University of Chicago Press, 1992), 140.

11 Simon Wiesenthal, *Die Sonnenblume:Eine Erzählung von Schuld und Vergebung* (Vienna: Ullstein, 1984), 29.

12 Jean Améry, *At the Mind's Limits: Contemplations by a Survivor on Auschwitz and Its Realities* (Bloomington: Indiana University Press, 1980), 31; Jean Améry, *Jenseits von Schuld und Sühne: Bewältigungsversuche eines Überwältigten* (Stuttgart: Klett-Cotta, 2014), 67.

13 Améry, *At the Mind's Limits,* 25.

14 Ibid., 28; Améry, *Jenseits von Schuld und Sühne,* 62.

15 Améry, *At the Mind's Limits,* 32.

16 Ibid., 35.

17 See ibid.

18 Ibid.

19 Ibid., 25. In characterizing the torturer's sadism as evil, Améry is reprimanding Hannah Arendt for arguing a few years earlier that Eichmann's evil was merely banal, a critique that recent investigations have vindicated. "When I speak of the banality of evil," Arendt famously wrote, "I do so only on the strictly factual level, pointing to a phenomenon which stared one in the face at the trial … Except for an extraordinary diligence in looking out for his personal advancement, he had no motives at all … He merely, to put the matter colloquially, *never realized what he was doing.*" Hannah Arendt, *Eichmann in Jerusalem: A Report on the Banality of Evil* (New York: Penguin Books, 2006), 287. Bettina Stangneth demolished the thesis, showing that Eichmann was a fanatical, unrepentant killer. Bettina Stangneth, *Eichmann Before Jerusalem: The Unexamined Life of a Mass Murderer* (New York: Random House, 2014).

20 Améry, *At the Mind's Limits,* 32.

21 Ibid., 25; see 46.

22 On Jankélévitch, see "Le judaïsme, problème intérieur," in *La conscience juive: Données et débats,* ed. Éliane Amado Lévy-Valensi and Jean Halperin (Paris: Presses Universitaires de France, 1963), 54–79; and "Ressembler ou dissembler," in *Tentations et actions de la conscience juive: Données et débats,* ed. Éliane Amado Lévy-Valensi and Jean Halperin (Paris: Presses Universitaires de France, 1971), 17–34. See also Dana Hollander, *Living Together: Jacques Derrida's Communities of Violence and Peace* (New York: Fordham University Press, 2013); and Jonathan Judaken, "Vladimir Jankélévitch at the Colloques des intellectuels juifs de langue française," in *Vladimir Jankélévitch and the Question of Forgiveness,* ed. Alan Udoff (Lanham, MD: Lexington Books, 2013), 3–26. On Améry, see *At the Mind's Limits,* 50.

23 The distinction often goes unnoticed, especially in legal trials evaluating the

credibility of witnesses' accounts. See Elizabeth A. Phelps, "Emotion's Impact on Memory," *Memory and Law*, eds. Lynn Nadel and Walter P. Sinnot-Armstrong (New York: Oxford University Press, 2012), 7–28.

24 See Tom Segev, *Simon Wiesenthal: The Life and Legends* (New York: Doubleday, 2010), 237–8.

25 Ibid., 238.

26 In his essay "Historical Memory and Collective Memory," Halbwachs wrote, "Collective memory ... retains from the past only what still lives or is capable of living in the consciousness of the groups keeping the memory alive." Maurice Halbwachs, *The Collective Memory*, ed. Mary Douglas, trans. Francis J. Ditter Jr. and Vidayazdi Ditter (New York: Harper Colophon, 1980), 80.

27 Jean Améry, *At the Mind's Limits*, xi.

28 Stanley B. Klein and Shaun Nichols, "Memory and the Sense of Personal Identity," *Mind* 121 (2012): 677.

29 Klein and Nichols, "Memory and the Sense of Personal Identity," 695.

30 I use the term "survivors" as a reference to those under scrutiny in my argument, and not necessarily as an attempt at generalization.

31 Halbwachs, "*The Social Frameworks of Memory*," 140.

32 See Janna Thompson, "Historical Injustice and Reparation: Justifying Claims of Descendants," *Ethics* 112 (2001): 114–35.

33 Richard Vernon, *Historical Redress: Must We Pay for the Past?* (New York: Continuum, 2012), 109.

34 Halbwachs, "*The Social Frameworks of Memory*," 140.

35 Hella Pick, *Simon Wiesenthal: A Life in Search of Justice* (Boston: Northeastern University Press, 1996), 44.

36 Améry, *At the Mind's Limits*, 82.

37 Jacob Katz, *Tradition and Crisis: Jewish Society at the End of the Middle Ages* (New York: Schocken Books, 1961). Katz regarded the introduction of Jews at the end of the eighteenth century to the open society as an indication of the collapse of traditional society.

38 To "be a man in the street and a Jew at home" is the formulation submitted by the Russian Jew Judah Leib Gordon in his poem *Hakitzah ami*, in 1863, two years after the Russian emancipation of serfs.

39 Jan Gross, in *Neighbors: The Destruction of the Jewish Community in Jedwabne, Poland* (New York: Penguin Books, 2002), galvanized attention to the phenomenon of local killing by examining the turn of events against Jewish residents in one small Polish village. See Dennis Klein, "Locality and the Hidden Realities of Genocide," *Historical Reflections/Reflexions Historiques* 39 (2013): 30–9.

40 Omer Bartov, "On Eastern Galicia's Past and Present," *Daedalus* 136 (2007): 116.

41 Omer Bartov, "Communal Genocide: Personal Accounts of the Destruction of Buczacz, Eastern Galicia, 1941–1944," in *Shatterzone of Empires: Coexistence and Violence in the German, Habsburg, Russian, and Ottoman Borderlands*, ed. Omer Bartov and Eric D. Weitz (Bloomington: Indiana University Press, 2013).

42 Ibid., 406.

43 Frank Golczewski, "Shades of Grey: Reflections on Jewish-Ukrainian and German-Ukrainian Relations in Galicia," in *The Shoah in Ukraine: History, Testimony, Memorialization,* ed. Ray Brandon and Wendy Lower (Bloomington: Indiana University Press, 2008), 146. As of January 1, 2017, Yad Vashem, the Holocaust documentation, research, education, and commemoration center in Israel, recognized 2,573 Ukrainians among the "Righteous Among the Nations."

44 Golczewski, "Shades of Grey," 145.

45 Natalya Lazar, "Czernowitz Jews and the Holocaust: Interethnic Relations, Violence, and Survival in a Borderland City, 1941–1946" (PhD diss. proposal, Clark University, 2015).

46 Eva Hoffman, *Shtetl: The Life and Death of a Small Town and the World of Polish Jews* (Boston: Houghton Mifflin, 1997), 161.

47 Ibid., 247.

48 Ibid., 256.

49 Ibid., 247–8.

50 Peter Gay, *Freud, Jews and Other Germans* (New York: Oxford University Press, 1978), 161.

51 Ibid., 94.

52 Theodor Herzl, *The Jewish State,* in *Theodor Herzl: A Portrait for This Age*, ed. Ludwig Lewisohn, trans. Sylvie d'Avigdor (Cleveland: The World Publishing Co., 1955), 235.

53 Ibid., 239.

54 Ibid., 244. See Carl E. Schorske, *Fin-de-siècle Vienna: Politics and Culture* (New York: Knopf, 1979), 146–75.

55 Herzl, *The Jewish State,* 240.

56 Götz Aly, *Why the Germans? Why the Jews?: Envy, Race, Hatred, and the Preshistory of the Holocaust* (New York: Metropolitan Books, 2014), 6.

57 Aly, *Why the Germans? Why the Jews?*; see Friedrich Meinecke, *The German Catastrophe: Reflections and Recollections* (Cambridge, MA: Harvard University Press, 1950), in which he argued that Jews' good fortune provoked considerable disfavor.

58 Hannah Arendt, *Eichmann in Jerusalem: A Report on the Banality of Evil* (New York: Penguin Books, 1963).

59 Hannah Arendt, *The Origins of Totalitarianism* (New York: Harcourt Brace Jovanovich, 1973), 23.

60 Ibid., 57.

61 For example, Beer Isaac Berr, *Lettre d'un citoyen, membre de la ci-devant Communauté des Juifs de Lorraine, à ses confrères, à l'occasion du droit de citoyen actif, rendu aux Juifs par le décret du 28 septembre 1791* (Nancy: H. Haener, 1791).

62 Arendt, *The Origins of Totalitarianism,* 66.

63 Herzl, *The Jewish State,* 240.

64 Avashai Margalit, *The Ethics of Memory* (Cambridge, MA: Harvard University Press, 2008).

65 Ibid., 8.

66 Ibid., 45.

67 Ibid., 7.

68 Ibid., 33.

69 Ibid., 44.

70 Ibid., 42.

71 Ibid., 34.

72 Ibid., 37; see Carolyn L. Hafner, et al., "Extreme Harmdoing: A View from the Social Psychology of Justice," in *Explaining the Breakdown of Ethnic Relations: Why Neighbors Kill,* ed. Victoria M. Esses and Richard A. Vernon (Malden, MA: Blackwell Publishing, 2008), 17–40.

73 Margalit, *The Ethics of Memory,* 8.

74 Referring to sunflowers above the graves of German soldiers as a connection with the living world, Wiesenthal was "seized with a childish longing to have a sunflower of my own." Wiesenthal, *The Sunflower,* 63; see 14–15.

75 Freddie Knoller and John Landaw, *Living with the Enemy: My Secret Life on the Run from the Nazis* (London: Metro Publishing, 2005), 26.

76 Margalit, *The Ethics of Memory,* 45.

77 Sigmund Freud, "Negation," in *The Standard Edition of the Complete Psychological Works of Sigmund Freud,* Vol. 19, ed. and trans. James Strachey (London: Hogarth Press, 1961): 235–6.

78 Améry, *At the Mind's Limits,* 11.

79 For a discussion of the neural science of affective realism, see Eric Anderson, et al., "Out of Sight, but Not Out of Mind: Unseen Affective Faces Influence Evaluations and Social Impressions," *Emotion* 12 (2012): 1210–21. The article ends, "An exciting line of future research will be to leverage the current CFS paradigm to explore how affective realism contributes to real world social interactions."

80 Hannah Arendt, *The Human Condition* (Chicago: Chicago University Press, 1958), 246.

81 Ibid., 244.

82 Ibid., 243–7.

83 Lynn Hunt, *Inventing Human Rights: A History* (New York: W. W. Norton & Co., 2007), 64–5.

84 See Hunt, *Inventing Human Rights*. For a seminal phenomenological investigation of the idea of primordial "experiencing with one another" as constituent of fellow-feeling (*Mitgefühl*), see Max Scheler, *The Nature of Sympathy*, trans. Peter Heath (Hamden: Archon Books, 1970).

85 Adam Smith, *The Theory of Moral Sentiments* (Los Angeles: Enhanced Media Publishing, 2016), 13.

86 Améry, *At the Mind's Limits*, 70. Updating Smith, Améry privileged the subject, not the object, as the destination of sympathetic emotions in relationships, a consistent position in his accounts that preferred Jews as free agents over their common, pre-war other-directed attachments.

87 Johann Wolfgang von Goethe, *The Sorrows of Young Werther*, trans. Elizabeth Mayer and Louise Bogan (New York: Vintage Books, 1990), 118.

88 Ibid., 129–30.

89 Wiesenthal, *The Sunflower*, 87.

90 Vladimir Jankélévitch, *Forgiveness*, trans. Andrew Kelley (Chicago: University of Chicago Press, 2005), 161.

91 Marianne Hirsch and Leo Spitzer, *Ghosts of Home: The Afterlife of Czernowitz in Jewish Memory* (Berkeley: University of California Press, 2011), 90–1, citing Vera Hacken, "Kinder- und Jugendjahre mit Eliesar Steinbarg." Hirsch and Spitzer observed (286–87), "They had all maintained a surprising attachment to the place and its surrounding region."

92 Améry, *At the Mind's Limits*, 41–61. "One must have a home in order not to need it." Améry, *At the Mind's Limits*, 46.

93 Hoffman, *Shtetl*, 14.

94 Ibid., 19.

95 Herzl, *The Jewish State*, 302.

96 Ibid., 238.

97 Ibid., 302.

98 Ibid., 244.

99 Herzl, in a diary entry written during his work on *The Jewish State*; in Herzl, *The Jewish State*, 221.

100 Sigmund Freud, *The Interpretation of Dreams*, ed. and trans. James Strachey (New York: Avon Books, 1967), xxiv.

101 As cited in Ernst Simon, "Sigmund Freud, the Jew," *The Leo Baeck Institute Yearbook 2* (1957), 247. See Dennis B. Klein, *Jewish Origins of the Psychoanalytic Movement* (New York: Praeger, 1981), 24.

102 Freud, *The Interpretation of Dreams*, 225.

103 Carl Girska, *Wahlrede des Dr. C. Giskra für die Landtags-Candidaten des II. Bezirks in Brünn*, 1. Quoted in Pieter M. Judson, *Exclusive Revolutionaries, Liberal Politics, Social Experience, and National Identity in the Austrian Empire, 1848–1914* (Ann Arbor: The University of Michigan Press, 1996), 69.

104 Freud, *The Interpretation of Dreams*, 229.

105 As cited in Ernst Simon, "Sigmund Freud, the Jew," *The Leo Baeck Institute Yearbook 2* (1957), 274. See Klein, *Jewish Origins*, 227.

106 Freud, *The Interpretation of Dreams*, 224.

107 Ibid., 226.

108 Ibid.

109 Ibid., 229.

110 Ibid.

111 Freud's reference to "the promised land" implied something ancestral in the longing for fulfillment. That he strongly identified with Moses is clear from the references he made to the Hebrew prophet in letters as well as in his publications—"The Moses of Michelangelo" (1913) and *Moses and Monotheism* (1939). Moses, the Hebrew prophet, knew he would have to settle for seeing the promised land only from a distance: "Look at it well, for you shall not go across yonder Jordan." Denied entry, he resigned to looking from afar. But the gaze was urgently expressive, as well—an emotional supplication: "Let me, I pray, cross over and see the good land on the other side of the Jordan, that good hill country, and the Lebanon." Hanns Sachs, one of Freud's closest colleagues, commented that Freud "followed one of the oldest Jewish traditions. This is the belief that all Jews, born and unborn alike, were present on Mount Sinai and have there taken on themselves 'the yoke of the Law.'" In this, we understand that for Moses, as for Freud, the longing was not only a culmination of a long journey but a return to something familiar, a land he already knew. Freud's mission was not unlike the will of Jewish survivors, who encountered antisemitism as it turned violent: a yearning, far from realization, for home. See Deut. 3:23-28 in *Tanakh: A New Translation of the Holy Scriptures According to the Traditional Hebrew Text*, ed. Harry M. Orlinsky, H. L. Ginsberg and Ephraim A. Speiser (Philadelphia: The Jewish Publication Society, 1985), 279. Hanns Sachs, *Freud: Master and Friend* (Cambridge, MA: Harvard University Press, 1944), 152. For a discussion of Freud's Moses identity, see Klein, *Jewish Origins*, 94–5.

112 David Engel argued that witnesses' accounts do not meet the objective standards of scholarship; David Engel, *Facing the Holocaust: The Polish Government-in-Exile and the Jews, 1943–1945* (Chapel Hill: University of North Carolina Press, 1993), 1–14. Debórah Dwork and Robert van Pelt, in *The Holocaust: A History* (New

York: W. W. Norton & Co., 2002), maintained that witness' accounts are most effectively used to illustrate historical events. They preferred other documents for historical reconstruction.

113 Wiesenthal interview (1992) with Maria Sporrer and Herbert Steiner, as quoted in Segev, *Simon Wiesenthal*, 31.

114 Cited by Hirsch and Spitzer, *Ghosts of Home*, 95.

115 Wiesenthal, *The Sunflower*, 13.

116 Ibid., 69.

117 Ibid., 70.

118 Améry, *At the Mind's Limits*, 50.

119 Bartov "Communal Genocide," 405.

120 Ibid., 407.

121 Klein and Nichols, "Memory and the Sense of Personal Identity," 690.

122 Wiesenthal, *The Sunflower*, 7.

123 Klein and Nichols, "Memory and the Sense of Personal Identity," 690.

124 See Thomas Suddendorf and Michael C. Corballis, "Mental Time Travel and the Evolution of the Human Mind," *Genetic, Social, and General Psychology Monographs* 123 (1997): 133–67; and Thomas Suddendorf and Michael C. Corballis, "The Evolution of Foresight: What is Mental Time Travel and is it Unique to Humans?" *Behavioural Brain Sciences* 30 (2007): 299–313. Primo Levi wrote that his love for literature not only "saved" him from despair, but also "made it possible for me to re-establish a link with the past." Primo Levi, "The Intellectual in Auschwitz," in Primo Levi, *The Drowned and the Saved*, trans. Raymond Rosenthal (New York: Summit Books, 1988), 139. Levi's connection with the past through literature is, perhaps, "thinner" than compatriots', but even the thinness confirms the strength of mental continuity.

125 See John Kleinig, *On Loyalty and Loyalties: The Contours of a Problematic Virtue* (New York: Oxford University Press, 2014) and "The Virtue in Patriotism," in *The Ethics of Patriotism: A Debate*, ed. John Kleinig, Simon Keller, and Igor Primoratz (Hoboken, NJ: Wiley-Blackwell, 2015), 19–47.

126 Améry, *At the Mind's Limits*, 50.

127 Ruth Kluger, *Still Alive: A Holocaust Girlhood Remembered* (New York: The Feminist Press, 2001), 206. The negative "never" suggests a stronger fidelity than its positive counterpart, "ever."

128 Arendt, *On the Origins of Totalitarianism*, 25.

129 Ibid.

130 Saul Friedländer, *The Years of Extermination: Nazi Germany and the Jews, 1939–1945* (New York: HarperCollins, 2007), 10.

131 Ibid., 9.

132 Herzl, *The Jewish State*, 238.

133 Ibid., 250.

134 Ibid.

135 Gershom Scholem, *On Jews and Judaism in Crisis: Selected Essays* (Philadelphia: Schocken Books, 1976), 62.

136 Ibid., 63.

137 Ibid., 62.

138 Segev, *Simon Wiesenthal,* 40–1.

139 For an evaluation of German–Jewish leaders in Nazi Germany, see Avraham Barkai, "Jewish Self-Help in Nazi Germany, 1933–1939: The Dilemmas of Cooperation," in *Jewish Life in Nazi Germany: Dilemmas and Responses,* ed. Francis R. Nicosia and David Scrase (New York: Berghahn Books, 2010), 71–88.

140 Wiesenthal, *The Sunflower,* 24.

141 Ibid.

142 Ibid.

143 Ibid.

144 Wiesenthal interview (1992) with Maria Sporrer and Herbert Steiner, as quoted in Segev, *Simon Wiesenthal,* 40.

145 Havi Ben-Sasson, "Polish–Jewish Relations During the Holocaust:A Changing Jewish Viewpoint." In *Rethinking Poles and Jews: Troubled Past, Brighter Future,* ed. Robert Cherry and Annamaria Orla-Bukowska (New York: Rowman and Littlefield, 2007), 95.

146 Lee Ann Fujii, *Killing Neighbors: Webs of Violence in Rwanda* (Ithaca, NY: Cornell University Press, 2009), 19–20.

147 Jürgen Matthäus, "Assault and Destruction," in *The Hidden History of the Kovno Ghetto,* ed. Dennis B. Klein (Boston: Little, Brown & Co., 1997), 15. See also Anne Kelly Knowles, et al., eds, *Geographies of the Holocaust* (Bloomington: Indiana University Press, 2014) for the local and sometimes improvised multiplication of the concentration camp and subcamp system.

148 Gross, *Neighbors,* 18.

149 Ibid.

150 Ibid., 38, 80.

151 Ibid., 22–3.

152 Ibid., 18.

153 Ibid.

154 Ibid., 19.

155 Ibid., 17–18.

156 Ibid., 42.

157 Scholem, *On Jews and Judaism in Crisis,* 62.

158 Tony Judt, *Postwar: A History of Europe Since 1945* (New York: Penguin Books, 2006), 815.

159 Ibid., 810.

160 Ibid., 811.

161 Jan Grabowski, *Hunt for the Jews: Betrayal and Murder in German-Occupied Poland* (Bloomington: Indiana University Press, 2013), 63.

162 Ibid., 72.

163 Gross, *Neighbors,* 35.

164 Halbwachs, "*The Social Frameworks of Memory,*" 49.

165 Améry, *At the Mind's Limits,* 50.

166 Ibid., 51.

167 Ibid.

168 Gross, *Neighbors,* 36.

169 Ibid., 39.

170 David Rohde, *Endgame: The Betrayal and Fall of Srebrenica, Europe's Worst Massacre Since World War II* (New York: Penguin, 2012), 184.

171 Philip Gourevitch, *We Wish to Inform You That Tomorrow We Will Be Killed with Our Families: Stories from Rwanda* (New York: Farrar, Straus and Giroux, 1998), 141.

172 Immaculée Ilibagiza, *Left to Tell: Discovering God Amidst the Rwandan Holocaust* (Carlsbad, CA: Hay House, 2007), 203–4.

173 Herman Melville, "Hawthorne and His Mosses," http://people.virginia.edu/~sfr/enam315/hmmosses.html (accessed July 6, 2016). The essay originally appeared as two installments in the August 17 and 24, 1850, editions of *The Literary World.*

174 Paul Ricoeur, *Memory, History, Forgetting* (Chicago: University of Chicago Press, 2004), 416–17.

175 Ibid., 429.

176 Ibid., 429–30.

177 Jankélévitch, *Forgiveness,* 5.

178 Ibid., 155.

179 Ibid., 36.

180 See Wiesenthal, *The Sunflower,* 25.

181 Ricoeur, *Memory, History, Forgetting,* 430.

182 Améry, *At the Mind's Limits,* 33.

Chapter 3: Narrative Disclosure: Jean Améry

1 Jean Améry, *At the Mind's Limits: Contemplations by a Survivor on Auschwitz and Its Realities* (Bloomington: Indiana University Press, 1980), 63.

2 James M. Deem, *The Prisoners of Breendonk* (New York: Houghton Mifflin, 2015).

3 Améry, *At the Mind's Limits*, 35.
4 Ibid., 11.
5 Ibid., 94–5.
6 Ibid., 94.
7 Ibid.
8 Ibid.
9 Ibid., 100.
10 Ibid., 59–60.
11 Ibid., 60.
12 Ibid., 28.
13 Ibid.
14 Ibid. For a useful discussion of Améry's "expectation of help," see Jay M. Bernstein, *Torture and Dignity: An Essay on Moral Injury* (Chicago: University of Chicago Press, 2015), 99–115.
15 Améry, *At the Mind's Limits*, 42.
16 Ibid.
17 Ibid., 50.
18 Ibid., 8.
19 Ibid., 50.
20 Ibid.
21 Ibid., 51.
22 Ibid.
23 Ibid., 92.
24 Ibid., 91.
25 Ibid., xi.
26 Ibid., 67.
27 Ibid., 100.
28 Ibid., 80.
29 Ibid., 85.
30 Ibid., 88.
31 Ibid., 89.
32 Ibid., 91.
33 Ibid., 90.
34 Ibid., 92.
35 Ibid.
36 Ibid., 99–100.
37 Ibid., 79.
38 Ibid., 90.
39 Ibid., 97.
40 Ibid., 96.

41 Ibid., 40.

42 Ibid., 70. For classic discussions of the loneliness and isolation torture victims endure, see Elaine Scarry, *The Body in Pain* (Oxford: Oxford University Press, 1968), and Lawrence Weschler, *A Miracle, a Universe: Settling Accounts with Torturers* (Chicago: University of Chicago Press, 1998).

43 Améry, *At the Mind's Limits,* 95. Améry used the term "trust" as a "thick" concept implying a sense of kinship and familiarity, though it can also mean an impersonal, "thin" relationship among strangers, as in an alliance. For a useful discussion of the term, see Florencia Torche and Eduardo Valenzuela, "Trust and Reciprocity: A Theoretical Distinction of the Sources of Social Capital," *European Journal of Social Theory* 14 (2011): 181–98.

44 Améry, *At the Mind's Limits,* 81.

45 Ibid., xi.

46 Ibid., 70.

47 Ibid., 95.

48 Ibid., 96.

49 Bruno Bettelheim, "Individual and Mass Behavior in Extreme Situations," *Journal of Abnormal Psychology* 38 (1943): 442.

50 Eliezer Wiesel, Unpublished ms. [*Night*, Hebrew version], n.d., as reported in Ofer Aderet, "Newly Unearthed Version of Elie Wiesel's Seminal Work Is a Scathing Indictment of God, Jewish World," *Haaretz,* May 1, 2016, http://www.haaretz.com/jewish/news/.premium-1.717093 (accessed June 28, 2016).

51 Vladimir Jankélévitch, "Should We Pardon Them?," *Critical Inquiry* 22 (1996): 570.

52 Ibid.

53 Améry, *At the Mind's Limits,* 87.

54 Ibid.

55 Ibid., xiii.

56 Ibid., 51.

57 Ibid., 79.

58 Ibid., 39.

59 Ibid., 68.

60 Ibid., 81.

61 Ibid., 51, 79.

62 Harold Bloom, *A Map of Misreading* (New York: Oxford University Press, 1980), 71.

63 Ibid., 10.

64 Harold Bloom, *The Anxiety of Influence: A Theory of Poetry* (New York: Oxford University Press, 1997), 14.

65 Lucretius, *On the Nature of Things,* trans. Frank O. Copley (New York: W. W. Norton & Co., 2011), 34.

66 Améry, *At the Mind's Limits*, 9.
67 Ibid.
68 Ibid., 16.
69 Ibid., 9.
70 Ibid.
71 Ibid., 10.
72 Ibid., 9.
73 Ibid., 7.
74 Ibid., 11.
75 Ibid., 8.
76 Ibid., 12.
77 Ibid., 9–10.
78 Ibid., 9.
79 Ibid., 13.
80 Ibid., 14.
81 Ibid., 15.
82 Ibid., 14.
83 Ibid.
84 Ibid., 29.
85 Ibid., 100.
86 Ibid., 43.
87 Ibid., 70.
88 Ibid., 78.
89 Ibid., 79.
90 Ibid., 78.
91 Ibid.
92 Ibid., 79.
93 Ibid.
94 Ibid., 39.
95 Ibid., 28.
96 Ibid., 39.
97 Sigmund Freud, "Negation," in *The Standard Edition of the Complete Psychological Works of Sigmund Freud*, Vol. 19, ed. and trans. James Strachey (London: Hogarth Press, 1961): 235–6.
98 Edward S. Casey, *Remembering: A Phenomenological Study* (Bloomington: Indiana University Press, 2000), 225.
99 Améry, *At the Mind's Limits*, xiv.
100 Ibid., 30. Améry referred directly to his broadcasts in the essays; see pages 80 and 94.
101 Ibid., 69.

102 Ibid., xiv.
103 Susanne Langer, *Philosophy in a New Key* (Cambridge, MA: Harvard University Press, 1951), 153.
104 Albert Camus, *The Rebel* (New York: Vintage Books, 1956), 263.
105 Améry, *At the Mind's Limits,* 28.
106 Thomas Brudholm, "Revisiting Resentments: Jean Améry and the Dark Side of Forgiveness and Reconciliation," *Journal of Human Rights* 5 (2006): 16; Améry, *At the Mind's Limits,* 70. See Thomas Brudholm, *Resentment's Virtue: Jean Améry and the Refusal to Forgive* (Philadelphia: Temple University Press, 2008).
107 Améry, *At the Mind's Limits,* 44.
108 Ibid., 47.
109 Ibid., 48.
110 Ibid.
111 Ibid., 83.
112 Ibid., 83–4.
113 Ibid., 97.
114 Ibid., 98.
115 Ibid., 97.
116 Johann Gottfried von Herder, *Reflections on the Philosophy of the History of Mankind*, trans. T. O. Churchill (Chicago: University of Chicago Press, 1968), 38.
117 Améry, *At the Mind's Limits,* 97.
118 Ibid., 84.
119 Ibid., 48.
120 Ibid., 84.
121 Ibid., 100.
122 Ibid., 60.
123 Ibid., 57.
124 Simon Schama, *Landscape and Memory* (New York: Harper Perennial, 2004).
125 W. G. Sebald, *On the Natural History of Destruction,* trans. Anthea Bell (New York: Random House, 2003), 83.
126 Améry, *At the Mind's Limits,* 50–1; Jean Améry, *Jenseits von Schuld und Sühne: Bewältigungsversuche eines Überwältigten* (Stuttgart: Klett-Cotta, 2014), 97.
127 Améry, *At the Mind's Limits,* 51, 60–1.
128 See Celia Applegate, *A Nation of Provincials: The German Idea of Heimat* (Berkeley: University of California Press, 1990).
129 Améry, *At the Mind's Limits,* 57.
130 Ibid., 51.
131 Ibid.; Améry, *Jenseits von Schuld und Sühne,* 98.
132 Améry, *At the Mind's Limits,* 49.
133 Ibid.

134 Ibid., 48.
135 Ibid., xiv.
136 Ibid., 72.
137 Ibid., 73.
138 Ibid., 78.
139 Ibid., 68.
140 John Kleinig, *On Loyalty and Loyalties: The Contours of a Problematic Virtue* (New York: Oxford University Press, 2014), 279.
141 Isa. 54:7-8 as rendered in *Tanakh: A New Translation of the Holy Scriptures According to the Traditional Hebrew Text,* ed. Harry M. Orlinsky, H. L. Ginsberg, and Ephraim A. Speiser (Philadelphia: The Jewish Publication Society, 1985), 734–5.
142 Camus, *The Rebel,* 276.
143 Lawrence L. Langer, *Versions of Survival: The Holocaust and the Human Spirit* (Albany: State University of New York Press, 1982), 133.
144 Améry, *At the Mind's Limits,* 11.
145 Ibid., 28.
146 Ibid., 25.
147 Ibid., xi, 18.
148 Ibid., 20.
149 Ibid., 25.
150 Ibid., 95.
151 Ibid., 28.

Chapter 4: Betrayal and Its Vicissitudes

1 "American Rage: The Esquire/NBC News Survey," last modified March 18, 2016, http://www.esquire.com/news-politics/a40693/american-rage-nbc-survey/?src=social-email (accessed May 6, 2016). See Avishai Margalit, *On Betrayal* (Cambridge, MA: Harvard University Press, 2017). Margalit is concerned with the "ungluing" of relationships between friends and family: "It is the injury to the relationship that makes [an offense] betrayal … A *serious* breach of a *serious* trust … Betrayal is an act that undermines a thick relation." Margalit, *On Betrayal,* 83–5.
2 Hannah Arendt, *The Human Condition* (Chicago: University of Chicago Press, 1958), 246.
3 "Displaced Iraqis Traumatized by Islamic State, Betrayed by Neighbors," last modified August 20, 2014, http://www.pbs.org/newshour/bb/displaced-iraqis-traumatized-betrayed-islamic-militants/ (accessed March 21, 2015).

4 Margalit drew the distinction between intentional and normative betrayal in a conversation I had with him on December 11, 2014.

5 Jennifer J. Freyd and Pamela J. Birrell, *Blind to Betrayal: Why We Fool Ourselves We Aren't Being Fooled* (Hoboken, NJ: John Wiley & Sons, 2013), 9.

6 Jean Améry, *At the Mind's Limits: Contemplations by a Survivor on Auschwitz and Its Realities* (Bloomington: Indiana University Press, 1980), 69.

7 Ibid., ix.

8 Ibid., 40.

9 Margaret Urban Walker, "Resentment and Assurance," in *Setting the Moral Compass: Essays by Women Philosophers*, ed. Cheshire Calhoun (New York: Oxford University Press, 2004), 146. I removed her emphasis on "*threats to expectations based on norms*," which makes sense in the context of her argument, in order to preserve a succinct definition of resentment. See also Pablo de Greiff, *The Age of Apology: Facing Up to the Past* (Philadelphia: University of Pennsylvania Press, 2008), 128; and Richard Wallace, *Responsibilities and the Moral Sentiments* (Cambridge, MA: Harvard University Press, 1994), 12.

10 Améry, *At the Mind's Limits,* 28.

11 Havi Ben-Sasson, "Polish–Jewish Relations During the Holocaust: A Changing Jewish Viewpoint" (unpublished manuscript, 2014), 9–10.

12 Ibid., 11–12.

13 Marianne Hirsch and Leo Spitzer, *Ghosts of Home: The Afterlife of Czernowitz in Jewish Memory* (Berkeley: University of California Press, 2011), 73.

14 Eliezer Wiesel, Unpublished ms. [*Night*, Hebrew version], n.d. as reported in Ofer Aderet, "Newly Unearthed Version of Elie Wiesel's Seminal Work Is a Scathing Indictment of God, Jewish World," *Haaretz,* May 1, 2016, http://www.haaretz.com/jewish/news/.premium-1.717093 (accessed June 28, 2016).

15 Elie Wiesel, *Legends of Our Time* (New York: Schocken Books, 1982), 191.

16 Ibid., 189.

17 Lawrence L. Langer, *Versions of Survival: The Holocaust and the Human Spirit* (Albany: State University of New York Press, 1982), 141.

18 Ibid., 142.

19 Ibid., 133.

20 See Lawrence L. Langer, *Holocaust Testimonies: The Ruins of Memory* (New Haven, CT: Yale University Press, 1991), 38.

21 Emanuel Ringelblum, *Polish–Jewish Relations During the Second World War,* ed. Joseph Kermish and Shmuel Krakowski, trans. Dafna Allon, Danuta Dabrowski, and Dana Keren (Evanston, IL: Northwestern University Press, 1992), 77–8.

22 Ibid., 77.

23 See, for example, Omer Bartov, "Communal Genocide: Personal Accounts of the Destruction of Buczacz, Eastern Galicia, 1941–1944," in *Shatterzone of Empires:*

Coexistence and Violence in the German, Habsburg, Russian, and Ottoman Borderlands (Bloomington: Indiana University Press, 2013), 399–422; Frank Golczewski, "Shades of Grey: Reflections on Jewish-Ukrainian and German-Ukrainian Relations in Galicia," in *The Shoah in Ukraine: History, Testimony, Memorialization,* ed. Ray Brandon and Wendy Lower (Bloomington: Indiana University Press, 2008), 114–55; Natalya Lazar, "Czernowitz Jews and the Holocaust: Interethnic Relations, Violence, and Survival in a Borderland City, 1941–1946" (PhD diss. proposal, Clark University, 2015).

24 Simon Wiesenthal, *The Sunflower: On the Possibilities and Limits of Forgiveness* (New York: Schocken Books, 1998), 35.

25 Ibid., 68.

26 Ibid., 13, 55.

27 Ibid., 68.

28 Ibid.

29 Ibid., 35.

30 Ibid.

31 Ibid., 9.

32 Ibid., 57; Simon Wiesenthal, *Die Sonnenblume:Eine Erzählung von Schuld und Vergebung* (Vienna: Ullstein, 1984), 64.

33 Wiesenthal, *The Sunflower,* 56.

34 Ibid., 57.

35 Ibid., 22.

36 Ibid., 18.

37 Ibid., 19.

38 Ibid.

39 Ibid., 20.

40 Ibid., 8.

41 Ibid., 9.

42 Tony Judt, *Postwar: A History of Europe Since 1945* (New York: Penguin Books, 2006), 803–31; Jan Grabowski, *Hunt for the Jews: Betrayal and Murder in German-Occupied Poland* (Bloomington: Indiana University Press, 2013).

43 Jonathan Lear referred to cultural strategies—including ritual, myths, and customs—that support a psychological process of "psychic integration" against the threat of "incomprehensible catastrophe." Jonathan Lear, "Mourning and Moral Psychology," *Psychoanalytic Psychology* 31 (2014): 475. I would add the act of writing, and specifically, writing memoirs and other accounts, as another proven strategy. See Terrence Des Pres, *The Survivor: An Anatomy of Life in the Death Camps* (New York: Oxford University Press, 1976), 35, on Wiesel's act of writing as process: he "attempts to interpret, not the experience itself, but the survivor's relation to it in retrospect."

44 See Orlando Patterson, *Slavery and Social Death* (New York: Cambridge University Press, 1982), which introduced the term "social death." He defined it as a condition of personal subjection, expulsion from the normative social and moral community, and chronic dishonor. For a description of its conditions in Nazi Germany, see Marion A. Kaplan, *Between Dignity and Despair: Jewish Life in Nazi Germany* (New York: Oxford University Press, 1998).
45 Ringelblum, *Polish–Jewish Relations,* 59.
46 Améry, *At the Mind's Limits,* 78.
47 Omer Bartov, "Guilt and Accountability in the Postwar Courtroom: The Holocaust in Czortków and Buczacz, East Galicia, as Seen in West German Legal Discourse," *Historical Reflections/Reflexions Historiques* 39 (2013): 96–123; see Devin O. Pendas, *The Frankfurt Auschwitz Trial, 1963–1965: Genocide, History, and the Limits of the Law* (Cambridge: Cambridge University Press, 2006), 216–17.
48 Wiesenthal, *The Sunflower,* 97.
49 Améry, *At the Mind's Limits,* xiii.
50 Wiesenthal, *The Sunflower,* 97.
51 See Pendas, *The Frankfurt Auschwitz Trial,* 258.
52 Vladimir Jankélévitch, "Should We Pardon Them?," *Critical Inquiry* 22 (1996): 571. See Améry, *At the Mind's Limits,* 71.
53 For an analysis of public debates and national legislation in Europe dealing with statutory limitations, see Ruth A. Kok, *Statutory Limitations in International Criminal Law* (The Hague: T. M. C. Asser Press, 2007), esp. 37–51, 141–245. See Peter Banki, "The Survival of the Question: Simon Wiesenthal's *The Sunflower,*" in *Terror and the Roots of Poetics,* ed. J. R. Champlin (New York: Atropos Press, 2013), 110–38, http://handle.uws.edu.au:8081/1959.7/528611 (accessed February 19, 2016).
54 Améry, *At the Mind's Limits,* 72.
55 Ibid., 70.
56 Jankélévitch, "Should We Pardon Them?," 571.
57 Ibid., 557.
58 Tom Segev, *Simon Wiesenthal: The Life and Legends* (New York: Doubleday, 2010), 237–8.
59 Wiesenthal, *The Sunflower,* 47, 87.
60 Ibid., 29.
61 Ibid., 78.
62 Ibid., 43.
63 Ibid., 7; Wiesenthal, *Die Sonnenblume,* 11.
64 Wiesenthal, *The Sunflower*, 84.
65 Quoted in Antony Polonsky and Joanna B. Michlic, eds, *The Neighbors Respond:*

The Controversy over the Jedwabne Massacre in Poland (Princeton, NJ: Princeton University Press, 2004), 13.

66 Langer, *Versions of Survival,* 142, 146.

67 See Bruno Bettelheim, *The Informed Heart: Autonomy in a Mass Age* (New York: Avon, 1971), 134: "Forcing nonsensical labor on the prisoners was a deliberate effort to speed their decline from self-respecting adults to obedient children." The figure of the Muselmann, literally "the Muslim," is an extreme example of utter helplessness in Nazi concentration camps. "Men of decay," in Primo Levi's terms, often succumbed to muted exhaustion, submission, and resignation. "They suffer and drag themselves along in an opaque intimate solitude." Primo Levi, *Survival in Auschwitz: The Nazi Assault on Humanity* (New York: Collier Books, 1993), 89. For an analysis, see Giorgio Agamben, *Remnants of Auschwitz: The Witness and the Archive* (New York: Zone Books, 2002), 41–86, and Shoshana Felman, *The Juridical Unconscious: Trials and Traumas in the Twentieth Century* (Cambridge, MA: Harvard University Press, 2002), 131–68. Stanley Elkins compared U.S. slavery to concentration camps precisely because both compelled childlike dependency. Levi and Elkins noted the exceptions; indeed, depending on conditions and personalities, victims, no matter the age, could transmute traumatic injury into resilience.

68 Jennifer L. Freyd, "Betrayal Trauma: Traumatic Amnesia as an Adaptive Response to Child Abuse," *Ethics and Behavior* 4 (1994): 307–29; Jennifer L. Freyd, *Betrayal Trauma: The Logic of Forgetting Childhood* (Cambridge, MA: Harvard University Press, 1996).

69 Freyd, "Betrayal Trauma," 318.

70 Ibid., 319–20.

71 Alice Miller, *Thou Shalt Not Be Aware: Society's Betrayal of the Child* (New York: Farrar, Straus and Giroux, 1998), 66.

72 Ibid.

73 Améry, *At the Mind's Limits,* 36.

74 Jankélévitch, "Should We Pardon Them?," 554.

75 Dominick LaCapra, *Writing History, Writing Trauma* (Baltimore: The Johns Hopkins Press, 2001), 92; Sidra DeKoven Ezrahi, "Representing Auschwitz," *History and Memory* 7 (1996): 121–56.

76 Melanie Klein, *Contributions to Psycho-Analysis* (London: Hogarth Press, 1950). See also Melanie Klein, "Love, Guilt, and Reparation," in Melanie Klein, *Love, Guilt and Reparation and Other Works, 1921–1945* (New York: The Free Press, 1975), 306–43.

77 Melanie Klein, "Mourning and Its Manic-Depressive States," *International Journal of Psycho-Analysis* 21 (1940): 125–53.

78 Sigmund Freud, "Mourning and Melancholia," in *The Standard Edition of the Complete Psychological Works of Sigmund Freud*, Vol. 14, ed. and trans. James Strachey (London: Hogarth Press, 1957): 243.

79 Ibid., 246.
80 Ibid., 244.
81 Améry, *At the Mind's Limits,* 40.
82 Freud, "Mourning and Melancholia," 245.
83 Ibid., 249.
84 Améry, *At the Mind's Limits,* 68.
85 Herbert Lehman, "A Conversation Between Freud and Rilke," *Psychoanalytic Quarterly* 35 (1966): 423–7; Max Schur, *Freud Living and Dying* (London: Hogarth Press, 1972), 302.
86 Sigmund Freud, "On Transience," in *Collected Papers,* Vol. 5, ed. and trans. James Strachey (London: Hogarth Press, 1950): 79.
87 Ibid., 80.
88 Ibid.
89 Ibid.
90 Ibid., 82.
91 Ibid., 81.
92 Ibid., 82.
93 Jankélévitch, "Should We Pardon Them?," 554.
94 Améry, *At the Mind's Limits,* 33.
95 Ibid., x.
96 Freud, "On Transience," 82; originally published in Janos Landau and Eugen Zabel, eds., *Das Land Goethes, 1914–1916: Ein vaterländisches Gedenkbuch* (Stuttgart and Berlin: Deutsche Verlang-Anstalt, 1916), 37–8.
97 Freud, "On Transience," 82.
98 See Dennis B. Klein, *Jewish Origins of the Psychoanalytic Movement* (New York: Praeger, 1981).
99 See Sigmund Freud, *The Interpretation of Dreams,* ed. and trans. James Strachey (New York: Avon Books, 1967), 229: "In the higher classes I began to understand for the first time what it meant to belong to an alien race, and anti-semitic feelings among the other boys warned me that I must take up a definite position." See also Klein, *Jewish Origins,* 48–55.
100 Freud, "On Transience," 82. One of Freud's followers, Otto Rank, discerned early on in Freud's *Interpretation of Dreams* a tendency to find a way out of predicaments and triumph over rivals and obstacles. See, for example, Rank's comments on Freud's interpretation of his own "Frau Doni" dream in E. James Lieberman and Robert Kramer, eds., *The Letters of Sigmund Freud and Otto Rank: Inside Psychoanalysis* (Baltimore: The Johns Hopkins Press, 2012), 315–22; and Dennis Klein, "Rank Contra Freud: Freud's Frau Doni Dream and the Struggle for the Soul of Psychoanalysis," *Annual of Psychoanalysis* 38 (2015): 40–51.

101 Sigmund Freud, *The Ego and the Id*, in *The Standard Edition of the Complete Psychological Works of Sigmund Freud*, Vol. 19, ed. and trans. James Strachey (London: Hogarth Press, 1961): 12–66.
102 See Sigmund Freud, "Remembering, Repeating, and Working Through," in *The Standard Edition of the Complete Psychological Works of Sigmund Freud*, Vol. 12, ed. and trans. James Strachey (London: Hogarth Press, 1958): 145–56. Consistent with his theoretical revisions in the 1920s, Freud modified the prospects of working through in deference to what he came to recognize as the inordinate might of repression. See Sigmund Freud, "Inhibitions, Symptoms, and Anxieties," in *The Standard Edition of the Complete Psychological Works of Sigmund Freud*, Vol. 20, ed. and trans. James Strachey (London: Hogarth Press, 1959): 87–176.
103 Jeffrey M. Blustein, *Forgiveness and Remembrance: Remembering Wrongdoing in Personal and Public Life* (New York: Oxford University Press, 2014).
104 Wiesel, unpublished ms., n.d., as reported in Ofer Aderet, "Newly Unearthed Version of Elie Wiesel's Seminal Work."
105 Blustein, *Forgiveness and Remembrance*, 93.
106 Ibid., 94.
107 Améry, *At the Mind's Limits*, 42.
108 Ibid., 51.
109 Ibid.
110 Ibid., 62.
111 Margalit, *On Betrayal*, 4.
112 Ibid., 289–304.

Chapter 5: Critical Forgiveness

1 Jean Améry, *At the Mind's Limits: Contemplations by a Survivor on Auschwitz and Its Realities* (Bloomington: Indiana University Press, 1980), 72.
2 Ibid., 69.
3 Ibid., 71.
4 Ibid., 69.
5 Simon Wiesenthal, *The Sunflower: On the Possibilities and Limits of Forgiveness* (New York: Schocken Books, 1998), 73.
6 Primo Levi, *The Drowned and the Saved* (New York: Summit Books, 1988), 137.
7 Ruth Kluger, "Forgiving and Remembering," *PLMA* 117 (2002): 313.
8 Ibid., 311–12.
9 Vladimir Jankélévitch, "Should We Pardon Them?," *Critical Inquiry* 22 (1996): 556.
10 Ibid., 567. When not referring specifically to official acts of state, Jankélévitch's translators used "pardon" and "forgive" interchangeably.

11 See Marcel Mauss, *The Gift: Forms and Functions of Exchange in Archaic Societies* (New York: W. W. Norton & Co., 1967).

12 Vladimir Jankélévitch, *Forgiveness,* trans. Andrew Kelley (Chicago: University of Chicago Press, 2005), 127.

13 See, for example, ibid., 126.

14 Ibid., 152.

15 Ibid., 34.

16 See Jacques Derrida, *On Cosmopolitanism and Forgiveness* (New York: Routledge, 2001). Recognizing forgiveness's other-worldliness, Paul Ricoeur wonders, "Is there some forgiveness for us?" Paul Ricoeur, *Memory, History, Forgetting* (Chicago: University of Chicago Press, 2004), 469.

17 Maurice Blanchot, *The Writing of Disaster* (Lincoln: University of Nebraska Press, 1995), 53.

18 Specifically, Jankélévitch, "Should We Pardon Them?"; Derrida, *On Cosmopolitanism and Forgiveness*; Ricoeur, *Memory, History, Forgetting.*

19 See Austin Sarat and Nasser Hussain, eds., *Forgiveness, Mercy, and Clemency* (Stanford: Stanford University Press, 2007).

20 Ricoeur, *Memory, History, Forgetting,* 468.

21 Jankélévitch, *Forgiveness,* 129.

22 Ibid., 127.

23 Hannah Arendt, *The Human Condition* (Chicago: University of Chicago Press, 1958), 241.

24 Lyn S. Graybill, *Truth and Reconciliation in South Africa: Miracle or Model?* (Boulder, CO: Lynne Rienner Publishers, 2002), 50.

25 Other truth commission chairs have encouraged forgiveness. Bishop J. C. Humper, chair of the Sierra Leone Truth and Reconciliation Commission, proclaimed in his foreword to the commission report, "Those who have confronted the past will be able to forgive others for the wrongs committed against them. Where the act of forgiveness is genuine it does not matter whether the perpetrator declines to express remorse. Learning to forgive those who have wronged us is the first step we can take towards healing our traumatised nation." J. C. Humper, *Witness to Truth: Report of the Sierra Leone Truth & Reconciliation Commission,* Vol. 1 (Accra, Ghana: GPL Press, 2004), 3.

26 Colleen Murphy, *A Moral Theory of Political Reconciliation* (Cambridge: Cambridge University Press, 2010), 11.

27 See David A. Crocker, "Punishment, Reconciliation, and Democratic Deliberation," in *Taking Wrongs Seriously: Apologies and Reconciliations*, ed. Elazar Barkan and Alexander Karn (Stanford: Stanford University Press, 2006), 50–82.

28 See Margaret Urban Walker, "Resentment and Assurance," in *Setting the Moral*

Compass: Essays by Women Philosophers, ed. Cheshire Calhoun (New York: Oxford University Press, 2004), 145–60.

29 Jeffrie Murphy, *Getting Even: Forgiveness and Its Limits* (New York: Oxford University Press, 2003), 19.

30 Desmond Mpilo Tutu, *No Future Without Forgiveness* (New York: Doubleday, 1999).

31 Thomas Brudholm, "Revisiting Resentments: Jean Améry and the Dark Side of Forgiveness and Reconciliation," *Journal of Human Rights* 5 (2006):15.

32 See Bernard R. Boxill, "Self-Respect and Protest," *Philosophy and Public Affairs* 6 (1976): 58–69. See Jeffrey Blustein, *Forgiveness and Remembrance: Remembering Wrongdoing in Personal and Public Life* (New York: Oxford University Press, 2014), 57–9.

33 Nancy Wood, *Modernity, Culture and the "Jew,"* ed. Bryan Cheyette and Laura Marcus (Stanford: Stanford University Press, 1998), 257–67; Arne Johan Vetlesen, "A Case for Resentment: Jean Améry Versus Primo Levi," *Journal of Human Rights* 5 (2006): 27–44.

34 Améry, *At the Mind's Limits*, ix.

35 Resentment is an "opportunity and ability to get transgressors back within bounds, to impose some corrective action on them, or at the very least to summon support from others for a clear repudiation of what transgressors have done." Walker, "Resentment and Assurance," 153.

36 Brudholm, "Revisiting Resentments," 21.

37 Améry, *At the Mind's Limits*, 81.

38 Ibid., 80.

39 Ibid., 81. Jean Améry, *Jenseits von Schuld und Sühne: Bewältigungsversuche eines Überwältigten* (Stuttgart: Klett-Cotta, 2014), 144.

40 Améry, *At the Mind's Limits*, 80.

41 Jankélévitch, "Should We Pardon Them?," 571.

42 Ibid.

43 Ibid., 556.

44 Wiesenthal, *The Sunflower*, 93.

45 Ibid.

46 Ibid., 97.

47 Améry, *At the Mind's Limits*, 69.

48 "Cultural imperialism" is another apt expression for what survivors saw as a regnant demand to forget the past and to move on. See Iris Marion Young, *Justice and the Politics of Difference* (Princeton, NJ: Princeton University Press, 1990).

49 I am grateful to Devin O. Pendas for his scrupulous and helpful review of the discussion that follows. For an overview of the trial, see Hermann Langbein, *Auschwitz-Proceß: Eine Dokumentation*, 2 vols. (Frankfurt am Main: EVA, 1965).

50 Depending on interpretations of the Lüneberg trial, the Frankfurt trial might be

considered the third Auschwitz trial. See Devin O. Pendas et al., "Auschwitz Trials: The Jewish Dimension," *Yad Vashem Studies* 41 (2013): 139–71.

51 Technically, the West German code complied with international law in disavowing superior orders as a legitimate defense, but in recognizing accessory crimes, it effectively validated the defense as grounds for mitigation. The code was formulated in the Wilhelmine period with emendations in 1940 redefining murder and revived in the 1950s after the period of Allied occupation and the establishment of the Federal Republic of Germany. See Adalbert Rückerl, *NS-Verbrechen vor Gericht: Versuch einer Vergangenheitsbewältigung* (Heidelberg: C. F. Müller, 1982). For a critical overview of the prosecution of Nazi crimes since the Second World War, see Helge Grabitz, "Problems of Nazi Trials in the Federal Republic of Germany," *Holocaust Genocide Studies* 3 (1988): 209–22.

52 West German courts, challenging ex post facto law, ceased prosecuting crimes against humanity—the standard, codified in Control Council Law No. 10, during the occupation period—in 1950; a 1954 statute declaring genocide illegal exempted the crime of genocide as grounds for prosecuting former Nazis.

53 Devin O. Pendas, *The Frankfurt Auschwitz Trial, 1963–1965: Genocide, History, and the Limits of the Law* (Cambridge: Cambridge University Press, 2006), 56–9. See also Rebecca Wittmann, *Beyond Justice: The Auschwitz Trial* (Cambridge, MA: Harvard University Press, 2005). Pendas and Wittmann were concerned with the limits of the law in dealing with genocide. Both are valuable sources for their overview of the proceedings. For an analysis of West German jurisprudential policy after the war, see Omer Bartov, "Guilt and Accountability in the Postwar Courtroom: The Holocaust in Czortków and Buczacz, East Galicia, as Seen in West German Legal Discourse," *Historical Reflections/Reflexions Historiques* 39 (2013): 96–123.

54 See Norbert Frei, *Adenauer's Germany and the Nazi Past: The Politics of Amnesty and Integration,* trans. Joel Golb (New York: Columbia University Press, 2002); Jeffrey Herf, *Divided Memory: The Nazi Past in the Two Germanys* (Cambridge, MA: Harvard University Press, 1997).

55 Ibid., 271.

56 Ibid., 271–2.

57 Ibid., 295.

58 Jean-Paul Bier, "The Holocaust and West Germany: Strategies of Oblivion, 1947–1979," *New German Critique* 19 (1980): 9–29.

59 Frei, *Adenauer's Germany,* xiii.

60 Jankélévitch, "Should We Pardon Them?," 557.

61 Wiesenthal, *The Sunflower,* 97.

62 Statutory limitations for most other crimes of violence, such as assault, lapsed in 1955.

63 See Marc von Miquel, *Ahnden oder Amnestieren: Westdeutsche Justiz und Vergangenheitspolitik in den sechziger Jahren* (Göttigen: Wallstein Verlag, 2004).

64 Pendas, *The Frankfurt Auschwitz Trial,* 254–5.

65 Jankélévitch, "Should We Pardon Them?," 557.

66 On a technicality, the 1965 debate resulted in a four-year extension, to 1969—twenty years after the withdrawal of the Allies and the establishment of an independent West German judiciary. In 1969 the prescribed period became thirty years, to 1979. In that year, the parliament exempted limitations altogether. For an analysis of parliamentary decisions in Europe, see Ruth A. Kok, *Statutory Limitations in International Criminal Law* (The Hague: T. M. C. Asser Press, 2007), 37–47.

67 Wittmann, *Beyond Justice,* 2.

68 Herf, *Divided Memory,* 338.

69 See Gollwitzer's introduction to Emmi Bonhoeffer, *Zeugen im Auschwitz-Prozess: Begegnungen und Gedanken* (Wuppertal-Barmen: Johannes Kiefel Verlag, 1965), 7. See also Pendas, *The Frankfurt Auschwitz Trial,* 255–8.

70 Herf, *Divided Memory,* 339.

71 Pendas, *The Frankfurt Auschwitz Trial,* 255; see Hans-Peter Moehl, "Bonn gegen Lex Auschwitz," *Neue Rhein und Ruhr Zeitung,* November 18, 1964.

72 John R. Gillis, "Memory and Identity: The History of a Relationship," *Commemorations: The Politics of National Identity,* ed. John R. Gillis (Princeton, NJ: Princeton University Press, 1994), 3–24.

73 The failure to prove "base motives" produced relatively lenient verdicts—six received life penalties; three were acquitted; the rest (eleven) received short-term imprisonment sentences, including one juvenile sentence. Two were released for medical reasons.

74 Thomas Hobbes, *Leviathan,* ed. A. P. Martinich and Brian Battiste (Ontario: Broadview Press, 2011), 416.

75 Ralph Giordano, "Auschwitz—und kein Ende (II)," January 29, 1965, qtd in Pendas, *The Frankfurt Auschwitz Trial,* 268.

76 Ralph Giordano, "Leben—mit Auschwitz: Epilog auf den Frankfurter Prozeß," August 27, 1965, qtd in Pendas, *The Frankfurt Auschwitz Trial,* 269.

77 Améry, *At the Mind's Limits,* 73.

78 Ibid., 75.

79 Ibid.

80 Jankélévitch, "Should We Pardon Them?," 557.

81 Améry, *At the Mind's Limits,* xiii. It was Améry's decision to challenge and engage with public opinion that ended his period of silence. Before the 1960s survivors generally talked about their ordeal for archival documentation or within intimate, communal settings among family members, at displaced persons camps, and in

Jewish social circles. See Hasia Diner, *We Remember with Reverence and Love: American Jews and the Myth of Silence After the Holocaust, 1945–1962* (New York: New York University Press, 2009); David Cesarani and Eric J Sundquist, eds, *After the Holocaust: Challenging the Myth of Silence* (New York: Routledge, 2012); and François Azouvi, *Le mythe du grand silence: Auschwitz, les français, la mémoire* (Paris: Fayard, 2012). What is important is the belief Wiesenthal and Améry held that they were once again—as they were twenty years before during their ordeal—pressured into silence by the hostility toward the trial, but that this time they would react openly and strongly.

82 Cited by Dana Hollander, *Living Together: Jacques Derrida's Communities of Violence and Peace* (New York: Fordham University Press, 2013), 145.
83 Jankélévitch, *Forgiveness,* 158.
84 Jankélévitch, "Should We Pardon Them?," 565.
85 Améry, *At the Mind's Limits,* 75; Wiesenthal, *The Sunflower,* 97.
86 Jankélévitch, *Forgiveness,* 143.
87 Ibid., 30.
88 Ibid., 158.
89 Ibid., 35.
90 Emmanuel Levinas, *Nine Talmudic Readings* (Bloomington: Indiana University Press, 1994), 25.
91 Jankélévitch added disdainfully, "What matters [to Germans] is knowing whether Heidegger has been slandered." Jankélévitch, "Should We Pardon Them?," 568.
92 Wiesenthal, *The Sunflower,* 85.
93 Améry, *At the Mind's Limits,* 71.
94 Ibid.
95 Ibid., 72.
96 See ibid., 71.
97 Jankélévitch, "Should We Pardon Them?," 557.
98 Améry, *At the Mind's Limits,* 69.
99 Jankélévitch, "Should We Pardon Them?," 553.
100 Améry, *At the Mind's Limits,* 71.
101 Ibid., 78–9.
102 Ibid.
103 Ibid., 41–61.
104 See Jankélévitch, *Forgiveness,* 153.
105 Ibid., 152–3.
106 Ibid., 119, 140. In arguing for unconditional forgiveness, Derrida did not credit Jankélévitch for making the same argument in *Forgiveness,* perhaps, as Jonathan Judaken suggests, to single out "Should We Pardon Them?," with its reservations, for criticism. But he did arouse interest in his work. See Derrida, *On*

Cosmopolitanism and Forgiveness, 36; Jonathan Judaken, *Vladimir Jankélévitch and the Question of Forgiveness* (Lanham, MD: Lexington Books, 2013), 25 n.51.

107 Wiesenthal, *The Sunflower,* 55.

108 Ibid., 54.

109 Ibid., 55.

110 Ibid., 75.

111 Ibid., 97, 98.

112 Simon Wiesenthal, *Die Sonnenblume: Eine Erzählung von Schuld und Vergebung* (Frankfurt: Ullstein, 1998), 107–8.

113 Brudholm recognized in Améry's reprimands a "wish for a constitution (or restoration) of a moral community between former enemies" and even that "his whole endeavor was aimed toward a reconciliation between people"; Brudholm, "Revisiting Resentments," 16; and Thomas Brudholm and Valerie Rosoux, "The Unforgiving: Reflections on the Resistance to Forgiveness After Atrocity," *Law and Contemporary Problems* 72 (2009): 40. But he also argued that Améry was "unforgiving." The apparent discrepancy involves Améry's adoption of the conventional concept of forgiveness: Améry refused to forgive because he understood the term to involve forgetting or to mean forgiving for the sake of moving on. But Brudholm conceded that Améry's values and commitments were compatible with "some well-reflected approaches to forgiveness." See Brudholm and Rosoux, "The Unforgiving," 37–8.

114 Joseph Butler, *The Works of Joseph Butler, in two volumes,* Vol. 2, *Sermons, etc.*, ed. W. E. Gladstone (Oxford: Clarendon, 1896), 158.

115 Ibid.; see Charles L. Griswold, *Forgiveness: A Philosophical Exploration* (New York: Cambridge University Press, 2007), 19–37.

116 Friedrich Nietzsche, *On the Genealogy of Morality* (Indianapolis: Hackett Publishing Co., 1998), 21.

117 Eva Kor, "If I Met Mengele Now, I'd Forgive What He Did to Me," *Guardian Unlimited Network,* January 8, 2005, http://www.theguardian.com/world/2005/jan/09/secondworldwar.theobserver (accessed March 26, 2015).

118 Eva Kor, "Miriam and I," http://theforgivenessproject.com/stories/eva-kor-poland/ (last modified March 29, 2010; accessed March 26, 2015). Kor is the founder of C.A.N.D.L.E.S., a Holocaust museum in Terre Haute, Indiana. The acronym stands for "Children of Auschwitz—Nazi's Deadly Lab Experiments Survivors." Münch was acquitted after survivors testified on his behalf, saying that he saved their lives. In a separate incident, he was convicted for inciting racial hatred after making disparaging remarks in 2001 on French radio about Roma and Sinti.

119 Margalit also argued that forgiveness is something "we may owe … to ourselves," even if the offender repents: "This duty stems from not wanting to live with feelings of resentment and the desire for revenge. Those are poisonous attitudes

and states of mind." Avishai Margalit, *The Ethics of Memory* (Cambridge, MA: Harvard University Press, 2008), 207. For a psychoanalytic view on forgiveness as "intrapsychic," see Melvin R. Lansky, "Hidden Shame, Working Through, and the Problem of Forgiveness in *The Tempest*," *Journal of the American Psychoanalytic Association* 49 (2001): 1005–33.

120 Margalit, *The Ethics of Memory,* 198.

121 See Berel Lang, *The Future of the Holocaust: Between History and Memory* (Ithaca, NY: Cornell University Press, 1999), 137.

122 Arendt, *The Human Condition,* 237.

123 Butler, *The Works of Joseph Butler,* 158.

124 Arendt, *The Human Condition,* 237.

125 Ibid., 246.

126 Ibid., 243.

127 Ibid., 242.

128 Ibid., 238.

129 Ibid., 240–80.

130 Ibid., 243.

131 Ibid., 178.

132 Ibid., 237.

133 Ibid., 240.

134 "So little is known" about offenses "we call 'radical evil' …, even to us who have been exposed to one of their rare outbursts on the public scene." Arendt, *The Human Condition,* 241.

135 Pumla Gobodo-Madikizela, *A Human Being Died That Night: A South African Woman Confronts the Legacy of Apartheid* (Boston: Houghton Mifflin, 2004), 98. Her story is the basis of a dramatic production that premiered in the United States in 2015.

136 For Desmond Mpilo Tutu's defense, see his "Foreword by Chairperson," *Truth and Reconciliation Commission of South Africa Report*, Vol. 1 (1998), 1–23, http://www.justice.gov.za/trc/report/finalreport/Volume%201.pdf (accessed April 15, 2015).

137 Jankélévitch, "Should We Pardon Them?," 572.

138 Ibid.

139 Wiesenthal, *The Sunflower,* 66; see 82.

140 Ibid., 53.

141 Primo Levi, *The Periodic Table,* trans. Raymond Rosenthal (New York: Schocken Books, 1984), 221–23.

142 Levinas, *Nine Talmudic Readings,* 19.

143 Jankélévitch, *Forgiveness,* 158.

144 Levinas, *Nine Talmudic Readings,* 16.

145 Kluger, "Forgiving and Remembering," 313.

146 Levi, *The Periodic Table,* 215.
147 Jankélévitch, "Should We Pardon Them?," 568.
148 Ibid., 567.
149 Jankélévitch, *Forgiveness,* 124.
150 Ibid., 127.
151 Derrida, *On Cosmopolitanism and Forgiveness,* 34. Derrida explored the idea of unconditional forgiveness in a seminar on forgiveness and perjury from 1997 to 2000.
152 For an example of divine forgiveness, see Num. 19:1-22.
153 Derrida, *On Cosmopolitanism and Forgiveness,* 39.
154 Griswold, *Forgiveness: A Philosophical Exploration,* 124.
155 Ricoeur, *Memory, History, Forgetting,* 457–506.
156 Améry, *At the Mind's Limits,* xiii.
157 Wiesenthal, *The Sunflower,* 97.
158 Ibid.
159 Jankélévitch, *Forgiveness,* 151.
160 Ibid., 154.
161 Ibid., 153.
162 For Arendt's analysis of Eichmann, see her polemic, originally published in 1963, *Eichmann in Jerusalem.* For a persuasive revision of Arendt's evaluation of Eichmann, see Bettina Stangneth, *Eichmann Before Jerusalem: The Unexamined Life of a Mass Murderer* (New York: Knopf, 2014). The logic of Arendt's argument mirrors aspects of the rationale of the FRG penal code. In contrast to international legal standards, the code regarded misdeeds committed by those who were deemed not to have integrated the base motives of perpetrators as accessory crimes. The nature of evil is left unexplored in her analysis of forgiveness, but by twinning it with intention—"the extremity of crime and willed evil" (239)—presumably unknowing misdeeds, in her view, are not radical crimes.
163 Arendt, *The Human Condition,* 238.
164 Ibid., 241. Strangely, in her otherwise strong reading of Arendt, Susan Rubin Suleiman argued that Arendt's conception of forgiveness was conditional, predicated on the offender's repentance. See Susan Rubin Suleiman, *Crises of Memory and the Second World War* (Cambridge, MA: Harvard University Press, 2006), 227–31.
165 Arendt, *The Human Condition,* 177.
166 Ibid., 178.
167 Ibid., 247.
168 Ibid., 178.
169 Ibid.
170 Ibid., 246.

171 Ibid., 244.

172 Ibid., 238.

173 Julia Kristeva and Alison Rice, "Forgiveness: An Interview," *PMLA* 117 (2002): 281.

174 Derrida, *On Cosmopolitanism and Forgiveness,* 39.

175 Ibid., 32.

176 Ibid., 39.

177 Ibid.

178 Jankélévitch, *Forgiveness,* 126.

179 Arendt, *The Human Condition,* 242.

180 Ibid., 241.

181 Ibid., 243.

182 Ibid., 242.

183 Ibid., 243.

184 See Martha Nussbaum, *Political Emotions: Why Love Matters for Justice* (Cambridge, MA: Harvard University Press, 2013) for a persuasive critique of ideal political theories.

185 See Ricoeur, *Memory, History, Forgetting,* 472. Amnesty, on the other hand, was an officially authorized forgetting, a practice that the South African Truth and Reconciliation Commission reversed with its charter legislative mandate for complete disclosures as a precondition of forgiveness.

186 Ricoeur, *Memory, History, Forgetting,* 490. See Blustein, *Forgiveness and Remembrance,* 171: "Forgiveness does not disable protest against wrongdoing, or against forgetting wrongdoing, but can in fact coexist with a readiness to protest wrongdoing if and when the need arises." Like Arendt, Blustein considered mediate circumstances of forgiveness, in his case, a victim's "non-retributive" emotions that permit forgiveness as opposed to "retributive" emotions, such as revenge and retaliation. Butler, too, acknowledged that awareness of the offense was consistent with an act of forgiveness, so long as the emotional feeling of resentment deferred to forgiveness. Butler, *The Works of Joseph Butler,* 158.

187 Ricoeur, *Memory, History, Forgetting,* 490.

188 Jacques Derrida, "Le siècle et le pardon," *Le Monde des débats* 9 (1999): 10–17. Qtd by Ricoeur, *Memory, History, Forgetting,* 605 n.44.

189 Kristeva and Rice, "Forgiveness: An Interview," 283.

190 Julia Kristeva, *Hannah Arendt: Life Is a Narrative* (Toronto: University of Toronto Press, 2001), 80. See Margaret R. Holmgren, *Forgiveness and Retribution: Responding to Wrongdoing* (New York: Cambridge University Press, 2014).

191 Margalit, *The Ethics of Memory,* 183–209, made the important distinction between forgetting the crime and "disregarding" it, arguing that "successful forgiveness" manages to remember the injury without "reliving" it. By sidestepping severe injuries, this formulation, however, fails to offer a paradigm of forgiveness after

atrocity. Under extreme circumstances, survivors, if inclined to forgive, cannot but relive the past.

192 Wiesenthal, *The Sunflower*, 95. See Jankélévitch, *Forgiveness*, 143, 162; Améry, *At the Mind's Limits*, 35.

193 Kristeva and Rice, "Forgiveness: An Interview," 283.

194 Ricoeur, *Memory, History, Forgetting*, 493.

195 Derrida, "Le siècle et le pardon," qtd by Ricoeur, *Memory, History, Forgetting*, 605 n.44.

196 Immanuel Kant, *The Metaphysics of Morals*, cited in Stephen Darwall, *The Second-Person Standpoint: Morality, Respect, and Accountability* (Cambridge, MA: Harvard University Press, 2006), 132–4. Butler, on the other hand, could not imagine "that we are required to love them [our enemies] with any peculiar kind of affection," preferring the more disinterested pose of recognizing the enemy's humanity. Butler, *The Works of Joseph Butler*, 160.

197 Bruno Bettelheim, writing in 1960, recognized "a real person" in a commanding SS officer at Buchenwald, but he saw him that way for negative reasons—to reduce his fear of him—rather than confirm a human connection with him. Bruno Bettelheim, *The Informed Heart: Autonomy in a Mass Age* (New York: Avon, 1971), 220.

198 Derrida, *On Cosmopolitanism and Forgiveness*, 44–5.

199 Kristeva and Rice, "Forgiveness: An Interview," 285.

200 Derrida, *On Cosmopolitanism and Forgiveness*, 51.

201 Kristeva and Rice, "Forgiveness: An Interview," 285.

202 Ricoeur, *Memory, History, Forgetting*, 490.

203 Kristeva and Rice, "Forgiveness: An Interview," 282.

204 Jankélévitch, *Forgiveness*, 161.

205 Scholars tend to downplay the historical conditions of survivors' appeal to human fellowship. Kristeva, Charles Griswold, and Avishai Margalit, for example, refer in passing to prior relations—to "remembered intimacy," as Margalit remarked—as a precondition of forgiveness. In fact, remembered intimacy or historical attachments form a critical part in setting the stage for survivors' inclinations to renegotiate their relationships. See Kristeva and Rice, "Forgiveness: An Interview," 283; Griswold, *Forgiveness: A Philosophical Exploration*, 58; and Margalit, *The Ethics of Memory*, 204.

206 Améry, *At the Mind's Limits*, 68.

207 Wiesenthal, *The Sunflower*, 40–3.

208 Ibid., 95; Wiesenthal, *Die Sonnenblume*, 105. Note that this judgment contravened penal deliberations in the FRG at the time, which condemned criminals for their base motives, showing leniency only toward criminals who didn't perpetrate, or instigate, crimes.

209 Wiesenthal, *The Sunflower*, 56.

210 Ibid., 57.

211 Ibid., 47; Wiesenthal, *Die Sonnenblume,* 54. *Schrecklich* referred to an object—"*Es gibt nichts, das so schrecklich wäre*"—rather than a person, which could have been rendered as *Es gibt niemanden.*

212 Wiesenthal, *The Sunflower,* 43.

213 Ibid., 51.

214 Ibid., 53.

215 Ibid., 66.

216 Ibid., 95.

217 Ibid., 81.

218 Ibid., 52.

219 Ibid., 36.

220 Jankélévitch, "Should We Pardon Them?," 565.

221 Ibid., 570.

222 Ibid., 565.

223 Ibid., 567.

224 Ibid., 572.

225 Ibid., 555.

226 Ibid., 562.

227 Ibid., 558.

228 Jankélévitch, *Forgiveness,* 164.

229 Ibid., 162.

230 Jankélévitch, "Should We Pardon Them?," 555.

231 Ibid., 556.

232 Jankélévitch, *Forgiveness,* 161.

233 Wiesenthal, *The Sunflower,* 7.

234 Jankélévitch, "Should We Pardon Them?," 572.

235 Ibid., 567–8.

236 Jankélévitch, *Forgiveness,* 162.

237 Ibid., 147.

238 Jankélévitch, "Should We Pardon Them?," 553. He reprised the point at the end of *Forgiveness*: "Forgiveness is strong like wickedness; but it is not stronger than it." Jankélévitch, *Forgiveness,* 165.

239 Ibid., 158.

240 Ibid., 156.

241 "L'esprit de l'homme oscille entre ces deux triomphes simultanément vrais, mais alternativement conçus: car ils se démentent l'un l'autre." (The human spirit oscillates between these two triumphs that are simultaneously true, yet alternately conceived: for they contradict one another.) Vladimir Jankélévitch, *Le Pardon* (Paris: Aubier-Montaigne, 1967), 212; *Forgiveness,* 163.

242 Ibid, 144.

243 Ibid.
244 Ibid., 73.
245 Ibid., 162.
246 Améry, *At the Mind's Limits,* 35.
247 Ibid., 24.
248 Ibid., 31.
249 Ibid., 27.
250 Ibid., 28.
251 Ibid., 34.
252 Ibid., 35–6.
253 Ibid., 35.
254 Ibid.
255 Ibid.
256 Ibid. Transitively, he noted the fellowship of tormentor and victim in commenting—three times in a passage on sadism—that the tormentor abused his "fellow man." For Jankélévitch, see his *Le sérieux de l'intention,* Vol. 1 of *Traité des vertus* (Paris: Bordas/Flammarion, 1989), 245: Man is "amphibious, simultaneously angel and beast, detained in the mixed zone of existence." As quoted in Joëlle Hansel, "Forgiveness and 'Should We Pardon Them?': The Pardon and the Imprescriptible," in *Vladimir Jankélévitch and the Question of Forgiveness* (Lanham, MD: Lexington Books, 2013), 114.
257 Améry, *At the Mind's Limits,* 25.
258 Ibid., 40.
259 Ibid., 70.
260 Ibid.
261 Ibid.
262 Ibid.
263 Jankélévitch, *Forgiveness,* 143.
264 Wiesenthal, *The Sunflower,* 32–6.
265 Ibid., 38.
266 Améry, *At the Mind's Limits,* 35.
267 Ibid., 78.
268 Jankélévitch, *Forgiveness,* 143.
269 Améry, *At the Mind's Limits,* 70.
270 Ibid., xi.
271 Ibid., 72.
272 Ibid., 68.
273 Ibid., 78.
274 Brudholm stated that the story of the SS man represented a "wish" but argued that it was more than that: "The surviving victim cannot 'move on' in/with a society

that has not recognized the moral horror of the crime committed in its name and which has been tolerated by the masses." Brudholm, "Revisiting Resentments," 16. This interpretation is inconsistent with Améry's achievement of standing: social amelioration begins with the victim, who, in the process, acquires agency. He hardly depended on German society's prior acknowledgment of wrongdoing. Dreaming about it—yearning for it—was subjective.

275 Améry, *At the Mind's Limits,* 71.

276 Ibid., 35.

277 Ibid.

278 Ibid., 28.

279 Ibid. Primo Levi wrote in agreement that a moral code constituting an expectation of help, which Améry believed was once "one of the fundamental experiences of human beings" (28), was no longer relevant: A "need to ask for help" was a "refuge" only for believers. Primo Levi, *The Drowned and the Saved,* trans. Raymond Rosenthal (New York: Summit Books, 1988), 145–6. He said a code of selfishness replaced it, "the shame of the world": "There are those who, faced by the crime of others or their own, turn their backs so as not to see it and not feel touched by it." Levi, *The Drowned and the Saved,* 85.

280 Wiesenthal, *The Sunflower,* 54.

Chapter 6: Deep Transitions: A Conclusion Resisting Finality

1 Jean Améry, *At the Mind's Limits: Contemplations by a Survivor on Auschwitz and Its Realities* (Bloomington: Indiana University Press, 1980), 35; Jean Améry, *Jenseits von Schuld und Sühne: Bewältigungsversuche eines Überwältigten* (Stuttgart: Klett-Cotta, 2014), 73–4.

2 Vladimir Jankélévitch, "Should We Pardon Them?," *Critical Inquiry* 22 (1996): 558.

3 Vladimir Jankélévitch, *Forgiveness,* trans. Andrew Kelley (Chicago: University of Chicago Press, 2005), 155.

4 Simon Wiesenthal, *The Sunflower: On the Possibilities and Limits of Forgiveness* (New York: Schocken Books, 1998), 70.

5 Améry, *At the Mind's Limits,* 48.

6 Havi Ben-Sasson, "Polish–Jewish Relations During the Holocaust: A Changing Jewish Viewpoint" (unpublished manuscript, 2014), 9–10.

7 Omer Bartov, "Communal Genocide: Personal Accounts of Destruction of Buczacz, Eastern Galicia, 1941–1944," in *Shatterzone of Empires: Coexistence and Violence in the German, Habsburg, Russian, and Ottoman Borderlands* (Bloomington: Indiana University Press, 2013).

8 Améry, *At the Mind's Limits,* 35.

9 Ibid., 25.
10 Wiesenthal, *The Sunflower,* 7.
11 Améry, *At the Mind's Limits,* 70.
12 Jankélévitch, *Forgiveness,* 161.
13 Ibid., 152–3.
14 Améry, *At the Mind's Limits,* 78.
15 Ibid., xiv.
16 Wiesenthal, *The Sunflower,* 97; Simon Wiesenthal, *Die Sonnenblume: Eine Erzählung von Schuld und Vergebung* (Vienna: Ullstein, 1984), 108.
17 Stephanie Vieille, "Transitional Justice: A Colonizing Field?," *Amsterdam Law Forum* 4 (2012): 58–68.
18 Ernesto Verdeja, *Unchopping a Tree: Reconciliation in the Aftermath of Political Violence* (Philadelphia: Temple University Press, 2009), 22.
19 Edward Casey, *Remembering: A Phenomenological Study* (Bloomington: Indiana University Press, 2000), 235–6. See Jeffrey Blustein, *Forgiveness and Remembrance: Remembering Wrongdoing in Personal and Public Life* (New York: Oxford University Press, 2014), 171–5. On "Counter-Memorials," see James E. Young, *The Texture of Memory: Holocaust Memorials and Meaning* (New Haven, CT: Yale University Press, 1993), and Kerry Whigham, "Affective Echoes: Affect, Resonant Violence, and the Processing of Collective Trauma in Post-Genocidal Societies" (Ph.D. diss., New York University, 2016). For recent discussions of citizen activism, see Iosif Kovras, *Grassroots Activism and the Evolution of Transitional Justice: The Families of the Disappeared* (New York: Cambridge University Press, 2017); and Dennis B. Klein, ed. *Societies Emerging from Conflict: The Aftermath of Atrocity* (Newcastle upon Tyne: Cambridge Scholars Publishing. Forthcoming, 2017).
20 Impunity Watch, an NGO (non-governmental organization), is concerned with "victim communities" and other "local actors and bottom-up processes" toward promoting more effective political intervention. See Vasuki Nesiah, *Transitional Justice Practice: Looking Back, Moving Forward,* May 2016, http://www.impunitywatch.org/docs/scoping_study_FINAL.pdf (accessed July 11, 2016).
21 P. F. Strawson developed the idea of reactive attitudes in *Studies in the Philosophy of Thought and Action* (Oxford: Oxford Clarendon Press, 1968). An attitude frames a response to others' actions that presumes a moral stance behind their behavior. Responses to inscrutable actions acquire positive or negative inflection based on beliefs in others' generosity, esteem, or affection on the one hand, or, on the other, indifference, contempt, or broken promises. Since betrayal plays a significant role in survivors' accounts, we are interested in the reactive attitude of resentment.
22 Améry, *At the Mind's Limits,* 99.
23 Ibid., 95.
24 Ibid., 99; see 87.

25 Ibid., 99.
26 Ibid., 93.
27 Ibid., 86.
28 Ibid., 87.
29 Ibid.
30 Ibid., 100.
31 Ibid., 96.
32 Ibid., 95.
33 Ibid., 93.
34 Ibid., 101.
35 Ibid., 100.
36 See Hisham D. Aide, *Rebel Music: Race, Empire, and the New Muslim Youth Culture* (New York: Vintage, 2014), xiii. See also Aida Alami, "An Online Megaphone Nudges Focus Away from the Center of Paris," *New York Times,* July 4, 2015, 9.
37 The term "conflict" might suggest two belligerent parties actively opposing each other. For our purposes, the term describes conditions of distrust and discord between two parties. We are interested in encounters characterized by strife that involved power relationships. "Reconciliation" is one important model of transition but not the only one. Partition is sometimes seen as preferable to reconciliation where adversaries inhabit different territories and, in the aftermath of conflict, sometimes seek political independence. The violence within India between Muslims and Hindus leading, in 1947, to the establishment of independent Pakistan, mainly for Muslims, and independent India, mainly for Hindus and, some twenty-five years later, Bangladesh's war of independence with Pakistan serve as examples. We are interested in circumstances involving distinctive ethnic groups sharing the same physical space, as was the case of Jews in European societies. See Verdeja, *Unchopping a Tree,* 5–6. Pablo de Greiff regarded reconciliation as a "final aim," with "a just social order" as the "ultimate aim." "A Normative Conception of Transitional Justice," *Politorbis* 50 (2010): 28.
38 Verdeja, *Unchopping a Tree,* 25.
39 P. E. Digeser, *Political Forgiveness* (Ithaca, NY: Cornell University Press, 2001), 65–71.
40 See Amy Gutmann and Dennis Thompson, *Democracy and Disagreement: Why Moral Conflict Cannot Be Avoided in Politics, and What Should Be Done About It* (Cambridge, MA: Harvard University Press, 1996).
41 David A. Crocker, "Punishment, Reconciliation, and Democratic Deliberation," in *Taking Wrongs Seriously: Apologies and Reconciliations*, ed. Elazar Barkan and Alexander Karn (Stanford, CA: Stanford University Press, 2006), 61. See Verdeja, *Unchopping a Tree,* 22.

42 Stephen Darwall, "Respect and the Second-Person Standpoint," *Proceedings and Addresses of the American Philosophical Association* 78 (2004): 54. See Immanuel Kant, *Practical Philosophy* (Cambridge: Cambridge University Press, 1996).
43 Margaret Urban Walker, "Truth Telling as Reparations," *Metaphilosophy* 41 (2010): 536.
44 Ibid., 537.
45 Erin Daly, "Truth Skepticism: An Inquiry into the Value of Truth in Times of Transition," *International Journal of Transitional Justice* 2 (2008): 29, 37.
46 De Greiff, "A Normative Conception of Transitional Justice," 22.
47 Walker, "Truth Telling as Reparations," 532.
48 Margaret Urban Walker, *Moral Repair: Reconstructing Moral Relations After Wrongdoing* (New York: Cambridge University Press, 2006), 26.
49 Colleen Murphy, *A Moral Theory of Political Reconciliation* (Cambridge: Cambridge University Press, 2010), 30. See also Pablo de Greiff, *The Age of Apology: Facing Up to the Past* (Philadelphia: University of Pennsylvania Press, 2008), 125–6.
50 Richard Wallace, *Responsibilities and the Moral Sentiments* (Cambridge, MA: Harvard University Press, 1994), 18–50.
51 De Greiff, "A Normative Conception of Transitional Justice," 26.
52 John Hope Franklin, *The Color Line: Legacy for the Twenty-First Century* (Columbia: University of Missouri Press, 1993), 74–5.
53 Bryan Stevenson, *Just Mercy: A Story of Justice and Redemption* (New York: Spiegel & Grau, 2014), 300.
54 See Bryan Stevenson, "We Need to Talk About an Injustice," TED Talk, https://www.ted.com/talks/bryan_stevenson_we_need_to_talk_about_an_injustice/transcript?language=en at 20:27 (posted March 2012, accessed January 18, 2016); Martin Luther King, Jr., "Keep Moving from This Mountain," Sermon at Temple Israel of Hollywood, February 26, 1965, transcribed from the audio by Michael E. Eidenmuller, http://www.americanrhetoric.com/speeches/PDFFiles/MLK%20Temple%20Israel%20Hollywood.pdf (accessed January 18, 2015); Theodore Parker, *Ten Sermons of Religion* (Boston: Crosby, Nichols, and Co., 1853), 84–5.
55 Améry, *At the Mind's Limits*, xi.
56 Linda Radzik, *Making Amends* (New York: Oxford University Press, 2009), 169–70; Crocker, "Punishment, Reconciliation, and Democratic Deliberation," 66.
57 Jaime Malamud-Goti, "Transitional Governments in the Breach: Why Punish State Criminals?," *Human Rights Quarterly* 12 (1990): 2–3.
58 Jankélévitch, "Should We Pardon Them?," 572.
59 Paul van Zyl, "Dilemma of Transitional Justice: The Case of South Africa's Truth and Reconciliation Commission," *Journal of International Affairs* 52 (1999): 661.

60 See Ruti G. Teitel, *Transitional Justice* (New York: Oxford University Press, 2000), 28–9, 67; Raquel Aldana, "A Victim-Centered Reflection on Truth Commissions and Prosecutions as a Response to Mass Atrocities," *Journal of Human Rights* 5 (2006): 120.
61 Jankélévitch, "Should We Pardon Them?," 557.
62 Teitel, *Transitional Justice*, 34–39.
63 Améry, *At the Mind's Limits*, 98. The Frankfurt trial tried twenty defendants, convicting six to life sentences and eleven to prison terms from three-plus years to fourteen years. Three were acquitted.
64 Teitel, *Transitional Justice*, 60–6. The German parliament abolished the limitations statute for radical crimes in 1979.
65 Jankélévitch, "Should We Pardon Them?," 557.
66 Jankélévitch, *Forgiveness*, 127.
67 Jankélévitch, "Should We Pardon Them?," 555. During the occupation period under international jurisdiction, Wiesenthal commenced an active search for former Nazis in order to bring their cases to trial. He continued his activities afterward, reflecting in *The Sunflower* that the work "might help me regain my faith in humanity." Wiesenthal, *The Sunflower*, 84.
68 Améry, *At the Mind's Limits*, 28.
69 Wiesenthal, *The Sunflower*, 57.
70 Ibid., 92.
71 Ibid., 70.
72 Ibid.
73 Jankélévitch, *Forgiveness*, 128.
74 Desmond Mpilo Tutu, *No Future Without Forgiveness* (New York: Doubleday, 1999), 19.
75 See Teitel, *Transitional Justice*, 40.
76 Jaime Malamud-Goti, an adviser to Argentine president Raúl Alfonsín after a period of military dictatorship and political repression, argued that lower ranks were not criminally responsible since peer pressure, in institutional–military contexts, neutralized perpetrators' personal motivations. Malamud-Goti, "Transitional Governments in the Breach," 9.
77 See www.facebook.com/stevenspielbergjewishfilmarchive/posts/10152282744993513 (accessed July 12, 2016).
78 Radzik, *Making Amends*, 155; Lucy Allais, "Restorative Justice, Retributive Justice, and the South African Truth and Reconciliation Commission," *Philosophy and Public Affairs* 39 (2011): 350.
79 Among institutional reforms are the 1985 UN Declaration of Basic Principles of Justice for Victims of Crime and Abuse of Power. The Rome Statute of the International Criminal Court and ICC Rules entered into force in 2002 to support

victims' rights during proceedings. See Aldana, "A Victim-Centered Reflection," 111–15.

80 Malamud-Goti, "Transitional Governments in the Breach," 4–5, 14.

81 Jacques Derrida, *On Cosmopolitanism and Forgiveness* (New York: Routledge, 2001), 39.

82 Paul Ricoeur, *Memory, History, Forgetting* (Chicago: University of Chicago Press, 2004), 458.

83 Julia Kristeva and Alison Rice, "Forgiveness: An Interview," *PMLA* 117 (2002): 283.

84 Tutu, *No Future Without Forgiveness,* 145.

85 Ibid., 272.

86 Murphy, *A Moral Theory of Political Reconciliation,* 10.

87 Verdeja, *Unchopping a Tree,* 16; see Aldana, "A Victim-Centered Reflection," 116–17; Lyn S. Graybill, *Truth and Reconciliation in South Africa: Miracle or Model?* (Boulder, CO: Lynne Rienner Publishers, 2002).

88 Sisonke Msimang, "The End of the Rainbow Nation Myth," *New York Times,* April 12, 2015. http://www.nytimes.com/2015/04/13/opinion/the-end-of-the-rainbow-nation-myth.html?&_r=0 (accessed February 1, 2016).

89 Améry, *At the Mind's Limits,* 69.

90 Jeffrie Murphy, *Getting Even: Forgiveness and Its Limits* (New York: Oxford University Press, 2003), 20; Aldana, "A Victim-Centered Reflection," 117.

91 Murphy, *A Moral Theory of Political Reconciliation,* 11–12.

92 See Yazier Henri and Heidi Grunebaum, "Re-historicising Trauma: Reflections on Violence and Memory in Current-day Cape Town." Direct Action Center for Peace and Memory occasional papers series, no. 6 (Cape Town: DACPM, 2005).

93 Murphy, *A Moral Theory of Political Reconciliation,* 12.

94 Malamud-Goti, "Transitional Governments in the Breach," 16.

95 Aldana, "A Victim-Centered Reflection," 116–17.

96 Tony F. Marshall, "Criminal Justice Conferencing Calls for Caution," *VOMA Quarterly* 8 (1997): 5–6, 9.

97 Tony F. Marshall, *A Restorative Justice Reader* (Portland, OR: Willan, 2003); Nick Smith, "The Categorical Apology," *Journal of Social Philosophy* 36 (2005): 473–96; Radzik, *Making Amends.*

98 See John Braithwaite, "Repentance Rituals and Restorative Justice," *Journal of Political Philosophy* 8 (2000): 123–24.

99 De Greiff, *The Age of Apology.*

100 Janna Thompson, "Is Political Apology a Sorry Affair?," *Social and Legal Studies* 21 (2012): 215–25. For comparison, see Hannah Arendt's seminal essay, "Collective Responsibility" in *Responsibility and Judgment*, ed. Jerome Kohn (New York: Schocken Books, 2003), 147–58.

101 See http://www.sahistory.org.za/archive/challenge-church-theological-comment-political-crisis-south-africa-kairos-document-1985 (accessed June 7, 2015).

102 Volker Nerlich, "The Contribution of Criminal Justice," in *Justice and Reconciliation in Post-Apartheid South Africa,* ed. Francois du Bois and Antje du Bois-Pedain (Cambridge: Cambridge University Press, 2008), 90–115.

103 See Allais, "Restorative Justice."

104 Quoted in Graybill, *Truth and Reconciliation in South Africa: Miracle or Model?,* 42; See Crocker, "Punishment, Reconciliation, and Democratic Deliberation," 63.

105 Jankélévitch, *Forgiveness,* 143, 162.

106 Améry, *At the Mind's Limits,* 49.

107 Wiesenthal, *The Sunflower,* 47, 87.

108 Ibid., 40.

109 Ibid., 53.

110 Ibid., 84.

111 Jankélévitch, *Forgiveness,* 66, 161.

112 Ibid., 70.

113 Ibid., 162.

114 Jacques Derrida, "Le siècle et le pardon," *Le Monde des débats* 9 (1999): 3.

115 Jankélévitch, *Forgiveness,* 158.

116 See Michael Ignatieff, *Truth and Lies: Stories from the Truth and Reconciliation Commission in South Africa,* ed. Jillian Edelstein (Milpark, South Africa: M&G Books, 2001), 20.

117 See Jill Scott, *A Poetics of Forgiveness: Cultural Responses to Loss and Wrongdoing* (New York: Palgrave Macmillan, 2010), 141–66; Blustein, *Forgiveness and Remembrance,* 213–19. The Chilean National Commission on Truth and Reconciliation was a subject of public scrutiny: The country's president appeared on national television to announce the establishment of the commission and, eventually, the results of its investigations. Newspapers published reports for weeks. See Walker, "Truth Telling as Reparations," 535.

118 Daly, "Truth Skepticism," 23–30; David A. Crocker, "Reckoning with Past Wrongs: A Normative Framework," *Ethics and International Affairs* 13 (1999): 50–1; Aldana, "A Victim-Centered Reflection," 113.

119 Marshall, *A Restorative Justice Reader,* 34–40; Radzik, *Making Amends,* 157–8; Crocker, "Reckoning with Past Wrongs," 61; Walker, *Moral Repair,* 214; Walker, "Truth Telling as Reparations," 535.

120 Améry, *At the Mind's Limits,* 70; Jankélévitch, "Should We Pardon Them?," 567.

121 Wiesenthal, *Die Sonnenblume,* 107–8.

122 Améry, *At the Mind's Limits,* 72.

123 De Greiff, "A Normative Conception of Transitional Justice," 23.

124 Ibid., 26.

125 De Greiff, *The Age of Apology,* 126.

126 Jankélévitch, "Should We Pardon Them?," 567–8.

127 Theodor Herzl, *The Jewish State,* in *Theodor Herzl: A Portrait for This Age,* ed. Ludwig Lewisohn, trans. Sylvie d'Avigdor (Cleveland, OH: The World Publishing Company, 1955), 238.

128 Freddie Knoller and John Landaw, *Living with the Enemy: My Secret Life on the Run from the Nazis* (London: Metro Publishing, 2005), 26.

129 Améry, *At the Mind's Limits,* 50.

130 Wiesenthal, *The Sunflower,* 70.

131 Jankélévitch, "Should We Pardon Them?," 569.

132 Améry, *At the Mind's Limits,* xi.

133 Ibid., 40.

134 Wiesenthal, *The Sunflower,* 46.

135 Améry, *At the Mind's Limits,* 28.

136 Digeser, *Political Forgiveness,* 68.

137 Ibid., 76.

138 Ibid., 70.

139 Ibid., 81.

140 Ibid., 72.

141 Ibid., 77.

142 Some 7,000 perpetrators applied for amnesty. The government's manifest efforts at prosecuting those who did not qualify for amnesty were anemic: "The contribution of criminal justice to dealing with the apartheid past was negligible." Nerlich, "The Contribution of Criminal Justice," 105. See also Allais, "Restorative Justice," 333–4; Crocker, "Punishment, Reconciliation, and Democratic Deliberation," 63. Referring to the Promotion of Natural Unity and Reconciliation Act No. 34 of 1995, *Truth and Reconciliation Commission of South Africa Report* (hereafter, *TRC Report*) made note that "the way was left open" for prosecution "in cases where amnesty applications were not made or were unsuccessful." *TRC Report,* Vol. 1 (1998): 119, http://www.justice.gov.za/trc/report/finalreport/Volume%201.pdf (accessed June 7, 2015).

143 Teitel, *Transitional Justice,* 56–9.

144 Marshall, *A Restorative Justice Reader,* 36.

145 Aldana, "A Victim-Centered Reflection," 118–19, 122.

146 Jankélévitch, *Forgiveness,* 143.

147 Améry, *At the Mind's Limits,* 70.

148 Jankélévitch, *Forgiveness,* 161.

149 Ibid., 128.

150 Ibid., 159.

151 Ibid., 158.

152 Ibid., 155.
153 Jankélévitch, "Should We Pardon Them?," 567.
154 Améry, *At the Mind's Limits,* 78.
155 Ibid., 25.
156 Ibid., xiv.
157 Ibid., 47.
158 Ibid., 50.
159 See ibid., 47.
160 Jankélévitch, *Forgiveness,* 163.
161 Ibid., 164.
162 Améry, *At the Mind's Limits,* 78.
163 Jankélévitch, *Forgiveness,* 78–9.
164 Jankélévitch, "Should We Pardon Them?," 566.
165 Ibid., 567.
166 Wiesenthal, *The Sunflower,* 83.
167 Ibid., 9.
168 Ibid., 10.
169 Ibid., 35; see 72.
170 Ibid., 12; see 85.
171 Wiesenthal, *Sonnenblume,* 108. By the late 1960s, the phrase "never again" gained currency with the founding of the Jewish Defense League, though it appeared in a similar context at the end of the 1961 documentary *Mein Kampf* as "It must never happen again—never again," and was used earlier by prisoners at the liberation of Buchenwald as well as by Jewish Resistance fighters in the Warsaw Ghetto. See "Is There a New Antisemitism? A Conversation with Raul Hilberg," *Logos: A Journal of Modern Society and Culture* 6 (2007): n.p., http://www.logosjournal.com/issue_6.1-2/hilberg.htm (accessed March 23, 2015).
172 Murphy, *A Moral Theory of Political Reconciliation;* Walker, *Moral Repair,* 222.
173 Murphy, *A Moral Theory of Political Reconciliation,* 11; see Aldana, "A Victim-Centered Reflection," 116; Jeffrie Murphy, *Forgiveness and Mercy* (Cambridge: Cambridge University Press, 1988), 16–17; de Greiff, *The Age of Apology,* 128–9.
174 Walker, *Moral Repair,* 223.
175 Ibid., 222; See Crocker, "Punishment, Reconciliation, and Democratic Deliberation," 61, and Murphy, *Getting Even: Forgiveness and Its Limits,* 17–26.
176 Améry, *At the Mind's Limits,* 62–81.
177 Ibid., 81.
178 Ibid., 67; Murphy, *A Moral Theory of Political Reconciliation,* 11.
179 Jankélévitch, "Should We Pardon Them?," 572.
180 Tutu, *No Future Without Forgiveness,* 31.
181 *TRC Report,* Vol. 1, 116.

182 Desmond Mpilo Tutu, "Foreword by Chairperson," *TRC Report,* Vol. 1, 9.
183 Tutu, "Foreword by Chairperson," 9.
184 *TRC Report,* Vol. 1, 116.
185 De Greiff, "A Normative Conception of Transitional Justice," 25.
186 Ibid.
187 Walker, "Truth Telling as Reparations," 532–3.
188 Christopher Kutz, "Justice in Reparations: The Cost of Memory and the Value of Talk," *Philosophy and Public Affairs* 32 (2004): 283.
189 Murphy, *A Moral Theory of Political Reconciliation,* 33.
190 Kutz, "Justice in Reparations," 283.
191 Marshall, *A Restorative Justice Reader,* 32.
192 Digeser, *Political Forgiveness,* 81.
193 Ibid., 71.
194 Murphy, *A Moral Theory of Political Reconciliation,* 11 n.24; see Malamud-Goti, "Transitional Governments in the Breach," who argued for reforming the Argentine military.
195 Murphy, *A Moral Theory of Political Reconciliation,* 13.
196 Teitel, *Transitional Justice,* 67.
197 Jankélévitch, "Should We Pardon Them?," 572.
198 Améry, *At the Mind's Limits,* 67.
199 Ibid.
200 Ibid., 77.
201 Ibid., 66.
202 Wiesenthal, *The Sunflower,* 91.
203 Ibid., 7.
204 Ibid., 96.
205 Ibid., 85.
206 See Trudy Govier and Wilhelm Verwoerd, "Trust and the Problem of National Reconciliation," *Philosophy of the Social Sciences* 32 (2002): 178–205; de Greiff, *The Age of Apology: Facing Up to the Past,* 125.
207 Tutu, *No Future Without Forgiveness,* 31.
208 Ibid., 32.
209 For an overview, see Walker, "Truth Telling as Reparations," 526–7. For an enumeration of official apologies, which reveals a spate of declarations starting modestly in the late 1980s and accelerating from 2000, http://www.humanrightscolumbia.org/ahda/political-apologies (accessed August 18, 2016).
210 Crocker, "Punishment, Reconciliation, and Democratic Deliberation," 61; see also Verdeja, *Unchopping a Tree,* 22, and Kutz, *Justice in Reparations,* 312: "A central task of Europe's nascent democracies is establishing the mutual relationships of respect and reciprocity constitutive of common citizenship."

211 Crocker, "Punishment, Reconciliation, and Democratic Deliberation," 61.
212 Darwall, "Respect and the Second-Person Standpoint," 45; Walker, "Truth Telling as Reparations," 538. See Crocker, "Punishment, Reconciliation, and Democratic Deliberation," 62.
213 Radzik, *Making Amends,* 159.
214 Darwall, "Respect and the Second-Person Standpoint," 51.
215 Hannah Arendt, *The Human Condition* (Chicago: University of Chicago Press, 1958), 243.
216 Crocker, "Punishment, Reconciliation, and Democratic Deliberation," 62; Walker, "Truth Telling as Reparations," 538.
217 Walker, *Moral Repair,* 209.
218 Judy Barsalou and Victoria Baxter, *The Urge to Remember: The Role of Memorials in Social Reconstruction and Transitional Justice* (Washington, DC: United States Institute of Peace, 2007), 5.
219 Walker, *Moral Repair,* 210.
220 Verdeja, *Unchopping a Tree,* 23.
221 Digeser, *Political Forgiveness,* 69–70.
222 De Greiff, "A Normative Conception of Transitional Justice," 23.
223 Ibid.
224 Ibid., 18 n.4.
225 Nils Christie argued that victims and offenders, rather than the state and its civil and criminal justice system, should resolve conflicts. The argument is a classic premise of the restorative justice movement. Nils Christie, "Conflicts of Property," *British Journal of Criminology* 17 (1977): 1–26.
226 Wiesenthal, *The Sunflower,* 9. The persistence of resentment in a post-conflict era of national reconciliation is apparent in independent Namibia: "I just kept silent because our founding president talked about national reconciliation," one Herero remarked, until a decision by a local city council concerning the Herero section of the municipal cemetery offended Hereros and piqued their residual anger. *The New York Times,* January 22, 2017, 9.
227 Walker, "Truth Telling as Reparations," 532.
228 Améry, *At the Mind's Limits,* 51.
229 De Greiff, "A Normative Conception of Transitional Justice," 26.
230 Ibid., 23. Quote from Annette C. Baier, *Moral Prejudices: Essays on Ethics,* ed. Annette C. Baier (Cambridge, MA: Harvard University Press, 1994), 133.
231 Jankélévitch, "Should We Pardon Them?," 567.
232 Ibid., 566.
233 In the U.S., healing and reconciliation is the presumed response to conflict; at least, that's the position of the United States Institute of Peace (USIP), an institution funded by Congress to promote the nation's potential for managing

international conflict without violence. It recognizes the role of grievances in the process but ultimately seeks the resolution of conflict and a "lasting peace." Had the 2015 forum it sponsored included witnesses to conflicts among its main speakers, who in the end were USIP staff members, it would have more likely acknowledged the persistence of grievances in the aftermath of conflict, http://www.usip.org/ (accessed February 3, 2016).

234 Améry, *At the Mind's Limits,* 71, 81.

235 Améry referred to Scheler's 1912 essay on resentment, *Vom Umsturz der Werte, Gesammelte Werke,* Vol. 3, ed. Maria Scheler (Bern: Francke, 1955), 33–147.

236 Max Scheler, *The Nature of Sympathy,* trans. Peter Heath (New Brunswick, NJ: Transaction Publishers, 2008), 101. Améry provided a reason for the Nazis' persecution of intellectuals' work like Scheler's: National Socialism "hated the word 'humanity' like the pious person hates sin, and that is why it spoke of 'sentimental humanitarianism.'" Améry, *At the Mind's Limits,* 31. The observation is self-reflective as well, for his dreams of fellowship placed him ideologically on the other side of Nazism's tribalism, even as his humanitarianism was anything but sentimental. See Améry, *At the Mind's Limits,* 60–1.

237 Jankélévitch, *Forgiveness,* 147; Scheler, *Vom Umsturz der Werte, Gesammelte Werke,* Vol. 3, 159. Even though forgiveness, for Jankélévitch, did not require an offender's promises, and that love, for Scheler, did not "desire a change in the thing loved" (158), they both imagined the possible influence of generosity on inspiring new, moral worldly relationships. But as we have argued, an offender's change of heart was, for Jankélévitch, essentially wishful. Forgiveness might make moral change possible—the offender "capable of getting back up" (147)—but given his contemporaries' resistance to self-examination, unconditional forgiveness was, in the end, subjective.

238 Scheler, *Vom Umsturz der Werte, Gesammelte Werke,* Vol. 3, 161.

239 The similarity of passages in *Forgiveness* and *The Nature of Sympathy* suggests Jankélévitch's intellectual indebtedness to Scheler's philosophy. Compare the prodigal son passages in *Forgiveness,* 155, with *The Nature of Sympathy,* 159.

240 Améry, *At the Mind's Limits,* 73.

241 Ibid., 74.

242 Wiesenthal, *The Sunflower,* 83.

243 Ibid., 84.

244 Ibid.; Wiesenthal, *Sonnenblume,* 94.

245 Jankélévitch, *Forgiveness,* 36.

246 "The Rule of St. Augustine," Ch. 1, Rule 2, http://www.op.org/sites/www.op.org/files/public/documents/fichier/rule_augustine_en.pdf (accessed June 20, 2015).

247 G. W. F. Hegel, *Early Theological Writings,* trans. T. M. Knox (Philadelphia: University of Pennsylvania Press, 1996), 238–9.

248 Jankélévitch, *Forgiveness,* 158.

249 Améry, *At the Mind's Limits,* 94.

250 Ibid., 100.

251 Wiesenthal, *The Sunflower,* 97.

252 Améry, *At the Mind's Limits,* 44.

253 Primo Levi, *The Drowned and the Saved,* trans. Raymond Rosenthal (New York: Summit Books, 1988), 85.

254 Charles Villa-Vicencio, "The Politics of Reconciliation," in *Telling the Truths: Truth-Telling and Peace Building in Post-Conflict Societies,* ed. Tristan Anne Borer (Notre Dame, IN: Notre Dame University Press, 2006), 62.

255 Ibid., 61.

256 Ibid., 60–2.

257 Améry, "Introduction," xi.

258 Edna O'Brien, *The Little Red Chairs* (Boston: Little, Brown & Co., 2016).

259 For an articulation of historical disruption, or discontinuity, this stark, where the succession of events are experienced as new temporalities, see Reinhart Koselleck, *Futures Past: On the Semantics of Historical Time,* trans. Keith Tribe (New York: Columbia University Press, 2004). Experience, he argued, shatters the "horizon of expectation," a conception of "disposable" history challenging classical conceptions that presumed the past as prologue. Survivors' counter-narratives, of course, flow in the opposite direction by summoning ancestral memories. By incorporating aspects of the past in the present as longing, survivors regard the past as a *historia magistra vitae* (history as a school of life). The narrative contradiction in the same account—here, as manifest historical discontinuity and counter-narrative historical continuity—is another example of locutionary incongruity that distinguishes the accounts we are investigating.

260 See Leo Strauss, *Rebirth of Classical Political Rationalism: An Introduction to the Thought of Leo Strauss,* ed. Thomas L. Pangle (Chicago: University of Chicago Press, 1989). Strauss observed the tension between intellectual traditions, specifically, "the conflict between the Biblical and the philosophical notions of the good life" (270). He contended that each person should adhere to one tradition but remain open to the challenge of the other. Ibram X. Kendi's 2016 study of racism in America argued that Americans historically live the conflict between racial progress and racist ideas, a challenge to regnant conceptions of racial progress as inexorable: John Hope Franklin's admonition to "turn our history around … [and] avoid doing what we have done for so long"; Martin Luther King, Jr.'s unforgettable hymn to the "moral arc of history"; and Barack Obama's "The long sweep of America has been defined by forward motion." Kendi recognized the enduring contradictions in America's experiences with race: "The outlawing of chattel slavery in 1865 brought on racial progress. Then, the legalization of

Jim Crow brought on the progression of racist policies in the late nineteenth century. The outlawing of Jim Crow in 1964 brought on racial progress. Then, the legalization of superficially unintentional discrimination brought on the progression of racist policies in the late twentieth century." Ibram X. Kendi, *Stamped from the Beginning: The Definitive History of Racist Ideas in America* (New York: Nation Books, 2016), 8. His references to progress in one camp as a "backlash" to the other diminishes his argument that racial progress and the progression of racist policies are "simultaneous" (9), that discordant traditions, ideas, and policies coexist independently, indeed, simultaneously, and not only in reaction to each other.

261 Primo Levi, "Revisiting the Camps," in *The Art of Memory: Holocaust Memorials in History,* ed. James Young (New York: Prestel-Verlag, 1994), 185.

262 Wiesenthal, *The Sunflower,* 46.

263 Jankélévitch, *Forgiveness,* 141.

264 Améry, *At the Mind's Limits,* 28.

265 Wiesenthal, *The Sunflower,* 96.

266 Jankélévitch, *Forgiveness,* 141.

267 Améry, *At the Mind's Limits,* 33.

268 Ibid., 88.

269 Eliezer Wiesel, unpublished ms. [*Night,* Hebrew version], n.d., as reported in Ofer Aderet, "Newly Unearthed Version of Elie Wiesel's Seminal Work Is a Scathing Indictment of God, Jewish World," *Haaretz,* May 1, 2016, http://www.haaretz.com/jewish/news/.premium-1.717093 (accessed June 28, 2016).

270 Améry, *At the Mind's Limits,* 47.

271 Murphy, *A Moral Theory of Political Reconciliation,* 30.

272 Améry, *At the Mind's Limits,* 46–7.

273 Virginia Held, *The Ethics of Care: Personal, Political, and Global* (New York: Oxford University Press, 2006), 12.

274 Jankélévitch, *Forgiveness,* 141.

275 See, for comparison, Nico van Hout, *The Unfinished* (New York: Harry N. Abrams, 2013).

276 Améry, *At the Mind's Limits,* 47.

Bibliography

7th Mauthausen Memorial Dialogue Forum (2015). Available online: https://eventmaker.at/mauthausen_memorial/7th_mauthausen_memorial_dialogue_forum (accessed June 11, 2016).

Agamben, Giorgio. *Remnants of Auschwitz: The Witness and the Archive.* New York: Zone Books, 2002.

Aide, Hisham D. *Rebel Music: Race, Empire, and the New Muslim Youth Culture.* New York: Vintage Books, 2014.

Alami, Aida. "An Online Megaphone Nudges Focus Away from the Center of Paris." *New York Times,* July 4, 2015.

Aldana, Raquel. "A Victim-Centered Reflection on Truth Commissions and Prosecutions as a Response to Mass Atrocity." *Journal of Human Rights* 5 (2006): 107–26.

Aleksiun, Natalia. "The Central Jewish Historical Commission in Poland, 1944–1947," *Polin: Studies in Polish Jewry* 20 (2007): 74–97.

Alexander, Jeffrey C. *Cultural Trauma and Collective Identity*, edited by Jeffrey C. Alexander. Berkeley: University of California Press, 2004.

Allais, Lucy. "Restorative Justice, Retributive Justice, and the South African Truth and Reconciliation Commission." *Philosophy and Public Affairs* 39 (2011): 331–63.

Aly, Götz. *Why the Germans? Why the Jews?: Envy, Race, Hatred, and the Prehistory of the Holocaust.* New York: Metropolitan Books, 2014.

"American Rage: The Esquire/NBC News Survey." *Esquire,* January 3, 2016. Last modified March 18, 2016. Available online: http://www.esquire.com/news-politics/a40693/american-rage-nbc-survey/ and http://www.esquire.com/news-politics/a40693/american-rage-nbc-survey/ (both accessed May 6, 2016).

Améry, Jean. *At the Mind's Limits: Contemplations by a Survivor on Auschwitz and Its Realities.* Bloomington: Indiana University Press, 1980.

Améry, Jean. *Jenseits von Schuld und Sühne: Bewältigungsversuche eines Überwältigten.* Stuttgart: Klett-Cotta, 2014.

Anderson, Eric, Dominique White, Erika Siegel, and Lisa Barrett. "Out of Sight, but Not Out of Mind: Unseen Affective Faces Influence Evaluations and Social Impressions." *Emotion* 12 (2012): 1210–21.

Applegate, Celia. *A Nation of Provincials: The German Idea of Heimat.* Berkeley: University of California Press, 1990.

Arendt, Hannah. *The Human Condition.* Chicago: University of Chicago Press, 1958.

Arendt, Hannah. *The Origins of Totalitarianism.* New York: Harcourt Brace Jovanovich, 1973.

Arendt, Hannah. "Collective Responsibility." In *Responsibility and Judgment,* edited by Jerome Kohn. New York: Schocken Books, 2003.

Arendt, Hannah. *Eichmann in Jerusalem: A Report on the Banality of Evil.* New York: Penguin Books, 2006.

Azouvi, François. *Le mythe du grand silence: Auschwitz, les français, la mémoire.* Paris: Fayard, 2012.

Baier, Annette C. *Moral Prejudices: Essays on Ethics.* Cambridge, MA: Harvard University Press, 1994.

Banki, Peter. "The Survival of the Question: Simon Wiesenthal's *The Sunflower.*" In *Terror and the Roots of Poetics,* edited by J. R. Champlin, 110–38. New York: Atropos Press, 2013. Available online: http://handle.uws.edu.au:8081/1959.7/528611 (accessed February 19, 2016).

Barkai, Avraham. "Jewish Self-Help in Nazi Germany, 1933–1939: The Dilemma of Cooperation." In *Jewish Life in Nazi Germany: Dilemmas and Responses,* edited by Francis R. Nicosia and David Scrase, 71–88. New York: Berghahn Books, 2010.

Barsalou, Judy and Victoria Baxter. *The Urge to Remember: The Role of Memorials in Social Reconstruction and Transitional Justice.* United States Institute of Peace, Stabilization and Reconstruction Series No. 5, Washington, DC, January 2007.

Bartov, Omer. "On Eastern Galicia's Past and Present." *Daedalus* 136 (2007): 115–18.

Bartov, Omer. "Eastern Europe as the Site of Genocide." *Journal of Modern History* 80 (2008): 557–93.

Bartov, Omer. "Communal Genocide: Personal Accounts of the Destruction of Buczacz, Eastern Galicia, 1941–1944." In *Shatterzone of Empires: Coexistence and Violence in the German, Habsburg, Russian, and Ottoman Borderlands,* edited by Omer Bartov and Eric D. Weitz, 399–422. Bloomington: Indiana University Press, 2013.

Bartov, Omer. "Guilt and Accountability in the Postwar Courtroom: The Holocaust in Czortków and Buczacz, East Galicia, as Seen in West German Legal Discourse." *Historical Reflections/Reflexions Historiques* 19 (2013): 96–123.

Ben-Sasson, Havi. "Polish-Jewish Relations During the Holocaust: A Changing Jewish Viewpoint." In *Rethinking Poles and Jews: Troubled Past, Brighter Future,* edited by Robert Cherry and Annamaria Orla-Bukowska, 89–98. New York: Rowman and Littlefield, 2007.

Ben-Sasson, Havi. "Polish-Jewish Relations During the Holocaust: A Changing Jewish Viewpoint." Unpublished manuscript, 2014.

Bergson, Henri. *TK.* Paris: Presses Universitaires de France, 1989.

Bernstein, Jay M. *Torture and Dignity: An Essay on Moral Injury.* Chicago: University of Chicago Press, 2015.

Berr, Isaac. *Lettre d'un citoyen, membre de la ci-devant Communauté des Juifs de Lorraine, à ses confrères, à l'occasion du droit de citoyen actif, rendu aux Juifs par le décret du 28 septembre 1791.* Nancy: H. Haener, 1791.

Bettelheim, Bruno. "Individual and Mass Behavior in Extreme Situations." *Journal of Abnormal Psychology* 38 (1943): 417–52.

Bettelheim, Bruno. *The Informed Heart: Autonomy in a Mass Age*, 189–220. New York: Avon, 1971.

Bier, Jean-Paul. "The Holocaust and West Germany: Strategies of Oblivion 1947–1979." *New German Critique* 19 (1980): 9–29.

Blanchot, Maurice. *The Writing of Disaster.* Lincoln: University of Nebraska Press, 1995.

Bloom, Harold. *A Map of Misreading.* New York: Oxford University Press, 1980.

Bloom, Harold. *The Anxiety of Influence: A Theory of Poetry.* New York: Oxford University Press, 1997.

Bloxham, Donald. *The Final Solution: A Genocide.* New York: Oxford University Press, 2009.

Blustein, Jeffrey M. *The Moral Demands of Memory.* New York: Cambridge University Press, 2008.

Blustein, Jeffrey M. *Forgiveness and Remembrance: Remembering Wrongdoing in Personal and Public Life.* New York: Oxford University Press, 2014.

Boder, David P. *I Did Not Interview the Dead.* Urbana: University of Illinois Press, 1949.

Boder, David P. *Topical Autobiographies of Displaced People Recorded Verbatim in Displaced Persons Camps, with a Psychological and Anthropological Analysis.* Chicago: David P. Boder, 1950–7.

Boxill, Bernard R. "Self-Respect and Protest." *Philosophy and Public Affairs* 6 (1976): 58–69.

Braithwaite, John. "Repentance Rituals and Restorative Justice." *Journal of Political Philosophy* 8 (2000): 115–31.

Brison, Susan J. "Trauma Narratives and the Remaking of the Self." In *Acts of Memory: Cultural Recall in the Present,* edited by Mieke Bal, Jonathan Crewe, and Leo Spitzer, 39–54. Hanover, NH: University Press of New England, 1999.

Broszat, Martin, and Saul Friedländer. "Martin Broszat/Saul Friedländer: A Controversy about the Historicization of National Socialism." *Yad Vashem Studies* 19 (1988): 1–47.

Brudholm, Thomas. "Revisiting Resentments: Jean Améry and the Dark Side of Forgiveness and Reconciliation." *Journal of Human Rights* 5 (2006): 7–26.

Brudholm, Thomas. *Resentment's Virtue: Jean Améry and the Refusal to Forgive.* Philadelphia: Temple University Press, 2008.

Brudholm, Thomas, and Valerie Rosoux. "The Unforgiving: Reflections on the Resistance to Forgiveness After Atrocity." *Law and Contemporary Problems* 72 (2009): 33–49.

Butler, Joseph. *The Works of Joseph Butler, in two volumes.* Vol. 2, *Sermons, etc,* edited by W. E. Gladstone. Oxford: Clarendon, 1896.

Camus, Albert. *The Rebel.* New York: Vintage Books, 1956.

Casey, Edward S. *Remembering: A Phenomenological Study.* Bloomington: Indiana University Press, 2000.

Cesarani, David and Eric J. Sundquist, eds. *After the Holocaust: Challenging the Myth of Silence.* New York: Routledge, 2012.

Christie, Nils. "Conflicts of Property." *British Journal of Criminology* 17 (1977): 1–26.

Crocker, David A. "Reckoning with Past Wrongs: A Normative Framework." *Ethics and International Affairs* 13 (1999): 43–64.

Crocker, David A. "Punishment, Reconciliation, and Democratic Deliberation." In *Taking Wrongs Seriously: Apologies and Reconciliations,* edited by Elazar Barkan and Alexander Karn, 50–82. Stanford, CA: Stanford University Press, 2006.

Daly, Erin. "Truth Skepticism: An Inquiry into the Value of Truth in Times of Transition." *International Journal of Transitional Justice* 2 (2008): 23–41.

Darwall, Stephen. "Respect and the Second-Person Standpoint." *Proceedings and Addresses of the American Philosophical Association* 78 (2004).

Darwall, Stephen. *The Second-Person Standpoint: Morality, Respect, and Accountability.* Cambridge, MA: Harvard University Press, 2006.

Davidson, Basil. *The African Past.* Boston: Little, Brown & Co., 1964.

Dawidowicz, Lucy S. *The Holocaust and the Historian.* Cambridge, MA: Harvard University Press, 1981.

Deem, James A. *The Prisoners of Breendonk.* New York: Houghton Mifflin, 2015.

Delbo, Charlotte. *Auschwitz and After*, translated by Rosette C. Lamont. New Haven, CT: Yale University Press, 1995.

Delbo, Charlotte. *Days and Memory*, translated by Rosette C. Lamont. Evanston, IL: Marlboro Press/Northwestern, 2001.

Derrida, Jacques. "Le siècle et le pardon." *Le Monde des débats* 9 (1999): 10–17.

Derrida, Jacques. *On Cosmopolitanism and Forgiveness,* 27–60. New York: Routledge, 2001.

Des Pres, Terrence. *The Survivor: An Anatomy of Life in the Death Camps.* New York: Oxford University Press, 1976.

Digeser, P. E. *Political Forgiveness.* Ithaca, NY: Cornell University Press, 2001.

Diner, Hasia. *We Remember with Reverence and Love: American Jews and the Myth of Silence After the Holocaust, 1945–1962.* New York: New York University Press, 2009.

"Displaced Iraqis Traumatized by Islamic State, Betrayed by Neighbors." PBS *Newshour,* August 20, 2014. Last modified March 24, 2016. Available online http://www.pbs.org/newshour/bb/displaced-iraqis-traumatized-betrayed-islamic-militants/ (accessed March 21, 2015).

Dwork, Debórah and Robert van Pelt. *The Holocaust: A History.* New York: W. W. Norton & Co., 2002.

Endelman, Todd. *Leaving the Jewish Fold: Conversion and Radical Assimilation in Modern Jewish History.* Princeton, NJ: Princeton University Press, 2015.

Engel, David. *Facing the Holocaust: The Polish Government-in-Exile and the Jews, 1943–1945.* Chapel Hill: University of North Carolina Press, 1993.

Ezrahi, Sidra DeKoven. "Representing Auschwitz." *History and Memory* 7 (1996): 121–56.

Falzeder, Ernst and Eva Brabant, eds. *The Correspondence of Sigmund Freud and Sándor Ferenczi, Volume 3, 1920–1933*, translated by Peter T. Hoffer. Cambridge, MA: Harvard University Press, 2000.

Feiner, Shmuel. *The Jewish Enlightenment*, translated by Chaya Naor. Philadelphia: University of Pennsylvania Press, 2004.

Felman, Shoshana *The Juridical Unconscious: Trials and Traumas in the Twentieth Century.* Cambridge, MA: Harvard University Press, 2002.

Felman, Shoshana and Dori Laub. *Testimony: Crises of Witnessing in Literature, Psychoanalysis, and History.* New York: Routledge, 1992.

Foucault, Michel. *Language, Counter-Memory, Practice,* edited by Donald F. Bouchard, translated by Donald F. Bouchard and Sherry Simon. Ithaca, NY: Cornell University Press, 1977.

Franklin, John Hope. *The Color Line: Legacy for the Twenty-First Century.* Columbia: University of Missouri Press, 1993.

Frei, Norbert. *Adenauer's Germany and the Nazi Past: The Politics of Amnesty and Integration*, translated by Joel Golb. New York: Columbia University Press, 2002.

Freud, Sigmund. "On Transience." In *Collected Papers*, Vol. 5, edited and translated by James Strachey, 79–82. London: Hogarth Press, 1950.

Freud, Sigmund. "Mourning and Melancholia." In *The Standard Edition of the Complete Psychological Works of Sigmund Freud,* Vol. 14, edited and translated by James Strachey, 243–58. London: Hogarth Press, 1957.

Freud, Sigmund. "Remembering, Repeating, and Working-Through." In *The Standard Edition of the Complete Psychological Works of Sigmund Freud*, Vol. 12, edited and translated by James Strachey, 145–56. London: Hogarth Press, 1958.

Freud, Sigmund. "Inhibitions, Symptoms and Anxieties." In *The Standard Edition of the Complete Psychological Works of Sigmund Freud*, Vol. 20, edited and translated by James Strachey, 87–176. London: Hogarth Press, 1959.

Freud, Sigmund. "Negation." In *The Standard Edition of the Complete Psychological Works of Sigmund Freud*, Vol. 19, edited and translated by James Strachey, 235–39. London: Hogarth Press, 1961.

Freud, Sigmund. "*The Ego and the Id*." In *The Standard Edition of the Complete Psychological Works of Sigmund Freud,* Vol. 19, edited and translated by James Strachey, 12–66. London: Hogarth Press, 1961.

Freud, Sigmund. *The Interpretation of Dreams,* edited and translated by James Strachey. New York: Avon Books, 1967.

Freyd, Jennifer. "Betrayal Trauma: Traumatic Amnesia as an Adaptive Response to Childhood Abuse." *Ethics and Behavior* 4 (1994): 307–29.

Freyd, Jennifer. *Betrayal Trauma: The Logic of Forgetting Childhood.* Cambridge, MA: Harvard University Press, 1996.

Freyd, Jennifer and Pamela J. Birrell. *Blind to Betrayal: Why We Fool Ourselves We Aren't Being Fooled.* Hoboken, NJ: Wiley, 2013.

Friedländer, Saul. "Trauma, Transference, and 'Working Through' in Writing the History of the Shoah." *History and Memory* 4 (1992): 39–59.

Friedländer, Saul. *The Years of Extermination: Nazi Germany and the Jews, 1939–1945.* New York: HarperCollins, 2007.

Fujii, Lee Ann. *Killing Neighbors: Webs of Violence in Rwanda.* Ithaca, NY: Cornell University Press, 2009.

Gay, Peter. *Freud, Jews, and Other Germans.* New York: Oxford University Press, 1978.

Gillis, John R. "Memory and Identity: The History of a Relationship." In *Commemorations: The Politics of National Identity,* edited by John R. Gillis, 3–24. Princeton, NJ: Princeton University Press, 1994.

Gobodo-Madikizela, Pumla. *A Human Being Died That Night: A South African Woman Confronts the Legacy of Apartheid.* Boston: Houghton Mifflin, 2004.

Goddard, Jean-Christophe. "Vladimir Jankélévitch (1903–85)." In *The Columbia History of Twentieth-Century Thought*, edited by Lawrence D. Kritzman, 551–3. New York: Columbia University Press, 2006.

Goethe, Johann Wolfgang von. *The Sorrows of Young Werther.* New York: Vintage Books, 1990.

Golczewski, Frank. "Shades of Grey: Reflections on Jewish-Ukrainian and German-Ukrainian Relations in Galicia." In *The Shoah in Ukraine: History, Testimony, Memorialization,* edited by Ray Brandon and Wendy Lower, 114–55. Bloomington: Indiana University Press, 2008.

Gollwitzer, Helmut. *Zeugen im Auschwitz-Prozess: Begegnungen und Gedanken.* Wuppertal-Barmen: Johannes Kiefel Verlag, 1965.

Gourevitch, Philip. *We Wish to Inform You That Tomorrow We Will Be Killed with Our Families: Stories from Rwanda.* New York: Farrar, Straus and Giroux, 1998.

Govier, Trudy and Wilhelm Verwoerd. "Trust and the Problem of National Reconciliation." *Philosophy of the Social Sciences* 32 (2002): 178–205.

Grabitz, Helge. "Problems of Nazi Trials in the Federal Republic of Germany." *Holocaust Genocide Studies* 3 (1988): 209–22.

Grabowski, Jan. *Hunt for the Jews: Betrayal and Murder in German-Occupied Poland.* Bloomington: Indiana University Press, 2013.

Graybill, Lyn S. *Truth and Reconciliation in South Africa: Miracle or Model?* Boulder, CO: Lynne Rienner, 2002.

Greene, Joshua M. and Shiva Kumar, eds. *Witness: Voices from the Holocaust.* New York: Free Press, 2000.

Greiff, Pablo de. *The Age of Apology: Facing Up to the Past.* Philadelphia: University of Pennsylvania Press, 2008.

Greiff, Pablo de. "A Normative Conception of Transitional Justice." *Politorbis* 50 (2010): 17–29.

Griswold, Charles L. *Forgiveness: A Philosophical Exploration.* New York: Cambridge University Press, 2007.

Gross, Jan T. *Neighbors: The Destruction of the Jewish Community of Jedwabne, Poland.* New York: Penguin Books, 2002.

Gutmann, Amy and Dennis Thompson. *Democracy and Disagreement: Why Moral Conflict Cannot Be Avoided in Politics, and What Should Be Done About It.* Cambridge, MA: Harvard University Press, 1996.

Hafner, Carolyn L., James M. Olson, and Alexandra A. Peterson. "Extreme Harmdoing: A View from the Social Psychology of Justice." In *Explaining the Breakdown of Ethnic Relations: Why Neighbors Kill*, edited by Victoria M. Esses and Richard A. Vernon, 17–40. Malden: Blackwell Publishing, 2008.

Halbwachs, Maurice, *The Collective Memory*, edited by Mary Douglas, translated Francis J. Ditter Jr. and Vidayazdi Ditter. New York: Harper Colophon, 1980.

Halbwachs, Maurice. "*The Social Frameworks of Memory*." In *On Collective Memory*, edited and translated by Lewis A. Coser, 37–189. Chicago: University of Chicago Press, 1992.

Hansel, Joëlle. "Forgiveness and 'Should We Pardon Them?': The Pardon and the Imprescriptible." In *Vladimir Jankélévitch and the Question of Forgiveness*, edited by Alan Udoff, 111–25. Lanham, MD: Lexington Books, 2013.

Hartman, Geoffrey. *The Longest Shadow: In the Aftermath of the Holocaust.* Bloomington: Indiana University Press, 1996.

Hausner, Gideon. *Justice in Jerusalem.* New York: Harper & Row, 1966.

Hegel, G. W. F. *Early Theological Writings*, translated by T. M. Knox. Philadelphia: University of Pennsylvania Press, 1996.

Heidelberger-Leonard, Irene. *The Philosopher of Auschwitz: Jean Améry and Living with the Holocaust.* London: I.B. Tauris, 2010.

Held, Virginia. *The Ethics of Care: Personal, Political, and Global.* New York: Oxford University Press, 2006.

Henri, Yazir and Heidi Grunebaum. "Re-historicising Trauma: Reflections on Violence and Memory in Current-day Cape Town." Direct Action Center for Peace and Memory occasional papers series, no. 6. Cape Town, South Africa: DACPM, 2005. Available online: https://www.medico.de/download/report26/ps_henrigrunebaum_en.pdf (accessed June 6, 1016).

Herder, Johann Gottfried von. *Reflections on the Philosophy of the History of Mankind*, translated by T. O. Churchill. Chicago: University of Chicago Press, 1968.

Herf, Jeffrey. *Divided Memory: The Nazi Past in the Two Germanys.* Cambridge, MA: Harvard University Press, 1997.

Herzl, Theodor. "The Jewish State." In *Theodor Herzl: A Portrait for This Age*, translated by Ludwig Lewisohn and translated by Sylvie d'Avigdor, 233–303. Cleveland: World Publishing Company, 1955.

Hirsch, Marianne and Leo Spitzer. "The Witness in the Archives." *Holocaust Studies/ Memory Studies* 2 (2009): 151–70.

Hobbes, Thomas. *Leviathan.* Ontario: Broadview Press, 2011.

Hoffman, Eva. *Shtetl: The Life and Death of a Small Town and the World of Polish Jews.* Boston: Houghton Mifflin, 1997.

Hollander, Dana. *Living Together: Jacques Derrida's Communities of Violence and Peace.* New York: Fordham University Press, 2013.

Holmgren, Margaret R. *Forgiveness and Retribution: Responding to Wrongdoing.* New York: Cambridge University Press, 2014.

Hout, Nico van. *The Unifinished.* New York: Harry N. Abrams, 2013.

Humper, J. C. *Witness to Truth: Report of the Sierra Leone Truth & Reconciliation Commission,* Vol. 1. Accra, Ghana: GPL Press, 2004.

Hunt, Lynn. *Inventing Human Rights: A History.* New York: W. W. Norton & Co., 2007.

Hyman, Paula E. *Gender and Assimilation in Modern Jewish Society: The Roles and Representation of Women.* Seattle: University of Washington Press, 1997.

Ignatieff, Michael. *Truth and Lies: Stories from the Truth and Reconciliation Commission in South Africa,* edited by Jillian Edelstein. Milpark, South Africa: M&G Books, 2001.

Ilibagiza, Immaculée. *Left to Tell: Discovering God Amidst the Rwandan Holocaust.* Carlsbad, CA: Hay House, 2007.

Isaiah. In *Tanakh: A New Translation of the Holy Scriptures According to the Traditional Hebrew Text,* edited by Harry M. Orlinsky, H. L. Ginsberg, and Ephraim A. Speiser. Philadelphia: Jewish Publication Society, 1985.

Jankélévitch, Vladimir. "Le judaïsme, problème intérieur." In *La conscience juive: Données et débats,* edited by Éliane Amado Lévy-Valensi and Jean Halpérin, 54–79. Paris: Presses Universitaires de France, 1963.

Jankélévitch, Vladimir. "Introduction au thème du pardon." In *La conscience juive: Face à l'histoire: le pardon,* edited by Éliane Amado Lévy-Valensi and Jean Halpérin, 247–61. Paris: Presses Universitaires de France, 1965.

Jankélévitch, Vladimir. *Le Pardon.* Paris: Aubier-Montaigne, 1967.

Jankélévitch, Vladimir. "Ressembler ou dissembler." In *Tentations et actions de la conscience juive: Données et débats,* edited by Éliane Amado Lévy-Valensi, and Jean Halpérin, 17–34. Paris: Presses Universitaires de France, 1971.

Jankélévitch, Vladimir. *Le sérieux de l'intention.* Vol. 1, *Traité des vertus.* Paris: Bordas/Flammarion, 1989.

Jankélévitch, Vladimir. "Should We Pardon Them?" *Critical Inquiry* 22 (1996): 552–72.

Jankélévitch, Vladimir. *Forgiveness,* translated by Andrew Kelley. Chicago: University of Chicago Press, 2005.

Jockusch, Laura. *Collect and Record!: Jewish Holocaust Documentation in Early Postwar Europe.* New York: Oxford University Press, 2012.

Jockusch, Laura. "Historiography in Transit: Survivor Historians and the Writing of Holocaust History in the Late 1940s." *Leo Baeck Institute Year Book* 58 (2013): 76.

Judaken, Jonathan. "Vladimir Jankélévitch at the Colloques des intellectuels juifs de langue française." In *Vladimir Jankélévitch and the Question of Forgiveness,* edited by Alan Udoff, 3–26. Lanham, MD: Lexington Books, 2013.

Judson, Pieter M. *Exclusive Revolutionaries: Liberal Politics, Social Experience, and*

National Identity in the Austrian Empire, 1848–1914. Ann Arbor: University of Michigan Press, 1996.

Judt, Tony. *Postwar: A History of Europe Since 1945*. New York: Penguin Books, 2006.

Kant, Immanuel. *Practical Philosophy*. Cambridge: Cambridge University Press, 1996.

Kaplan, Marion A. *Between Dignity and Despair: Jewish Life in Nazi Germany*. New York: Oxford University Press, 1998.

Kassow, Samuel D. *Who Will Write Our History?: Rediscovering the Hidden Archive from the Warsaw Ghetto*. New York: Vintage Books, 2009.

Katz, Jacob. *Tradition and Crisis: Jewish Society at the End of the Middle Ages*. New York: Schocken Books, 1961.

Kendi, Ibram X. *Stamped from the Beginning: The Definitive History of Racist Ideas in America*. New York: Nation Books, 2016.

Kertész, Imre. "Nobel Lecture," translated by Ivan Sanders, 2002. Available online: http://www.nobelprize.org/nobel_prizes/literature/laureates/2002/kertesz-lecture-e.html (accessed May 11, 2015).

King Jr., Martin Luther. "Keep Moving from This Mountain." Sermon delivered at Temple Israel of Hollywood, Hollywood, California, February 26, 1965. Available online: http://www.americanrhetoric.com/speeches/PDFFiles/MLK%20Temple%20Israel%20Hollywood.pdf (accessed January 18, 2015).

Klein, Dennis. *Jewish Origins of the Psychoanalytic Movement*. New York: Praeger, 1981.

Klein, Dennis. "Forgiveness and History: A Reinterpretation of Post-Conflict Testimony." In *Memory, Narrative, and Forgiveness: Perspectives on the Unfinished Journey of the Past*, edited by Pumla Gobodo-Madikizela, 113–29. Newcastle upon Tyne: Cambridge Scholars Publishing, 2009.

Klein, Dennis. "Locality and the Hidden Realities of Genocide." *Historical Reflections/Reflexions Historiques* 39 (2013): 30–9.

Klein, Dennis. "Rank Contra Freud: Freud's Frau Doni Dream and the Struggle for the Soul of Psychoanalysis." *Annual of Psychoanalysis* 38 (2015): 40–51.

Klein, Dennis. *Societies Emerging from Conflict: The Aftermath of Atrocity*, ed. Newcastle upon Tyne: Cambridge Scholars Publishing. Forthcoming, 2017.

Klein, Melanie. "Mourning and Its Manic-Depressive States." *International Journal of Psycho-Analysis* (1940): 125–53.

Klein, Melanie. *Contributions to Psycho-Analysis*. London: Hogarth Press, 1950.

Klein, Melanie. "Love, Guilt and Reparation." In *Love, Guilt and Reparation and Other Works, 1921–1945*, 306–43. London: Hogarth Press, 1975.

Klein, Stanley B. and Shaun Nichols. "Memory and the Sense of Personal Identity." *Mind* 121 (2012): 677–702.

Kleinig, John. *On Loyalty and Loyalties: The Contours of a Problematic Virtue*. New York: Oxford University Press, 2014.

Kleinig, John. "The Virtue in Patriotism." In *The Ethics of Patriotism: A Debate*, John Kleinig, Simon Keller, and Igor Primoratz, eds 19–47. Malden, MA: John Wiley & Sons, 2015.

Kluger, Ruth. "Forgiving and Remembering." *PMLA* 117 (2002): 311–13.

Kluger, Ruth. *Still Alive: A Holocaust Girlhood Remembered.* New York: The Feminist Press, 2001.

Knoller, Freddie and John Landaw. *Living with the Enemy: My Secret Life on the Run from the Nazis.* London: Metro Publishing, 2005.

Knowles, Anne Kelly, Tim Cole, and Alberto Giordano, eds. *Geographies of the Holocaust.* Bloomington: Indiana University Press, 2014.

Kok, Ruth A. *Statutory Limitations in International Criminal Law.* The Hague: T. M. C. Asser Press, 2007.

Kolk, Bessel A. van der "Dissociation and the Fragmentary Nature of Traumatic Memories: Overviews and Exploratory Study." *Journal of Trauma Stress* 8 (1995): 505–25.

Kolk, Bessel A. van der. and Onno Van der Hart. "The Intrusive Past: The Flexibility of Memory and the Engraving of Trauma." In *Trauma: Explorations in Memory*, edited by Cathy Caruth, 158–82. Baltimore: Johns Hopkins University Press, 1995.

Kor, Eva. "If I Met Mengele Now, I'd Forgive What He Did to Me." *Guardian Unlimited Network,* January 8, 2005. Available online: https://www.theguardian.com/world/2005/jan/09/secondworldwar.theobserver (accessed March 26, 2015).

Kor, Eva. "Miriam and I." The Forgiveness Project, March 29, 2010. Available online: http://theforgivenessproject.com/stories/eva-kor-poland/ (accessed March 26, 2015).

Koselleck, Reinhart. *Futures Past: On the Semantics of Historical Time.* New York: Columbia University Press, 2004.

Kristeva, Julia. *Hannah Arendt: Life Is a Narrative.* Toronto: University of Toronto Press, 2001.

Kristeva, Julia and Alison Rice. "Forgiveness: An Interview." *PMLA* 117 (2002): 278–87.

Kutz, Christopher. "Justice in Reparations: The Cost of Memory and the Value of Talk." *Philosophy and Public Affairs* 32 (2004): 277–312.

LaCapra, Dominick. "Representing the Holocaust: Reflections on the Historians' Debate." In *Probing the Limits of Representation: Nazism and the "Final Solution,"* edited by Saul Friedländer, 108–27. Cambridge: Harvard University Press, 1992.

LaCapra, Dominick. *Writing History, Writing Trauma,* 86–113. Baltimore: Johns Hopkins University Press, 2001.

Lang, Berel. *The Future of the Holocaust: Between History and Memory.* Ithaca, NY: Cornell University Press, 1999.

Langbein, Hermann. *Auschwitz-Proceß: Eine Dokumentation.* Frankfurt am Main: EVA, 1965.

Langer, Lawrence L. *Versions of Survival: The Holocaust and the Human Spirit.* Albany: State University of New York Press, 1982.

Langer, Lawrence L. *Holocaust Testimonies: The Ruins of Memory.* New Haven, CT: Yale University Press, 1991.

Langer, Lawrence L. "Remembering Survival." In *Holocaust Remembrance: The*

Shapes of Memory, edited by Geoffrey Hartman, 70–80. Cambridge, MA: Blackwell, 1994.

Langer, Susanne. *Philosophy in a New Key*. Cambridge, MA: Harvard University Press, 1951.

Lansky, Melvin R. "Hidden Shame, Working Through, and the Problem of Forgiveness in *The Tempest*." *Journal of the American Psychoanalytic Association* 49 (2001): 1005–33.

Laub, Dori. "Bearing Witness, or the Vicissitudes of Listening." In *Testimony: Crises of Witnessing in Literature, Psychoanalysis, and History*, edited by Shoshana Felman and Dori Laub, 57–74. New York: Routledge, 1992.

Lazar, Natalya. "Czernowitz Jews and the Holocaust: Interethnic Relations, Violence, and Survival in a Borderland City, 1941–1946." Ph.D. diss. proposal, Clark University, 2015.

Lear, Jonathan. "Mourning and Moral Psychology." *Psychoanalytic Psychology* 31 (2014): 470–81.

Lehman, Herbert. "A Conversation Between Freud and Rilke." *Psychoanalytic Psychology* 35 (1966): 423–37.

Lemkin, Raphael. *Axis Rule in Occupied Europe: Laws of Occupation, Analysis of Government, Proposals for Redress*. Washington, DC: Carnegie Endowment for International Peace, 1944.

Levi, Primo. *The Periodic Table*, translated by Raymond Rosenthal. New York: Schocken Books, 1984.

Levi, Primo. *The Drowned and the Saved*, translated by Raymond Rosenthal. New York: Summit Books, 1988.

Levi, Primo. *Survival in Auschwitz: The Nazi Assault on Humanity*. translated by Stuart Woolf. New York: Collier Books, 1993.

Levi, Primo. "Revisiting the Camps." In *The Art of Memory: Holocaust Memorials in History*, edited by James Young, 185. New York: Prestel, 1994.

Levi, Primo. *Moments of Reprieve*, translated by Ruth Feldman. New York: Penguin Books, 1995.

Levinas, Emmanuel. *Nine Talmudic Readings*, translated by Annette Aronowicz. Bloomington: Indiana University Press, 1994.

Levy, Daniel and Natan Sznaider. "Memory Unbound: The Holocaust and the Formation of Cosmopolitan Memory." *European Journal of Social Theory* 5 (2002): 87–106.

Lieberman, E. James and Robert Kramer, eds. *The Letters of Sigmund Freud and Otto Rank: Inside Psychoanalysis*. Baltimore: Johns Hopkins Press, 2012.

Lucretius. *On the Nature of Things*, translated by Frank O Copley. New York: W. W. Norton & Co., 2011.

Malamud-Goti, Jaime. "Transitional Governments in the Breach: Why Punish State Criminals?" *Human Rights Quarterly* 12 (1990): 1–16.

Margalit, Avishai. *The Ethics of Memory*. Cambridge, MA: Harvard University Press, 2008.

Margalit, Avishai. *On Betrayal.* Cambridge, MA: Harvard University Press, 2017.

Marshall, Tony F. "Criminal Justice Conferencing Calls for Justice." *VOMA Quarterly* 8 (1997): 5–6, 9.

Marshall, Tony F. *A Restorative Justice Reader.* Portland, OR: Willan, 2003.

Matthäus, Jürgen. "Assault and Destruction." In *Hidden History of the Kovno Ghetto,* edited by Dennis B. Klein, 15–24. Boston: Little, Brown & Co., 1997.

Mauss, Marcel. *The Gift: Forms and Functions of Exchange in Archaic Societies.* New York: W. W. Norton & Co., 1967.

Meinecke, Friedrich. *The German Catastrophe: Reflections and Recollections.* Cambridge, MA: Harvard University Press, 1950.

Melville, Herman. "Hawthorne and His Moses." *The Literary World,* August 17 and 24, 1850. Available online: http://people.virginia.edu/~sfr/enam315/hmmosses.html (accessed July 6, 2016).

Memmi, Albert. *Portrait of a Jew,* translated by Elisabeth Abbott. New York: Orion Press, 1962.

Miller, Alice. *Thou Shalt Not Be Aware: Society's Betrayal of the Child,* translated by Hildegarde and Hunter Hannum. New York: Noonday Press, 1998.

Miquel, Marc von. *Ahnden oder Amnestieren: Westdeutsche Justiz und Vergangenheitspolitik in den sechziger Jahren.* Göttigen: Wallstein Verlag, 2004.

Moehl, Hans-Peter. "Bonn gegen Lex Auschwitz," *Neue Rhein und Ruhr Zeitung* November 18, 1964.

Moses, A. Dirk. "Empire, Colony, Genocide: Keywords and the Philosophy of History." In *Empire, Colony, Genocide: Conquest, Occupation and Subaltern Resistance in World History,* 36, 39–40. New York: Berghahn Books, 2008.

Moses, A. Dirk. "Revisiting a Founding Assumption of Genocide Studies." *Genocide Studies and Prevention* 6 (2011): 287–300.

Moyn, Samuel. *The Last Utopia: Human Rights in History.* Cambridge, MA: Harvard University Press, 2010.

Msimang, Sisonke. "The End of the Rainbow Nation Myth." *The New York Times,* April 12, 2015. Available online: http://www.nytimes.com/2015/04/13/opinion/the-end-of-the-rainbow-nation-myth.html?&_r=0 (accessed February 1, 2016).

Murphy, Colleen. *A Moral Theory of Political Reconciliation.* Cambridge: Cambridge University Press, 2010.

Murphy, Jeffrie. *Getting Even: Forgiveness and Its Limits.* New York: Oxford University Press, 2003.

Nabert, Jean. *Éléments pour une éthique.* Paris: Aubier, 1962.

Nerlich, Volker. "The Contribution of Criminal Justice." In *Justice and Reconciliation in Post-Apartheid South Africa,* edited by François du Bois and Antje du Bois-Pedain, 90–115. Cambridge: Cambridge University Press, 2008.

Nesiah, Vasuki. *Transitional Justice Practice: Looking Back, Moving Forward.* Impunity Watch, May 2016. Available online: http://www.impunitywatch.org/docs/scoping_study_FINAL.pdf (accessed July 11, 2016).

Nietzsche, Friedrich. *The Birth of Tragedy from the Spirit of Music*. In *The Birth of Tragedy and the Genealogy of Morals*, translated by Francis Golffing, 19–146. Garden City, NY: Doubleday & Company, Inc., 1956.

Nietzsche, Friedrich. *On the Genealogy of Morality*. Indianapolis: Hackett Publishing Co., 1998.

Nir, Yehuda. *The Lost Childhood*. New York: Harcourt Brace Jovanovich, 1989.

Nora, Pierre. "Between Memory and History: Les Lieux de Memoire." *Representations* 26 (1989): 144–9.

Nussbaum, Martha. *Political Emotions: Why Love Matters for Justice*. Cambridge, MA: Harvard University Press, 2013.

O'Brien, Edna. *The Little Red Chairs*. Boston: Little, Brown & Co., 2016.

Parker, Theodore. *Ten Sermons of Religion*. Boston: Crosby, Nichols, 1853.

Patterson, Orlando. *Slavery and Social Death*. New York: Cambridge University Press, 1982.

Pendas, Devin O. *The Frankfurt Auschwitz Trial, 1963–1965: Genocide, History, and the Limits of the Law*. Cambridge: Cambridge University Press, 2006.

Pendas, Devin O., Laura Jockusch, and Gabriel N. Finder. "Auschwitz Trials: The Jewish Dimension." *Yad Vashem Studies* 41 (2013): 139–71.

Phelps, Elizabeth A. "Emotion's Impact on Memory." *Memory and Law*, edited by Lynn Nadel and Walter P. Sinnot-Armstrong, 7–28. New York: Oxford University Press, 2012.

Pick, Hella. *Simon Wiesenthal: A Life in Search of Justice*. Boston: Northeastern University Press, 1996.

Polonsky, Antony and Joanna B. Michilic, eds. *The Neighbors Respond: The Controversy over the Jedwabne Massacre in Poland*. Princeton, NJ: Princeton University Press, 2004.

Postel, Danny. "Revisiting the Brink: The Architect of 'Critical Oral History' Sheds New Light on the Cold War." *Chronicle of Higher Education* (October 18, 2002).

Radzik, Linda. *Making Amends: Atonement in Morality, Law, and Politics*. New York: Oxford University Press, 2009.

Ricoeur, Paul. *Memory, History, Forgetting*. Chicago: University of Chicago Press, 2004.

Ringelblum, Emanuel. *Polish-Jewish Relations During the Second World War*, edited by Joseph Kermish and Shmuel Krakowski, translated by Dafna Allon, Danuta Dabrowska, and Dana Keren. Evanston, IL: Northwestern University Press, 1992.

Robertson, Ritchie. *The German-Jewish Dialogue: An Anthology of Literary Texts, 1749–1993*. New York: Oxford University Press, 1999.

Rohde, David. *Endgame: The Betrayal and Fall of Srebrenica, Europe's Worst Massacre Since World War II*. New York: Penguin, 2012.

Rosenfeld, Alvin H. *A Double Dying: Reflections on Holocaust Literature*. Bloomington: Indiana University Press, 1980.

Rosenfeld, Alvin H. *Thinking About the Holocaust: After Half a Century*. Bloomington: Indiana University Press, 1997.

Rosenfeld, Sidney. "Afterword: Jean Améry: The Writer in Revolt." In Jean Améry, *At the Mind's Limits: Contemplations by a Survivor on Auschwitz and Its Realities,* translated by Sidney Rosenfeld and Stella P. Rosenfeld, 104–9. Bloomington: Indiana University Press, 1980.

Rosensaft, Hadassah. *Yesterday: My Story.* New York: Yad Vashem, 2005.

Rothberg, Michael. "The Work of Testimony in the Age of Decolonization: *Chronicle of a Summer,* Cinema Verité, and the Emergence of the Holocaust Survivor." *PMLA* 119 (2004): 1231–46.

Rothberg, Michael. *Multidirectional Memory: Remembering the Holocaust in the Age of Decolonization.* Stanford, CA: Stanford University Press, 2009.

Rückerl, Adalbert. *NS-Verbrechen vor Gericht: Versuch einer Vergangenheitsbewältigung.* Heidelberg: C. F. Müller, 1982.

Sachs, Hanns. *Freud: Master and Friend.* Cambridge, MA: Harvard University Press, 1944.

Salsitz, Norman and Amalie Petranker Salsitz. *Against All Odds: A Tale of Two Survivors.* New York: Holocaust Library, 1990.

Sands, Philippe. *East West Street: On the Origins of "Genocide" and "Crimes Against Humanity."* New York: Alfred A. Knopf, 2016.

Sanyal, Debarati. *Memory and Complicity: Migrations of Holocaust Remembrance.* New York: Fordham University Press, 2015.

Sarat, Austin and Nasser Hussain, eds. *Forgiveness, Mercy, and Clemency.* Stanford: Stanford University Press, 2007.

Scarry, Elaine. *The Body in Pain.* Oxford: Oxford University Press, 1968.

Schama, Simon. *Landscape and Memory.* New York: Harper Perennial, 2004.

Scheler, Max. *Vom Umsturz der Werte, Gesammelte Werke,* Vol. 3, edited by Maria Scheler. Bern: Francke, 1955.

Scheler, Max. *The Nature of Sympathy,* translated by Peter Heath. New Brunswick, NJ: Transaction Publishers, 2008.

Scholem, Gershom. *On Jews and Judaism in Crisis: Selected Essays.* Philadelphia: Schocken Books, 1976.

Schorske, Carl E. *Fin-de-siècle Vienna: Politics and Culture.* New York: Knopf, 1979.

Schur, Max. *Freud Living and Dying.* London: Hogarth Press, 1972.

Scott, Jill. *A Poetics of Forgiveness: Cultural Responses to Loss and Wrongdoing.* New York: Palgrave Macmillan, 2010.

Sebald, W. G. *On the Natural History of Destruction,* translated by Anthea Bell. New York: Random House, 2003.

Seeberg, Mary Louise, Irene Levin, and Claudia Lenz. *The Holocaust as Active Memory: The Past in the Present.* New York: Routledge, 2013.

Segev, Tom. *Simon Wiesenthal: The Life and Legends.* New York: Doubleday, 2010.

Semprún, Jorge. *Literature or Life,* translated by Linda Coverdale. New York: Viking Penguin, 1997.

Semprún, Jorge and Elie Wiesel. *Se taire est impossible.* Paris: Mille et une nuits, 1995.

Simon, Ernst. "Sigmund Freud, the Jew." *Leo Baeck Institute Yearbook* 2 (1957): 274.

Smith, Adam. *The Theory of Moral Sentiments.* Los Angeles: Enhances Media Publishing, 2016.

Smith, Nick. "The Categorical Apology." *Journal of Social Philosophy* 36 (2005): 473–96.

Stangneth, Bettina. *Eichmann Before Jerusalem: The Unexamined Life of a Mass Murderer.* New York: Knopf, 2014.

Stevenson, Bryan. *Just Mercy: A Story of Justice and Redemption.* New York: Spiegel & Grau, 2014.

Stevenson, Bryan. "We Need to Talk About an Injustice." TED Talk, March 2012. Available online: https://www.ted.com/talks/bryan_stevenson_we_need_to_talk_about_an_injustice (accessed January 18, 2016).

Strauss, Leo. *Rebirth of Classical Political Rationalism: An Introduction to the Thought of Leo Strauss.* Chicago: University of Chicago Press, 1989.

Strawson, P. F. *Studies in the Philosophy of Thought and Action.* Oxford: Oxford Clarendon Press, 1968.

Suddendorf, Thomas and Michael Corballis. "Mental Time Travel and the Evolution of the Human Mind." *Genetic, Social and General Psychology Monographs* 123 (1997): 133–67.

Suddendorf, Thomas and Michael Corballis. "The Evolution of Foresight: What is Mental Time Travel, and is it Unique to Humans?" *Behavioral and Brain Sciences* 30 (2007): 299–313.

Suleiman, Susan Rubin. *Crises of Memory and the Second World War.* Cambridge, MA: Harvard University Press, 2006.

Teitel, Ruti G. *Transitional Justice.* New York: Oxford University Press, 2000.

Thompson, Janna. "Historical Injustice and Reparation: Justifying Claims of Descendants." *Ethics* 112 (2001): 114–35.

Thompson, Janna. "Is Political Apology a Sorry Affair?" *Social and Legal Studies* 21 (2012): 215–25.

Torche, Florencia and Eduardo Valenzuela. "Trust and Reciprocity: A Theoretical Distinction of the Sources of Social Capital." *European Journal of Social Theory* 14 (2011): 181–98.

Tutu, Desmond Mpilo. *No Future Without Forgiveness.* New York: Doubleday, 1999.

Tutu, Desmond Mpilo. "Foreword by Chairperson." In *Truth and Reconciliation Commission of South Africa Report,* Vol. 1, presented on October 29, 1998, 1–23. Available online: http://www.justice.gov.za/trc/report/finalreport/Volume%201.pdf (accessed April 15, 2015).

Verdeja, Ernesto. *Unchopping a Tree: Reconciliation in the Aftermath of Political Violence.* Philadelphia: Temple University Press, 2009.

Vernon, Richard. *Historical Redress: Must We Pay for the Past?* New York: Continuum, 2012.

Vetlesen, Arne Johan. "A Case for Resentment: Jean Améry versus Primo Levi." *Journal of Human Rights* 5 (2006): 27–44.

Vieille, Stephanie. "Transitional Justice: A Colonizing Field?" *Amsterdam Law Forum* 4 (2012): 58–68.

Villa-Vicencio, Charles. "The Politics of Reconciliation." In *Telling the Truths: Truth-Telling and Peace Building in Post-Conflict Societies,* edited by Tristan Anne Borer, 59–82. Notre Dame, IN: Notre Dame University Press, 2006.

Walker, Margaret Urban. "Resentment and Assurance." In *Setting the Moral Compass: Essays by Women Philosophers,* edited by Cheshire Calhoun, 145–60. New York: Oxford University Press, 2004.

Walker, Margaret Urban. *Moral Repair: Reconstructing Moral Relations After Wrongdoing.* New York: Cambridge University Press, 2006.

Walker, Margaret Urban. "Truth Telling as Reparations." *Metaphilosophy* 41 (2010): 525–45.

Wallace, Richard. *Responsibilities and the Moral Sentiments.* Cambridge, MA: Harvard University Press, 1994.

Waxman, Zoë Vania. *Writing the Holocaust: Identity,Testimony, Representation.* New York: Oxford University Press, 2006.

Weschler, Lawrence. *A Miracle, a Universe: Settling Accounts with Torturers.* Chicago: University of Chicago Press, 1998.

Whigham, Kerry. "Affective Echoes: Affect, Resonant Violence, and the Processing of Collective Trauma in Post-Genocidal Societies." PhD diss., New York University, 2016.

Wiesel, Elie. *Legends of Our Time.* New York: Schocken Books, 1982.

Wiesel, Elie. *Dimensions of the Holocaust,* edited by Elliot Lefkowitz. Evanston, IL: Northwestern University Press, 1990.

Wiesel, Elie. "The Holocaust as Literary Inspiration," *Dimenions of the Holocaust,* ed. Elliot Lefkowitz (Evanston, IL: Northwestern University Press, 1990).

Wiesel, Elie. *All Rivers Run to the Sea: Memoirs.* New York: Schocken Books, 1995.

Wiesel, Elie. *Night.* New York: Hill and Wang, 2006.

Wiesel, Eliezer. *Un di velt hot geshvign* [*And the World Was Silent*]. Buenos Aires: Tsentral-Farband fun Poylische Yidn in Argentine, 1956.

Wiesel, Eliezer. Unpublished ms. [*Night,* Hebrew version], n.d. as reported in Ofer Aderet, "Newly Unearthed Version of Elie Wiesel's Seminal Work Is a Scathing Indictment of God, Jewish World," *Haaretz,* May 1, 2016. Available online: http://www.haaretz.com/jewish/news/.premium-1.717093http://www.haaretz.com/jewish/news/.premium-1.717093 (accessed June 28, 2016).

Wiesenthal, Simon. *Die Sonnenblume: Eine Erzählung von Schuld und Vergebung.* Vienna: Ullstein, 1984.

Wiesenthal, Simon. *The Sunflower: On the Possibilities and Limits of Forgiveness.* New York: Schocken Books, 1998.

Wieviorka, Annette. *The Era of the Witness.* Ithaca, NY: Cornell University Press, 2006.

Wisse, Ruth R. *The Modern Jewish Canon: A Journey Through Language and Culture.* New York: Free Press, 2000.

Wittman, Rebecca. *Beyond Justice: The Auschwitz Trial.* Cambridge, MA: Harvard University Press, 2005.

Wood, Nancy. *Modernity, Culture, and the "Jew,"* edited by Bryan Cheyette and Laura Marcus. Stanford, CA: Stanford University Press, 1998.

Yones, Eliyahu. *Smoke in the Sand: The Jews of Lvov in the War Years, 1939–1944.* Jerusalem: Gefen, 2004.

Young, Iris Marion. *Justice and the Politics of Difference.* Princeton, NJ: Princeton University Press, 1990.

Young, James E. *The Texture of Memory: Holocaust Memorials and Meaning.* New Haven, CT: Yale University Press, 1993.

Zimmerer, Jürgen. "Colonialism and the Holocaust: Towards an Archeology of Genocide." In *Genocide and Settler Society*, edited by A. Dirk Moses, 49–76. Oxford: Berghahn Books, 2004.

Zimmerer, Jürgen. "The Birth of the Ostland out of the Spirit of Colonialism: A Postcolonial Perspective on the Nazi Policy of Conquest and Extermination." *Patterns of Prejudice* 39 (2005): 218.

Zimmerer, Jürgen and Joachim Zeller, eds. "Völkermord in Deutsch-Südwest-Afrika: Der Kolonialkrieg (1904–1908)". In *Namibia und seine Folgen.* Berlin: Christoph Links, 2003.

Zyl, Paul van. "Dilemma of Transitional Justice: The Case of South Africa's Truth and Reconciliation Commission." *Journal of International Affairs* 52 (1999): 647–67.

Index

CPSIA information can be obtained
at www.ICGtesting.com
Printed in the USA
LVHW080232030919
629751LV00007B/153/P

9 781350 112315